**W9-AJR-360**

# Complete American Presidents Sourcebook

# Complete American Presidents Sourcebook

## Volume 5
### John F. Kennedy through George W. Bush
### 1961–2001

*Roger Matuz*
*Lawrence W. Baker, Editor*

AN IMPRINT OF THE GALE GROUP

DETROIT · NEW YORK · SAN FRANCISCO
LONDON · BOSTON · WOODBRIDGE, CT

Roger Matuz

## Staff

Lawrence W. Baker, *U•X•L Senior Editor*
Gerda-Ann Raffaelle, *U•X•L Contributing Editor*
Carol DeKane Nagel, *U•X•L Managing Editor*
Thomas L. Romig, *U•X•L Publisher*

Rita Wimberley, *Senior Buyer*
Dorothy Maki, *Manufacturing Manager*
Evi Seoud, *Assistant Manager, Composition Purchasing and Electronic Prepress*
Mary Beth Trimper, *Manager, Composition Purchasing and Electronic Prepress*

Cynthia Baldwin, *Senior Art Director*
Michelle DiMercurio, *Senior Art Director*
Kenn Zorn, *Product Design Manager*

Shalice Shah-Caldwell, *Permissions Associate (text and pictures)*
Maria L. Franklin, *Permissions Manager*
Kelly A. Quin, *Editor, Imaging and Multimedia Content*
Pamela A. Reed, *Imaging Coordinator*
Leitha Etheridge-Sims, *Image Cataloger*
Mary Grimes, *Image Cataloger*
Robert Duncan, *Imaging Specialist*
Dan Newell, *Imaging Specialist*
Randy A. Bassett, *Image Supervisor*
Barbara J. Yarrow, *Imaging and Multimedia Content Manager*

Marco Di Vita, Graphix Group, *Typesetting*

**Library of Congress Cataloging-in-Publication Data**

Matuz, Roger.
    Complete American presidents sourcebook / Roger Matuz ; Lawrence W. Baker, editor.
        p. cm.
    Includes bibliographical references and indexes.
    ISBN 0-7876-4837-X (set) — ISBN 0-7876-4838-8 (v. 1) — ISBN 0-7876-4839-6 (v. 2) — ISBN 0-7876-4840-X (v. 3) — ISBN 0-7876-4841-8 (v. 4) — ISBN 0-7876-4842-6 (v. 5)
        1. Presidents—United States—Biography—Juvenile literature. 2. Presidents' spouses—United States—Biography—Juvenile literature. 3. United States—Politics and government—Sources—Juvenile literature. I. Baker, Lawrence W. II. Title.

E176.1 .M387 2001
973'.09'9—dc21
[B]
                                                                    00-056794

Cover illustration of Abraham Lincoln is reproduced courtesy of the Library of Congress; Franklin and Eleanor Roosevelt, reproduced by permission of the Corbis Corporation; George W. Bush, reproduced by permission of Archive Photos; Thomas Jefferson, reproduced by permission of the National Portrait Gallery, Smithsonian Institution; Washington Monument, reproduced by permission of PhotoDisc, Inc.; Clintons, Bushes, Reagans, Carters, and Fords, reproduced by permission of Archive Photos; Theodore Roosevelt, reproduced by permission of Archive Photos.

Printed in the United States of America

10 9 8 7 6 5 4 3 2 1

# Contents

# Volume 2

# Volume 3

# Volume 4

# Volume 5

# Reader's Guide

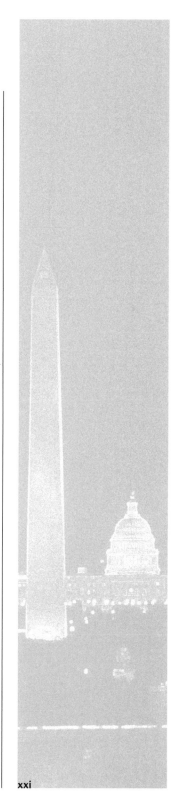

An "embarrassed pause" fell on the gathering of delegates at the Constitutional Convention of 1787 when James Wilson of Pennsylvania suggested the idea of a chief executive. Wanting "no semblance of a monarch," as Edmund Randolph of Virginia put it, delegates moved on to other matters.

So went the first real "discussion" about the office of president, according to Virginia delegate James Madison. Madison, later nicknamed "the Father of the Constitution," took lengthy notes on the proceedings. They were published in 1840 in a book, *Journal of the Federal Convention*.

The Convention was called to address the weakness of the American government formed under the Articles of Confederation that was approved in 1781. By the end of the Convention of 1787, delegates had cautiously agreed on a new system. They had debated ideas of government ranging in history from ancient Greece and Rome to the "Age of Enlightenment" (eighteenth century) in Europe; they considered the workings of the Iroquois confederacy of Native American tribes as well as the state governments in America; and they held to their ideals of liberty and their dislike of monarchy, a system in which one person rules a country for life. The delegates eventually returned to Wilson's suggestion and debated it. The new system of government they cautiously agreed to in the end did indeed include an elected chief executive—the president.

"President" was a title used for the position of governor in three states—Delaware, Pennsylvania, and New Hampshire. They were among the first nine states to ratify the Constitution, helping provide the majority (nine of thirteen states) needed for the Constitution to become legally binding.

The process of ratification was not easy. In Virginia, for example, which finally approved the Constitution in 1788 by a slim majority (89-79), there were significant concerns about the powers of the president. Former Continental congressman and former Virginia governor Patrick Henry called it "a squint toward monarchy."

The delegates of Virginia, however, had an example of the kind of leader envisioned when the office of president was created. George Washington had presided over the Constitutional Convention. He introduced no ideas and seldom participated in debates, but he kept delegates focused on the cause of improving the system of government. Washington was known for his honesty and for not being overly ambitious. Americans had turned to him to lead their military struggle in the Revolutionary War (1775–81). After the Constitution was ratified (approved), delegates turned to him to lead the new nation as its first president.

Washington's example as president reveals the realities of political leadership. He was voted unanimously into office, and left office in the same high regard, but he had faced resistance in between. Some viewed his version of the federal government as being too powerful: he had called on state militias to put down a rebellion in Pennsylvania against taxes; and for economic reasons, he sided in foreign relations with Great Britain—still a hated enemy to some Americans— over France, the nation that had assisted Americans in winning independence.

Washington was among those presidents who made firm decisions, then awaited the consequences. Some had viewed the presidency as being more impartial. Such are the perils of the presidency. John Adams, the second president, followed the more forceful actions of members of his party and became so unpopular that he had no real hope for reelection. Thomas Jefferson, whose ideals shaped the Declaration of Independence, lost much popularity by the time he left office as the third president. Jefferson had ordered foreign trade restrictions to assert America's strength and to demand respect from Great Britain and France, but the action ended up hurting the American economy.

Like the Constitution, the office of the president was never intended to be perfect. The Constitution is flexible, meant to be used and adapted to form "a more perfect union." The presidency has ranged at times from being a near monarchy to having little real strength. President Andrew Jackson was dubbed "King Andrew" by his opponents, who felt he overstepped his power in several instances. Franklin D. Roosevelt was given tremendous powers and support, first in 1933 to combat the effects of the Great Depression (1929–41), and later to direct the nation's economy during World War II (1939–45). But when Roosevelt tried to change the Supreme Court, he was met with swift criticism. Roosevelt was the only president elected to office four times, the last time being 1944. (In 1945, he died only three months into his fourth term.) By 1951, a constitutional amendment was passed to limit presidents to two terms in office.

Other presidents were far less powerful or effective. Prior to the Civil War, two presidents from the North (Franklin Pierce and James Buchanan) supported the rights for states to decide whether to permit slavery. Abraham Lincoln was elected to challenge that notion, and the Civil War (1861–65) followed. Lincoln took a more aggressive approach than his two predecessors, and he emerged in history as among the greatest presidents.

After Lincoln's assassination in 1865, the presidency was dominated by Congress. In 1885, future president Woodrow Wilson criticized that situation in a book he wrote, *Congressional Government*, while he was a graduate student at Johns Hopkins University. By the time Wilson was elected president in 1912, a series of strong presidents—Grover Cleveland, William McKinley, and Theodore Roosevelt—had reasserted the president's power to lead.

The presidency, then, has passed through various stages of effectiveness. The dynamics of change, growth, and frustration make it fascinating to study. Different ideas of leadership, power, and the role of government have been pursued by presidents. Chief executives have come from various backgrounds: some were born in poverty, like Andrew Johnson and Abraham Lincoln, and others had the advantages of wealth, like the Roosevelts and Bushes; some were war heroes, like Ulysses S. Grant and Dwight D. Eisenhower, others were more studious, like Thomas Jefferson and Woodrow Wilson. Some came to the presidency by accident, like John Tyler and Gerald R. Ford, others campaigned long and hard for the position, like Martin Van Buren and Richard Nixon.

There are various ways to present information on the presidency. In 2000, a Public Broadcasting System (PBS) television series called *The American President* divided presidents into ten categories (such as presidents related to each other, those who were prominent military men, and chief executives who became compromise choices of their parties). The same year, a group of presidential scholars also used ten categories (such as crisis leadership, administrative skills, and relations with Congress) to rank presidents in order of effectiveness

*Complete American Presidents Sourcebook* uses a chronological approach, beginning with George Washington in 1789, and ending with George W. Bush in 2001. Each president's section contains three types of entries.

### Biography of the president

Each of the forty-two men who have served in the nation's top political office is featured in *Complete American Presidents Sourcebook*.

- Each entry begins with a general overview of the president's term(s) in office, then follows his life from birth, through his service as president, to his post-presidency (if applicable).

- Outstanding events and issues during each presidential administration are described, as are the president's responses in his role as the nation's highest elected official.

- Sidebar boxes provide instant facts on the president's personal life; a timeline of key events in his life; a "Words to

Know" box that defines key terms related to the president; results of the president's winning election(s); a list of Cabinet members for each administration; and a selection of homes, museums, and other presidential landmarks.

• A final summary describes the president's legacy—how his actions and the events during his administration influenced the historical period and the future.

## Biography of the first lady

Forty-four first ladies are featured in *Complete American Presidents Sourcebook*. Though some of the women died before their husbands became president, all had an important influence on the men who would serve as president. The profiles provide biographical information and insight into the ways in which the women lived their lives and defined their public roles. Like the presidents, first ladies have responded in different ways to their highly public position.

## Primary source entry

Another important feature of interest to students is a selection of forty-eight primary source documents—speeches, writings, executive orders, and proclamations of the presidents. At least one primary source is featured with each president.

In the presidents' own words, the documents outline the visions and plans of newly elected presidents, the reasons for certain actions, and the responses to major world events. Students can learn more about key documents (such as the Declaration of Independence and the Monroe Doctrine); famous speeches (such as George Washington's Farewell Address and Abraham Lincoln's Gettysburg Address); presidential orders (the Emancipation Proclamation issued by Abraham Lincoln in 1863 and Harry S. Truman's executive order on military desegregation in 1946); responses to ongoing issues, from tariffs (William McKinley) to relations between the government and Native Americans (Chester A. Arthur); different views on the role of the federal government (from extensive programs advocated by Franklin D. Roosevelt and Lyndon B. Johnson, to reducing the influence of government by Warren G. Harding and Ronald Reagan); and many inaugural addresses, including the memorable speeches of Abraham Lincoln and John F. Kennedy.

Each document (or excerpt) presented in *Complete American Presidents Sourcebook* includes the following additional material:

- **Introduction** places the document and its author in a historical context.

- **Things to remember** offers readers important background information and directs them to central ideas in the text.

- **What happened next** provides an account of subsequent events, both during the presidential administration and in future years.

- **Did you know** provides significant and interesting facts about the excerpted document, the president, or the subjects discussed in the excerpt.

- **For further reading** lists sources for more information on the president, the document, or the subject of the excerpt.

*Complete American Presidents Sourcebook* also features sidebars containing interesting facts and short biographies of people who were in some way connected with the president or his era. Within each entry, boldfaced cross-references direct readers to other presidents, first ladies, primary sources, and sidebar boxes in the five-volume set. Finally, each volume includes approximately 70 photographs and illustrations (for a total of 350), a "Timeline of the American Presidents" that lists significant dates and events related to presidential administrations, a general "Words to Know" section, research and activity ideas, sources for further reading, and a cumulative index.

This wealth of material presents the student with a variety of well-researched information. It is intended to reflect the dynamic situation of serving as the leader of a nation founded on high ideals, ever struggling to realize those ideals.

### Acknowledgments from the author

Many individuals, many institutions, and many sources were consulted in preparing *Complete American Presidents Sourcebook*. A good portion of them are represented in bibliographies and illustration and textual credits sprinkled throughout the five volumes. The many excellent sources and the ability to access them ensured a dynamic process that made the project lively and thought-provoking, qualities reflected in the presentation.

Compilation efforts were organized through Manitou Wordworks, Inc., headed by Roger Matuz with contributions from Carol Brennan, Anne-Jeanette Johnson, Allison Jones, Mel Koler, and Gary Peters. On the Gale/U•X•L side, special recognition goes to U•X•L publisher Tom Romig for his conceptualization of the project. Thanks, too, to Gerda-Ann Raffaelle for filling in some editorial holes; Pam Reed, Kelly A. Quin, and the rest of the folks on the Imaging team for their efficient work; and Cindy Baldwin for another dynamite cover.

The author benefited greatly through his association and friendship with editor Larry Baker and his personal library, tremendous patience, and great enthusiasm for and knowledge of the subject matter.

Finally, with love to Mary Claire for her support, interest (I'll miss having you ask me the question, "So what new thing did you learn about a president today?"), and understanding from the beginning of the project around the time we were married through my frequent checking of the latest news before and after the election of 2000.

**Acknowledgments from the editor**

The editor wishes to thank Roger Matuz for a year and a half of presidential puns, for putting up with endless Calvin Coolidge tidbits, and—above all—for producing a tremendously solid body of work. You've got my vote when Josiah Bartlet's time in office is up. Thank you, Mr. Author.

Thanks also to typesetter Marco Di Vita of The Graphix Group who always turns in top-quality work and is just a lot of fun to work with; Terry Murray, who, in spite of her excellent-as-usual copyediting and indexing, still couldn't resist suggesting a sidebar for Zachary Taylor's horse, Old Whitey (um, no . . . maybe if we do *Complete American Presidents' Pets Sourcebook);* and proofer Amy Marcaccio Keyzer, whose sharp eye kept the manuscript clean and whose election e-mails kept me laughing.

In addition, the editor would be remiss if he didn't acknowledge his first family. Decades of thanks go to Mom & Dad, for starting it all by first taking me to the McKinley Memorial in Canton, Ohio, all those years ago. Love and appreciation go to editorial first lady Beth Baker, for putting up with all of the presidential homes and museums and grave markers and books, but who admits that touring FDR's Campobello during a nor'easter storm is pretty cool. And to Charlie & Dane—please don't fight over who gets to be president first!

Finally, a nod to Al Gore and George W. Bush for adding some real-life drama to the never-ending completion of this book . . . and who *did* fight over who got to be president first!

### Comments and suggestions

We welcome your comments on the *Complete American Presidents Sourcebook* and suggestions for other topics in history to consider. Please write: Editors, *Complete American Presidents Sourcebook,* U•X•L, 27500 Drake Rd., Farmington Hills, Michigan 48331-3535; call toll-free: 800-877-4253; fax to 248-414-5043; or send e-mail via http://www.galegroup.com.

# Timeline of the American Presidents

1776    The Declaration of Independence is written, approved, and officially issued.

1781    The Articles of Confederation are approved, basing American government on cooperation between the states. Congress is empowered to negotiate treaties, but has few other responsibilities.

1787    A national convention called to strengthen the Articles of Confederation develops the U.S. Constitution instead, defining a new system of American government. The powers of Congress are broadened. Congress forms the legislative branch of the new government, and the Supreme Court forms the judicial

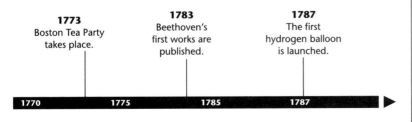

**1773**
Boston Tea Party
takes place.

**1783**
Beethoven's
first works are
published.

**1787**
The first
hydrogen balloon
is launched.

1770          1775          1785          1787

branch. An executive branch is introduced and will be led by an elected official, the president. The president and vice president are to be inaugurated on March 4 of the year following their election (a date that remains in practice until 1933, when the Twentieth Amendment is ratified, changing inauguration day to January 20).

**1787** Three of the original thirteen colonies—Delaware, Pennsylvania, and New Jersey—ratify the Constitution, thereby becoming the first three states of the Union.

**1788** Eight of the original thirteen colonies—Georgia, Connecticut, Massachusetts, Maryland, South Carolina, New Hampshire, Virginia, and New York—ratify the Constitution, thereby becoming the fourth through eleventh states of the Union. The Constitution becomes law when New Hampshire is the ninth state to ratify it (two-thirds majority of the thirteen states had to approve the Constitution for it to become legally binding).

**1789** One of the original thirteen colonies—North Carolina—ratifies the Constitution, thereby becoming the twelfth state of the Union.

**1789** The first presidential election is held. Voting is done by electors appointed by each state, and the number of electors are based on the state's population. Each elector votes for two candidates. Whomever finishes with the most votes becomes president, and whomever finishes second becomes vice president.

**1789** Revolutionary War hero George Washington is elected president, receiving votes from each elector.

**1789** The French Revolution begins.

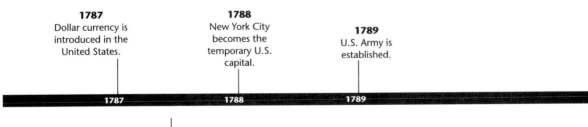

**1787**
Dollar currency is introduced in the United States.

**1788**
New York City becomes the temporary U.S. capital.

**1789**
U.S. Army is established.

1787     1788     1789

1789    George Washington is inaugurated in New York City. A site for the national capital is selected along the Potomac River in Washington, D.C., and the federal government will be situated in Philadelphia, Pennsylvania, until the new capital is completed.

1789    One of the original thirteen colonies—Rhode Island—ratifies the Constitution, thereby becoming the thirteenth state of the Union.

1789    Political factions solidify. Federalists, who support a strong federal government, are led by Secretary of the Treasury Alexander Hamilton, and Anti-Federalists, who support limited federal power and strong states' rights, are led by Secretary of State Thomas Jefferson.

1791    Vermont becomes the fourteenth state of the Union.

1792    President George Washington is reelected unanimously.

1792    Kentucky becomes the fifteenth state of the Union.

1794    American forces defeat a confederacy of Native American tribes at the Battle of Fallen Timbers in Ohio, opening up the midwest for settlement.

1796    When Vice President John Adams finishes first and former Secretary of State Thomas Jefferson finishes second in the presidential election, two men with conflicting political views and affiliations serve as president and vice president. Political parties—the Federalists and the Democratic-Republicans—become established.

1796    Tennessee becomes the sixteenth state of the Union.

1798    The United States engages in an undeclared naval war with France.

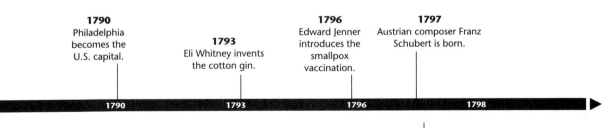

**1790**
Philadelphia
becomes the
U.S. capital.

**1793**
Eli Whitney invents
the cotton gin.

**1796**
Edward Jenner
introduces the
smallpox
vaccination.

**1797**
Austrian composer Franz
Schubert is born.

1790      1793      1796      1798

1798    Federalists in Congress pass and President John Adams signs into law the Alien and Sedition Acts. The laws, which expand the powers of the federal government, prove unpopular and bolster the prospects of anti-Federalists.

1800    The seat of government moves from Philadelphia, Pennsylvania, to Washington, D.C.; President John Adams and first lady Abigail Adams move into the White House (officially called The Executive Mansion until 1900).

1800    In the presidential election, Vice President Thomas Jefferson and former New York senator Aaron Burr (both of the Democratic-Republican Party) finish tied with the most electoral votes. The election is decided in the House of Representatives, where Jefferson prevails after thirty-six rounds of voting.

1803    The historic *Marbury v. Madison* decision strengthens the role of the U.S. Supreme Court to decide constitutional issues.

1803    The Louisiana Purchase more than doubles the size of the United States.

1803    Ohio becomes the seventeenth state of the Union.

1804    The Twelfth Amendment to the Constitution mandates that electors must distinguish between whom they vote for president and vice president (to avoid repeating the problem of the 1800 election, where most voters selected both Jefferson and Burr with their two votes).

1804    President Thomas Jefferson wins reelection. He selects a new running mate, New York governor George Clinton, to replace Vice President Aaron Burr.

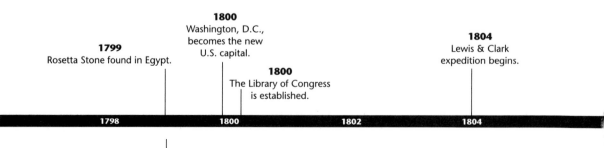

**1800**
Washington, D.C.,
becomes the new
U.S. capital.

**1799**
Rosetta Stone found in Egypt.

**1800**
The Library of Congress
is established.

**1804**
Lewis & Clark
expedition begins.

| 1798 | 1800 | 1802 | 1804 |

**1804**    After losing an election for governor of New York, outgoing vice president Aaron Burr kills former U.S. secretary of the treasury Alexander Hamilton in a duel. Hamilton had influenced voters against Burr in the presidential campaign of 1800 and during Burr's campaign to be governor of New York in 1804.

**1806**    The Lewis and Clark expedition, commissioned by President Thomas Jefferson, is completed when explorers Meriwether Lewis and William Clark return to St. Louis, Missouri, after having traveled northwest to the Pacific Ocean.

**1807**    President Thomas Jefferson institutes an embargo on shipping to England and France, attempting to pressure the nations to respect American rights at sea. The embargo is unsuccessful and unpopular.

**1807**    Former vice president Aaron Burr is tried and acquitted on charges of treason.

**1808**    Secretary of State James Madison, the "Father of the Constitution," is elected president. Vice President George Clinton campaigns and places third as a member of the Independent Republican Party after having accepted Madison's offer to continue in his role as vice president.

**1811**    At the Battle of Tippecanoe, American forces (led by future president William Henry Harrison) overwhelm a Native American confederacy led by Shawnee chief Tecumseh.

**1811**    Vice President George Clinton casts the tie-breaking vote in the U.S. Senate (a responsibility of the vice president under the U.S. Constitution) against rechartering the National Bank, and against President James Madison's wishes.

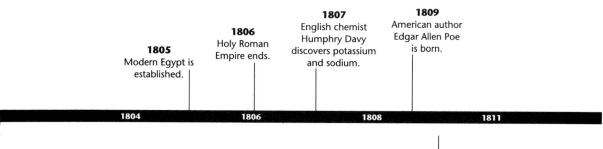

**1805**
Modern Egypt is established.

**1806**
Holy Roman Empire ends.

**1807**
English chemist Humphry Davy discovers potassium and sodium.

**1809**
American author Edgar Allen Poe is born.

1804      1806      1808      1811

| 1812 | War of 1812 (1812–15) begins. |
|---|---|
| 1812 | President James Madison is reelected. |
| 1812 | Louisiana becomes the eighteenth state of the Union. |
| 1813 | After having suffered military defeats in Canada, U.S. naval forces win control of the Great Lakes. |
| 1814 | British military forces burn the White House and the Capitol during the War of 1812. |
| 1815 | The Battle of New Orleans, where American forces (led by future president Andrew Jackson) rout a superior British force, occurs after an armistice was agreed on, but news had not yet reached Louisiana. The War of 1812 officially ends a month later. |
| 1816 | Secretary of State James Monroe is elected president. The "Era of Good Feelings" begins: the war is over, America is expanding, and Monroe is a popular president. |
| 1816 | Indiana becomes the nineteenth state of the Union. |
| 1817 | President James Monroe moves into an incompletely reconstructed White House. |
| 1816 | Mississippi becomes the twentieth state of the Union. |
| 1818 | Illinois becomes the twenty-first state of the Union. |
| 1819 | Alabama becomes the twenty-second state of the Union. |
| 1819 | Bank Panic slows economic growth. |
| 1820 | President James Monroe is reelected by winning every state. One elector casts a vote for John Quincy Adams as a symbolic gesture to ensure that George Washington remains the only president to win all electoral votes in an election. |

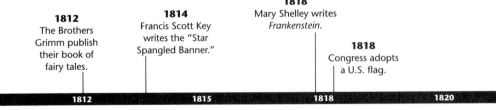

**1812**
The Brothers Grimm publish their book of fairy tales.

**1814**
Francis Scott Key writes the "Star Spangled Banner."

**1818**
Mary Shelley writes *Frankenstein.*

**1818**
Congress adopts a U.S. flag.

1812    1815    1818    1820

**1820** The Missouri Compromise sets a boundary (the southern border of present-day Missouri): slavery is not permitted north of that boundary for any prospective territory hoping to enter the Union.

**1820** Maine, formerly part of Massachusetts, becomes the twenty-third state of the Union.

**1821** Missouri becomes the twenty-fourth state of the Union.

**1823** In his annual message to Congress, President James Monroe introduces what will become known as the Monroe Doctrine. Although not very significant at the time, the Doctrine, which warns European nations against expansionist activities in the Americas, sets a foreign policy precedent several later presidents will invoke.

**1824** Electoral votes are based on the popular vote for the first time. Tennessee senator Andrew Jackson bests Secretary of State John Quincy Adams with over 45,000 more popular votes and a 99-84 Electoral College lead, but does not win a majority of electoral votes, split among four candidates. The election is decided in Adams's favor by the House of Representatives. The support of powerful Speaker of the House Henry Clay, who finished fourth in the election, helps sway the House in favor of Adams. When Adams names Clay his secretary of state, Jackson supporters claim a "corrupt bargain" had been forged between Adams and Clay.

**1824** John Quincy Adams is the fourth straight and last president from the Democratic-Republican Party, which held the White House from 1800 to 1829. The party splits into factions around Adams and his elec-

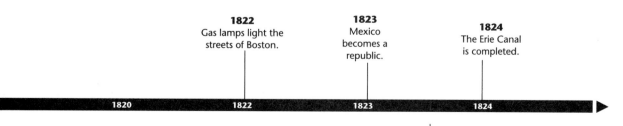

**1822**
Gas lamps light the streets of Boston.

**1823**
Mexico becomes a republic.

**1824**
The Erie Canal is completed.

1820      1822      1823      1824

tion opponent, Andrew Jackson (called Jacksonian Democrats), respectively.

1826    Former presidents John Adams and Thomas Jefferson die on the same day, July 4—fifty years to the day after the Declaration of Independence was officially issued.

1828    Former Tennessee senator Andrew Jackson defeats President John Quincy Adams. Modern-day political parties are established: Jackson leads the Democratic Party, and Adams leads the National Republican Party. The National Republicans are also represented in the 1832 presidential election, but most party members are joined by anti-Jackson Democrats to form the Whig Party in 1834.

1832    President Andrew Jackson is reelected. Candidates from the Nullifier Party (based on the proposition that states have the right to nullify federal laws) and the Anti-Masonic Party receive electoral votes. Future president Millard Fillmore was elected to the U.S. House of Representatives in 1831 as a member of the Anti-Masonic Party (a pro-labor group against social clubs and secret societies).

1832    The Black Hawk War leads to the taking of Native American land west to the Mississippi River. Future president Abraham Lincoln is among those fighting.

1832    President Andrew Jackson vetoes the charter for the Second National Bank (the federal banking system), creating great controversy between Democrats (favoring states' rights) and proponents for a strong federal government, who gradually unite to form the Whig Party in 1834.

1833    Running water is installed in the White House.

**1826**
James Fenimore Cooper writes *The Last of the Mohicans.*

**1827**
Contact lenses are invented.

**1831**
Nat Turner leads slave rebellion.

**1833**
The Whig Party is formed.

1826    1828    1830    1833

1834    Congress censures (publicly rebukes) President Andrew Jackson for having taken funds from the federal bank and depositing them in various state banks.

1836    Vice President Martin Van Buren is elected president after defeating three Whig candidates. Whigs hoped that their three regional candidates would win enough electoral votes to deny Van Buren a majority and throw the election to the House of Representatives, where Whigs held the majority.

1836    The last surviving founding father, James Madison, dies the same year the first president born after the American Revolution (Martin Van Buren) is elected.

1836    Arkansas becomes the twenty-fifth state of the Union.

1837    The Panic of 1837 initiates a period of economic hard times that lasts throughout President Martin Van Buren's administration.

1837    Michigan becomes the twenty-sixth state of the Union.

1840    Military hero and Ohio politician William Henry Harrision (known as "Old Tippecanoe") defeats President Martin Van Buren.

1841    President William Henry Harrison dies thirty-one days after being inaugurated president. A constitutional issue arises because the document is unclear as to whether Vice President John Tyler should complete Harrison's term or serve as an interim president until Congress selects a new president. Tyler has himself sworn in as president. Controversy follows, but Tyler sets a precedent on presidential succession.

1841    The President's Cabinet, except for Secretary of State Daniel Webster, resigns, and some congressmen con-

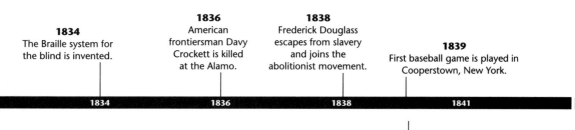

**1834**
The Braille system for the blind is invented.

**1836**
American frontiersman Davy Crockett is killed at the Alamo.

**1838**
Frederick Douglass escapes from slavery and joins the abolitionist movement.

**1839**
First baseball game is played in Cooperstown, New York.

1834     1836     1838     1841

sider impeachment proceedings against President John Tyler (but the impeachment fails to materialize). Though a member of the Whig Party, Tyler opposes the Whig program for expanding federal powers. He is kicked out of the Whig Party.

1842    The Webster-Ashburton Treaty settles a border dispute between Maine and Quebec, Canada, and averts war between the United States and Great Britain.

1844    Congress approves a resolution annexing Texas.

1844    Tennessee politician James K. Polk, strongly associated with former president Andrew Jackson, is elected president. The years beginning with Jackson's presidency in 1829 and ending with Polk's in March 1849 are often referred to historically as The Age of Jackson.

1845    Congress passes and President James K. Polk signs legislation to have presidential elections held simultaneously throughout the country on the Tuesday following the first Monday in November.

1845    Florida becomes the twenty-seventh and Texas the twenty-eighth states of the Union.

1845    The U.S. Naval Academy opens.

1846    The Mexican War begins.

1846    Iowa and Wisconsin expand the Union to thirty states.

1848    Gas lamps are installed in the White House to replace candles and oil lamps.

1848    The Mexican War ends. The United States takes possession of the southwest area from Texas to California.

1848    General Zachary Taylor, a Mexican War hero, is elected president in a close race. He had joined the Whig

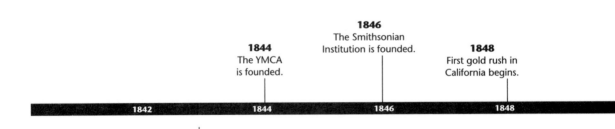

**1846**
The Smithsonian
Institution is founded.

**1844**
The YMCA
is founded.

**1848**
First gold rush in
California begins.

1842      1844      1846      1848

Party but promised to remain above partisan causes and announced that he was against the expansion of slavery into new territories. Ex-president Martin Van Buren finishes a distant third as a candidate for the Free-Soil Party that also opposes the expansion of slavery into new territories. Van Buren likely drew enough votes from the Democratic candidate, former Michigan senator Lewis Cass, to tip the election to Taylor.

1849   The California Gold Rush brings thousands of people into the new American territory.

1850   President Zachary Taylor dies in office, and Vice President Millard Fillmore becomes president.

1850   President Millard Fillmore supports and signs into law the series of bills called the Compromise of 1850 that the late president Zachary Taylor had opposed. The Fugitive Slave Act, which forces northern states to return runaway slaves, becomes law.

1850   California becomes the thirty-first state of the Union.

1850   The Pony Express begins operation, providing mail service to the far west.

1852   Former New Hampshire senator Franklin Pierce is elected president.

1852   *Uncle Tom's Cabin,* by Harriet Beecher Stowe, is published and further fuels growing support in the North for complete abolition of slavery.

1853   The Gadsden Purchase adds southern areas of present-day New Mexico and Arizona as American territory.

1854   The Republican Party is formed by those against the expansion of slavery and by abolitionists wanting to outlaw the institution, drawing from the Whig Party

**1851**
*The New York Times* begins publication.

**1853**
Steinway pianos begin manufacturing.

**1854**
The Kansas-Nebraska Act returns slavery decisions to states.

1849          1850          1852          1854

(which becomes defunct) and Democrats opposed to slavery.

1854    Diplomatic and trade relations begin between the United States and Japan.

1856    Civil war breaks out in Kansas Territory between pro- and anti-slavery proponents.

1856    Former secretary of state James Buchanan, a states' rights advocate, is elected president. Former California senator John Frémont finishes second as the Republican Party's first presidential candidate. Former president Millard Fillmore finishes third with about twenty percent of the popular vote and eight electoral votes, as the nominee of the American Party (also nicknamed the Know-Nothing Party).

1857    The *Dred Scott* decision by the U.S. Supreme Court limits the power of Congress to decide on slavery issues in American territories petitioning to become states.

1858    The Lincoln-Douglas debates in Illinois, between U.S. Senate candidates Abraham Lincoln and incumbent Stephen Douglas, receive national press coverage.

1858    Minnesota becomes the thirty-second state of the Union.

1859    Abolitionist John Brown leads a raid on a federal arsenal in Harper's Ferry, Virginia (now West Virginia), hoping to spark and arm a slave rebellion.

1859    Oregon becomes the thirty-third state of the Union.

1860    Former Illinois congressman Abraham Lincoln is elected president despite winning less than forty percent of the popular vote. Democratic votes are split among three candidates. One of the party's candidates, Illi-

**1856**
Neanderthal man fossils are found.

**1858**
Ottawa becomes the capital of Canada.

**1859**
Charles Darwin publishes his theory of evolution.

**1860**
Early form of the typewriter is invented.

1854      1856      1858      1860

nois senator Stephen Douglas, finishes second in the popular vote but places fourth in electoral votes.

1860    South Carolina secedes from the Union.

1861    Confederate States of America formed; Civil War begins.

1861    Kansas becomes the thirty-fourth state of the Union.

1863    President Abraham Lincoln, sitting in what is now called the Lincoln Bedroom in the White House, signs the Emancipation Proclamation, freeing slaves in the states in rebellion.

1863    West Virginia becomes the thirty-fifth state of the Union.

1863    President Abraham Lincoln proposes a policy for admitting seceded states back into the Union on moderate terms.

1864    Pro-Union Republicans and Democrats unite as the National Union Party under President Abraham Lincoln (Republican) and Tennessee senator Andrew Johnson, who had remained in Congress after his southern colleagues walked out. The Lincoln-Johnson ticket wins 212 of 233 electoral votes.

1864    Nevada becomes the thirty-sixth state of the Union.

1865    The Civil War ends.

1865    President Abraham Lincoln is assassinated, and Vice President Andrew Johnson succeeds him as president.

1865    The Thirteenth Amendment to the Constitution, outlawing slavery, is ratified.

1867    Over objections and vetoes by President Andrew Johnson, Congress passes harsher Reconstruction

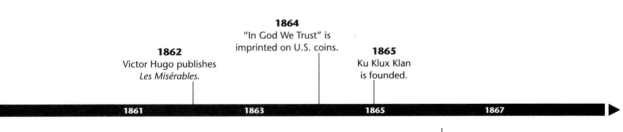

**1864**
"In God We Trust" is imprinted on U.S. coins.

**1862**
Victor Hugo publishes
*Les Misérables.*

**1865**
Ku Klux Klan
is founded.

1861          1863          1865          1867

policies (terms under which former Confederate states can operate) than the Johnson (and Lincoln) plans.

1867    Nebraska becomes the thirty-seventh state of the Union.

1867    The United States purchases Alaska (a deal called "Seward's Folly" after Secretary of State William H. Seward, who negotiated the acquisition) from Russia.

1868    President Andrew Johnson becomes the first president to be impeached by the House of Representatives. He is acquitted by one vote in a trial in the U.S. Senate.

1868    Civil War hero Ulysses S. Grant is elected president.

1869    The Transcontinental railroad is completed.

1869    President Ulysses S. Grant fails in attempts to annex the Dominican Republic.

1872    President Ulysses S. Grant is reelected. His opponent, newspaper publisher Horace Greeley, dies shortly after the election, and his electoral votes are dispersed among several other Democrats.

1873    The Crédit Mobilier scandal reflects widespread corruption among some officials in the Ulysses S. Grant administration and some congressmen.

1876    Colorado becomes the thirty-eighth state of the Union.

1876    In the hotly contested presidential election, the Democratic candidate, New York governor Samuel J. Tilden, outpolls the Republican nominee, Ohio governor Rutherford B. Hayes, by over two hundred thousand votes, but falls one electoral vote short of a majority when twenty electoral votes (from the states of Florida, South Carolina, Louisiana, and Oregon) are contested with claims of fraud. The House of Representatives fails to resolve the issue.

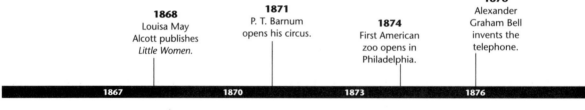

**1868**
Louisa May Alcott publishes *Little Women.*

**1871**
P. T. Barnum opens his circus.

**1874**
First American zoo opens in Philadelphia.

**1876**
Alexander Graham Bell invents the telephone.

1867        1870        1873        1876

1877    A special Electoral Commission is established to resolve the 1876 presidential election controversy. Days before the scheduled inauguration of the new president in March, the Commission awards the 20 disputed votes to Republican Rutherford B. Hayes, who edges Democrat Samuel J. Tilden, 185-184, in the Electoral College. Some historians refer to the decision as the Compromise of 1877, believing that Republicans and southern Democrats struck a deal: Hayes would be president, and Reconstruction (federal supervision of former Confederate states) would end.

1877    Federal troops are withdrawn from South Carolina and Louisiana, where troops had been stationed since the end of the Civil War to enforce national laws. Reconstruction ends, and southern states regain the same rights as all other states.

1878    Attempting to reform the civil service (where jobs were often provided by the party in power to party members), President Rutherford B. Hayes suspends fellow Republican Chester A. Arthur (a future U.S. president) as the powerful head of the New York Custom's House (which collects import taxes).

1879    The first telephone is installed in the White House. The phone number: 1.

1879    Thomas Edison invents the incandescent light bulb.

1880    Ohio congressman James A. Garfield is elected president.

1881    President James A. Garfield is assassinated by an extremist who lost his job under civil service reform. Chester A. Arthur becomes the fourth vice president to assume the presidency upon the death of the chief executive. Like the previous three (John Tyler, Millard

**1877**
The first Wimbledon
tennis championship
is played.

**1879**
British Zulu War
takes place.

**1880**
Gilbert and
Sullivan compose
"The Pirates of
Penzance."

1877      1878      1880      1881

Fillmore, and Andrew Johnson), Arthur is not selected by his party to run for the presidency after completing the elected president's term.

1883    The Pendleton Act, mandating major civil service reform, is signed into law by President Chester A. Arthur.

1884    New York governor Grover Cleveland is elected as the first Democrat to win the presidency since 1856. Tariffs (taxes on imported goods) and tariff reform become major issues during his presidency and the following three elections.

1885    The Statue of Liberty is dedicated.

1886    President Grover Cleveland marries Frances Folsom, becoming the only president to marry at the White House.

1888    Former Indiana senator Benjamin Harrison is elected president despite receiving 90,000 fewer popular votes than President Grover Cleveland. Harrison wins most of the more populated states for a 233-168 Electoral College advantage.

1889    North Dakota, South Dakota, Montana, and Washington enter the Union, expanding the United States to forty-two states.

1890    Idaho and Wyoming become the forty-third and forty-fourth states of the Union.

1891    Electric wiring is installed in the White House.

1892    Former president Grover Cleveland becomes the first person to win non-consecutive presidential terms by defeating incumbent president Benjamin Harrison (in the popular vote *and* the Electoral College). Iowa politician James B. Weaver of the People's Party (also

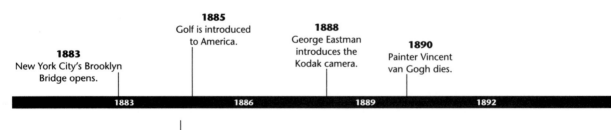

**1885**
Golf is introduced to America.

**1883**
New York City's Brooklyn Bridge opens.

**1888**
George Eastman introduces the Kodak camera.

**1890**
Painter Vincent van Gogh dies.

1883      1886      1889      1892

known as the Populists) finishes a distant third in the popular vote but garners twenty-two electoral votes.

1893     Lame duck (an official completing an elected term after having failed to be reelected) President Benjamin Harrison presents a treaty to annex Hawaii to the U.S. Congress.

1893     President Grover Cleveland rescinds former president Benjamin Harrison's treaty for the annexation of Hawaii and calls for an investigation of the American-led rebellion that overthrew the Hawaiian native monarchy.

1894     An economic downturn and numerous strikes paralyze the American economy.

1895     With gold reserves (used to back the value of currency) running low, President Grover Cleveland arranges a gold purchase through financier J. P. Morgan.

1896     Ohio governor William McKinley, the Republican Party nominee, is elected president over the Democratic candidate, former Nebraska congressman William Jennings Bryan.

1896     Utah becomes the forty-fifth state of the Union.

1898     The Spanish-American War takes place. The United States wins quickly and takes possession of overseas territories (the former Spanish colonies of Cuba, Puerto Rico, and the Philippines).

1898     President William McKinley reintroduces the Hawaii annexation issue and Congress approves it.

1899     President William McKinley expands U.S. trade with China and other nations through his Open Door Policy.

1900     President William McKinley is reelected by defeating William Jennings Bryan a second time.

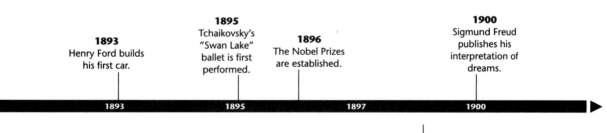

**1893**
Henry Ford builds his first car.

**1895**
Tchaikovsky's "Swan Lake" ballet is first performed.

**1896**
The Nobel Prizes are established.

**1900**
Sigmund Freud publishes his interpretation of dreams.

1893      1895      1897      1900

1900    Chinese nationalists take arms against growing for-
        eign influences in their country, an uprising called
        the Boxer Rebellion. American military forces join
        those of other foreign nations to put down the upris-
        ing. American military forces are also stationed in the
        Philippines to combat revolts.

1901    President William McKinley is assassinated; Vice Pres-
        ident Theodore Roosevelt assumes the presidency
        and, at age 42, becomes the youngest man to become
        president.

1902    To combat the growing influence of trusts (business
        combinations intended to stifle competition), Presi-
        dent Theodore Roosevelt orders vigorous enforcement
        of antitrust laws, and an era of business and social re-
        form gains momentum.

1903    The United States quickly recognizes and supports a
        rebellion in the nation of Colombia through which
        Panama becomes an independent nation. Through the
        Panama Canal treaty, which provides a strip of land to
        be developed by the United States, President Theodore
        Roosevelt spearheads plans to build a canal across
        Panama, linking the Atlantic and Pacific oceans.

1904    Theodore Roosevelt becomes the first president who
        assumed office upon the death of the elected presi-
        dent to win election for a full term.

1905    President Theodore Roosevelt serves as mediator dur-
        ing the Russo-Japanese War. His success at helping
        end the conflict earns him a Nobel Peace Prize.

1907    Oklahoma becomes the forty-sixth state.

1908    William Howard Taft, who served in the William
        McKinley and Theodore Roosevelt administrations, is

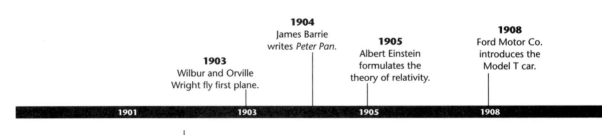

**1904**
James Barrie
writes *Peter Pan.*

**1905**
Albert Einstein
formulates the
theory of relativity.

**1908**
Ford Motor Co.
introduces the
Model T car.

**1903**
Wilbur and Orville
Wright fly first plane.

1901          1903          1905          1908

elected president. William Jennings Bryan loses in his third presidential bid.

1909    In a sign of the times, President William Howard Taft purchases official automobiles and has the White House stable converted into a garage.

1909    The North Pole is reached.

1912    New Jersey governor Woodrow Wilson is elected president. Former president Theodore Roosevelt, running as the Progressive Party candidate (nicknamed "the Bull Moose Party"), finishes second. Roosevelt outpolls his successor, President William Howard Taft, by about seven hundred thousand popular votes and wins eighty more electoral votes.

1912    New Mexico and Arizona enter the Union, expanding the United States to forty-eight states.

1912    The Sixteenth Amendment, authorizing the collection of income taxes, is ratified.

1912    The Federal Reserve, which regulates the nation's money supply and financial institutions, is established.

1913    The Seventeenth Amendment changes the system for electing U.S. senators. The popular vote replaces the system where most senators were elected by state legislatures.

1914    World War I begins.

1914    U.S. military forces begin having skirmishes with Mexican rebels in a series of incidents that last until 1916.

1914    The Panama Canal is opened.

1916    President Woodrow Wilson is reelected by a slim Electoral College margin, 277-254. He defeats the Repub-

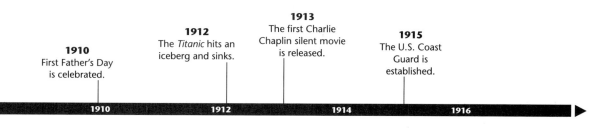

**1910**
First Father's Day is celebrated.

**1912**
The *Titanic* hits an iceberg and sinks.

**1913**
The first Charlie Chaplin silent movie is released.

**1915**
The U.S. Coast Guard is established.

1910    1912    1914    1916

lican candidate, former U.S. Supreme Court justice Charles Evans Hughes.

1916    President Woodrow Wilson acts as mediator for the nations in conflict in World War I.

1917    Citing acts of German aggression, President Woodrow Wilson asks Congress to declare war. The United States enters World War I. The Selective Service (a system through which young men are called on for military duty) is established.

1918    World War I ends.

1919    Congress rejects the Treaty of Versailles negotiated by President Woodrow Wilson and other leaders representing the nations involved in World War I. Congress also rejects American participation in the League of Nations that Wilson had envisioned.

1919    Attempting to rally support of the Treaty of Versailles and the League of Nations during a long speaking tour, President Woodrow Wilson collapses with a debilitating stroke. The public is not made aware of the severity of the affliction that leaves Wilson bedridden.

1919    The Eighteenth Amendment, outlawing the manufacture and sale of alcohol, is ratified.

1920    Women are able to participate in national elections for the first time.

1920    Ohio senator Warren G. Harding is elected president.

1922    Illegal deals are made by some officials of the Warren G. Harding administration. Two years later, they are implicated in the Teapot Dome scandal.

1923    President Warren G. Harding dies in San Francisco, California; Vice President Calvin Coolidge assumes the presidency.

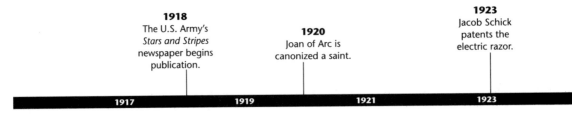

**1918**
The U.S. Army's
*Stars and Stripes*
newspaper begins
publication.

**1920**
Joan of Arc is
canonized a saint.

**1923**
Jacob Schick
patents the
electric razor.

1917          1919          1921          1923

**1924** Calvin Coolidge is elected president in a landslide, defeating West Virginia politician John W. Davis, the Democratic candidate. Progressive Party candidate Robert M. LaFollette, a future Wisconsin senator, garners over thirteen percent of the popular vote and wins thirteen electoral votes.

**1925** The Scopes Trial is held in Dayton, Tennessee, after a public school teacher instructs his class on the theory of evolution in defiance of a state law.

**1927** Charles Lindbergh becomes the first pilot to fly solo across the Atlantic Ocean.

**1928** Former secretary of commerce Herbert Hoover, who also supervised international relief efforts during World War I, wins his first election attempt in a landslide (by over six million popular votes and a 444-87 Electoral College triumph).

**1929** The stock market crashes.

**1930** President Herbert Hoover assures the nation that "the economy is on the mend," but continued crises become the Great Depression that lasts the entire decade.

**1932** The Bonus March, in which World War I veterans gather in Washington, D.C., to demand benefits promised to them, ends in disaster and death when military officials forcibly remove them and destroy their campsites.

**1932** New York governor Franklin D. Roosevelt defeats President Herbert Hoover by over seven million popular votes and a 472-59 margin in the Electoral College.

**1933** President Franklin D. Roosevelt calls a special session of Congress to enact major pieces of legislation to combat the Great Depression. Over a span called The

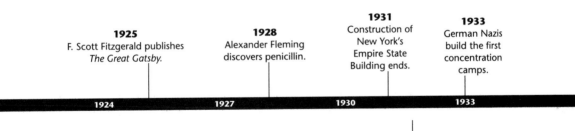

**1925**
F. Scott Fitzgerald publishes *The Great Gatsby*.

**1928**
Alexander Fleming discovers penicillin.

**1931**
Construction of New York's Empire State Building ends.

**1933**
German Nazis build the first concentration camps.

1924    1927    1930    1933

Hundred Days, much of Roosevelt's New Deal program of social and economic relief, recovery, and reform is approved.

1933   As part of the Twentieth Amendment to the Constitution, the inauguration date of the president is changed to January 20 of the year following the election.

1933   The Twenty-first Amendment repeals prohibition.

1936   President Franklin D. Roosevelt is reelected by a popular vote margin of eleven million and wins the Electoral College vote, 523-8.

1937   Frustrated when the U.S. Supreme Court declares several New Deal programs unconstitutional, President Franklin D. Roosevelt initiates legislation to add more justices to the court and to set term limits. His attempt to "stack the court" receives little support.

1939   World War II begins.

1939   Physicist Albert Einstein informs President Franklin D. Roosevelt about the possibility for creating nuclear weapons and warns him that Nazi scientists are already pursuing experiments to unleash atomic power.

1940   President Franklin D. Roosevelt wins an unprecedented third term by slightly less than five million popular votes and a 449-82 win in the Electoral College.

1941   Pearl Harbor, Hawaii, is attacked; the United States enters World War II.

1942   The success of the first nuclear chain reaction is communicated to President Franklin D. Roosevelt through the code words, "The eagle has landed." A secret program for manufacturing and testing atomic bombs begins.

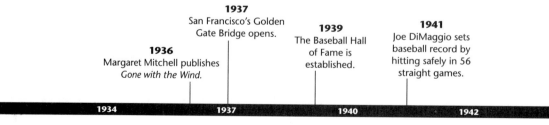

**1936**
Margaret Mitchell publishes
*Gone with the Wind.*

**1937**
San Francisco's Golden
Gate Bridge opens.

**1939**
The Baseball Hall
of Fame is
established.

**1941**
Joe DiMaggio sets
baseball record by
hitting safely in 56
straight games.

1934     1937     1940     1942

**1944** President Franklin D. Roosevelt is elected to a fourth term by over five million popular votes and a 432-99 Electoral College triumph.

**1945** President Franklin D. Roosevelt attends the Yalta Conference and meets with British prime minister Winston Churchill and Soviet leader Joseph Stalin to discuss war issues and the postwar world.

**1945** President Franklin D. Roosevelt dies; Vice President Harry S. Truman becomes president. It is only then that Truman learns about development and successful testing of the atomic bomb.

**1945** World War II ends in Europe.

**1945** The United States drops atomic bombs on Japan. Japan surrenders, and World War II ends.

**1946** The U.S. government seizes coal mines and railroads to avoid labor strikes and business practices that might contribute to inflation.

**1947** An economic aid package called the Marshall Plan, named after its architect, Secretary of State George C. Marshall, helps revive war-torn Europe.

**1947** The Cold War, a period of strained relations and the threat of nuclear war between the United States and the Soviet Union, and their respective allies, settles in and continues for more than forty years.

**1948** Renovation of the White House begins. Four years later, the project has completely reconstructed the interior and added two underground levels.

**1948** Despite the *Chicago Daily Tribune* headline "DEWEY DEFEATS TRUMAN" on the morning after election day, President Harry S. Truman wins the presidency,

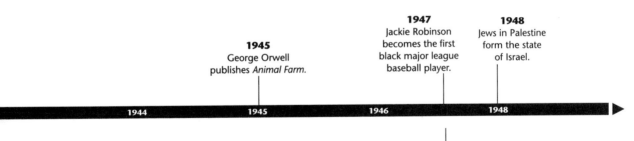

**1945**
George Orwell
publishes *Animal Farm.*

**1947**
Jackie Robinson
becomes the first
black major league
baseball player.

**1948**
Jews in Palestine
form the state
of Israel.

1944    1945    1946    1948

taking over two million more popular votes and winning 303-189 in the Electoral College. The State's Rights Party candidate, South Carolina governor J. Strom Thurmond, places third, slightly outpolling the Progressive Party candidate, former vice president Henry Wallace, and winning thirty-nine electoral votes. Thurmond led a contingent of Southern politicians away from the Democratic Party in protest of Truman's support for civil rights legislation.

1949    The North Atlantic Treaty Organization (NATO) is formed by the United States and its European allies to monitor and check acts of aggression in Europe.

1950    The United States becomes involved in a police action to protect South Korea from invasion by communist North Korea. The police action intensifies into the Korean War.

1951    The Twenty-second Amendment to the Constitution is ratified, limiting presidents to two elected terms and no more than two years of a term to which someone else was elected.

1952    Dwight D. "Ike" Eisenhower, famous as the Supreme Commander of Allied Forces during World War II, is elected president.

1953    An armistice is signed in Korea.

1954    The Army-McCarthy hearings are held. Wisconsin senator Joseph McCarthy presents accusations that the U.S. military and Department of State are deeply infiltrated by communists. McCarthy is eventually disgraced when most of his accusations prove groundless.

1954    In *Brown v. Board of Education,* the U.S. Supreme Court rules that racially segregated public schools are un-

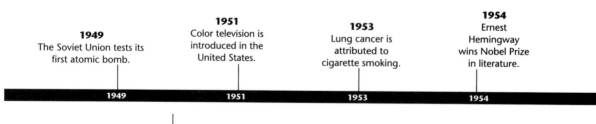

**1949**
The Soviet Union tests its first atomic bomb.

**1951**
Color television is introduced in the United States.

**1953**
Lung cancer is attributed to cigarette smoking.

**1954**
Ernest Hemingway wins Nobel Prize in literature.

1949          1951          1953          1954

constitutional. In 1957, President Dwight D. Eisenhower sends troops to Little Rock, Arkansas, to enforce desegregation of schools.

1956    An uprising in Hungary against Soviet domination is quickly crushed.

1956    President Dwight D. Eisenhower wins reelection, his second straight triumph over his Democratic challenger, former Illinois governor Adlai Stevenson.

1957    The Soviet Union launches the first space satellite, *Sputnik I.*

1958    The United States launches its first space satellite, *Explorer I,* and the National Aeronautics and Space Agency (NASA) is created.

1959    Alaska and Hawaii enter the Union as the forty-ninth and fiftieth states.

1960    The Cold War deepens over the *U2* incident, where a U.S. spy plane is shot down inside the Soviet Union.

1960    Massachusetts senator John F. Kennedy outpolls Vice President Richard Nixon by slightly more than 100,000 votes while winning 303-219 in the Electoral College. Kennedy, at age 43, is the youngest elected president. A dispute over nine thousand votes in Illinois, that might have resulted in Nixon winning that state instead of Kennedy, is stopped by Nixon. A change of electoral votes in Illinois would not have affected the overall electoral majority won by Kennedy.

1961    The District of Columbia is allowed three electoral votes.

1961    An invasion of Cuba by American-supported rebels at the Bay of Pigs fails when an internal rebellion does

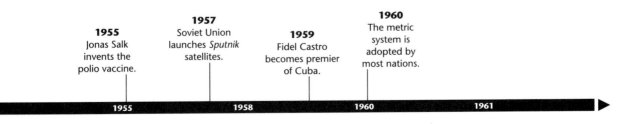

**1955**
Jonas Salk invents the polio vaccine.

**1957**
Soviet Union launches *Sputnik* satellites.

**1959**
Fidel Castro becomes premier of Cuba.

**1960**
The metric system is adopted by most nations.

1955         1958         1960         1961

not materialize and President John F. Kennedy refuses to provide military backing.

1962   The Cuban Missile Crisis puts the United States and the Soviet Union on the brink of nuclear war after the Soviets are discovered building missile launch sites in Cuba. After a tense, ten-day standoff, the missiles are removed.

1963   A military coup overthrows the political leader of South Vietnam, where American military advisors are assisting South Vietnamese to repel a communist takeover.

1963   A large civil rights march on Washington, D.C., culminates with the famous "I Have a Dream" speech by Rev. Martin Luther King Jr.

1963   President John F. Kennedy is assassinated; Vice President Lyndon B. Johnson assumes the presidency.

1964   President Lyndon B. Johnson steers major civil rights legislation through Congress in memory of the late president John F. Kennedy. The Twenty-fourth Amendment to the Constitution is ratified and ensures the right of citizens of the United States to vote shall not be denied "by reason of failure to pay any poll tax or other tax."

1964   President Lyndon B. Johnson is elected in a landslide, winning almost sixteen million more popular votes than Arizona senator Barry Goldwater.

1965   The Vietnam conflict escalates. President Lyndon B. Johnson is given emergency powers by Congress. Massive bombing missions begin, and U.S. military troops begin engaging in combat, although the U.S. Congress never officially declares war.

**1962**
Rachel Carson publishes environmental classic *Silent Spring*.

**1963**
Golfer Jack Nicklaus wins his first Masters Tournament.

**1964**
Musical *Fiddler on the Roof* opens.

**1965**
Astronauts walk in space for the first time.

1962    1963    1964    1965

**1966** An unmanned American spacecraft lands on the moon.

**1967** Protests, including a march on Washington, D.C., escalate against American involvement in the Vietnam War.

**1967** Thurgood Marshall becomes the first African American Supreme Court justice.

**1967** The Twenty-fifth Amendment to the Constitution is ratified and provides clear lines of succession to the presidency: "Section 1. In case of the removal of the President from office or of his death or resignation, the Vice President shall become President. Section 2. Whenever there is a vacancy in the office of the Vice President, the President shall nominate a Vice President who shall take office upon confirmation by a majority vote of both Houses of Congress."

**1968** Civil rights leader Rev. Martin Luther King Jr. is assassinated in April, and leading Democratic presidential candidate Robert F. Kennedy is assassinated in June.

**1968** Former vice president Richard Nixon is elected president, winning with 500,000 more popular votes than incumbent vice president Hubert H. Humphrey and a 301-191 Electoral College edge. Former Alabama governor George C. Wallace of the American Independent Party (for state's rights and against racial desegregation) nets over nine million popular votes and wins forty-six electoral votes.

**1969** American troop withdrawals from South Vietnam begin.

**1969** U.S. astronaut Neil Armstrong becomes the first man to walk on the moon.

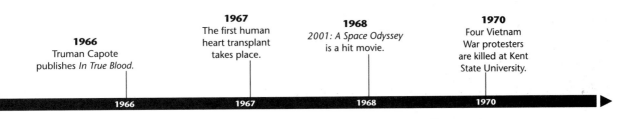

**1966**
Truman Capote publishes *In True Blood.*

**1967**
The first human heart transplant takes place.

**1968**
*2001: A Space Odyssey* is a hit movie.

**1970**
Four Vietnam War protesters are killed at Kent State University.

1966     1967     1968     1970

**1972** President Richard Nixon reestablishes U.S. relations with the People's Republic of China that were ended after a communist takeover in China in 1949. He visits China and the Soviet Union, where he initiates a policy of détente (a relaxing of tensions between rival nations).

**1972** An investigation of a burglary of Democratic National Headquarters at the Watergate Hotel and Office Complex in Washington, D.C., begins and leads to connections with officials in the Richard Nixon administration.

**1972** President Richard Nixon is reelected in a landslide.

**1973** The Paris Peace Agreement, between the United States and North Vietnam, ends American military involvement in the Vietnam War.

**1973** Vice President Spiro T. Agnew resigns over income tax evasion; he is replaced by Michigan congressman Gerald R. Ford.

**1974** Nationally televised U.S. Senate hearings on the Watergate scandal confirm connections between the 1972 burglary and officials of the Richard Nixon administration as well as abuses of power.

**1974** The House Judiciary Committee begins impeachment hearings and plans to recommend to the House the impeachment of President Richard Nixon.

**1974** President Richard Nixon resigns from office over the Watergate scandal. Vice President Gerald R. Ford assumes office.

**1974** President Gerald R. Ford issues a pardon, protecting former president Richard Nixon from prosecution in an attempt to end "our national nightmare."

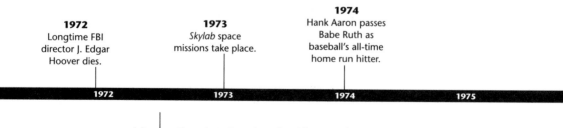

**1972**
Longtime FBI director J. Edgar Hoover dies.

**1973**
*Skylab* space missions take place.

**1974**
Hank Aaron passes Babe Ruth as baseball's all-time home run hitter.

1972    1973    1974    1975

1976    In a close election, former Georgia governor Jimmy Carter defeats President Gerald R. Ford.

1977    Beset by rising fuel costs and a continued sluggish economy, President Jimmy Carter calls an energy shortage "the moral equivalent of war" and attempts to rally conservation efforts.

1979    The Camp David Accords, the result of negotiations spearheaded by President Jimmy Carter, is signed by the leaders of Egyptian president Anwar Sadat and Israeli prime minister Menachem Begin in Washington, D.C.

1979    Fifty-two Americans are taken hostage in Iran following a religious revolution in that nation in which the American-supported leader was overthrown. The hostage crisis lasts 444 days, with the hostages released on the day President Jimmy Carter leaves office.

1980    Former California governor Ronald Reagan wins a landslide (489-49 in the Electoral College) over President Jimmy Carter. Independent candidate John Anderson, a longtime Republican congressman from Illinois, polls over five million votes. Reagan becomes the oldest president.

1981    Sandra Day O'Connor becomes the first female U.S. Supreme Court justice.

1982    Economic growth begins after a decade of sluggish performance.

1984    President Ronald Reagan is reelected in another landslide, drawing the most popular votes ever (54,455,075) and romping in the Electoral College, 525-13.

1987    A sudden stock market crash and growing federal deficits threaten economic growth.

**1976**
The United States celebrates its bicentennial.

**1978**
Pope John Paul II begins reign as leader of the Catholic Church.

**1985**
Microsoft releases Windows.

**1986**
The space shuttle *Challenger* explodes.

1976    1980    1984    1987

**1988** George Bush becomes the first sitting vice president since Martin Van Buren in 1836 to be elected president.

**1989** Several East European nations become independent from domination by the U.S.S.R. Reforms in the U.S.S.R. eventually lead to the breakup of the Soviet Union; the former Soviet states become independent nations in 1991, and the Cold War ends.

**1991** After the Iraqi government fails to comply with a United Nations resolution to abandon Kuwait, which its military invaded in August of 1990, the Gulf War begins. Within a month, Kuwait is liberated by an international military force. President George Bush's popularity soars over his leadership in rallying U.N. members to stop Iraqi aggression.

**1992** An economic downturn and a huge budget deficit erode President George Bush's popularity. Arkansas governor Bill Clinton defeats Bush for the presidency. The Reform Party candidate, Texas businessman H. Ross Perot, draws 19,221,433 votes, the most ever for a third-party candidate, but wins no electoral votes. Clinton and running mate Al Gore are the youngest president–vice president tandem in history.

**1994** An upturn in the economy begins the longest sustained growth period in American history.

**1996** President Bill Clinton is reelected.

**1998** President Bill Clinton is implicated in perjury (false testimony under oath in a court case) and an extramarital affair. The House Judiciary Committee votes, strictly on party lines, to recommend impeachment of the president, and the House impeaches the president for perjury and abuse of power.

**1989**
The Berlin Wall is torn down.

**1990**
Soviet president Mikhail Gorbachev wins the Nobel Peace Prize.

**1993**
Toni Morrison becomes the first African American to win the Nobel Prize in literature.

**1998**
Mark McGwire hits 70 home runs.

1988    1991    1994    1998

**1999**   President Bill Clinton remains in office after being acquitted in a Senate trial.

**2000**   In the closest and most hotly contested election since 1876, Texas governor George W. Bush narrowly defeats Vice President Al Gore in the Electoral College, 271-266. Gore wins the popular vote by some three hundred thousand votes. The final victor cannot be declared until after a recount in Florida (with its twenty-five electoral votes at stake) takes place. Five weeks of legal battles ensue and Gore officially contests the results before Bush is able to claim victory in the state and, therefore, in the national election.

**2000**   Hillary Rodham Clinton becomes the first first lady to be elected to public office when she is elected U.S. senator from New York.

**2000**   In one of his last functions as president, Bill Clinton attends an international economic summit in Asia and visits Vietnam, twenty-five years after the end of the conflict that deeply divided Americans.

**2001**   George W. Bush is inaugurated the nation's forty-third president and becomes the second son of a president to become president himself.

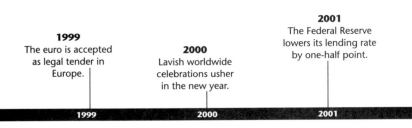

**1999**
The euro is accepted as legal tender in Europe.

**2000**
Lavish worldwide celebrations usher in the new year.

**2001**
The Federal Reserve lowers its lending rate by one-half point.

1999          2000          2001

# Words to Know

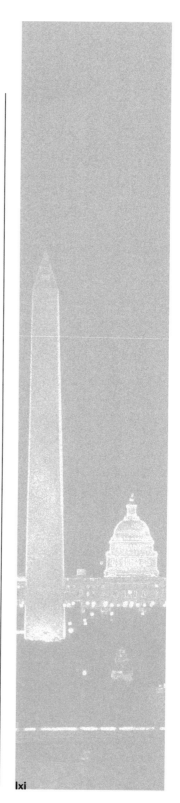

## A

**Abolitionists:** People who worked to end slavery.

**Agrarian:** One who believes in and supports issues beneficial to agriculture.

**Alien and Sedition Acts:** Four bills—the Naturalization Act, Alien Act, Alien Enemies Act, and Sedition Act—passed by Congress in 1798 and signed into law by President John Adams. The Naturalization Act extended from five to fourteen years the waiting period before citizenship—and with it, the right to vote—could be obtained by new immigrants. The two Alien acts gave the president the right to deport or jail foreign citizens he deemed a threat to the nation's stability, especially during wartime. The Sedition Act criminalized criticism of the government. To write or publish views that disparaged the administration was punishable by harsh fines and jail terms.

**Allied forces (allies):** Alliances of countries in military opposition to another group of nations. Twenty-eight nations made up the Allied and Associated powers in World War I. In World War II, the Allied powers included Great Britain, the United States, and the Soviet Union.

**Anarchist:** One against any form of government.

**Annexing:** Adding a new state or possession to the existing United States of America.

**Annual Message to Congress:** A speech the president delivers before Congress each year. Originally called the Annual Message to Congress and delivered each November, the speech became known as the State of the Union Address and is delivered each January.

**Anti-Federalists:** A group who wanted a limited federal government and more power for individual states.

**Antitrust:** Government action against businesses that dominate a certain industry or market and that are alleged to have stifled competing businesses.

**Appropriations:** Funds authorized for a particular project.

**Armistice:** An agreement to cease fire while warring parties negotiate a peace settlement.

**Articles of Confederation:** From March 1, 1781, to June 21, 1788, the Articles served as the equivalent of the Constitution (1787). The Constitution replaced the Articles, which had failed to produce a strong central government, and the present-day United States was formed.

**Axis:** The countries that fought together against the Allies in World War II. Germany, Italy, and Japan formed the first coalition; eventually, they were joined by Hungary, Romania, Slovakia, Finland, and Bulgaria.

# B

**Bar:** A term that encompasses all certified lawyers—those who have passed all official requirements (the bar exam) to be certified as lawyers.

**Bar exam:** A test that lawyers must pass in order to become legally certified to practice law.

**Battle of the Bulge:** Battles surrounding the last German offensive (1944–45) during World War II. Allied forces moving toward Germany from France following the D-Day invasion were stalled by bad weather along the German border. Germans launched a counteroffensive to divide American and British forces. Germans created a "bulge" in the Allied lines, but they were halted and then withdrew.

**Bay of Pigs invasion:** Failed U.S.-backed invasion of Cuba at the Bay of Pigs by fifteen hundred Cuban exiles opposed to Fidel Castro, on April 17, 1961.

**"Big stick" foreign policy:** Theodore Roosevelt's theory that in diplomatic efforts, it was wise to "speak softly and carry a big stick," meaning that one should attempt peaceful solutions while at the same time being prepared to back up the talk with action when necessary.

**Bill of Rights:** The first ten amendments to the American Constitution of rights and privileges guaranteed to the people of the United States.

**Black Codes:** Laws and provisions that limited civil rights and placed economic restrictions on African Americans.

**"Bleeding Kansas":** The conflict in Kansas in 1854 between slavery advocates and abolitionists—in the form of both residents and transients, and two different governments—that led to bloodshed. It was the first indication that the issue of slavery would not be settled diplomatically.

**Bloc:** A unified group able to wield power through its size and numbers.

**Boston Tea Party:** An event in 1773 in which colonists spilled shipments of tea into Boston harbor to protest taxes imposed on various products.

**Bull market:** A stock market term that describes a period of aggressive buying and selling of stock that proves profitable for most investors; in contrast, "bear market" is used to describe a more sluggish trading period.

**Bureaucracy:** A government or big business set up to be run by bureaus, or departments, that strictly follow rules and regulations and a chain of authority.

# C

**Camp David Accords:** An agreement of peace following negotiations led by President Jimmy Carter and signed by Israeli prime minister Menachem Begin and Egyptian president Anwar Sadat on March 26, 1979.

**Capitol Hill:** A nickname for Congress, since the Capitol building where Congress holds sessions is located on a small hill.

**Carpetbaggers:** A term of contempt used by Southerners about agents, humanitarians, politicians, and businessmen who came to the South to assist or to exploit Reconstruction policies. The term suggests that Northerners could stuff everything they owned into a bag made from carpet.

**Caucus:** An organized vote by registered and designated members of a political party to determine the amount of support within a state for the party's presidential candidates.

**Censure:** To publicly condemn an individual; in Congress, the act of censure expresses Congress's condemnation of an individual's actions and is entered into the *Congressional Record*.

**Central Intelligence Agency (CIA):** A U.S. government agency charged with accumulating information on foreign countries.

**Checks and balances:** The system in which the three branches of the U.S. government can review and dismiss acts passed by one of the other branches.

**Civil service:** Positions under the authority of the federal government.

**Civil War:** Conflict that took place from 1861 to 1865 between the Northern states (Union) and the Southern seceded states (Confederacy); also known in the South as the War between the States and in the North as the War of the Rebellion.

**Coalitions:** Groups of people supporting a political issue or cause.

**Cold War:** A term that describes a period from 1945 to the late 1980s characterized by tense conflicts and failed diplomacy between the Soviet Union and the United States and their respective allies.

**Communism:** A system in which the government controls the distribution of goods and services and limits individual freedom.

**Compromise of 1850:** Legislation passed by Congress and signed into law by President Millard Fillmore consisting of five bills: (1) California was admitted as a free state; (2) Texas was compensated for the loss of territory in a boundary dispute with New Mexico; (3) New Mexico was granted territorial status; (4) the slave trade—but not slavery itself—was abolished in Washington, D.C; (5) and most controversially, the Fugitive Slave Law was enacted, allowing slaveowners to pursue fleeing slaves and recapture them in free states.

**Confederate States of America (Confederacy):** The eleven Southern states that seceded (separated) from the United States during the 1860s and fought the Union during the American Civil War.

***Congressional Record:*** A document that records all speeches and votes made in Congress.

**Conservative:** A political philosophy of limited government influence and support for conventional social values.

**Constitutional Convention:** The 1787 convention attended by delegates to strengthen the Articles of Confederation. Instead, delegates adopted the American Constitution that formed the United States.

**Constructionist:** One who bases decisions on literal readings of the Constitution.

**Consul:** A diplomat stationed in a foreign country who advises people from his or her own country on legal matters.

**Continental Army:** The American army during the Revolutionary War against Great Britain.

**Continental Congress:** The group of representatives who met to establish the United States.

**Coup:** A sudden overthrow of a government, often by the country's military.

**Covert operations:** Secret, undercover acts used to help influence the outcome of events.

**Cuban missile crisis:** A showdown in October 1962 that brought the Soviet Union and the United States close to war over the existence of Soviet nuclear missiles in Cuba.

# D

**D-Day:** A military term that describes the day when an event can be scheduled. D-Day in World War II was June 6, 1944, when Allied forces landed in Normandy, France.

**Dark horse:** A little-known candidate with modest chances for success who might emerge surprisingly strong.

**Delegate:** A member of a party or organization who has a vote that represents a larger group and helps determine the leader of that party or organization.

**Democratic Party:** One of the oldest political parties in the United States, developed out of the Democratic-Republican Party of the late eighteenth century. Andrew Jackson was one of its first leaders. In the years before the Civil War (1861–65), Democrats became increasingly associated with the South and slavery. Following the war, the party gradually transformed and became associated with urban voters and liberal policies. In the twentieth and twenty-first centuries, Democrats have generally favored freer trade, more international commitments, greater government regulations, and social programs.

**Democratic-Republican Party:** One of the first political parties in the United States, led by Thomas Jefferson and James Madison in the 1790s to oppose the Federalist Party and close ties with Great Britain. It was also called the Republican Party and the Jeffersonian Republican Party at the time, but the term Democratic-Republican helps distinguish that early political group from the Democratic and Republican parties that were formed later. The Democratic-Republican Party dissolved in the 1820s. Many former members began supporting the formation of the Democratic Party led by Andrew Jackson, who was elected president in 1828 and 1832. The modern-day Republican Party was formed in 1854.

**Depression:** *See* **Great Depression.**

**Deregulation:** Removal of guidelines and laws governing a business or financial institution.

**Détente:** A relaxing of tensions between rival nations, marked by increased diplomatic, commercial, and cultural contact.

**Draft cards:** From the mid-1960s through the mid-1970s, all males had to register for the draft upon turning eighteen. After registering, an individual received a draft card that contained a draft number. A lottery system was used to determine which available males would be "drafted"—required to serve in the military.

# E

**Election board:** A group authorized to operate elections and count votes.

**Electoral College:** A body officially responsible for electing the president of the United States. In presidential elections, the candidate who receives the most popular votes in a particular state wins all of that state's electoral votes. Votes are distributed among states in ratios based on population. A candidate must win a majority of electoral votes (over fifty percent) in order to win the presidency.

**Electoral votes:** The votes a presidential candidate receives for having won a majority of the popular vote in a state. In presidential elections, the candidate who receives the most popular votes in a particular state wins all of that states' electoral votes. Votes are distributed among states in ratios based on population. A candidate must win a majority of electoral votes (over fifty percent) in order to win the presidency.

**Emancipation:** The act of freeing people from slavery.

**Enfranchisement:** Voting rights.

**Expansionism:** The policy of a nation that plans to enlarge its size or gain possession of other lands.

**Exploratory committee:** A group established by a potential political candidate to examine whether enough party, public, and financial support exists for the potential candidate to officially announce that he or she is running for an elected position.

# F

**Federal budget:** The list of all planned expenditures the federal government expects to make over a year.

**Federal budget deficit:** When government spending exceeds income (from taxes and other revenue).

**Federal Reserve System:** The central banking system of the United States, which serves as the banker to the financial sector and the government, issues the national currency, and supervises banking practices.

**Federalist:** A proponent for a strong national (federal) government.

**Federalist Party:** An American political party of the late eighteenth century that began losing influence around 1820. Federalists supported a strong national government. Growing sentiments for states' rights and rural regions led to the demise of the party. Many Federalists became Democratic-Republicans until that party was split into factions in the mid-1820s. Those favoring states' rights became Jackson Democrats and formed the Democratic Party in 1832.

**First Continental Congress:** A group of representatives from the thirteen colonies who met in Philadelphia in 1774 to list grievances (complaints) against England.

**Fiscal:** Relating to financial matters.

**Fourteen Points:** Famous speech given by Woodrow Wilson that includes reasons for American involvement in war, terms for peace, and his vision of a League of Nations.

**Freedmen's Bureau:** An agency that provided federal help for freed slaves.

**Fugitive Slave Law:** The provision in the Compromise of 1850 that allowed Southern slaveowners to pursue and capture runaway slaves into Northern states.

# G

**General assembly:** A state congressional system made up only of representatives from districts within that particular state.

**Gerrymandering:** A practice whereby the political party in power changes boundaries in a voting area to include more people likely to support the party in power. This can occur when Congressional districts are rezoned (marked off into different sections) following the national census that occurs every ten years.

**Gold standard:** The economic practice whereby all of the money printed and minted in a nation is based on the amount of gold the nation has stored. (Paper money is printed; coins are minted, or stamped.)

**GOP:** Short for "Grand Old Party," a nickname of the Republican Party.

**Grand jury:** A group empowered to decide whether a government investigation can provide enough evidence to make criminal charges against a citizen.

**Grass roots:** A term that describes political activity that begins with small groups of people acting without the influence of large and powerful groups.

**Great Depression:** The worst financial crisis in American history. Usually dated from 1929, when many investors lost money during a stock market crash, to 1941, when the last Depression-related relief effort to help impoverished and unemployed people was passed by the government. When America entered World War II (1939–45) in 1941, many more employment opportunities became available in war-related industries.

**Great Society:** A set of social programs proposed by President Lyndon B. Johnson designed to end segregation and reduce poverty in the United States.

**Gross national product (GNP):** An economic measurement of a nation's total value of goods and services produced over a certain period (usually a year); the GNP became an official economic statistic in 1947.

# H

**House of Burgesses:** A representative body made up of Virginia colonists but under the authority of British rule.

**Human rights:** Principles based on the belief that human beings are born free and equal; governments must respect those rights or they can be accused of human rights violations.

# I

**Immunity:** Protection from prosecution; usually extended to someone who can help the prosecution win its case.

**Impeachment:** A legislative proceeding charging a public official with misconduct. Impeachment consists of the formal accusation of such an official and the trial that follows. It does not refer to removal from office of the accused.

**Imperialism:** The process of expanding the authority of one government over other nations and groups of people.

**Incumbent:** The person currently holding an elected office during an election period.

**Independent counsel:** A federal position established during the 1970s to investigate federal officials accused of crimes. The Independent Counsel Act, intended to perform in a nonpartisan manner in rare occasions, was not renewed in 1999.

**Indictment:** An official charge of having committed a crime.

**Industrialization:** The use of machinery for manufacturing goods.

**Inflation:** An economic term that describes a situation in which money loses some of its value, usually because the cost of goods is more expensive.

**Infrastructure:** The system of public works—the physical resources constructed for public use, such as bridges and roads—of a state or country.

**Injunction:** A legal maneuver that suspends a certain practice until a legal decision can be reached.

**Insurrections:** Armed rebellions against a recognized authority.

**Integration:** The bringing together of people of all races and ethnic backgrounds without restrictions; desegregation.

**Interest rates:** The percentage of a loan that a person agrees to pay for borrowing money.

**Internationalism:** Interest and participation in events involving other countries.

**Iran-Contra scandal:** A scandal during the Ronald Reagan administration during which government officials made illegal sales of weapons to Iran. Money made from those sales were diverted to secret funds provided to the Contras in the civil war in El Salvador. This was illegal, since Congress must authorize foreign aid.

**Iran hostage crisis:** A 444-day period from November 4, 1979, to Inauguration Day 1981 when Iran held 52 American embassy officials hostage following the toppling of the American-backed Shah of Iran.

**Iron Curtain:** A term describing Eastern European nations dominated by the Soviet Union.

**Isolationism:** A national policy of avoiding pacts, treaties, and other official agreements with other nations in order to remain neutral.

# K

**Kansas-Nebraska Act:** A U.S. law authorizing the creation of the states of Kansas and Nebraska and specifying that the inhabitants of the territories should decide whether or not to allow slaveholding.

**Keynote address:** The most important speech during opening ceremonies of an organized meeting.

**Korean War:** A war from 1950 to 1953 fought between communist North Korea and non-communist South Korea; China backed North Korea and the United Nations backed South Korea.

# L

*Laissez faire:* A French term (roughly translated as "allow to do") commonly used to describe noninterference by government in the affairs of business and the economy.

**Lame duck:** An official who has lost an election and is filling out the remainder of his or her term.

**League of Nations:** An organization of nations, as proposed by President Woodrow Wilson, that would exert moral leadership and help nations avoid future wars.

**Legal tender:** Bills or coin that have designated value.

**Lobbyist:** A person hired to represent the interests of a particular group to elected officials.

**Louisiana Purchase:** A vast region in North America purchased by the United States from France in 1803 for $15 million.

**Loyalists:** Americans who remained loyal to Great Britain during the Revolutionary War (1775–83).

# M

**Manifest Destiny:** The belief that American expansionism is inevitable and divinely ordained.

**Marshall Plan:** A post–World War II program led by Secretary of State George C. Marshall that helped rebuild European economies (also benefiting U.S. trade) and strengthened democratic governments.

**Martial law:** A state of emergency during which a military group becomes the sole authority in an area and civil laws are set aside.

**Medicare:** A government program that provides financial assistance to poor people to help cover medical costs.

**Mercenaries:** Soldiers hired to serve a foreign country.

**Merchant marine:** Professional sailors and boat workers involved with commercial marine trade and maintenance (as opposed to branches of the military such as the navy and the coast guard).

**Midterm elections:** Congressional elections that occur halfway through a presidential term. These elections can affect the president's dealings with Congress. A president is elected every four years; representatives (members of the House of Representatives), every two years; and senators, every six years.

**Military dictatorships:** States in which military leaders have absolute power.

**Military draft:** A mandatory program that requires that all males register for possible military service. Those who pass a medical test receive a draft number. A lottery system is used to determine which available males must serve in the military. Those whose numbers are drawn are "drafted" into military service.

**Military governments:** Governments supervised or run by a military force.

**Military tribunal:** A court presided over by military officials to try cases in an area under a state of war.

**Militia:** A small military group, not affiliated with the federal government, organized for emergency service.

**Missing in action:** A term that describes military personnel unaccounted for. They might have been captured by the enemy, in which case they become prisoners of war; they might be hiding out and attempting to return to safety; or they might have been killed.

**Missouri Compromise:** Legislation passed in 1820 that designated which areas could enter the Union as free states and which could enter as slave states. It was repealed in 1854.

**Monarchy:** A form of government in which a single person (usually a king or queen) has absolute power.

**Monroe Doctrine:** A policy statement issued during the presidency of James Monroe (1817–25) that explained the position of the United States on the activities of European powers in the western hemisphere; of major significance was the stand of the United States against European intervention in the affairs of the Americas.

**Muckrakers:** A circle of investigative reporters during Theodore Roosevelt's term in office who exposed the seamier (unwholesome) side of American life. These reporters thoroughly researched their stories and based their reports on provable facts.

# N

**National Security Council:** A group of military advisors assisting the president.

**Nationalism:** Loyalty to a nation that exalts that quality above all other nations.

**Nazi:** The abbreviated name for the National Socialist German Workers' Party, the political party led by Adolf Hitler, who became dictator of Germany. Hitler's Nazi Party controlled Germany from 1933 to 1945. The Nazis promoted racist and anti-Semitic (anti-Jewish) ideas and enforced complete obedience to Hitler and the party.

**Neutrality:** A position in which a nation is not engaged with others and does not take sides in disputes.

**New Deal:** A series of programs initiated by the administration of President Franklin D. Roosevelt to create jobs and stimulate the economy during the Great Depression (1929–41).

**North Atlantic Treaty Organization (NATO):** An alliance for collective security created by the North Atlantic Treaty in 1949 and originally involving Belgium, Canada, Denmark, France, Great Britain, Iceland, Italy, Luxembourg, the Netherlands, Norway, Portugal, and the United States.

**Nuclear test ban treaty:** An agreement to stop testing nuclear weapons.

**Nullification:** Negatation; the Theory of Nullification was proposed by John C. Calhoun, a South Carolina congressman who later served as vice president to Andrew Jackson. In Calhoun's theory, a state has the right to nullify federal laws that it deems harmful to the state's interests.

# O

**Open Door Policy:** A program introduced by President William McKinley to extend trade and relations with China, opening up a vast new market.

**Oppression:** Abuse of power by one party against another.

# P

**Pacifist:** A person opposed to conflict.

**Panic of 1837:** An economic slump that hit the United States in 1837.

**Pardon:** A power that allows the president to free an individual or a group from prosecution for a crime.

**Parliamentary government:** A system of government in which executive power resides with Cabinet-level officials responsible to the nation's legislature. The highest-ranking member of the political party with a majority in such a system of government is usually made the nation's chief executive.

**Partisan:** Placing the concerns of one's group or political party above all other considerations.

**Patronage system:** Also called spoils system; a system in which elected officials appoint their supporters to civil service (government) jobs.

**Peace Corps:** A government-sponsored program that trains volunteers for social and humanitarian service in underdeveloped areas of the world.

**Peacekeeping force:** A military force sponsored by the United Nations that polices areas that have been attacked by another group clearly defined as aggressors.

**Pearl Harbor:** An American naval station in Hawaii attacked without warning by Japanese forces in December 1941.

**Pendleton Civil Service Reform Act:** A congressional act signed into law by President Chester A. Arthur that established the Civil Service Commission, an organization that oversees federal appointments and ensures that appointees do not actively participate in party politics while holding a federal job.

**Perjury:** The voluntary violation of an oath or a vow; answering falsely while under oath (having previously sworn to tell the truth).

**Platform:** A declaration of policies that a candidate or political party intends to follow if the party's candidate is elected.

**Political boss:** A politically powerful person who can direct a group of voters to support a particular candidate.

**Political dynasty:** A succession of government leaders from the same political party.

**Political machine:** An organized political group whose members are generally under the control of the leader of the group.

**Populism:** An agricultural movement of rural areas between the Mississippi River and the Rocky Mountains of the late nineteenth century that united the interests of farmers and laborers. In 1891, the movement formed a national political party, the People's Party, whose members were called Populists. Populist ideals remained popular even when the party faded early in the twentieth century.

**Presidential primaries:** Elections held in states to help determine the nominees of political parties for the general election. Each party disperses a certain number of delegates to each state. A candidate must win support of a majority of those delegates to win the party's presidential nomination. In states that hold primary elections, delegates are generally awarded to candidates based on the percentage of votes they accumulate; in some states, the leading vote-getter wins all of those state's delegates.

**Presidential veto:** When a president declines to sign into law a bill passed by Congress.

**Primaries:** *See* **Presidential primaries.**

**Progressive "Bull Moose" Party:** Party in which Theodore Roosevelt ran as a third-party candidate in 1912. He came in second to incumbent president William Howard Taft, but lost to New Jersey governor Woodrow Wilson.

**Progressivism:** A movement that began late in the nineteenth century whose followers pursued social, economic, and government reform. Generally located in urban areas, Progressivists ranged from individuals seeking to improve local living conditions to radicals who pursued sweeping changes in the American political and economic system.

**Prohibition:** The constitutional ban on the manufacture and sale of alcohol and alcoholic beverages from 1920 to 1933.

**Prosecuting attorney:** The attorney who represents the government in a law case.

**Protectorate:** A relationship in which an independent nation comes under the protection and power of another nation.

**Proviso:** A clause in a document making a qualification, condition, or restriction.

# R

**Racial desegregation:** A policy meant to ensure that people of all racial origins are treated equal.

**Rapprochement:** Reestablishment of relations with a country after it has undergone a dramatic change in government.

**Ratification:** A vote of acceptance. A majority of the representatives from each of the thirteen colonies had to vote for the U.S. Constitution (1787) in order for the document to become legally binding.

**Recession:** A situation of increasing unemployment and decreasing value of money.

**Recharter:** To renew a law or an act.

**Reciprocal trade agreements:** When participating nations promise to trade in a way that will benefit each nation equally.

**Reconstruction:** A federal policy from 1865 to 1877 through which the national government took an active part in assisting and policing the former Confederate states.

**Reconstruction Act of 1867:** An act that placed military governments (governments supervised by a military force) in command of states of the South until the Fourteenth Amendment was ratified in 1868.

**Regulation:** Monitoring business with an established set of guidelines.

**Reparations:** Payments for damage caused by acts of hostility.

**Republican government:** A form of government in which supreme power resides with citizens who elect their leaders and have the power to change their leaders.

**Republican Party:** Founded in 1854 by a coalition (an alliance) of former members of the Whig, Free-Soil, and Know-Nothing parties and of northern Democrats dissatisfied with their party's proslavery stands. The party quickly rose to become one of the most important parties in the United States, and the major opposition to the Democratic Party. Republicans are generally associated with conservative fiscal and social policies. The Republican Party is not related to the older Democratic-Republican Party, although that party was often called the Republicans before the 1830s.

**Riders:** Measures added on to legislation. Riders are usually items that might not pass through Congress or will be vetoed by the president if presented alone. Congressmen attempt to attach such items to popular bills, hoping they will "ride" along with the more popular legislation.

# S

**Sanctions:** Punishment against a nation involved in activities considered illegal under international law; such punishment usually denies trade, supplies, or access to other forms of international assistance to the nation.

**Satellite nations:** Countries politically and economically dominated by a larger, more powerful nation.

**Secession:** Formal withdrawal from an existing organization. In 1860–61, eleven Southern states seceded from the Union to form the Confederate States of America.

**Second Continental Congress:** A group of representatives from the thirteen colonies who began meeting in Philadelphia in 1775 and effectively served as the American government until the Constitution was adopted in 1787.

**Sectionalism:** The emphasis that people place on policies that would directly benefit their area of the country.

**Segregation:** The policy of keeping groups of people from different races, religions, or ethnic backgrounds separated.

**Social Security:** A government program that provides pensions (a regular sum of money) to American workers after they reach age sixty-five.

**Social welfare:** A term that encompasses government programs that provide assistance, training, and jobs to people.

**Solicitor:** An attorney who represents a government agency.

**Solicitor general:** An attorney appointed by the president to argue legal matters on behalf of the government.

**South East Asia Treaty Organization:** An alliance of nations founded in 1954 to prevent the spread of communism in Asian and Pacific island nations. Original members included Australia, France, Great Britain, New Zealand, Pakistan, the Philippines, Thailand, and the United States. The alliance disbanded in 1977.

**Speaker of the House:** The person in charge of supervising activity in the House of Representatives. The Speaker is elected by colleagues of the party with a majority in Congress.

**Spin doctoring:** A late twentieth-century term that describes the practice of having political aides offer the best possible interpretation of a political statement or the effects of an event on their political boss.

**State militia:** An organized military unit maintained by states in case of emergency; often called the National Guard.

**Stock market crash:** A sudden decline in the value of stocks that severely affects investors.

**Strategic Arms Limitation Treaty (SALT):** Missile reduction program between the United States and the Soviet Union.

**Strategic Defense Initiative (SDI):** A proposed—but never approved—technological system (nicknamed "Star Wars," after the popular movie) that combined several advanced technology systems that could, in theory, detect and intercept missiles fired by enemies of the United States.

**Subpoena:** A formal legal document that commands a certain action or requires a person to appear in court.

# T

**Taft-Hartley Act:** Act that outlawed union-only workplaces, prohibited certain union activities, forbade unions to contribute to political campaigns, established loyalty oaths for union leaders, and allowed court orders to halt strikes that could affect national health or safety.

**Tariff:** A protective tax placed on imported goods to raise their price and make them less attractive than goods produced by the nation importing them.

**Teapot Dome scandal:** Incident that became public following the death of President Warren G. Harding that revealed that Navy secretary Edwin Denby transfered control of oil reserves in Teapot Dome, Wyoming, and Elk Hill, California, to the Department of the Interior, whose secretary, Albert Fall, secretly leased the reserve to two private oil operators, who paid Fall $400,000.

**Tenure of Office Act:** A law passed by Congress to limit the powers of the presidency.

**Terrorist:** A person who uses acts of violence in an attempt to coerce by terror.

**Theater:** A large area where military operations are occurring.

**Thirteenth Amendment:** An amendment to the U.S. Constitution that outlawed slavery.

**Tonkin Gulf Resolution:** Passed by Congress after U.S. Navy ships supposedly came under attack in the Gulf of Tonkin, this resolution gave President Lyndon B. Johnson the authority to wage war against North Vietnam.

**Tribunal:** A court of law.

**Truman Doctrine:** A Cold War–era program designed by President Harry S. Truman that sent aid to anticommunist forces in Turkey and Greece. The Union of Soviet Socialist Republics (U.S.S.R.) had naval stations in Turkey, and nearby Greece was fighting a civil war with communist-dominated rebels.

# U

**Underground railroad:** A term that describes a series of routes through which escaped slaves could pass through free Northern states and into Canada. The escaped slaves were assisted by abolitionists and free African Americans in the North.

**Union:** Northern states that remained loyal to the United States during the Civil War.

# V

**Veto:** The power of one branch of government—for example, the executive—to reject a bill passed by a legislative body and thus prevent it from becoming law.

**Vietcong:** Vietnamese communists engaged in warfare against the government and people of South Vietnam.

# W

**War of 1812:** A war fought from 1812 to 1815 between the United States and Great Britain. The United States wanted to protect its maritime rights as a neutral nation during a conflict between Great Britain and France.

**Warren Commission:** A commission chaired by Earl Warren, chief justice of the Supreme Court, that investigated President John F. Kennedy's assassination. The commission concluded that the assassination was the act of one gunman, not part of a larger conspiracy. That conclusion remains debated.

**Watergate scandal:** A scandal that began on June 17, 1972, when five men were caught burglarizing the offices of the Democratic National Committee in the Watergate complex in Washington, D.C. This led to a cover-up, political convictions, and, eventually, the resignation of President Richard Nixon.

**Welfare:** Government assistance to impoverished people.

**Whig Party:** A political party that existed roughly from 1836 to 1852, composed of different factions of the former Democratic-Republican Party. These factions refused to join the group that formed the Democratic Party led by President Andrew Jackson.

# Y

**Yalta Conference:** A 1944 meeting between Allied leaders Joseph Stalin, Winston Churchill, and Franklin D. Roosevelt in anticipation of an Allied victory in Europe over the Nazis. The leaders discussed how to manage lands conquered by Germany, and Roosevelt and Churchill urged Stalin to enter the Soviet Union in the war against Japan.

# Research and Activity Ideas

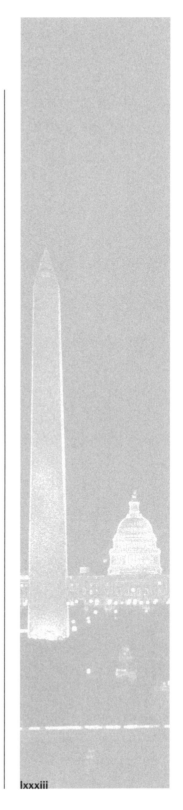

The following research and activity ideas are intended to offer suggestions for complementing social studies and history curricula, to trigger additional ideas for enhancing learning, and to suggest cross-disciplinary projects for library and classroom use.

- The aftermath of the 2000 race between George W. Bush and Al Gore renewed debate over whether the Electoral College system should be abandoned in favor of the popular vote. Research the reasons why the Founding Fathers instituted the Electoral College. Write a paper on arguments for and against the Electoral College, or take one side and have a partner take the other side.

- Several Web sites on presidents are listed in the "Where to Learn More" section. Additional Web sites, linked to presidential libraries and historical sites, are listed at the end of many individual president entries. Using a president of particular interest to you, compare the descriptions of his life and his presidency on the various Web sites. The comparison will show how presidents are appraised by different sources. Pretend you are a media critic. Write a review of the various sites, comparing their different features, the ways they treat the president, and what you find interesting and not useful in each site.

• Plan a debate or a series of debates on important issues in American history. One issue could be the powers of the federal government in relation to the states. That issue can be explored and debated by contrasting the views of a president who took a different view of federal power from the president who preceded him. Such contrasting pairs include John Adams and Thomas Jefferson; James Buchanan and Abraham Lincoln; Herbert Hoover and Franklin D. Roosevelt; and George Bush and Bill Clinton.

• In contemporary times, when a president makes his State of the Union address each year, television networks provide equal time for a member of the opposing party to present his or her party's views. After reading and making notes on one of the speeches in the primary documents section, prepare a response—a speech that takes an opposite view on issues presented by the president.

• Create a timeline of a fifty-year period to parallel the "Timeline of the American Presidents," found on pages xxix–lix. Your timeline might list important inventions, world events, or developments in science and technology. Placing the timelines side by side, consider ways in which the events on your timeline might be connected with events in the presidential timeline.

• Using the resources of your local library, find magazines and newspapers that were published near the time you were born, or pick a date earlier in time. What were some of the big national news stories back then? How did the press view the performance of the president concerning those issues?

• Pretend you are a reporter preparing to interview one of the presidents. Just before your interview is to begin, the president is informed about a major event (select one from the president's entry). You are allowed to follow the president as he plans a course of action. Write an article providing an "insider's view" of the president in action.

• The Congressional cable network C-Span commissioned presidential scholars to rate presidents in ten categories (see http://www.americanpresidents.org/survey/histori-ans/overall.asp). Compare that ranking with other sources that rank presidents in terms of effectiveness. How are the rankings similar and different? What criteria do they use for judging presidents? Consider whether or not you feel the rankings are fair, and write an essay supporting your view.

- Visit a historical site or Web sites devoted to a particular president. Listings for both can often be found in each president's entry. Using biographical information about the president's childhood, his schooling, and his career as president, write a short play in which the president is surrounded by loved ones and aides at a crucial moment during his presidency.

- There were many different kinds of first ladies. Some were politically active (such as Sarah Polk and Eleanor Roosevelt), others believed they should not participate in politics because they were not the one elected to office (such as Bess Truman and Pat Nixon). Compare and contrast those different approaches by profiling several first ladies.

- Research more about a leading opponent of a particular president, perhaps someone he faced in an election. Imagine that the opponent was able to convince voters that he or she should be elected. Write about how history would have been different if the opponent had become president. The focus could be on an election that was very close (such as Rutherford B. Hayes over Samuel Tilden in 1876 or George W. Bush over Al Gore in 2000) or one in which the victor won by a large margin (such as Franklin D. Roosevelt over Alfred Landon in 1936 or Ronald Reagan over Walter Mondale in 1984).

# Complete
# American
# Presidents
# Sourcebook

# John F. Kennedy

**Thirty-fifth president (1961–1963)**

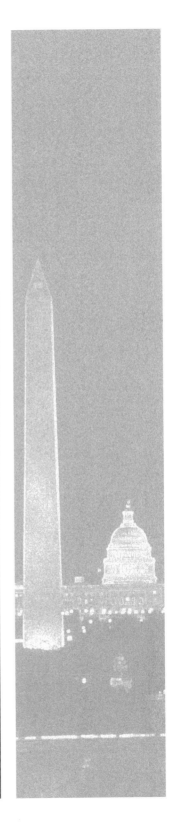

# John F. Kennedy

**Born May 29, 1917**
**Brookline, Massachusetts**
**Died November 22, 1963**
**Dallas, Texas**

**Thirty-fifth president of the United States**
**(1961–1963)**

**Assassination ended brief, energetic**
**Camelot presidency**

Youthful and full of energy, President John F. Kennedy represented those Americans seeking progressive social programs and improved interaction with other nations. Most of his administration's New Frontier programs, however, were barely underway when Kennedy was assassinated (murdered) nearly three years into his presidency. The killing of the widely popular president in November 1963 shocked the nation and left many people grieving around the world.

At age forty-three in 1960, Kennedy was the youngest elected president. His administration developed strongly after early setbacks. Three months into office, he accepted responsibility for a failed military operation in Cuba in 1961. The following year, he effectively pressured the Soviet Union to remove nuclear missiles from that island. Kennedy's reputation nationally and worldwide increased greatly over his handling of the Cuban missile crisis. During his presidency, Kennedy enjoyed triumphant tours and made inspiring speeches in such nations as France, West Germany, Ireland, and Mexico.

At home, Kennedy moved cautiously to establish his programs, having won a close election. With a Cabinet (group

"A man must have goals. There is not sufficient time, even in two terms to achieve those goals."

*John F. Kennedy*

**John F. Kennedy.**
*Courtesy of the John F. Kennedy Library.*

## Fast Facts about John F. Kennedy

**Full name:** John Fitzgerald Kennedy

**Born:** May 29, 1917

**Died:** November 22, 1963

**Burial site:** Arlington National Cemetery, Arlington, Virginia

**Parents:** Joseph Patrick and Rose Elizabeth Fitzgerald Kennedy

**Spouse:** Jacqueline Lee Bouvier (1929–1994; m. 1953)

**Children:** Daughter (stillborn 1956); Caroline Bouvier (1957– ); John Fitzgerald Jr. (1960–1999); Patrick Bouvier (1963–1963)

**Religion:** Roman Catholic

**Education:** Harvard University (B.S., 1940); Stanford University Graduate School of Business Administration (1940)

**Occupations:** Navy ensign; author; journalist

**Government positions:** U.S. representative and senator from Massachusetts

**Political party:** Democratic

**Dates as president:** January 20, 1961– November 22, 1963

**Age upon taking office:** 43

of presidential advisors) that included many younger men from the business world, he presented a burst of ideas while gradually building support. Among his successful efforts were a large increase in the American space program and expanded trade with democratic nations of Latin America and Europe. A sweeping civil rights bill and a tax cut were facing delays in Congress at the time of his death. His successor, **Lyndon B. Johnson** (1908–1973; see entry in volume 5), fought successfully for passage of that legislation in memory of Kennedy.

Overall, Kennedy's effectiveness is difficult to evaluate because his presidency ended early. Nevertheless, he remains among the most admired and discussed presidents, remembered for his ability to inspire young Americans and for programs he was actively pursuing at the time of his death.

## Happy childhood

The second of nine children of Joseph (1888–1969) and Rose Kennedy (1890–1995), John Fitzgerald Kennedy was born on May 29, 1917, in Brookline, Massachusetts. A bank president by age twenty-five, Joseph Kennedy expanded into shipbuilding, real estate, and other ventures and was very wealthy by age thirty, the year John was born. Rose was the daughter of Boston mayor John Francis "Honey Fitz" Fitzgerald (1863–1950). The wedding of Joseph and Rose united two of Boston's most powerful families.

During his happy childhood, Kennedy became an excellent swimmer and sailor. A back injury he suffered while playing football, however, would cause him lasting pain. As the Kennedy family grew in size and wealth, they moved to different homes in areas near Boston and New York City before establishing a home base at Hyannis Port on Cape Cod, Massachusetts, in 1928. Educated at private schools, Kennedy went on to study in 1935 at the London School of Economics and then enrolled at Princeton University.

Joseph Kennedy served as chairman of the Securities and Exchange Commission under President **Franklin D. Roosevelt** (1882–1945; see entry in volume 4) in 1934 and 1935. He was then appointed ambassador to Great Britain. Kennedy joined his father there in 1937 and in 1939. He became acquainted with reporters, diplomats, and political leaders, including Winston Churchill (1874–1965; see box in **Franklin D. Roosevelt** entry in volume 4), who became Britain's prime minister in 1940.

(see entry in volume 4)

On travels through Europe, Kennedy observed the tensions that erupted into World War II (1939–45). After the war broke out in September 1939, he accompanied his father to Scotland to meet American survivors of a British ship, the *Athenia*, that had been torpedoed by a Nazi submarine.

Meanwhile, Kennedy had transferred to Harvard University. He graduated from there in 1940. While there, Kennedy wrote a thesis (a scholarly paper) on the Munich Pact of 1938. In that agreement, Great Britain and France accepted the demands of Nazi leader Adolf Hitler (1889–1945) that the German-speaking Sudetenland, a region of Czechoslovakia, should be ceded (handed over) to Germany. The pact was later violated by Hitler in a series of actions that started World War II. Kennedy's thesis, primarily on how Great Britain failed to challenge Hitler at the time, was praised and later published as a book, *Why England Slept*.

## John F. Kennedy Timeline

**1917:** Born in Massachusetts

**1943:** Awarded a U.S. Navy and Marine Corps medal for heroism in a noncombat situation

**1947–53:** Serves as U.S. representative from Massachusetts

**1953–61:** Serves as U.S. senator from Massachusetts

**1957:** Awarded Pulitzer Prize for Biography for his book, *Profiles in Courage*

**1961–63:** Serves as thirty-fifth U.S. president

**1961:** Bay of Pigs invasion in Cuba fails

**1962:** Soviet Union and United States lock heads in Soviet missile crisis

**1963:** Assassinated in Dallas, Texas

## Words to Know

**Bay of Pigs invasion:** Failed U.S.-backed invasion of Cuba at the Bay of Pigs by fifteen hundred Cuban exiles opposed to Fidel Castro, on April 17, 1961.

**Central Intelligence Agency (CIA):** A U.S. government agency charged with accumulating information on foreign countries.

**Cold War:** A period of tension between nations from 1945 through 1989, with the United States and its allies on one side and a group of nations led by the Soviet Union on the other.

**Cuban missile crisis:** A showdown in October 1962 that brought the Soviet Union and the United States close to war over the existence of Soviet nuclear missiles in Cuba.

**Electoral College:** A body officially responsible for electing the president of the United States. In presidential elections, the candidate who receives the most popular votes in a particular state wins all of that state's electoral votes. Votes are distributed among states in ratios based on population. A candidate must win a majority of electoral votes (over fifty percent) in order to win the presidency.

**Peace Corps:** A government-sponsored program that trains volunteers for social and humanitarian service in underdeveloped areas of the world.

**Presidential primaries:** Elections held in states to help determine the nominees of political parties for the general election. Each party disperses a certain number of delegates to each state. A candidate must win support of a majority of those delegates to win the party's presidential nomination. In states that hold primary elections, delegates are awarded to candidates based on the percentage of votes the candidates accumulate.

Kennedy entered the Stanford University Graduate School of Business in 1940, traveled in South America, and volunteered for military duty in the spring of 1941. Because of his injured back, however, Kennedy was rejected from the military for medical reasons. After a demanding period of strengthening exercises, he was accepted into the U.S. Navy in September 1941.

## PT-109

Serving in the South Pacific Ocean during World War II, Kennedy reached the rank by 1943 of commander of a PT boat (patrol torpedo boat; a small patrol craft armed with tor-

## JFK and PT-109

In August 1943, John F. Kennedy was serving as commander of a PT boat, a small patrol craft. Kennedy's PT-109 was cruising slowly and quietly on a dark night a few miles from a group of islands in the South Pacific Ocean. A fog was settling in. PT-109 was among fifteen PT boats scattered around the area on the lookout for Japanese boats rumored to be moving forces to prepare an attack. After midnight, other PT boats were returning to base. PT-109 went for one last patrol before turning back as well.

Suddenly, from out of a mist, PT-109 was rammed by a Japanese destroyer. The PT boat was split in half, spilling all twelve men aboard. Gas tanks exploded into fire, and the men struggled for safety from the flames and the wake of the destroyer.

After the destroyer passed, Kennedy discovered that two of his men were dead and a third was badly burned. The surviving men clung for hours to wreckage, waiting for help. After three hours, they decided to try and reach shore. Holding on to a large plank, they swam three miles before reaching an island. Kennedy towed along the burned sailor, who was unable to swim, by clenching his teeth on the cord of the man's life preserver and pulling him along through the water.

**Naval lieutenant John F. Kennedy during World War II.** *Reproduced by permission of Archive Photos.*

Over the next four days, Kennedy and another man swam under the cover of darkness to nearby islands they were familiar with from patrol duty. On one island, they found a stash of candy on a wrecked Japanese boat. The sweets helped the exhausted and hungry men survive. They were eventually found by a couple of island natives who worked with Allied forces. The natives carried a message Kennedy carved on a coconut to Allied agents, who helped rescue Kennedy and his crew. Kennedy was rewarded for his heroism with a U.S. Navy and Marine Corps medal, and the PT-109 incident was later recounted in a *New Yorker* article.

pedoes). Commanding PT-109, he endured a frightening and ultimately heroic adventure when his boat was wrecked by a Japanese destroyer. Cited for courage, endurance, and excellent leadership, Kennedy received a U.S. Navy and Marine Corps medal for heroism in a noncombat situation (see box). The experience further weakened his back, however, and he also fell ill with malaria, an infectious disease caused by the bite of an infected mosquito.

As Kennedy recuperated and returned to active service, he learned that his older brother, Joseph Jr. (1915–1944), had died in a flying mission over Belgium. Kennedy's identity had been shaped somewhat by his rivalry with his brother Joe, an excellent student and soldier. For example, Kennedy chose to enter college at Princeton, instead of Harvard, the school his brother had attended. The death of Joe was a heavy loss for Kennedy and his family.

After receiving his discharge from the navy, Kennedy worked as a reporter for the Hearst International News Service. He was stationed in San Francisco in 1945 to cover the opening events of the newly established United Nations. Kennedy soon decided to follow the political aspirations of his late brother. Returning to Boston, he set up a political organization staffed by family, friends, and navy buddies and ran for a congressional seat that was being vacated by longtime Boston politician James M. Curley (1874–1958).

Running a well-organized campaign during which he met many voters and highlighted his military service, Kennedy won election in 1946. Serving three terms in the House of Representatives, Kennedy backed acts beneficial to his home state and supported most of the major policies of the administration of President **Harry S. Truman** (1884–1972; see entry in volume 4). Kennedy displayed a streak of independence as well, criticizing his fellow Democrat Truman for not providing sufficient support for China's leader, Chiang Kai-shek (1887–1975). Chiang was toppled from power in 1949 through a communist rebellion led by Mao Tse-tung (also spelled Mao Ze-dong; 1893–1976).

## Success and struggles

Kennedy set his sights on a U.S. Senate seat in 1952. He began campaigning early by traveling around Massachusetts making speeches and meeting voters. The Kennedy clan was deeply involved in the successful campaign, from financing by father Joseph to endless support work by Kennedy's attractive, youthful, and enthusiastic friends and family members. In a close race, Kennedy defeated his Republican opponent, incumbent senator Henry Cabot Lodge Jr. (1902–1985).

The early part of Kennedy's Senate term was filled with joy and pain. As a senator, Kennedy helped forge a voting bloc among New England congressmen for legislation favorable to the region. (In a legislative assembly, a bloc is a temporary combination of legislators from both parties.) On September 12, 1953, he married Jacqueline Lee Bouvier (1929–1994; see entry on **Jacqueline Kennedy** in volume 5), a photographer and journalist who came from a wealthy family.

 **The Lodge Connection**

The 1952 U.S. Senate race between John F. Kennedy and Henry Cabot Lodge Jr. had an interesting parallel. In 1916, Henry Cabot Lodge Sr. defeated "Honey" Fitzgerald, Kennedy's maternal grandfather, for a Senate seat. Lodge Sr. went on to become a vocal opponent of President Woodrow Wilson's plans for American involvement in the League of Nations. Kennedy won in 1952 against Lodge Jr. and became a vocal proponent for further American involvement in international affairs. Kennedy and Lodge were involved in another election eight years later when Kennedy and his running mate, Lyndon B. Johnson, defeated Richard M. Nixon and his running mate, Lodge, in the presidential election of 1960.

By 1954, however, Kennedy could only get around by using crutches because of back pain. He underwent a serious spinal operation that was not successful, then endured surgery a second time that helped relieve the pain and made him mobile. While recovering from those operations, Kennedy wrote a book, *Profiles in Courage,* published in 1956. A collection of essays on eight U.S. senators who risked their careers for just but unpopular causes, the book was a bestseller and won the prestigious Pulitzer Prize for Biography in 1957. Among the senators profiled were **John Quincy Adams** (1767–1848; see entry in volume 1), Daniel Webster (1782–1852; see box in **John Tyler** entry in volume 2), Edmund G. Ross (1826–1907; see box on impeachment proceedings in **Andrew Johnson** entry in volume 2), and Robert A. Taft (1889–1953; see box on Taft family in **William Howard Taft** entry in volume 3).

The Kennedys endured further hardships when Jacqueline suffered miscarriages in 1955 and 1956. (A miscarriage is a natural, unexpected ending of a pregnancy before the baby can survive on its own.) Daughter Caroline was born in 1957, and son John Jr. (1960–1999) in 1960.

Kennedy's national reputation was enhanced when he made the nominating speech for former Illinois governor Adlai Stevenson (1900–1965; see box in **Dwight D. Eisenhower** entry in volume 4) at the Democratic National Convention in 1956. Stevenson later surprised the convention by asking delegates to select his running mate. Presidential candidates usually select their own vice presidential running mate, who is then given a vote of approval by the convention. Kennedy, only thirty-nine years old, quickly emerged as a leading contender.

Kennedy was edged after three rounds of balloting, but the experience was very helpful. His excellent speech-making skills and vibrant personality were displayed on national television. The opportunity for Kennedy to become vice president led journalists to consider the question of whether a Roman Catholic could someday be elected president. No Roman Catholic had been elected to the nation's highest office; the only previous nominee, Alfred E. Smith (1873–1944; see box in **Herbert Hoover** entry in volume 4) in 1928, had met with some voter backlash (a strong negative reaction) over his religion. There was fear among some voters that a Catholic president would do whatever the pope—the leader of the Roman Catholic Church—told him to do.

## First Catholic president

Kennedy's standing in the Senate improved in 1957. He was active on the Foreign Relations Committee and the Senate Committee on Improper Activities in the Labor Management Field. His brother, Robert F. Kennedy (1925–1968; see box), served as a counsel for that committee. Kennedy was among the Democrats led by Senate majority leader **Lyndon B. Johnson** (1908–1973; see entry in volume 5) of Texas who helped Congress pass civil rights legislation supported by President **Dwight D. Eisenhower** (1890–1969; see entry in volume 4).

Kennedy was reelected in 1958 by the largest margin ever in a Massachusetts Senate race. He began an early, well-organized bid for the presidency in 1960. He was able to establish

momentum against more experienced candidates as his campaign geared up for the presidential primaries, the state elections held to help determine the nominees of each political party for the general presidential election. A decisive primary win in the predominantly Protestant state of West Virginia showed that his Catholicism would not prevent him from being elected.

Kennedy earned enough support to win the nomination on the first ballot of the Democratic National Convention. Texan Lyndon B. Johnson accepted Kennedy's invitation to run as vice president and helped Kennedy in southwestern states. Launching his campaign with an acceptance speech at the convention in which he announced that "We stand today on the edge of a new frontier," Kennedy campaigned tirelessly. His opponent, Vice President **Richard Nixon** (1913–1994; see entry in volume 5), campaigned with equal enthusiasm.

The close race was likely determined in a series of four televised debates—the first time the medium (method of

**Vice President Richard M. Nixon (left) and Senator John F. Kennedy (right) participate in the first televised presidential debates in 1960.**
*Reproduced by permission of the Corbis Corporation.*

## Election Results

### 1960

| Presidential / Vice presidential candidates | Popular votes | Presidential electoral votes |
|---|---|---|
| John F. Kennedy / Lyndon B. Johnson (Democratic) | 34,227,096 | 303 |
| Richard M. Nixon / Henry Cabot Lodge Jr. (Republican) | 34,107,647 | 219 |

communicating information) was used for that presidential forum. Kennedy proved in the debates that he was informed and experienced enough to handle the presidency. Additionally, his lively personality and good looks were contrasted by many with Nixon's more serious comments and stiff appearance. Those debates made appearance a factor in future presidential campaigns. Kennedy won the election by just over one hundred thousand popular votes and a 303-to-219-vote margin in the Electoral College, a body officially responsible for electing the president of the United States. (For more information on the Electoral College, see boxes in **George W. Bush** entry in volume 5.) In presidential elections, a candidate must win a majority of electoral votes (over fifty percent) in order to win the presidency.

The Kennedy presidency commenced with a stirring inaugural address (see **John F. Kennedy** primary source entry in volume 4) and widely reported social festivities. The personalities of the president and first lady, their attractive young children, and their social activities were constantly profiled in the media as "the Kennedy style."

## Troubles off the mainland

The establishment of the Peace Corps—a government-sponsored program that trains volunteers for social and humanitarian service in underdeveloped areas of the world—in March 1961 was an early highlight. Kennedy's New Frontier domestic (at home, as opposed to international) program moved forward gradually. Meanwhile, his foreign policy began with a major setback, followed by significant actions that earned him much international attention.

Upon assuming the presidency, Kennedy inherited a plan from the Eisenhower administration to support rebels in Cuba. A revolution there had resulted in the rise to power of Fidel Castro (1926– ) in 1959. Castro soon made clear his communist sympathies. Many U.S. companies operating in Cuba were shut down as property was nationalized (the Cuban government took over ownership and control). Castro developed strong ties with the Soviet Union, creating another wedge of Cold War tension between the United States and the Soviet Union. (The Cold War refers to a period of tension between nations from 1945 through 1989, with the United States and its allies on one side and a group of nations led by the Soviet Union on the other.)

Many anti-Castro Cubans, called nationalists, fled for the United States. A force of about one thousand nationalists was trained in military operations by the Central Intelligence Agency (CIA). The plan to overthrow Castro involved having those nationalists transported to the Cuban shore, where they would move inland and unite with nationalist forces operating inside the country. The United States was to back the effort with air support. Kennedy approved what was called the Bay of Pigs invasion, named after the beach area where the CIA-trained nationalists would land.

The Bay of Pigs invasion was a disaster. The anti-Castro forces within

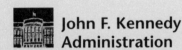 **John F. Kennedy Administration**

***Administration Dates***
January 20, 1961–November 22, 1963

***Vice President***
Lyndon Baines Johnson (1961–63)

***Cabinet***

**Secretary of State**
David D. Rusk (1961–63)

**Secretary of the Treasury**
Clarence D. Dillon (1961–63)

**Attorney General**
Robert F. Kennedy (1961–63)

**Postmaster General**
J. Edward Day (1961–63)
John A. Gronouski Jr. (1963)

**Secretary of the Interior**
Stewart L. Udall (1961–63)

**Secretary of Agriculture**
Orville L. Freeman (1961–63)

**Secretary of Labor**
Arthur J. Goldberg (1961–62)
William W. Wirtz (1962–63)

**Secretary of Commerce**
Luther H. Hodges (1961–63)

**Secretary of Defense**
Robert S. McNamara (1961–63)

**Secretary of Health, Education, and Welfare**
Abraham A. Ribicoff (1961–62)
Anthony J. Celebrezze (1961–63)

Cuba never appeared, and Kennedy refused to allow American air support. Such support could be considered an act of aggression. The insurgents (rebels) were quickly defeated and many were taken prisoner. Castro demanded money for their release, but Kennedy refused. Eventually, some $53 million in food and medical supplies was raised by businesses and private donors to free the prisoners. Kennedy accepted sole responsibility for the failed invasion. An anti-Kennedy faction (group) within the nation grew more vocal, but his forthrightness helped rally support as well.

Other foreign policy moves were more successful. Concerned about terrible economic conditions in the Caribbean and Latin America that might spark revolts, the Kennedy administration introduced a plan called the Alliance for Progress. Like the Marshall Plan (see George C. Marshall box in **Harry S. Truman** entry in volume 4)—which assisted democracies in post–World War II Europe—the Alliance for Progress helped fund the new economic life of Latin American nations.

The program won back U.S. support in the region after years of tension. Kennedy made triumphant visits to Colombia and Argentina in 1961 and to Mexico in 1962. Just a few years earlier, Vice President Nixon had been threatened by hostile crowds in Venezuela. Many South Americans had felt that the United States had long regarded the region solely for exploitation by American businesses (that is, unjust use for their own advantage).

The Kennedys made triumphant visits to France, England, Germany, and Ireland, among other nations, during his administration. So much attention was paid to first lady Jacqueline Kennedy in France that Kennedy remarked to the Paris press, "I am the man who accompanied Jacqueline Kennedy to Paris." Those high-spirited tours were balanced by more profoundly serious confrontations between Kennedy and Soviet premier Nikita Khrushchev (1894–1971; see box in **Dwight D. Eisenhower** entry in volume 4) and by a civil war in Southeast Asia.

## Eyeball to eyeball

Kennedy and Khrushchev met in Vienna, Austria, in June 1961. Soviet tension with the United States was high be-

Editorial cartoon shows the Cuban missile crisis as a potential old west shootout. President John F. Kennedy (left) is depicted as a cowboy (wearing white), with Soviet premier Nikita Khrushchev (wearing black) and Cuban president Fidel Castro (on a mule) approaching the U.S. president.
*Drawing by Leslie Gilbert Illingworth. Courtesy of the Library of Congress.*

cause of the U-2 incident, in which an American spy plane was shot down over the U.S.S.R. in 1960, and because of the Bay of Pigs invasion. Khrushchev believed that Kennedy was a weak leader, but Kennedy remained resolute. "It's going to be a long, cold winter," he said to reporters about the meeting.

In August 1961, the Soviet Union arranged for the construction of a wall to separate the German city of Berlin from the rest of East Germany. Kennedy asked Congress for increased military spending and called up reserve troops. Fifteen hundred armed troops began an announced and legal mission of traveling a route through East Germany to West Berlin. They were not challenged. Kennedy made another well-publicized and well attended trip, this time to West Berlin in 1963. Declaring "Ich bin ein Berliner" ("I am a Berliner," in German) to a cheering crowd, he was able to show American support for a united, democratic Berlin. However, the city would remain divided for more than two more decades.

The Berlin trip occurred after a serious crisis—which came to be known as the Cuban missile crisis—erupted between the United States and the Soviet Union. On October 14, 1962, photographs taken from spy plane missions over Cuba showed construction projects of nuclear missile facilities with Soviet supervision.

After Soviet leaders denied the accusation, Kennedy made a dramatic speech on national television and radio describing the situation to Americans. Noting that a nuclear attack from Cuba could be launched on any nation within the Western Hemisphere, he demanded immediate removal of the missiles and declared a quarantine zone—an area of isolation around Cuba where no ships could pass without U.S. inspection. Kennedy invoked the Monroe Doctrine (see **James Monroe** primary source entry in volume 1), a policy statement issued during the presidency of **James Monroe** (1758–1831; see entry in volume 1) that stressed the position of the United States against intervention by European nations in the affairs of the countries of the Americas. Dramatically, Kennedy said, "It shall be the policy of this nation to regard any nuclear missile launched from Cuba against any nation in the Western Hemisphere as an attack by the Soviet Union on the United States, requiring a full retaliatory response upon the Soviet Union." U.S. military personnel were on alert. The nation seemed on the brink of war, possibly a nuclear disaster.

After six tense days following Kennedy's nationwide address, the missiles were removed and inspections inside Cuba were authorized by Khrushchev. Cuba denied access to inspectors, but spy planes charted the progress of the removal of the construction sites. The two superpower nations had been at the brink of nuclear war. As the tension eased, Secretary of State Dean Rusk (1909–1994) observed, "We're eyeball to eyeball, and I think the other fellow just blinked."

By August 1963, the United States and the Soviet Union began having more positive relations. A limited Nuclear Test Ban treaty between the two nations and Great Britain was signed. The treaty outlawed testing of nuclear weapons in the air or water, but allowed for underground testing. The United States also agreed to sell wheat to the Soviet Union, which was beset by poor crops.

# Vietnam

Kennedy's concern about the expansion of communism became focused on Southeast Asia. In 1954, the French abandoned their colony of Indochina following a communist uprising. The area was partitioned into four nations: North and South Vietnam, Cambodia, and Laos. North Vietnam was controlled by communists, and the democratic government of South Vietnam was threatened by communist guerillas (persons who fight in an irregular military force, often with the support of the local population) called the National Liberation Front, a group that later became known as the Vietcong.

In 1962, a neutral government was established in Laos. South Vietnam, however, was threatened by unrest from communists and followers of the Buddhist religion who objected to the leadership of president Ngo Dinh Diem (1901–1963). Ngo proved to be more interested in maintaining his base of power than in instituting reforms in his corrupt government. He was killed in a rebellion in 1963.

After the French abandoned Indochina in 1954, President Eisenhower sent advisors to help the South Vietnamese army fight communist guerillas. In 1961, Kennedy increased the number of advisors from seven hundred to fifteen hundred. By 1963, there were over fifteen thousand American military advisors in South Vietnam.

The question of whether Kennedy would have continued to increase American involvement to combat and aerial bombing missions is impossible to determine. He was assassinated before U.S. troops and pilots became directly involved in the war in 1964. His most often quoted statement on the issue—"in the final analysis it is their [South Vietnam's] war,"—indicates that he might not have heightened American involvement into what many believed was a useless war that divided American opinion.

# The Kennedy style

At home, the Kennedy administration became part of popular culture. The White House became a center of social activity and was popularly named Camelot, after the legendary kingdom of King Arthur and the Knights of the Roundtable. Writers, artists, and scientists were regularly in-

# Robert F. Kennedy

Born on November 20, 1925, in Brookline, Massachusetts, Robert Kennedy was the seventh of Joseph and Rose Kennedy's nine children. Starting out as a poor student, he eventually began to excel academically. In 1946, after his discharge from the navy, Robert helped with brother John's campaign for the U.S. House of Representatives. In 1948, he graduated from Harvard, then earned his law degree from the University of Virginia in 1951.

In the early 1950s, Kennedy worked as an investigative lawyer for the Justice Department, interrupted in 1952 when he ran his brother John's U.S. Senate campaign. In 1953, he resigned his position on the Senate investigations committee in protest over the methods used by committee head Joseph R. McCarthy (1908–1957) in his hunt for communists in the government. The following year, after McCarthy's spectacular downfall, Kennedy returned as the committee's chief counsel (head lawyer). For six years, he worked on exposing organized crime's relationship with labor unions.

In 1960, Robert managed his brother's successful bid for the presidency. The new president then chose his brother to serve as attorney general. It was the first time a president's close relative had been appointed to a Cabinet position, which drew some criticism.

The brothers decided against trying to push a civil rights bill through Congress right away. Its passage would be difficult: John had won the presidency only narrowly, which made his influence in Congress weak. Instead, they focused first on enforcing existing civil rights laws. As attorney general, Robert supported the Freedom Riders, a group of black and white riders taking a well-publicized bus trip through the South to exercise the right of African Americans to sit anywhere on buses. The group was frequently threatened by white crowds as police stood by. Kennedy sent five hundred federal marshals to Montgomery, Alabama, where, reinforced by state troopers and the National Guard, they broke up a violent white crowd that had surrounded Martin Luther King Jr.'s Dexter Avenue Baptist Church.

Kennedy pushed for desegregation in schools and transportation. Like King, however, Kennedy thought that the most important job was protecting African Americans' right to vote. In many southern areas, African Americans had been prevented by local officials from registering. Kennedy promised support but was unsure of what legal right the government had to act as a police force over local organizations. His explanations about limits on federal powers did not satisfy civil rights leaders, and some began questioning the Kennedys' commitment to civil rights.

In June 1963, President Kennedy sent a bill to Congress that would ban segregation in all public places. Attorney General Kennedy took the lead in rallying sup-

**Robert F. Kennedy.**
*Reproduced by permission of Archive Photos.*

port for the bill. In August, African American leaders organized the March on Washington, in which over 250,000 people gathered to demonstrate their support for the bill. The crowd heard Martin Luther King Jr. deliver his famous "I Have a Dream" speech. As the Kennedy brothers had feared, the bill was soon stalled in Congress by southern senators. It was not until after John Kennedy's assassination in 1963 that Congress passed civil rights legislation. Under President Lyndon B. Johnson, the Civil Rights Act of 1964 (banning segregation in public places) and the Voting Rights Act of 1965 (allowing the government to protect citizens' voting rights) were enacted.

In 1964, Robert Kennedy decided to run for one of New York's two senate seats. He won easily, despite attacks against him for running in a state where he did not really live. He supported legislation for minorities and—hesitantly at first—began to attack Johnson's escalation of the Vietnam War (1954–75). Gradually the war was replacing civil rights as the dominant issue in American politics. In 1965 and 1966, Kennedy questioned whether the war was right; by 1967, he was openly condemning it as wrong. In early 1968, the war's unpopularity had led many to wonder if Kennedy would challenge Johnson for the Democratic presidential nomination.

Democratic senator Eugene McCarthy announced that he would enter the race against Johnson as an antiwar candidate. After McCarthy scored surprisingly well against Johnson in the New Hampshire primary, Kennedy announced in March 1968 that he would run. McCarthy supporters were furious; they believed that McCarthy had showed Johnson's weakness, and that Kennedy would use his famous name to take advantage of the situation. Two weeks later, Johnson withdrew from the race. After winning primaries in Indiana, Nebraska, and the District of Columbia, Kennedy lost to McCarthy in Oregon. The next primary, in California on June 4, was crucial.

Kennedy won the California primary, but shortly after giving his victory speech at Los Angeles's Ambassador Hotel, Robert Kennedy was shot. He died twenty-five hours later, on June 6, 1968.

vited to festivities, and Kennedy enjoyed good relations with the press. He spoke well during news conferences and displayed a quick wit. For instance, in a meeting with Soviet premier Nikita Khrushchev, Kennedy inquired about a medal Khrushchev was wearing. After the Russian leader identified it as a peace medal, Kennedy replied, "I hope you keep it."

The New Frontier program proceeded slowly. In 1961, Kennedy won approval for a bill to improve urban (city) housing and another to provide aid to economically depressed areas (poor areas, generally where jobs are rare and businesses cannot survive). His attempts at providing government medical assistance to the elderly was denied. So, too, were his attempts at civil rights legislation. Kennedy's plans for creating a Cabinet-level Department of Urban Affairs was rejected, at least partly because he planned to name an African American, Robert C. Weaver (1907–1997), to head the department. Kennedy's plans for a tax cut were also blocked.

In 1962, Kennedy intervened in a possible strike by steelworkers. An agreement that increased benefits for workers, but not their wages, was hailed by Kennedy as a solid compromise that would not lead to increases in steel prices and inflation (a sharp rise in the prices of goods and services because of an increase in the availability of money and credit). However, when steel companies soon announced price increases, Kennedy repealed the hikes, angering many business leaders.

Kennedy was successful increasing U.S. trade, arranging a financial deal that maintained the strength of the United Nations and winning a billion-dollar appropriation (reservation of funds) for the National Aeronautics and Space Agency (NASA), with the goal of landing a man on the moon by 1970.

## Civil rights

As his presidency gained momentum in 1963, Kennedy began more vigorous support for programs to conserve and develop natural resources, provide aid for education, revise inefficient farm programs, and support civil rights. Calling racial tension "a moral crisis" in June 1963, the president gave Attorney General Robert F. Kennedy the power to investigate cases of intimidation of (threats against) African American voters in the South. The president supported a planned civil rights march on Washington, D.C., in August 1963. At that march, civil rights leader Martin Luther King Jr. (1929–1968; see box) delivered his famous "I Have a Dream" address before more than two hundred thousand people.

Kennedy twice used his presidential authority to enforce existing civil rights laws through the use of federal troops. In 1962, Mississippi governor Ross R. Barnett (1898–1987) prevented the enrollment of an African American student, James Meredith (1933– ), to the University of Mississippi. After rioting broke out, Kennedy sent in federal troops to quiet the scene. Meredith was admitted to the university under escort of federal troops.

Racial segregation is the policy of keeping groups of people from different races separated; desegregation, also called integration, is the ending of such a policy. In June 1963, Alabama governor George Wallace (1919–1998) resisted court-ordered desegregation of school districts in three major Alabama cities. By the time school opened in September 1963, President Kennedy had federalized the state national guard (put the guard under federal authority) to enforce the integration ruling.

## Fateful trip

With the 1964 presidential election a year away, Kennedy planned a trip to the state of Texas, where his support was thin despite the presence of Vice President Johnson, a beloved Texan, in his administration. The period was difficult for the Kennedys, who had lost their newborn son, two-day-old Patrick, just weeks earlier.

Kennedy's Texas trip in November 1963 drew large, enthusiastic crowds. A motorcade (parade of, in this case, open cars) was arranged to transport Kennedy administration officials and Texas governor John C. Connally (1917–1993) to a speech in Dallas. Just after the motorcade slowed and turned a curve around 12:30 P.M., shots rang out. One bullet struck the president in the neck, passed through, and struck Connally, who was sitting in the front seat of the presidential limousine. A second bullet struck Kennedy in the head. After

**Martin Luther King Jr.**

Born on January 15, 1929, in Atlanta, Georgia, to Martin Luther and Alberta King, Martin Luther King Jr. was taught by his parents that he could overcome the humiliation of segregation. His father, who had grown up in poverty, rose to become a prominent Southern preacher. King grew up with racial segregation as a way of life. Blacks and whites had separate schools, hospital waiting rooms, and even drinking fountains. When both were allowed in the same room, lines were drawn on the floor to keep them divided.

Supported by his parents' teachings, King excelled at school, especially in public speaking. After completing high school early, King enrolled in Morehouse College in Atlanta in 1944. At this prestigious school for African American men, he majored in sociology and English and continued to participate in public-speaking contests. He had planned to attend medical or law school, but professors at Morehouse urged him to become a minister.

Upon his graduation in 1948, King went to Crozer Theological Seminary in Chester, Pennsylvania, to study religion. There he learned of the activities of Mohandas Gandhi (1869–1948), who used nonviolent means (boycotts, protests) to help free India from English rule. Gandhi's teachings greatly inspired King. After earning his degree from Crozer in 1951, King began doctoral studies at Boston University in philosophy and religion. He was awarded his doctorate (Ph.D.) in 1955. While at the university, he met and married Coretta Scott.

In 1954, King accepted the position of pastor at the Dexter Avenue Baptist Church in Montgomery, Alabama. That same year, the Supreme Court ruled in *Brown v. Board of Education of Topeka* that separate (segregated) but equal schools for blacks and whites were unconstitutional. The racial climate in America soon changed as many African Americans began to challenge other segregation laws. The bus system in Montgomery operated under such a law: blacks and whites had separate seats. On December 1, 1955, seamstress Rosa Parks (1913– ) was arrested for refusing to give up her seat to a white man. In response, King and other African American leaders urged Montgomery's black community to boycott the city's buses on December 5.

After the boycott began successfully, King and the others formed the Montgomery Improvement Association to work for fairer laws. Chosen the group's president, King negotiated with city officials to change segregation in the bus system. When his demands were refused, the boycott continued for 382 days. Finally, on December 21, 1956, the Supreme Court ruled that the segregation of city buses was unconstitutional. This victory convinced King and the others to spread the movement for civil rights across the South. In 1957, they organized the Southern Christian Leadership Conference. As the group's leader,

**Martin Luther King Jr.**
*Reproduced by permission of Archive Photos.*

King toured the country over the next few years, giving speeches, attending rallies, and setting up protests.

In 1963, King traveled to Birmingham, Alabama, to organize a protest against segregation in downtown department stores. The Birmingham police moved against protesters with clubs and attack dogs. King was arrested and placed in solitary confinement. He spent the time writing his famous "Letter from Birmingham Jail," eloquently arguing for the moral right of his movement. Because of the protestors' efforts, Birmingham's white businessmen agreed to halt their racial practices.

On August 28, 1963, over two hundred thousand people marched on Washington, D.C. Organized by King, this rally sought to raise the nation's awareness of civil rights and to encourage Congress to pass the civil rights bill submitted by President John F. Kennedy. At the end of the peaceful demonstration, King delivered his famous "I Have a Dream" speech.

For his leadership in the nonviolent fight for equality, King was awarded the Nobel Peace Prize in 1964, the youngest person ever to win the award at that time. Earlier that year, King had witnessed the signing of the Civil Rights Act of 1964. It forbid racial discrimination (racial prejudice resulting in the practice of segregation) in public places such as restaurants and theaters.

While continuing his work for civil rights, King widened his concern to include human rights. In 1967, he spoke out against the Vietnam War. Later that same year, he began a campaign to fight poverty in America. He toured the country to recruit people for a new march on Washington to demand economic rights for everyone. During this tour, he went to Memphis, Tennessee, to speak on behalf of striking sanitation workers. On April 4, 1968, while standing on the balcony of the Lorraine Motel in Memphis, King was shot and killed by an assassin identified as James Earl Ray (1928–1998). Ray later claimed that he had been part of a larger conspiracy. As was suspected in the assassination of John F. Kennedy in 1963, evidence suggests that more than one individual was involved in the assassination.

John F. Kennedy's alleged assassin, Lee Harvey Oswald (center), is shot and killed by Dallas nightclub owner Jack Ruby (right) while being transported to another facility on November 24, 1963.
*Reproduced by permission of Archive Photos.*

reeling back, Kennedy slumped forward. The presidential limousine sped away to Parkland Hospital in Dallas.

The president was declared dead shortly after 1:00 P.M. His body was placed in a casket that was put aboard Air Force One, where Mrs. Kennedy and Vice President Johnson were led for the return trip to Washington, D.C. Johnson was sworn in as the nation's thirty-sixth president.

The shots were identified as having come from a nearby warehouse. An employee there, Lee Harvey Oswald (1939–1963), fled the scene. He was accused of killing a policeman before being apprehended in a movie theater. On November 24, Oswald was shot by Dallas nightclub owner Jack Ruby (1911–1967) in front of reporters and live television cameras while being escorted from one jail to another. He died in the same hospital where the president was pronounced dead.

On the same day as the Oswald shooting, the president's flag-draped casket was drawn by caisson, a two-wheeled, horse-drawn cart, from the White House to the Capitol Rotunda. A state funeral attended by dignitaries (high-ranking representatives) from ninety-two nations was held the following day. An estimated one million people lined the route (and millions more watched on television) as the caisson took the casket to Arlington National Cemetery. Among many tributes, Willy Brandt (1913–1992), mayor of West Berlin and a future leader of West Germany, remarked, "a flame went out for all those who had hoped for a just peace and a better life."

## Legacy

Within a week after Lyndon B. Johnson assumed the presidency, he appointed a committee to investigate John F. Kennedy's assassination. The Warren Commission, named for its chairman, Supreme Court chief justice Earl Warren (1891–1974), supported the findings of the original investigation that determined a single gunman—Oswald—was responsible for killing the president.

Some people remained unsatisfied with the investigation, suspecting a conspiracy (an agreement between two or more persons to commit a crime)—to murder the president. Various conspiracy theories spread about groups that may have schemed to kill Kennedy. Unfortunately, those conspiracy theories are part of the Kennedy legacy. Furthermore, a congressional panel given the authority in 1977 to examine evidence overlooked by the Warren Commission reported in 1979 that there was a "probable conspiracy" and recommended further investigation.

While president, Kennedy increased the status of the United States internationally by issuing foreign policy initiatives (new legislative measures) that increased trade with developed nations and provided assistance for underdeveloped nations. In Berlin and Cuba, he challenged aggressive Soviet actions. Kennedy's Vietnam policy was unfinished at the time of his death: He was neither recalling American military advisors nor involving American combat forces.

At home Kennedy was extremely popular, but much of his domestic agenda was still being presented for debate at the time of his death. Civil rights legislation was soon enact-

## A Selection of Kennedy Landmarks

**Arlington National Cemetery.** Arlington, VA 22211. Burial site of John F. Kennedy and Jacqueline Kennedy Onassis. See http://www.arlingtoncemetery.org/historical_information/JFK.html (accessed on September 27, 2000).

**Hammersmith Farm.** Ocean Drive, Newport, RI 02840. (401) 846-7346. Childhood summer home of Jackie Kennedy. The reception for the wedding of John and Jackie Kennedy was held here.

**John F. Kennedy Hyannis Museum.** 397 Main St., Hyannis, MA 02601. (508) 790-3077. Artifacts memorialize John F. Kennedy's affection for Cape Cod. See http://www.hyannischamber.com/jfk.asp (accessed on September 27, 2000).

**John F. Kennedy National Historic Site.** 83 Beals St., Brookline, MA 02446. (617) 566-1689. Birthplace home of the late president. See http://www.nps.gov/jofi/ (accessed on September 27, 2000).

**John Fitzgerald Kennedy Library and Museum.** Columbia Point, Boston, MA 02125. (877) 616-4599. Exhibits advance the study of John F. Kennedy's life and career. The library is one of ten official presidential libraries in the country. See http://www.cs.umb.edu/jfklibrary/index.htm (accessed on September 27, 2000).

**The Sixth Floor Museum at Dealey Plaza.** 411 Elm St., Dallas, TX 75202-3308. (214) 747-6660. Displays and artifacts surrounding the Kennedy assassination are housed on the sixth floor of the former Texas Book Depository Building, from which Lee Harvey Oswald allegedly shot and killed the president in 1963. The Dealey Plaza National Historic Landmark District and the Kennedy Memorial Plaza are nearby. See http://www.jfk.org/ (accessed on September 27, 2000).

ed during the administration of his successor, Lyndon B. Johnson, who increased American involvement in Vietnam. The latter half of the 1960s saw America divided over that war, with antiwar protests in the streets. In evaluating Kennedy's presidency, the question of how much he influenced America is often overwhelmed by the example of how much America changed after his assassination in 1963.

## Where to Learn More

Bernstein, Irving. *Promises Kept: John F. Kennedy's New Frontier*. New York: Oxford University Press, 1991.

Beschloss, Michael R. *The Crisis Years: Kennedy and Khrushchev, 1960–1963.* New York: Harper Collins, 1991.

Burner, David. *John F. Kennedy and a New Generation.* Boston: Little Brown, 1988.

Chomsky, Noam. *Rethinking Camelot: JFK, the Vietnam War, and U.S. Political Culture.* Boston: South End Press, 1993.

Cole, Michael D. *John F. Kennedy: President of the New Frontier.* Springfield, NJ: Enslow, 1996.

Fairclough, Adam. *Martin Luther King, Jr.* Athens: University of Georgia Press, 1995.

Giglio, James. *The Presidency of John F. Kennedy.* Lawrence: University Press of Kansas, 1991.

*John Fitzgerald Kennedy Library and Museum.* [Online] http://www.cs.umb.edu/jfklibrary/index.htm (accessed on September 27, 2000).

Kennedy, John F. *Profiles in Courage.* New York: Harper, 1956. Reprint, 2000.

Kennedy, John F. *Why England Slept.* New York: Wilfred Funk, 1940. Reprint, Westport, CT: Greenwood Press, 1981.

King, Coretta Scott. *My Life with Martin Luther King, Jr.* New York: Holt, Rinehart and Winston, 1969. Reprint, New York: Puffin Books, 1994.

Manchester, William. *Death of a President: November 20–November 25, 1963.* New York: Harper & Row, 1967. Reprint, New York: Arbor House, 1985.

McAdams, John. *The Kennedy Assassination Home Page.* [Online] http://mcadams.posc.mu.edu/home.htm (accessed on September 28, 2000).

National Archives and Records Administration. *The President John F. Kennedy Assassination Records Collection.* [Online] http://www.nara.gov/research/jfk/index.html (accessed on September 28, 2000).

O'Donnell, Kenneth P., David F. Powers, and Joe McCarthy. *"Johnny, We Hardly Knew Ye": Memories of John Fitzgerald Kennedy.* Boston: Little, Brown, 1972.

Patterson, Lillie. *Martin Luther King, Jr., and the Freedom Movement.* New York: Facts on File, 1989.

Randall, Marta. *John F. Kennedy.* New York: Chelsea House, 1988.

Schlesinger, Arthur M., Jr. *Robert Kennedy and His Times.* Boston: Houghton Mifflin, 1978. Reprint, New York: Ballantine, 1996.

Schlesinger, Arthur M., Jr. *A Thousand Days: John F. Kennedy in the White House.* Boston: Houghton Mifflin, 1965. Reprint, New York: Greenwich House, 1983.

Schuster, Ralph. *John F. Kennedy Assassination Homepage.* [Online] http://www.informatik.uni-rostock.de/Kennedy/ (accessed on September 28, 2000).

Sidey, Hugh. *JFK for a New Generation.* Dallas: Southern Methodist University Press, 1996.

Thomas, Evan. *Robert Kennedy: His Life.* New York: Simon & Schuster, 2000.

# Jacqueline Kennedy

**Born July 28, 1929**
**Southampton, Long Island, New York**
**Died May 19, 1994**
**New York, New York**

**Concentrated on bringing art and culture
to the White House**

In 1960, the year that **John F. Kennedy** (1917–1963; see entry in volume 5) was elected president, the most popular play on Broadway was called *Camelot.* The musical about the court and castle of the legendary King Arthur had several popular songs, including one with the lyric, "Don't let it be forgot / That once there was a spot / For one brief shining moment / That was known as Camelot."

The name Camelot was soon applied to the Kennedy White House. As well as being the center of power of a great land, the White House was transformed into a showcase of American history and a setting for festive occasions during the Kennedy years. The president and first lady hosted elegant parties with guest lists that included foreign dignitaries, talented artists of all kinds, and accomplished scientists.

Most importantly, Jacqueline Kennedy restored the White House by recreating its historical past with antique items arranged among more contemporary designs. She was also responsible for much of what was called the "Kennedy style." A popular and trendsetting first lady, her appearance and fashions were regularly featured in magazines, and she

"Can anyone understand how it is to have lived in the White House and then, suddenly, to be living alone as the president's widow?"

*Jacqueline Kennedy*

**Jacqueline Kennedy.**
*Public Domain.*

charmed fans in many nations. Along with her attractive husband and their two young children, the first lady was photogenic (she photographed well) and made for interesting news stories beyond the political headlines. If Jacqueline Kennedy radiated grace and charm as a public person, she also showed great dignity during the tragedy of her husband's assassination and her own misfortunes.

## "Inquiring Camera Girl"

Jackie, as she was called, was born Jacqueline Lee Bouvier on July 28, 1929, in New York City. She came from a wealthy but troubled household. Her father, John Vernou Bouvier III (1892–1957), was a handsome and outgoing stockbroker. Her mother, Janet Lee (1908– ), was a stylish and reserved socialite (person active in high society). Her parents quarreled often, with many of the arguments stemming from her father's drinking and unfaithfulness to his wife. The couple separated in 1936 and soon divorced.

While growing up, Jackie spent summers at the family estate in East Hampton, New York, and lived during the winter with her mother in a large apartment in Manhattan. Her mother remarried in 1942 to Hugh D. Auchincloss (1897–1976), a wealthy lawyer based in Washington, D.C., with a large estate in Rhode Island. Jackie moved between the East Hampton and Rhode Island homes while developing into an excellent equestrienne (female horseback rider). She studied dance and ballet, and she loved to read and to write stories and poems. In school, she was both curious and mischievous.

Jackie attended Vassar College, studying art history, and spent a year at the Sorbonne in Paris, studying French language, art, and literature. In 1951, while she was a student at George Washington University in Washington, D.C., she won a contest sponsored by *Vogue* magazine against over one thousand other entries. Contestants were required to submit a personal profile, an entire magazine layout with articles on high fashion, and a five-hundred-word essay on "People I Wish I Had Known." Among Jackie's selections of people were three artists whom she credited as having produced moments of beauty amid the transience of life. The artists were Serge Diaghilev (1872–1929), a force in Russian ballet; French poet

Charles-Pierre Baudelaire (1821–1867); and English play-wright Oscar Wilde (1854–1900).

A one-year position at *Vogue* magazine—six months in New York and six months in Paris—was the prize. Jackie decided against taking the position, however. Instead, she secured a position at the *Washington Times-Herald* newspaper. As the "Inquiring Camera Girl," she contributed photographs and interviews of people in Washington, D.C. Among her first interview subjects was **Pat Nixon** (1912–1993; see entry in volume 5), wife of Vice President **Richard Nixon** (1913–1994; see entry in volume 5). Nixon was the subject of a later piece, as was a Massachusetts congressman, John Kennedy, whom most people called Jack.

## Jack and Jackie

Jack and Jackie had met before. Earlier in 1951, they were both invited to a dinner hosted by Washington newsman Charles Bartlett. He and his wife were playing matchmakers. Jack and Jackie dated a few times but did not develop a serious relationship. After Jackie received a marriage proposal from a stockbroker, Jack became more serious in his pursuit of Jackie. He called her regularly and occasionally sent post-cards when he was away from Washington, D.C., in 1952 campaigning for a Senate seat. After he returned to Washington as a senator early in 1953, he took her to movies, met her for lunch, and together they attended dinner parties.

Kennedy had a reputation as a womanizer (a man who pursued several women), and he had to win Jackie's confidence. In May 1953, she went to London on assignment to cover the coronation (crowning ceremony) of Queen Elizabeth II (1926– ). In communication over the phone and through letters, they both recalled later, they each seemed to be doing well on their own. But when Jackie returned, Kennedy was there to greet her at the airport, and she presented him with several gift books she had bought for him in London. Within twenty-four hours, they were engaged. The next day, the *Saturday Evening Post* ran a previously prepared article on Kennedy as the most eligible bachelor in Washington, D.C.

Their engagement was officially announced in late June 1953, and the wedding took place on September 12,

1953, near Newport, Rhode Island. The wedding was a huge social event, with six hundred guests at the ceremony and over seventeen hundred at the reception at Hammersmith Farm, Jackie's family's summer home.

Jackie helped broaden Kennedy's appreciation of the arts and fine dining. She was not politically minded, but she helped her husband by translating French reports on Indochina—the colony France vacated in 1954, part of which became North and South Vietnam.

## Early hardships

The Kennedys faced several hardships during their first three years of marriage. Kennedy had a back injury that required him to use crutches in order to move around. He had two spinal operations, one of which was so delicate that he was near death. During his recovery, Jackie read to him, and they played cards and board games. She arranged to have an acquaintance, actress Grace Kelly (1929–1982), dress as a nurse and announce to him that she would be his new caretaker; the joke failed when Kennedy did not recognize the famous celebrity.

As Kennedy recovered, he wrote a book, *Profiles in Courage,* about eight senators in American history who took courageous, unpopular stands. Jackie helped research the book and made notes on the text. Kennedy credited her in the preface for providing the encouragement, assistance, and criticism for him to complete the book, which became a bestseller and won the revered Pulitzer Prize for Biography in 1957.

Jackie, meanwhile, had her own hardships. She suffered miscarriages (the natural ending of a pregnancy before the baby can survive on its own) in 1955 and 1956. The Kennedy's marriage was strained by his extramarital affairs and her spending habits. The birth of Caroline Kennedy in November 1957 helped bring the couple closer together.

Kennedy was campaigning for the presidency when Jackie was pregnant with the couple's second surviving child, John Kennedy Jr. (1960–1999). John-John, as he was called, was born shortly after Kennedy was elected president. The couple were devoted parents, and images of the family charmed the public during the Kennedy White House years.

## The "Jackie look"

Having little interest in or knowledge of politics, Jackie was not expected to contribute much to Kennedy's presidential campaign except for photographic opportunities of the youthful, attractive, smartly dressed couple. However, the public soon found her to be witty, charming, and intelligent. She began holding her own press conferences, attended fundraising teas, and met with voters—from dairy farmers to shoppers at supermarkets to people in ethnic neighborhoods where she could speak to them in French, Spanish, or Italian. Kennedy once remarked, "I assure you that my wife can also speak English."

After moving into the White House, the Kennedys hosted parties that were informal and elegant, with opportunities for guests to mingle. Jackie's clothing choices were regularly reported on by magazines: From her pillbox hat, to her accessories, to her gowns, the "Jackie look" became a fashion sensation. Her popularity spread worldwide. She stirred great interest during a visit to France, where crowds cried out, "Vive Jackie!" ("Long live Jackie!") This prompted the president to jokingly introduce himself at a press conference as "the man who accompanied Jacqueline Kennedy to Paris." The first lady's trips to Pakistan and other Asian nations were also very successful.

Jacqueline Kennedy's most enduring legacy as first lady was her restoration of the White House. She hired museum curators (overseers), historians, and art experts to help bring out the historical significance of the building. She decorated with items found stacked away in storerooms—a chair from the Jackson administration, for example, and enough furnishings from the Monroe and Lincoln administrations to decorate entire bedrooms.

Her work prompted a book, *The Historic Guide to the White House,* and a television special in 1962 in which she served as guide. Forty-eight million viewers tuned in.

## That terrible year

A few months' span in 1963 turned tragic. Patrick Bouvier Kennedy, born in August 1963, died from an illness two days after being born. The Kennedys again drew closer together. Jackie decided to accompany her husband on a November trip to Texas, where he wanted to rally support for the 1964 presidential election.

The usual fanfare greeted the Kennedys. In Houston on November 21, a hotel manager brushed past the president to greet Mrs. Kennedy. Later that day, she met a group of Mexican Americans and spoke with them in Spanish. The next stop was Dallas, where there was a vocal anti-Kennedy group. As in other areas of the country, Kennedy had detractors (opponents) angry at his unwillingness to back military action against Cuba, his support for civil rights, and his attempts to improve relations with the Soviet Union. A full-page ad with his picture in the form of a criminal with the words "wanted for treason" appeared in a prominent Dallas newspaper.

Nevertheless, the route of the Kennedy motorcade (parade of cars) was lined with thousands of well-wishers. Kennedy ordered the protective "bubble" roof removed to enjoy a beautiful day. Jackie was instructed to wave to people on her side of the car (behind the driver) and the president to people on his side in order to double the number of potential voters greeted by the Kennedys.

Suddenly, a bullet struck the president. As she saw him crumple in pain and shouted, "He's been shot," a second bullet hit the president in the head and he slumped against her. The car sped away to a hospital, where Jackie watched as doctors tried to save the president. But Kennedy died a half hour after being shot. Two hours after the shooting, still wearing the same blood-stained dress, Jacqueline Kennedy stood next to Vice President **Lyndon Johnson** (1908–1973; see entry in volume 5) as he took the oath of office as president.

Back in Washington, D.C., she made all the funeral arrangements and decisions. From a symbol of youth and vitality, Jackie became a symbol of strength and courage during the funeral. She met foreign dignitaries, thanked the general public on national television for their sympathy, and lit the eternal flame at her husband's grave at Arlington National Cemetery.

Upon leaving the White House soon after, Jacqueline left a card in the Lincoln bedroom that she had restored and had shared with her husband. The card read, "In this room lived John Fitzgerald Kennedy with his wife Jacqueline during the two years, ten months, and two days he was president of the United States."

## In the news

Jackie Kennedy and her children remained in the news after leaving the White House. The former first lady worked hard to preserve the legacy of her husband, requesting that Cape Canaveral—site of American space launches—be renamed Cape Kennedy. She also oversaw construction of the John F. Kennedy Library in Boston, Massachusetts. She supported her brother-in-law, Robert (Bobby) Kennedy (1925–1968; see box in **John F. Kennedy** entry in volume 5), in his campaign for the presidency in 1968, only to be shocked again by the assassination of Robert Kennedy.

In 1969, she surprised many—and disappointed some—by marrying Aristotle Socrates Onassis (c.1900–1975), a wealthy Greek shipping businessman many years older than her. She explained to friends that she loved Onassis and found relief from the constant reminders of the Kennedy legacy. Upon his death in 1975, Jackie stated, "Aristotle Onassis saved me at a moment when my life was engulfed with shadows."

In 1975, Jacqueline Kennedy Onassis took a position with Viking Books as a consulting editor and then moved to Doubleday Books in 1978. She shunned publicity all the while, but she and her children continued to be hounded by photographers and written about regularly. Daughter Caroline became an attorney, married Ed Schlossberg in 1986, and had three children. Son John Jr. was admitted to the New York Bar in 1990, launched the political magazine *George* in 1995, and married Carolyn Bessette in 1996; he, his wife, and his sister-in-law died in a plane crash near Martha's Vineyard in 1999. The former first lady died of non-Hodgkin's lym-

John F. Kennedy's son, John Jr., salutes as his father's casket passes by en route to Arlington National Cemetery. Looking on are the president's daughter, Caroline (left), and (standing left to right) brother Edward Kennedy, wife Jacqueline Kennedy, and brother Robert Kennedy.
*Reproduced by permission of AP/Wide World Photos.*

Kennedy family members gather for a function at the John F. Kennedy Library on May 25, 1989. From left to right: Senator Edward Kennedy, Caroline Kennedy Schlossberg, John F. Kennedy Jr., and Jacqueline Kennedy Onassis.
*Reproduced by permission of the Corbis Corporation.*

phoma, a type of cancer, in 1994, and was buried next to President Kennedy.

## Where to Learn More

Andersen, Christopher P. *Jack and Jackie: Portrait of an American Marriage.* New York: William Morrow, 1996.

Heymann, C. David. *A Woman Named Jackie.* Secaucus, NJ: Carol Communications, 1989. Reprint, New York: Carol Pub. Group, 1994.

Santow, Dan. *Jacqueline Bouvier Kennedy Onassis, 1929–1994.* Danbury, CT: Children's Press, 1998.

Spoto, Donald. *Jacqueline Bouvier Kennedy Onassis: A Life.* New York: St. Martin's Press, 2000.

Wolff, Perry. *A Tour of the White House with Mrs. John F. Kennedy.* Garden City, NY: Doubleday, 1962.

# Kennedy's Inaugural Address

**Delivered January 20, 1961; excerpted from**
*Bartleby.com: Great Books Online* **(Web site)**

*Representing a new generation "born in this century," the*
*youthful president challenges Americans to "ask what you can do*
*for your country"*

Following a night of heavy snow, a bitterly cold wind swept through the capital on the day **John F. Kennedy** (1917–1963; see entry in volume 5) was inaugurated as the nation's thirty-fifth president. The oath of office was administered by Supreme Court chief justice Earl Warren (1891–1974); close to three years later, Justice Warren would head a commission investigating the assassination of President Kennedy.

Among the most memorable of inaugural addresses, Kennedy's set the tone for his administration by placing the United States firmly in the position as a world leader pursuing the highest ideals. That position also assumes the burden of living up to those ideals. To achieve that, Kennedy placed responsibility on each American citizen: "Ask not what your country can do for you," he implored his fellow citizens, "ask what you can do for your country."

That phrase was among several memorable statements in Kennedy's speech. As a classic piece of oratory, the speech contained many bold statements followed by challenges to uphold the ideals expressed. In some places,

"Let the word go forth from this time and place, to friend and foe alike, that the torch has been passed to a new generation of Americans—born in this century, tempered by war, disciplined by a hard and bitter peace, proud of our ancient heritage. . . ."

*John F. Kennedy*

John Kennedy delivers his inaugural address on January 20, 1961. Behind him (from left to right) are: Lady Bird Johnson, Jackie Kennedy, outgoing president Dwight D. Eisenhower, and Vice President Lyndon B. Johnson.
*Reproduced by permission of Archive Photos.*

Kennedy used repetitive phrases to create a rhythmic effect. Always, the phrases stressed an upbeat message.

## Things to remember while reading an excerpt from President Kennedy's inaugural address:

- Kennedy began his speech by declaring that the modern world was much different than when the nation was founded. Yet the values on which the nation was founded remained as significant. The third paragraph is often cited as an example of the youthful vigor that Kennedy brought to the nation as the first president born in the twentieth century.

- After Kennedy quickly extended his declarations on the virtues of a free society outward to include other nations, he spoke of possible conflict. In 1961, the threat of nuclear annihilation was very prominent: fresh in the

Complete American Presidents Sourcebook

minds of Americans were images of the destruction caused by the atomic bombs dropped on Japan in 1945, memories of the long struggle and the atrocities of World War II (1939–45), and ongoing tensions around the globe between communist and democratic nations.

- In the portion of the address not included in the excerpt, Kennedy discussed the ongoing struggle for peace, understanding, and human advancement. That led to his concluding statements. He declared that the present time offered a unique possibility to move forward. He concluded that such energy depended on Americans responding to the challenge, "ask what you can do for your country."

## *Excerpt from President Kennedy's inaugural address*

[We] observe today not a victory of party, but a celebration of freedom—symbolizing an end, as well as a beginning—signifying renewal, as well as change. For I have sworn before you and Almighty God the same solemn oath our **forebears prescribed** nearly a century and three quarters ago.

The world is very different now. For man holds in his mortal hands the power to abolish all forms of human poverty and all forms of human life. And yet the same revolutionary beliefs for which our forebears fought are still at issue around the globe—the belief that the rights of man come not from the generosity of the state, but from the hand of God.

We dare not forget today that we are the heirs of that first revolution. Let the word go forth from this time and place, to friend and foe alike, that the torch has been passed to a new generation of Americans—born in this century, tempered by war, disciplined by a hard and bitter peace, proud of our ancient heritage—and unwilling to witness or permit the slow undoing of those human rights to which this Nation has always been committed, and to which we are committed today at home and around the world.

Let every nation know, whether it wishes us well or ill, that we shall pay any price, bear any burden, meet any hardship, support

**Forebears:** Ancestors.

**Prescribed:** Laid down a rule.

*any friend, oppose any foe, in order to assure the survival and the success of liberty.*

*This much we pledge—and more.*

*To those **old allies** whose cultural and spiritual origins we share, we pledge the loyalty of faithful friends. United, there is little we cannot do in a host of cooperative ventures. Divided, there is little we can do—for we dare not meet a powerful challenge at odds and split **asunder**.*

*To those new States whom we welcome to the ranks of the free, we pledge our word that one form of **colonial** control shall not have passed away merely to be replaced by a far more iron **tyranny**. We shall not always expect to find them supporting our view. But we shall always hope to find them strongly supporting their own freedom—and to remember that, in the past, those who foolishly sought power by riding the back of the tiger ended up inside.*

*To those peoples in the huts and villages across the globe struggling to break the bonds of mass misery, we pledge our best efforts to help them help themselves, for whatever period is required—not because the Communists may be doing it, not because we seek their votes, but because it is right. If a free society cannot help the many who are poor, it cannot save the few who are rich.*

*To our sister republics south of our border, we offer a special pledge—to convert our good words into good deeds—in a new alliance for progress—to assist free men and free governments in casting off the chains of poverty. But this peaceful revolution of hope cannot become the prey of hostile powers. Let all our neighbors know that we shall join with them to oppose aggression or subversion anywhere in the Americas. And let every other power know that this Hemisphere intends to remain the master of its own house.*

*To that world assembly of sovereign states, the United Nations, our last best hope in an age where the instruments of war have far outpaced the instruments of peace, we renew our pledge of support—to prevent it from becoming merely a forum for **invective**—to strengthen its shield of the new and the weak—and to enlarge the area in which its **writ** may run.*

*Finally, to those nations who would make themselves our **adversary**, we offer not a pledge but a request: that both sides begin anew the quest for peace, before the dark powers of destruction unleashed by science engulf all humanity in planned or accidental self-destruction.*

**Old allies:** Kennedy is referring to European countries that the United States cooperated with during the two world wars.

**Asunder:** Apart.

**Colonial:** Refers to lands or countries ruled by another, faraway nation.

**Tyranny:** A form of leadership that dominates the lives of its people.

**Invective:** Anger.

**Writ:** Power.

**Adversary:** Enemy.

We dare not tempt them with weakness. For only when our arms are sufficient beyond doubt can we be certain beyond doubt that they will never be employed.

But neither can two great and powerful groups of nations take comfort from our present course—both sides overburdened by the cost of modern weapons, both rightly alarmed by the steady spread of the deadly atom, yet both racing to alter that uncertain balance of terror that stays the hand of mankind's final war.

So let us begin anew—remembering on both sides that civility is not a sign of weakness, and sincerity is always subject to proof. Let us never negotiate out of fear. But let us never fear to negotiate.

Let both sides explore what problems unite us instead of belaboring those problems which divide us.

Let both sides, for the first time, formulate serious and precise proposals for the inspection and control of arms—and bring the absolute power to destroy other nations under the absolute control of all nations.

Let both sides seek to invoke the wonders of science instead of its terrors. Together let us explore the stars, conquer the deserts, **eradicate** disease, tap the ocean depths, and encourage the arts and commerce.

Let both sides unite to heed in all corners of the earth the command of Isaiah—to "undo the heavy burdens . . . and to let the oppressed go free. . . ."

In the long history of the world, only a few generations have been granted the role of defending freedom in its hour of maximum danger. I do not shrink from this responsibility—I welcome it. I do not believe that any of us would exchange places with any other people or any other generation. The energy, the faith, the devotion which we bring to this endeavor will light our country and all who serve it—and the glow from that fire can truly light the world.

And so, my fellow Americans: ask not what your country can do for you—ask what you can do for your country.

My fellow citizens of the world: ask not what America will do for you, but what together we can do for the freedom of man.

Finally, whether you are citizens of America or citizens of the world, ask of us the same high standards of strength and sacrifice which we ask of you. With a good conscience our only sure reward,

**Eradicate:** Remove, eliminate, erase.

*with history the final judge of our deeds, let us go forth to lead the land we love, asking His blessing and His help, but knowing that here on earth God's work must truly be our own.* (Bartleby.com: Great Books Online *[Web site]*)

## What happened next . . .

Kennedy was able to rally support for many of his policies. Establishing the Peace Corps was an example of idealism (teaching those less advantaged) put into action. The struggle for human rights is ongoing. Kennedy was able to initiate civil rights legislation that eventually became law in 1964.

Kennedy's pledge to protect democracy abroad was acted on in several diplomatic confrontations with the Soviet Union and by sending military advisors to South Vietnam to help that country defend itself. The price for fighting the expansion of communism proved to be very high. Whether or not American involvement in Vietnam would have escalated under Kennedy remains unknown.

Kennedy's idealism, as expressed in his inaugural address, energized many Americans. They believed that, indeed, "the torch has been passed to a new generation of Americans." Those who believed that a new frontier had emerged were most dismayed at the Kennedy assassination. "We'll laugh again," said Kennedy's assistant secretary of labor, Daniel Patrick Moynihan (1927– ), after the assassination. "It's just that we'll never be young again."

## Did you know . . .

• John F. Kennedy was a lifelong supporter and advocate of the arts, what he called "our contribution to the human spirit." As president, Kennedy led fundraising efforts for the new National Cultural Center, holding special White House luncheons and receptions, appointing his wife, **Jacqueline Kennedy** (1929–1994; see entry in volume 5) and former first lady **Mamie Eisenhower** (1896–1979; see entry in volume 4) as honorary co-chairwomen.

• The John F. Kennedy Center for the Performing Arts, located on the banks of the Potomac River near the Lincoln Memorial in Washington, D.C., opened to the public in September 1971. But its roots date back to 1958, when President **Dwight D. Eisenhower** (1890–1969; see entry in volume 4) signed bipartisan legislation creating a National Cultural Center. Two months after President Kennedy's assassination in November 1963, Congress designated the National Cultural Center as a "living memorial" to Kennedy, and authorized $23 million to help build what was now known as the John F. Kennedy Center for the Performing Arts. In honor of Eisenhower's vision for such a facility, one of the Kennedy Center's theaters was named for him. "I am certain that after the dust of centuries has passed over our cities," President Kennedy once said, "we, too, will be remembered not for our victories or defeats in battle or in politics, but for our contribution to the human spirit."

## Where to Learn More

Goldzwig, Steven R. *In a Perilous Hour: The Public Address of John F. Kennedy.* Westport, CT: Greenwood Press, 1995.

Ions, Edmund S. *The Politics of John F. Kennedy.* New York: Barnes & Noble, 1967.

"John F. Kennedy: Inaugural Address." *Bartleby.com: Great Books Online.* [Online] http://www.bartleby.com/124/pres56.html (accessed on September 28, 2000).

Paper, Lewis J. *The Promise and the Performance: The Leadership of John F. Kennedy.* New York: Crown, 1975.

# Lyndon B. Johnson

**Thirty-sixth president (1963–1969)**

# Lyndon B. Johnson

**Born August 27, 1908**
**Stonewall, Texas**
**Died January 22, 1973**
**Johnson City, Texas**

**Thirty-sixth president of the United States**
**(1963–1969)**

**Began the War on Poverty and**
**Great Society programs to attack**
**social problems**

"Our institutions cannot be interrupted by an assassin's bullets."

*Lyndon B. Johnson*

**Lyndon B. Johnson.**
*Reproduced by permission of the Corbis Corporation.*

L yndon B. Johnson's presidency was marked by two major areas of involvement: his Great Society program—social legislation for civil rights, the "War on Poverty," and attempts to improve living standards; and his escalation (stepping up) of the American military presence in the Vietnam War (1954–75). Highlighting his impressive career as a persuasive political craftsman, Johnson's social programs made him among the most active and effective presidents. The Vietnam War, however, made him a troubled leader who left office at the low point of a distinguished career.

Johnson assumed the presidency amid national tragedy. The assassination (murder) of popular and idealistic President **John F. Kennedy** (1917–1963; see entry in volume 5) in 1963 stunned the nation. After Vice President Johnson was sworn in as president, he acted swiftly to restore stability to the grieving country. He was able to complete legislation Kennedy had put forward.

After winning a full term in 1964, the energetic Texan and his Cabinet (presidential advisors) made tremendous gains in passing progressive social legislation. His suc-

## Fast Facts about Lyndon B. Johnson

**Full name:** Lyndon Baines Johnson

**Born:** August 27, 1908

**Died:** January 22, 1973

**Burial site:** LBJ Ranch, near Johnson City, Texas

**Parents:** Samuel Ealy and Rebekah Baines Johnson

**Spouse:** Claudia Alta "Lady Bird" Taylor (1912– ; m. 1934)

**Children:** Lynda Bird (1944– ); Luci Baines (1947– )

**Religion:** Disciples of Christ

**Education:** Southwest Texas State College (B.S., 1930); attended Georgetown University Law School

**Occupations:** Teacher; rancher

**Government positions:** Congressional secretary; U.S. representative and senator from Texas; vice president under John F. Kennedy

**Political party:** Democratic

**Dates as president:** November 22, 1963–January 20, 1965 (first term); January 20, 1965–January 20, 1969 (second term)

**Age upon taking office:** 55

cess was much like that of President **Franklin D. Roosevelt** (1882–1945; see entry in volume 4) and his New Deal (see **Franklin D. Roosevelt** box in volume 4) legislative program during the 1930s, which was passed when Johnson first came to Washington, D.C.

As president, Johnson increased the commitment of U.S. troops and military hardware (weapons) in the battle against Southeast Asian communists with few positive results. Public debate over the Vietnam War grew increasingly tense. Demonstrations in the streets against the war and other issues became commonplace. Despite his social programs and the restraint Johnson showed by refusing to involve the United States in other international confrontations, his reelection chances in 1968 quickly faded. He dropped out of the race early, declaring he would instead devote his energies to resolving the conflict in Vietnam.

## Life lessons in Johnson City, Texas

Lyndon Baines Johnson was born on August 27, 1908, on a farm in central Texas, near Johnson City. Johnson came from a modest family that had strong political roots. A Johnson ancestor had served as governor of Kentucky. Johnson's maternal grandfather (his mother's grandfather) had served in the Texas state legislature. His paternal grandfather (his father's grandfather), Samuel Ealy Johnson Sr. (1838–1915), had been a soldier for the Confederacy (the Southern states during the Civil War [1861–65]). This grandfather settled the area that became Johnson City,

Texas. Father Sam Ealy Johnson (1877– 1937) farmed rough land and served in the Texas state legislature beginning in 1904.

Attending public schools in Johnson City, Johnson graduated from high school first in his class of six. His parents were firm about Johnson going on to college, but he headed west to California instead. As a teenager, Johnson worked odd jobs, such as picking cotton and shining shoes. He worked as a dishwasher in California and then returned home to work on a road-building crew. When he tired of the backbreaking work, Johnson entered Southwest Texas State Teachers College in San Marcos.

During his time at the college, Johnson took a year off to teach in Cotulla, Texas, in order to pay some of his growing personal debts. The school where he taught served the community's impoverished Mexican Americans, who lacked economic opportunities and faced long-standing racism. Johnson set high standards for his pupils, forcing them to speak English while on school grounds. When he learned that many came from homes in which food was scarce, he helped establish a free school lunch program. The experience of struggling to survive in Cotulla and Johnson City greatly influenced Johnson's later political policies.

## Lyndon B. Johnson Timeline

**1908:** Born in Texas

**1928–31:** Teaches school in Texas

**1931–35:** Serves as aide to Texas congressman Richard Kleberg

**1937–49:** Serves as U.S. representative from Texas

**1949–61:** Serves as U.S. senator from Texas

**1961–63:** Serves as vice president under John F. Kennedy

**1963–69:** Serves as thirty-sixth U.S. president following assassination of Kennedy

**1964:** Gulf of Tonkin incident prompts heightened U.S. involvement in the Vietnam War

**1973:** Dies in Texas

## Attracted to politics

After earning a teaching degree in 1930, Johnson taught for a year at a Houston high school. An interest in Democratic politics, however, was soon leading his career elsewhere. After campaigning for a fellow Texan who won election to the U.S. House of Representatives, Johnson was given a staff job assisting the new congressman in Washington, D.C. He

## Words to Know

**Appropriation:** A sum of money designated to fund or be spent on a specific project.

**Draft cards:** From the mid-1960s through the mid-1970s, all males had to register for the draft upon turning eighteen. After registering, an individual received a draft card that contained a draft number. A lottery system was used to determine which available males would be "drafted"—required to serve in the military.

**Enfranchisement:** Voting rights.

**Great Society:** A set of social programs proposed by President Lyndon B. Johnson designed to end segregation and reduce poverty in the United States.

**Hawks:** Supporters of war (named after a bird of prey); often contrasted with doves—those who favor peaceful solutions.

**National Aeronautics and Space Administration (NASA):** The agency in charge of the U.S. space program.

**New Deal:** The legislative program of President Franklin D. Roosevelt during the Great Depression (1929–41).

**Post-traumatic stress disorder:** A psychological symptom that was identified in the years following the Vietnam War. The disorder is felt after a stressful situation (such as fighting in war) is over.

**Quota system:** When referring to immigration, a system that determines how many individuals from specific countries may be allowed to enter the United States.

**Senate majority leader:** The person in charge of supervising activity in the Senate. The majority leader is elected by colleagues of the majority party in the Senate.

**Tonkin Gulf Resolution:** Passed by Congress after U.S. Navy ships supposedly came under attack in the Gulf of Tonkin, this resolution gave President Lyndon B. Johnson the authority to wage war against North Vietnam.

**Vietcong:** Vietnamese communists engaged in warfare against the government and people of South Vietnam.

**Warren Commission:** A commission chaired by Earl Warren, chief justice of the Supreme Court, that investigated President Kennedy's assassination. The commission concluded that the assassination was the act of one gunman, not part of a larger conspiracy. That conclusion remains debated.

soon became a great supporter of Franklin D. Roosevelt, who was elected president in 1932. Roosevelt started many government programs to counter the devastating effects of the Great Depression (1929–41), which had left millions of people jobless.

Johnson worked hard for New Deal programs, President Roosevelt's legislative measures during the Depression. His enthusiasm landed him a position in 1935 as the Texas director of the newly created National Youth Administration. This New Deal project provided educational and job opportunities, including part-time employment that helped recent high-school graduates afford college costs.

Meanwhile, Johnson met and soon wed University of Texas graduate Claudia Alta Taylor (1912– ; see entry on **Lady Bird Johnson** in volume 5) in 1934. "Lady Bird," as she was called, came from a wealthy family. Her father shared Johnson's aggressive personality traits and helped finance his successful 1936 campaign for a vacant seat as a U.S. representative from Texas.

Johnson's political standing in the state grew as he quickly became a powerful congressman. As a member of the House Naval Affairs committee, he secured the building of a naval training base in Corpus Christi, Texas. He helped pass an appropriation (legislation that authorizes federal funds for a specific use) for a program that brought electricity to his native rural region of Texas. When President Roosevelt toured the state in 1937, Johnson was at his side.

Johnson served six two-year terms in the House, interrupted only by World War II (1939–45) service. He became a lieutenant commander in the Navy. After an initial assignment reporting on the morale of American servicemen, Johnson began serving on flying missions. A plane in which he was flying experienced engine trouble and was chased and shot at by the Japanese but managed to land safely. Johnson won a Silver Star for his service in the South Pacific.

## Distinguished congressman

Before beginning military service, Johnson had experienced high and low points in his young political career: In 1940, he headed a Congressional Campaign Committee that helped keep a Democratic majority in Congress; in 1941, however, he lost a bid for the Senate. After that loss, he began to limit his complete enthusiasm for New Deal policies, which were beginning to lose appeal as the Depression ended. By 1948, when Texans elected him to the U.S. Senate, John-

*Lyndon B. Johnson was the first president to be sworn in by a woman judge (Sarah Hughes).*

*President Johnson signed the Voting Rights Act of 1965 on August 6, 1965, using the same pen that Abraham Lincoln had used when he signed the Emancipation Proclamation in 1862 that freed three million slaves.*

son cooled on civil rights legislation and support of unions. He became a Senate leader by stressing military preparedness and elimination of inefficiency and waste.

By 1954, Johnson was the Senate majority leader (the person in charge of activities in the Senate), gaining national attention at the age of forty-six. His persuasion skills helped form core groups of support to ensure legislation was passed. He helped pass programs favored by President **Dwight D. Eisenhower** (1890–1969; see entry in volume 4) that were being slowed by the president's own Republican Party. For example, Johnson's floor leadership brought about passage of a bill increasing the minimum wage and expanding the range of workers who would qualify.

After being slowed for six months following a heart attack in 1955, Johnson led the Senate in passing a civil rights bill Eisenhower supported. When the Soviet Union stunned the world by launching the first space mission—the *Sputnik* satellite—Americans questioned their own science and educational preparation. After leading a group that examined the American space program, Johnson chaired the congressional committee that formed the National Aeronautics and Space Administration (NASA), the agency in charge of the U.S. space program. He was selected by Eisenhower to make a speech before the United Nations on the need for international cooperation in space programs.

## Supportive role

Johnson set his sights on the presidency as the election of 1960 neared. He did not campaign actively, however, and was left trailing behind Massachusetts senator John F. Kennedy, who charmed the electorate with his youthful idealism and speech-making skills. Soon before the Democratic National Convention, Johnson spoke out, noting his superior experience and qualifications over the forty-three-year-old Kennedy.

Nevertheless, Kennedy won the nomination on the first ballot. He offered Johnson the position of vice president. Surprisingly, Johnson accepted. Even Kennedy was amazed that the ambitious and aggressive Johnson would accept second billing. Kennedy was fortunate, as well. Johnson campaigned effectively, especially in the South and Southwest where the Irish Catholic, Harvard-educated, and wealthy Kennedy was not expected to do well. Kennedy and Johnson won a narrow margin of popular votes (just over one hundred thousand out of sixty-nine million votes cast) and a close edge in the Electoral College over Republican candidate **Richard Nixon** (1913–1994; see entry in volume 5). (The Electoral College is a body of representatives officially responsible for electing the president of the United States. In presidential elections, a candidate must win a majority of electoral votes in order to win the presidency. For more information on the Electoral College, see boxes in **George W. Bush** entry in volume 5.)

## Johnson Becomes President

Lyndon B. Johnson became president of the United States following the death of John F. Kennedy. (See Kennedy entry for election results from the Kennedy/Johnson campaign.) This marked the eighth time in U.S. history that a vice president became president following the death of his predecessor. Johnson's victory in 1964 marked the fourth time that a former vice president finishing his predecessor's term was elected as president on his own in the next election.

Like many other dynamic men, Johnson disliked the office of vice president. Kennedy understood. He gave the tireless Johnson numerous responsibilities, and he made certain that Johnson stayed informed. Johnson chaired the Space Council as well as the Committee on Equal Employment Opportunity, and he traveled extensively. Johnson and his wife were following President and Mrs. Kennedy in an open-car motorcade (a parade of cars) through Dallas, Texas, on November 22, 1963, when sniper shots fired from a nearby building hit the president. Two cars behind, Johnson's vehicle followed the president's car to nearby Parkland Hospital. Kennedy died at the hospital from his wounds.

Johnson and Lady Bird accompanied **Jacqueline Kennedy** (1929–1994; see entry in volume 5) and the casket of her slain husband aboard Air Force One back to Washington, D.C. Ninety minutes after the president had been declared dead, Johnson was sworn in as president on the plane. The country was in great distress as news events concerning the assassination dominated television. "Our institutions cannot be interrupted by an assassin's bullets," declared Johnson. Fear over the continued functioning of the American government soon passed as deep grieving set in.

## Honoring Kennedy

"All I have I would have given gladly not to be standing here today," began Johnson in his first speech as president
before a joint session of Congress, just five days after
Kennedy's death. He moved quickly to set up an independent
commission to investigate the assassination. Named the Warren Commission (after its chairman, Supreme Court justice
Earl Warren [1891–1974]), the distinguished group concluded
that the sniper arrested for the shooting, Lee Harvey Oswald
(1939–1963), had acted alone. The alleged killer himself was
murdered live on national television, two days after Kennedy's

assassination, by Dallas nightclub owner Jack Ruby (1911–1967), during a jail transfer.

Johnson made it clear from the start that he planned to continue the Kennedy administration's goals and policies. One of Johnson's first tasks was to see that a sweeping Civil Rights Act, authored in part by the late president's brother, Attorney General Robert F. Kennedy (1925–1968; see box in **John F. Kennedy** entry in volume 5), passed Congress. "No memorial or eulogy," Johnson stated, "could more eloquently honor President Kennedy's memory than the earliest possible passage of the civil rights bill for which he fought so long." The hotly contested bill is considered one of the most significant pieces of legislation in American history. The bill outlawed all discrimination on the basis of race, religion, or ethnic origin, and it covered employment, education, housing, and public accommodations (travel lodgings, food, and services as well as space on public vehicles such as buses and trains). Johnson pressured congressional leaders to ensure all

**President Lyndon B. Johnson (far right) paid tribute to John F. Kennedy's memory by working hard on the civil rights issue. Here, he consults with civil rights leaders (left to right) Roy Wilkins, James Farmer, Martin Luther King Jr., and Whitney Young.** *Reproduced by permission of AP/Wide World Photos.*

| Presidential / Vice presidential candidates | Popular votes | Presidential electoral votes |
|---|---|---|
| Lyndon B. Johnson / Hubert H. Humphrey (Democratic) | 43,167,895 | 486 |
| Barry M. Goldwater / William E. Miller (Republican) | 27,175,770 | 52 |

of the bill's measures were passed. Johnson also championed a tax-cut bill that had been in the works under Kennedy; based on economic theories of John Maynard Keynes (1883–1946), the tax-cut bill was designed to help increase consumer spending and to stimulate more jobs that produced consumer goods.

## The Great Society

Easily winning his party's nomination on the 1964 presidential ticket, Johnson scored a landslide reelection by about 15 million popular votes and a 486 to 52 margin in the Electoral College. Prior to the November 1964 election, however, two significant events occurred that would shape the rest of the decade and would forever define Johnson's presidency. He announced plans for sweeping social legislation he called the Great Society (see **Lyndon B. Johnson** primary source entry in volume 5), and he began escalating American involvement in the Vietnam War.

The country was enjoying prosperity as a whole when Johnson announced in May 1964 that America's wealth could be used to erase poverty once and for all in the country. He declared a "War on Poverty" as the Great Society's first order of business. "Even the greatest of all past civilizations existed on the exploitation of the misery of the many," he stated. "This nation, this people, this generation, has man's first chance to create a Great Society: a society of success without squalor, beauty without barrenness, works of genius without the wretchedness of poverty."

## Lyndon B. Johnson Administration

**Administration Dates**
November 22, 1963–January 20, 1965
January 20, 1965–January 20, 1969

**Vice President**
None (1963–65)
Hubert H. Humphrey (1965–69)

**Cabinet**

**Secretary of State**
Dean Rusk (1963–69)

**Secretary of the Treasury**
C. Douglas Dillon (1963–65)
Henry H. Fowler (1965–68)
Joseph W. Barr (1968–69)

**Attorney General**
Robert F. Kennedy (1963–64)
Nicholas D. Katzenbach (1965–67)
William R. Clark (1967–69)

**Postmaster General**
John A. Gronouski Jr. (1963–65)
Lawrence F. O'Brien (1965–68)
William M. Watson (1968–69)

**Secretary of the Interior**
Stewart L. Udall (1963–69)

**Secretary of Agriculture**
Orville L. Freeman (1963–69)

**Secretary of Labor**
W. Willard Wirtz (1963–69)

**Secretary of Commerce**
Luther H. Hodges (1963–65)
John T. Connor (1965–67)
Alexander B. Trowbridge (1967–68)
Cyrus R. Smith (1968–69)

**Secretary of Defense**
Robert S. McNamara (1963–68)
Clark M. Clifford (1968–69)

**Secretary of Health, Education and Welfare**
Anthony J. Celebrezze (1963–65)
John W. Gardner (1965–68)
Wilbur J. Cohen (1968–69)

**Secretary of Housing and Urban Development**
Robert C. Weaver (1966–68)
Robert C. Wood (1969)

**Secretary of Transportation**
Alan S. Boyd (1967–69)

The Johnson administration used results and recommendations from fourteen different task forces (groups that study particular issues) to begin sending bills to Congress. Always an excellent consensus builder (one who excels at helping people agree on an issue), Johnson was able to bring together supporters of business and labor—from both parties—on many measures. Great Society legislation was far-reaching. The Economic Opportunity Act of 1964 established

*Lyndon Johnson became known as "Landslide Lyndon" after having received the largest-ever percentage of popular vote—61.1%—in 1964.*

an Office of Economic Opportunity (OEO) to oversee many new programs.

In the area of education, Johnson's Great Society reformed public schools, which had become overcrowded following a tremendous surge in births following World War II (the so-called baby boom generation). The Elementary and Secondary Education Act helped strengthen inadequate urban and rural schools, special education for the disabled, and remedial help (additional corrective help) for slower learners. Other programs included Head Start, a preschool program in low-income communities, and the Higher Education Act, which provided funding for colleges and universities for expansion to meet the growing enrollment.

The Higher Education Act also launched scholarships, work-study programs, and student loan programs. Johnson signed the act in the gymnasium of his alma mater (the college he had attended), Southwest Texas State College, on November 8, 1965. He spoke of the Mexican children he had taught in Cotulla and of his own battle to put himself through college. "For them and for this entire land of ours, it is the most important door that will ever open—the door to education."

To help citizens cope with rising medical costs, Johnson established the program of Medicare—the first successful government act to provide health care coverage (insurance for medical expenses) for the nation's growing elderly population. A related program, Medicaid, provided low-income Americans with similar access to health care. Meanwhile, the Voting Rights Act of 1965 ensured full political enfranchisement (voting rights) for all adults. The act authorized federal authorities to intervene if discriminatory practices were suspected. Johnson signed that bill into law on August 6, 1965.

The Fair Housing Act of 1968 barred landlords (people who own and rent out their property), sellers, or real estate agents from refusing to rent or to sell a property because of the buyer's race, ethnicity (ethnic background), or religion. The Model Cities Act provided federal funds for job training, community centers, medical clinics, and other social services in some of the country's most run-down urban areas. The programs often used residents of the community for staff and supervision.

An existing government agency was reorganized into the Cabinet-level Department of Housing and Urban Development in 1965 to better address the problems of urban decay. After World War II, a tremendous building boom in the United States occurred on the outskirts of major American cities, called suburbs. Meanwhile, houses and buildings within many large cities ("the inner city") fell into neglect and decay.

The Fair Labor Standards Act raised the federal minimum wage, the lowest wage allowed by law. An immigration reform act erased a long-standing quota system for immigration into the United States, which for decades had favored western Europeans. (A quota system determines how many individuals from specific countries may be allowed to enter the United States.) Johnson also pushed through Congress a bill authorizing the creation and funding of a National Foundation for the Arts and Humanities, which created the National Endowment for the Arts and the American Ballet The-

**President Lyndon B. Johnson (left) visits U.S. troops in Vietnam in 1966.** *Reproduced by permission of the Corbis Corporation.*

# Gulf of Tonkin Incident

The U.S. military presence in Vietnam increased regularly between 1960 and 1964. American combat troops were not present, but military advisors were assisting South Vietnamese forces. In 1964, the North Vietnamese attacked U.S. vessels in the Gulf of Tonkin, an area of the South China Sea bordered on the west by Vietnam and on the north by China. Johnson asked Congress for a resolution to increase U.S. military involvement without a formal declaration of war. The measure was passed by both houses.

By February 1965, U.S. planes began regular bombing raids over North Vietnam. On March 6, 1965, American marines landed at the South Vietnam port city of Da Nang, and by year's end the United States stationed two hundred thousand combat troops in Vietnam. Here is the text of Johnson's report to the nation on August 4, 1964, concerning the Gulf of Tonkin incident.

*My fellow Americans:*

*As President and Commander in Chief, it is my duty to the American people to report that renewed hostile actions against United States ships on the high seas in the Gulf of Tonkin have today required me to order the military forces of the United States to take action in reply.*

*The initial attack on the destroyer Maddox, on August 2, was repeated today by a number of hostile vessels attacking two U.S. destroyers with torpedoes. The destroyers and supporting aircraft acted at once on the orders I gave after the initial act of aggression. We believe at least two of the attacking boats were sunk. There were no U.S. losses.*

*The performance of commanders and crews in this engagement is in the highest tradition of the United States Navy. But repeated acts of violence against the Armed Forces of the United States must be met not only with alert defense, but with positive reply. That reply is being given as I speak to you tonight. Air action is now in execution against gunboats and certain supporting facilities in North Viet-*

ater, among other notable institutions; in 1967, he urged Congress to provide funds to create the Corporation for Public Broadcasting and National Public Radio; and the Water Quality Act and Clean Air Act were the first major legislative efforts to lower the growing percentage of deadly toxins (poisons) in the environment.

## Growing troubles

Along with the president's announcement of the Great Society program in 1964, a second significant event occurred when Johnson signed the Gulf of Tonkin Resolu-

Nam which have been used in these hostile operations.

In the larger sense this new act of aggression, aimed directly at our own forces, again brings home to all of us in the United States the importance of the struggle for peace and security in southeast Asia. Aggression by terror against the peaceful villagers of South Viet-Nam has now been joined by open aggression on the high seas against the United States of America.

The determination of all Americans to carry out our full commitment to the people and to the government of South Viet-Nam will be redoubled by this outrage. Yet our response, for the present, will be limited and fitting. We Americans know, although others appear to forget, the risks of spreading conflict. We still seek no wider war. I have instructed the Secretary of State [Dean Rusk] to make this position totally clear to friends and to adversaries and, indeed, to all. I have instructed Ambassador [Adlai] Stevenson to raise this matter immediately and urgently before the Security Council of the United Nations. Finally, I have today met with the leaders of both parties in the Congress of the United States and I have informed them that I shall immediately request the Congress to pass a resolution making it clear that our Government is united in its determination to take all necessary measures in support of freedom and in defense of peace in southeast Asia.

I have been given encouraging assurance by these leaders of both parties that such a resolution will be promptly introduced, freely and expeditiously debated, and passed with overwhelming support. And just a few minutes ago I was able to reach Senator [Barry] Goldwater [Johnson's opponent in the 1964 presidential election] and I am glad to say that he has expressed his support of the statement that I am making to you tonight.

It is a solemn responsibility to have to order even limited military action by forces whose overall strength is as vast and as awesome as those of the United States of America, but it is my considered conviction, shared throughout your Government, that firmness in the right is indispensable today for peace; that firmness will always be measured. Its mission is peace.

tion (see box). It declared that events in Southeast Asia were vital to international peace and security, and that the United States was prepared to "take all necessary steps, including the use of armed force" to help. The resolution came after the U.S. destroyer *Maddox* was hit by torpedoes from North Vietnamese vessels in August 1964. The attack was in revenge for increased American involvement in the Vietnam War.

The nations of North Vietnam and South Vietnam, as well as the bordering countries of Cambodia and Laos, were formed in 1954 after French forces abandoned their colony of Indochina after attacks by communist forces. President Eisen-

**Thurgood Marshall**

Thurgood Marshall was born on July 2, 1908, in Baltimore, Maryland. His mother was a teacher and his father a waiter and steward at a country club. Marshall graduated from Lincoln University and received his law degree from Howard University in 1933. While at Howard, he was influenced by a group of legal scholars who developed procedures for civil rights litigation (legal proceedings).

Marshall practiced law in Baltimore, Maryland, until 1938 and also served as counsel for the local branch of the National Association for the Advancement of Colored People (NAACP). In 1935, he successfully attacked segregation and discrimination in education, actions that helped lead to the desegregation of the University of Maryland Law School (where he had been denied admission because of race). Marshall became director of the NAACP's Legal Defense and Education Fund in 1939.

In 1938, Marshall was admitted to practice before the U.S. Supreme Court, the U.S. Circuit Court of Appeals, and the U.S. District Court for the Eastern District of Louisiana. Winning twenty-nine of the thirty-two civil rights cases before the Supreme Court (and sometimes threatened with death as he argued cases in the lower courts of some southern states), Marshall earned the reputation of one of America's most outstanding civil rights lawyers. Several important cases he argued became landmarks in the destruction of segregation: *Smith v. Allwright* (1944) overruled practices that had denied the rights of African Americans to vote in several Democratic primary elections; *Morgan v. Virginia* (1946) outlawed that state's segregation policy in interstate bus transportation; *Shelley v. Kramer* (1948) outlawed race restrictions in house selling; and *Sweatt v. Painter* (1950) required the admission of an African American student to the University of Texas Law School. The most famous case involving Marshall was the *Brown vs. Board of Education* (1954) decision that outlawed segregation in public schools and challenged all forms of legally sanctioned segregation.

The NAACP sent Marshall to Japan and Korea in 1951 to investigate complaints that African American soldiers convicted by U.S. Army court-martials had not received fair trials. His appeal arguments

hower had sent military advisors to help the South Vietnamese people defend their land from communists based in North Vietnam. About one thousand American advisors were there when Eisenhower left office in 1961. During President Kennedy's term, the number of advisors swelled to twenty-five thousand. Historians debate whether or not Kennedy

**Thurgood Marshall.**
*Courtesy of the Library of Congress.*

reduced the sentences of twenty-two men. President John Kennedy nominated Marshall as judge of the Second Court of Appeals in 1961; he was confirmed by the Senate a year later after undergoing intense hearings. In 1965, Marshall accepted President Lyndon Johnson's appointment as solicitor general. In that post, Marshall defended civil rights actions as an advocate for the American people instead of (as in his NAACP days) as a counsel strictly for African Americans; however, he personally did not argue cases in which he had previously been involved.

In 1967, President Johnson nominated Marshall as associate justice to the U.S. Supreme Court. Marshall's nomination was strongly opposed by several southern senators on the Judiciary Committee, but he was confirmed by a vote of 69 to 11. When he took his seat on October 2, 1967, he was the first African American justice to sit on the U.S. Supreme Court.

During his nearly quarter century on the Supreme Court, Marshall remained a strong advocate of individual rights and never wavered in his devotion to ending discrimination. He formed a key part of the Court's progressive majority that voted to uphold a woman's right to abortion. His majority opinions covered such areas as ecology and the right of appeal for persons convicted of narcotic charges, failure to report into the U.S. Armed Forces, and obscenity. After suffering several ailments, Marshall vacated his seat in 1991. He died in 1993 at the age of eighty-four.

would have continued increasing American involvement. One of his last policy statements said of the South Vietnamese, "It's their (war) to win."

President Johnson increased American involvement. His Republican opponent for the presidency in 1964, Arizona senator Barry Goldwater (1909–1998), had promised an immediate, large-scale escalation. Johnson moved more gradually. After a Vietcong (Vietnamese communists) attack on an American military base in February 1965, the president ordered air strikes (aerial bombings) against North Vietnam. By November 1965, over 165,000 American troops were stationed in South Vietnam. That number swelled to over 460,000 by May 1967. Combat was fierce in the largely jungle environment. As the American death toll rose (in 1964, 146; in 1965, 1,104; in 1966, 5,008; in 1967, 9,300), so too did debate begin to rage at home.

Hawks (supporters of the war) in Congress demanded even more aggressive bombing, mining, and combat missions. Meanwhile, the Vietnam protest movement grew large in numbers. At protest rallies, including a huge peace march on Washington, D.C., in 1967, young men often burned their draft cards. Draft cards were cards young men had to carry to prove that they had registered for possible military service. The peace movement was increasingly met with armed federal resistance. At that Washington, D.C., march, the image of protesters placing flowers in the barrels of guns held by federal troops became a symbol of the conflict at home. Some members of Congress, including South Dakota senator George McGovern (1922– ) and New York senator Robert Kennedy, began speaking out against the war.

## 1968: That violent year

Social unrest was widespread. Protest marches became commonplace. Demonstrations against the war expanded to marches for women's rights and environmental quality. Race riots had occurred in several major cities: Thirty-five people died during rioting in the Watts area of Los Angeles, California, in 1965, and over forty more in Detroit, Michigan, in 1967. Despite civil rights legislation and some notable events—for example, in 1967, President Johnson appointed well-known civil rights advocate Thurgood Marshall (1908–1993; see box) to the U.S. Supreme Court—racism was still widely practiced in the country.

In April 1968, civil rights leader Martin Luther King Jr. (1929–1968; see box in **John F. Kennedy** entry in volume 5) was murdered in Memphis, Tennessee. Two months later, Robert F. Kennedy, who was emerging as the leading Democratic presidential candidate, was shot after a rally in Los Angeles.

Meanwhile, fifteen thousand American soldiers had died in Vietnam as of November 1967; that figure would rise to fifty-seven thousand by early 1973, when the last American troops returned home, with most of the deaths occurring in 1968 and 1969. The Vietnam War persistently caused difficulties for the Johnson administration. The public began to feel that the government had misrepresented the situation in Vietnam—that Pentagon officials had known the situation was far more complicated than Americans had been informed. A "credibility gap" arose in which more Americans began to question their leaders.

Feelings against the war and against Johnson were highlighted when Wisconsin senator Eugene McCarthy (1916– ) finished about even with Johnson in the New Hampshire presidential primary—the first test on the road to the Democratic nomination for president. Finally, bowing to increasing public pressure to end the costly and deadly intervention (Congress had never officially declared war on North Vietnam), Johnson ordered an end to the aerial bombing of North Vietnam in March 1968 in an attempt to begin peace negotiations. At the end of the month, he shocked the country and even his closest aides with the televised announcement of his decision not to run for re-election that year. "With America's sons in the fields far away, with America's future under challenge right here at home, with our hopes and the world's hopes in the balance every day, I do not believe that I should devote an hour or a day of my time to any personal partisan causes or to any duties other than the awesome duties of this office," Johnson told the nation.

Vice President Hubert Humphrey (1911–1978; see box) became the leading candidate among older Democrats, while youths turned to McCarthy and then to Robert F. Kennedy. After Robert Kennedy's assassination, the party settled on Vice President Humphrey. Another image reflective of the state of the nation occurred during the Democratic convention that summer in Chicago, Illinois, where protesters and policemen clashed violently.

# Hubert Humphrey

Born in Wallace, South Dakota, Hubert Humphrey was influenced by the experiences of his family and neighbors in his home state. By the age of twenty-five, he had witnessed hardships from drought, bank failures, farm failures, and other depressed economic situations.

His father was a pharmacist and owner of several different drug stores in South Dakota. One of his drugstores became the first of the widespread Walgreen chain in the United States. In 1927, however, Humphrey's father was forced to sell their home to pay off business debts. The same situation happened in 1932, and Humphrey withdrew from the University of Minnesota to help support his family.

Humphrey enrolled at Capitol College of Pharmacy in Denver, Colorado. He graduated from this intensive program in six months and returned to work for his father. In Humphrey's words, "The drug store was my life and it seemed then it might always be." He remained a druggist from 1933 to 1937. He married Muriel Buck in 1936.

Humphrey returned to the University of Minnesota in 1937 and received his bachelor of arts degree in 1939. A year later, he received his master's degree in political science at Louisiana State University. He and his family returned to Minneapolis, Minnesota, where Humphrey performed further graduate work at the University of Minnesota. From 1941 to 1945, Humphrey held various public service jobs, including state director of war production training and assistant director of the War Manpower Commission. Humphrey's first attempt at elected public office occurred in 1943 when he ran for mayor of Minneapolis. He was narrowly defeated, but he learned from his loss. In 1945, he was elected mayor of Minneapolis and won reelection in 1947.

As mayor, Humphrey successfully passed a law supporting fair employment practices. In 1948, Humphrey had an opportunity to address civil rights at the Democratic national convention. As a member of the committee responsible for the party's platform (a statement of where the party stands on various issues), Humphrey challenged the leadership of the party on its weak stance on civil rights. In a speech before the convention, Humphrey stated, "There are those who say: This issue of civil rights is an infringement on State's rights. The time has arrived for the Democratic Party to get out of the shadow of State's rights and walk forth-rightfully into the bright sunshine of human rights." Some delegates were so excited at Humphrey's statements that they paraded around the convention floor and voted in favor of the stronger civil rights position. However, several conservative Southern Democrats walked out of that convention and established a splinter party, the Dixiecrats. Democratic candidate **Harry S. Truman** (1884–1972; see entry in volume 4) had to face Republican Thomas Dewey (1902–

**Hubert Humphrey.**
*Courtesy of the Library of Congress.*

1971) and Dixiecrat J. Strom Thurmond (1902– ).

Democrats were unable to pass civil rights legislation. The first modern civil rights law was adopted in 1957 under a Republican president, Dwight Eisenhower. Senate majority leader Lyndon B. Johnson, a Democrat, helped pass the bill through Congress. He worked with Humphrey, who served in the Senate from 1949 to 1965, when he became Johnson's vice president. As a senator, Humphrey supported the Peace Corps, the creation of a Food for Peace program (increasing agricultural trade), and legislation favoring labor unions, farmers, and the unemployed.

Humphrey ran for the presidency in 1960. His grass-roots campaign relied on bus transportation as opposed to the better financed campaign of John F. Kennedy. Humphrey withdrew from the race after losing to Kennedy in the West Virginia presidential primary. Later, as vice president under Johnson, who was elected president in 1964, he supported administration policies, including the increasing military involvement in the war in Vietnam. Johnson became unpopular because of the war and soon bowed out as a presidential candidate in 1968. Wisconsin senator Eugene McCarthy and New York senator Robert F. Kennedy emerged as favorites, with Humphrey lagging behind because of his support for the Vietnam War, even after he promised to end the conflict. Kennedy's effort ended in June when he was assassinated, but his supporters were reluctant to join Humphrey.

Humphrey became the Democratic candidate for the presidency in 1968 at the national convention in Chicago, where the streets were filled with antiwar rioters. When Humphrey campaigned on college campuses and in major American cities he was heckled by antiwar activists. He lost the election to Richard Nixon. Disappointed, Humphrey returned to Minnesota and served as a professor of public affairs at the University of Minnesota. In 1970 and again in 1976, Humphrey was reelected to the U.S. Senate. He died of cancer on January 14, 1978.

Johnson and his wife, Lady Bird, retired to their ranch in the Pedernales Mountains of Texas in 1969. The Johnsons lived quietly for the next three years. Johnson died of a heart attack on January 22, 1973, just nine days after the final and lasting cease-fire in Vietnam was formalized.

## Legacy

Like Franklin D. Roosevelt's presidency, Lyndon B. Johnson's began with an amazing number of new social programs designed to improve the nation. Some key pieces of legislation from both administrations were still in place as the calendar turned to the year 2000. Among Johnson's programs, the Clean Air Act forced automakers for the first time to meet federal emissions-control standards to limit the amount of toxic materials cars can release in their exhaust gases. The 1965 immigration reform law brought a large upsurge in Asian immigration during the 1960s and 1970s. As a result, Asian Americans play increasing economic, cultural, and political roles in the country. Latino immigration also benefited from the 1965 Immigration Act. Head Start still serves underprivileged communities in both urban and rural areas.

The Vietnam War, and Johnson's escalation of America's role, influenced the political landscape of the country. Historians note that the war literally seemed to divide the country: Even Johnson's Cabinet argued over U.S. policy. Along with university students, coalitions (alliances) of respected academics and clergy also spoke out against the war. During the Johnson years, the perception that the government was deceiving the public came to be tagged the "credibility gap."

Those who ran for president a generation later had to confront questions about their own military service, or lack thereof, during these years. Vietnam veterans returned to a nation indifferent and even hostile to them; many of them suffered psychological problems from what was eventually identified as post-traumatic stress disorder.

The events of the Johnson presidency remain central in the country's political debate in two important areas: the conduct of military actions, and the role the federal government can and should play in attempting to improve society.

## A Selection of Johnson Landmarks

**LBJ Museum of San Marcos.** 120 West Hopkins, Ste. 200, San Marcos, TX 78666. (512) 396-3247. Small museum of Johnson paraphernalia. See http://www.sanmarcostexas.com/lbj-museum/ (accessed on September 29, 2000).

**Lyndon B. Johnson National Historical Park.** P.O. Box 329, Johnson City, TX 78636. (830) 868-7128. Large acreage includes the president's reconstructed birth house, schoolhouse, ranch home, and gravesite. See http://www.nps.gov/lyjo/ (accessed on September 29, 2000).

**Lyndon Baines Johnson Library and Museum.** 2313 Red River St., Austin, TX 78705. (512) 916-5137. Exhibits, artifacts, and papers of President Johnson are housed here. The library is one of ten official presidential libraries in the country. See http://www.lbjlib.utexas.edu/ (accessed on September 29, 2000).

Johnson's swift assumption of confident leadership after the Kennedy assassination, his support of civil rights, and the successes among his sweeping social programs leave a more unquestionably positive legacy.

## Where to Learn More

Arthur, Joe. *The Story of Thurgood Marshall: Justice for All.* New York: Bantam Doubleday Dell Books for Young Readers, 1995.

Bornet, Vaughn Davis. *The Presidency of Lyndon B. Johnson.* Lawrence: University Press of Kansas, 1983.

Califano, Joseph A., Jr. *The Triumph and Tragedy of Lyndon Johnson.* New York: Simon & Schuster, 1991. Reprint, College Station: Texas A&M University Press, 2000.

Cohen, Dan. *Undefeated: The Life of Hubert H. Humphrey.* Minneapolis: Lerner Publications, 1978.

Dallek, Robert. *Flawed Giant: Lyndon Johnson and His Times, 1961-1973.* New York: Oxford University Press, 1998.

Eskow, Dennis. *Lyndon Baines Johnson.* New York: Franklin Watts, 1993.

Falkof, Lucille. *Lyndon B. Johnson: 36th President of the United States.* Ada, OK: Garrett Educational Corp., 1989.

Firestone, Bernard J., and Robert C. Vogt. *Lyndon Baines Johnson and the Uses of Power.* New York: Greenwood, 1988.

Hitzeroth, Deborah, and Sharon Leon. *Thurgood Marshall.* San Diego: Lucent Books, 1997.

Humphrey, Hubert. *The Education of a Public Man: My Life and Politics.*Garden City, NY: Doubleday, 1976. Reprint, Minneapolis: University of Minnesota Press, 1991.

Kaye, Tony. *Lyndon B. Johnson.* New York: Chelsea House, 1988.

Johnson, Lyndon Baines. *The Vantage Point: Perspectives of the Presidency, 1963–1969.* New York: Holt, Rinehart, 1971.

*Lyndon Baines Johnson Library and Museum.* [Online] http://www.lbjlib.utexas.edu/ (accessed on September 29, 2000).

Sidey, Hugh. *A Very Personal Presidency: Lyndon Johnson in the White House.* New York: Atheneum, 1968.

Unger, Irwin, and Debi Unger. *LBJ: A Life.* New York: Wiley, 1999.

# Lady Bird Johnson

**Born December 22, 1912**
**Karnack, Texas**

**Gracious southern belle helped beautify the nation and often tamed her sometimes fiery husband**

Claudia Alta Taylor Johnson—known all her life as "Lady Bird"—entered the White House under especially trying circumstances. While struggling with her husband, **Lyndon B. Johnson** (1908–1973; see entry in volume 5), to establish a sense of stability and continuity for the grieving nation following the assassination of President **John F. Kennedy** (1917–1963; see entry in volume 5), Lady Bird followed one of the most beloved first ladies in history, **Jacqueline Kennedy** (1929–1994; see entry in volume 5). During her husband's administration, Lady Bird devoted her energies to helping her husband cope with the strains of his presidency, while also traveling extensively to speak in support of his administration's Great Society program.

"For Bird, a lovely girl with ideals, principles, intelligence and refinement."

*From an inscription written by Lyndon B. Johnson*

## Shy girl

Claudia Alta Taylor was born on December 22, 1912, in Karnack, a town in eastern Texas. The Taylor family was relatively wealthy and had several servants; a nursemaid of the infant girl gave her the unusual and lasting nickname

**Lady Bird Johnson.**
*Courtesy of the Library of Congress.*

Lady Bird. Thomas Taylor, Lady Bird's father, was a prosperous storekeeper and farmer. Her mother, Minnie, died when Lady Bird was five.

Attending local schools, Lady Bird excelled academically, although she was painfully shy.

After high school, she attended a private junior college for women in Dallas. A friend convinced her to transfer to the University of Texas at Austin after two years. There she studied journalism and earned a teaching certificate.

Soon after she graduated in 1934, she was introduced to Lyndon B. Johnson by a college friend. Johnson asked her for a date the next day and soon proposed marriage. Lady Bird was both enchanted and intimidated by Johnson's tough personality, much in contrast to hers. True to form, Johnson was a persistent admirer. Everyone counseled her to wait except for her father, whose personality was much like Johnson's.

## Financed first campaign

The couple wed in November 1934, just three months after first meeting. They moved to an apartment in Washington, D.C., where Johnson worked as a congressional aide. Not yet twenty-two, Lady Bird did not even know how to cook. When a chance came for her husband to run for a suddenly vacant seat in the U.S. House of Representatives, Lady Bird learned that it would cost at least $10,000 to mount a campaign. Johnson had little money. (The wedding ring he bought for Lady Bird only cost $2.50.) She telephoned her father in Karnack and asked for an advance on her inheritance, which he wired the next day. After her husband won the election, Lady Bird carried the deposit slip for the $10,000 check in her purse as a good-luck charm.

Lady Bird knew that she had married an ambitious and confident man, but she was unaware of his episodes of depression. Johnson was first treated for it in the early 1940s, shortly before the birth of the first of the couple's two daughters, Lynda Bird (1944– ). Their second daughter, Lucy (Luci) Baines, was born in 1947.

Elected to the Senate in 1948, Johnson quickly became a leading southern Democrat on Capitol Hill, but his schedule affected him physically as well. In 1955, he suffered a heart attack and spent five weeks in the hospital, during which time his wife slept in the room next to his and used it as a substitute congressional office to help him continue his work.

When her husband was chosen as the running mate for John F. Kennedy on the Democratic presidential slate in 1960, Lady Bird campaigned tirelessly on their behalf. Democratic Party advisors came to call her the "Secret Weapon" for her charm and popularity.

Lady Bird spent nearly three years as the wife of the nation's vice president. She was with him in the motorcade on November 22, 1963, in Dallas, Texas, when a gunman killed Kennedy. She and her husband were just two cars behind.

## Difficult transition

Johnson became first lady during a time of tremendous national grief. Her husband set about continuing the Kennedy legacy and making the presidency his own. Lady Bird became especially active as a helpmate in his announced "War on Poverty." Attempting to raise awareness for the lives of dreadful poverty that many Americans lived, the first lady toured poorer parts of the nation, such as towns near coal mines in Pennsylvania and inner-city neighborhoods in major cities.

When her husband announced his bid for his own presidential term in 1964, Lady Bird campaigned for him across the Deep South, becoming the first spouse of a presidential candidate to stump (travel about making political speeches) on her own. Because of the Johnsons' support for sweeping civil-rights legislation that would end much of the generations-old segregation in the South, many politicians in those states were hostile to the president. His advisors even deemed it too risky for him to travel there. Lady Bird hired a speech coach to help her conquer her natural shyness. Using her genuine charm and belief in her husband's policies, she convinced many state and local politicians to campaign with her on a whistlestop train trip.

## Head Start and the nation's highways

One of the more enduring legacies of the Johnson era and its Great Society legislation was the Head Start preschool program. Lady Bird was said to have been influential in convincing her husband to push for the program. Recent studies had shown that when they entered school, five- and six-year-olds from poorer households were much less prepared socially and intellectually than were their more well-off counterparts. Head Start was designed to address that problem. The first lady announced the program at a tea in February 1965 and it began that summer.

Lady Bird would be linked by name with the Highway Beautification Act of 1965, which was deemed "Lady Bird's Bill." She had announced, as first lady, that her specific project would be "The Beauty of America." In speeches, she connected her program with her husband's War on Poverty and Great Society, asserting that crime was rooted in a sense of hopelessness and could be lessened somewhat by improving the physical environment.

After making numerous tours in her duties as first lady and viewing with dismay the increase of billboards and junkyards, she suggested to her husband a bill that would provide for the planting of trees and wildflowers along the nation's growing highway system. The legislation faced serious obstacles in Congress, but the president told his staff on more than one occasion, "You know, I love that woman and she wants that highway bill. By God, we're going to get it for her."

That attitude was typical of the Johnsons' relationship. On the one hand, the president was a demanding, bossy spouse; on the other hand, he was clearly devoted to his wife and valued her opinion on policy and political matters. His tongue-lashing lectures against his staff were legendary. Often Lady Bird was present during such an occasion; she was known to simply exit the room without a word. When he noticed her absence, Johnson would leave to find her. He would return in much better spirits.

## Drawn into antiwar protests

During their White House years, the Johnsons entertained extensively, offering guests Texas hospitality with the occasional barbecue or hoedown (square-dance party). In all, they hosted over two hundred thousand guests. One notorious visitor, however, was singer Eartha Kitt (c. 1927– ), who

**First lady Lady Bird Johnson plants flowers in the Capitol Mall in Washington, D.C., in 1965.**
*Reproduced by permission of the Corbis Corporation.*

had been invited to one of the first lady's "Women Doers" luncheons. After waiting until the president had made what was supposed to be a brief appearance, Kitt used her speaking time to scold the administration for attempting to improve life in the nation's inner cities while at the same time continuing a war that sent many eighteen-year-old men of color to the jungles of Vietnam. Lady Bird responded, her voice shaking, that the ongoing crisis in Southeast Asia "doesn't give us a free ticket not to try to work for better things" at home, such as crime prevention, improvements in education, and better health care.

Johnson was an active, engaged first lady—realizing rather unexpectedly, like many of her predecessors, that she was well-suited to the responsibilities and pace of the job. A sign on her office door read "Mrs. Johnson at Work" in forbidding capital letters. Nevertheless, she was relieved when her husband announced in March 1968 that he would not seek reelection. Daughter Luci supported the decision as well, in view of the noticeable decline in her father's health. But daughter Lynda, who had married Marine captain (and, later, Virginia governor and senator) Charles Robb (1939– ) at an extravagant White House wedding in December 1967, felt that her father was giving up the reins of leadership too quickly. She believed that another Johnson administration would bring a quicker end to the war.

## Back home in Texas

The Johnsons retired to their ranch near the Pedernales River in Texas, just a mile away from the home where her husband had been born. He died there, experiencing a third and fatal heart attack on the afternoon of January 22, 1973. Lady Bird was in a car near the recently dedicated Lyndon B. Johnson Presidential Library in Austin when she was informed of her husband's collapse. He was flown to a San Antonio hospital, and she met the plane there by helicopter, but he had already died.

At the close of the twentieth century, Lady Bird was the oldest surviving presidential spouse. She spent the years after her husband's death continuing her involvement with nature and conservation programs; she also served on the board of regents of her university, the University of Texas. Even in her late eighties, Lady Bird still swam daily, though she was legally blind and suffered from arthritis. Her son-in-law, Virginia senator Charles Robb, credited her with doing much to publicize conservation and other ecology issues during her term as first lady. "She made the environmental movement popular," Robb told *People* magazine in 2000.

# Where to Learn More

Gould, Lewis L. *Lady Bird Johnson: Our Environmental First Lacy.* Lawrence: University Press of Kansas, 1988. Reprint, 1999.

Johnson, Lady Bird. *A White House Diary.* New York: Holt, 1970.

Russell, Jan Jarboe. *Lady Bird: A Biography of Mrs. Johnson.* New York: Scribner, 1999.

# Johnson's "Great Society" Speech

**Delivered on May 22, 1964; excerpted from *Public Papers of the Presidents of the United States, Lyndon B. Johnson, Book I (1963–64)***

*President Johnson describes his vision of the "Great Society"*

Lyndon B. Johnson (1908–1973; see entry in volume 5) became president in November 1963 following the assassination of President **John F. Kennedy** (1917–1963; see entry in volume 5). A strong consensus builder in Congress for over twenty years previous to becoming vice president, Johnson rallied Congress as president to enact two pieces of legislation dear to Kennedy—a civil rights act and a tax cut.

Meanwhile, Johnson began laying plans for a sweeping domestic program as the presidential election of 1964 drew near. He occasionally used the expression "Great Society" to describe his vision. On May 22, 1964, in a commencement (graduation) speech at the University of Michigan, he emphasized the term as the overall title and goal of his program. Johnson wanted legislation that would improve the nation's cities, environment, education, and quality of life. The speech was given weeks before the Democratic National Convention, at which Johnson would be officially nominated for president.

"So, will you join in the battle to give every citizen the full equality which God enjoins and the law requires, whatever his belief, or race, or the color of his skin? Will you join in the battle to give every citizen an escape from the crushing weight of poverty?"

*Lyndon B. Johnson*

## Things to remember while reading an excerpt from President Johnson's "Great Society" speech:

- At the beginning of his speech, Johnson contrasted the "turmoil" of Washington, D.C., with the "tranquility" (peace) of the University of Michigan campus in the town of Ann Arbor. The turmoil reflected political debates occurring in the nation's capital. The tranquility referred to the fact that school was out and that graduates had reached a point of success in their lives. That theme of turmoil and tranquility was used throughout the address. Johnson's vision of a great society was one where a level of achievement and peace had been reached, but also one where work continued because new problems would arise that demanded new approaches.

- Johnson focused on three areas of concern: cities, the natural environment, and the quality of education. Attempts to improve these three areas were initiated through many pieces of legislation that were connected with Johnson's vision of the Great Society.

## *Excerpt from President Johnson's "Great Society" speech*

*I have come today from the turmoil of your Capital to the tranquility of your campus to speak about the future of your country.*

*The purpose of protecting the life of our Nation and preserving the liberty of our citizens is to pursue the happiness of our people. Our success in that pursuit is the test of our success as a Nation.*

*For a century we labored to settle and to subdue a continent. For half a century we called upon unbounded invention and untiring industry to create an **order of plenty** for all of our people.*

*The challenge of the next half century is whether we have the wisdom to use that wealth to enrich and elevate our national life, and to advance the quality of our American civilization.*

**Order of plenty:** Time of prosperity.

Your imagination, your initiative, and your **indignation** will determine whether we build a society where progress is the servant of our needs, or a society where old values and new visions are buried under **unbridled** growth. For in your time we have the opportunity to move not only toward the rich society and the powerful society, but upward to the Great Society.

The Great Society rests on abundance and liberty for all. It demands an end to poverty and racial injustice, to which we are totally committed in our time. But that is just the beginning.

The Great Society is a place where every child can find knowledge to enrich his mind and to enlarge his talents. It is a place where leisure is a welcome chance to build and reflect, not a feared cause of boredom and restlessness. It is a place where the city of man serves not only the needs of the body and the demands of commerce but the desire for beauty and the hunger for community.

It is a place where man can renew contact with nature. It is a place which honors creation for its own sake and for what it adds to the understanding of the race. It is a place where men are more concerned with the quality of their goals than the quantity of their goods.

But most of all, the Great Society is not a safe harbor, a resting place, a final objective, a finished work. It is a challenge constantly renewed, beckoning us toward a destiny where the meaning of our lives matches the marvelous products of our labor.

So I want to talk to you today about three places where we begin to build the Great Society—in our cities, in our countryside, and in our classrooms.

Many of you will live to see the day, perhaps 50 years from now, when there will be 400 million Americans—four-fifths of them in urban areas. In the remainder of this century urban population will double, city land will double, and we will have to build homes, highways, and facilities equal to all those built since this country was first settled. So in the next 40 years we must rebuild the entire urban United States.

[Greek philosopher] Aristotle said: "Men come together in cities in order to live, but they remain together in order to live the good life." It is harder and harder to live the good life in American cities today. The catalog of ills is long: there is the decay of the centers and the despoiling of the suburbs. There is not enough housing for our people or transportation for our traffic. Open land is vanishing and old landmarks are violated.

**Indignation:** Anger that surfaces due to something unjust.

**Unbridled:** Without restraint.

*Worst of all, expansion is eroding the precious and time honored values of community with neighbors and communion with nature. The loss of these values breeds loneliness and boredom and indifference.*

*Our society will never be great until our cities are great. Today the frontier of imagination and innovation is inside those cities and not beyond their borders. New experiments are already going on. It will be the task of your generation to make the American city a place where future generations will come, not only to live but to live the good life.*

*I understand that if I stayed here tonight I would see that Michigan students are really doing their best to live the good life.*

*This is the place where the* **Peace Corps** *was started. It is inspiring to see how all of you, while you are in this country, are trying so hard to live at the level of the people.*

*A second place where we begin to build the Great Society is in our countryside. We have always prided ourselves on being not only America the strong and America the free, but America the beautiful. Today that beauty is in danger. The water we drink, the food we eat, the very air that we breathe, are threatened with pollution. Our parks are overcrowded, our seashores overburdened. Green fields and dense forests are disappearing.*

*A few years ago we were greatly concerned about the "***Ugly American.***" Today we must act to prevent an ugly America.*

*For once the battle is lost, once our natural splendor is destroyed, it can never be recaptured. And once man can no longer walk with beauty or wonder at nature his spirit will wither and his* **sustenance** *be wasted.*

*A third place to build the Great Society is in the classrooms of America. There your children's lives will be shaped. Our society will not be great until every young mind is set free to scan the farthest reaches of thought and imagination. We are still far from that goal.*

*Today, 8 million adult Americans, more than the entire population of Michigan, have not finished 5 years of school. Nearly 20 million have not finished 8 years of school. Nearly 54 million—more than one-quarter of all America—have not even finished high school.*

*Each year more than 100,000 high school graduates, with proved ability, do not enter college because they cannot afford it. And if we cannot educate today's youth, what will we do in 1970*

**Peace Corps:** A volunteer, government-funded agency established by President John F. Kennedy that sends American teachers and craftspeople to underdeveloped countries.

**Ugly American:** A term that arose during the 1950s to reflect an unflattering image of Americans by people in foreign lands, who viewed the nation as domineering and bullying.

**Sustenance:** Nourishment.

*when elementary school enrollment will be 5 million greater than 1960? And high school enrollment will rise by 5 million. College enrollment will increase by more than 3 million.*

*In many places, classrooms are overcrowded and **curricula** are outdated. Most of our qualified teachers are underpaid, and many of our paid teachers are unqualified. So we must give every child a place to sit and a teacher to learn from. Poverty must not be a bar to learning, and learning must offer an escape from poverty.*

*But more classrooms and more teachers are not enough. We must seek an educational system which grows in excellence as it grows in size. This means better training for our teachers. It means preparing youth to enjoy their hours of leisure as well as their hours of labor. It means exploring new techniques of teaching, to find new ways to stimulate the love of learning and the capacity for creation.*

*These are three of the central issues of the Great Society. While our Government has many programs directed at those issues, I do not pretend that we have the full answer to those problems.*

*But I do promise this: We are going to assemble the best thought and the broadest knowledge from all over the world to find those answers for America. I intend to establish working groups to prepare a series of White House conferences and meetings—on the cities, on natural beauty, on the quality of education, and on other emerging challenges. And from these meetings and from this inspiration and from these studies we will begin to set our course toward the Great Society.*

*The solution to these problems does not rest on a massive program in Washington, nor can it rely solely on the strained resources of local authority. They require us to create new concepts of cooperation, a creative federalism, between the National Capital and the leaders of local communities.*

*[Former president] Woodrow Wilson once wrote: "Every man sent out from his university should be a man of his Nation as well as a man of his time."*

*Within your lifetime powerful forces, already loosed, will take us toward a way of life beyond the realm of our experience, almost beyond the bounds of our imagination.*

*For better or for worse, your generation has been appointed by history to deal with those problems and to lead America toward a new age. You have the chance never before afforded to any people in any*

**Curricula:** Educational courses.

*age. You can help build a society where the demands of morality, and the needs of the spirit, can be realized in the life of the Nation.*

*So, will you join in the battle to give every citizen the full equality which God enjoins and the law requires, whatever his belief, or race, or the color of his skin? Will you join in the battle to give every citizen an escape from the crushing weight of poverty?*

*Will you join in the battle to make it possible for all nations to live in enduring peace—as neighbors and not as mortal enemies?*

*Will you join in the battle to build the Great Society, to prove that our material progress is only the foundation on which we will build a richer life of mind and spirit?*

*There are those timid souls who say this battle cannot be won; that we are condemned to a soulless wealth. I do not agree. We have the power to shape the civilization that we want. But we need your will, your labor, your hearts, if we are to build that kind of society.*

*Those who came to this land sought to build more than just a new country.*

*They sought a new world. So I have come here today to your campus to say that you can make their vision our reality. So let us from this moment begin our work so that in the future men will look back and say: It was then, after a long and weary way, that man turned the exploits of his genius to the full enrichment of his life.*

*Thank you. Goodbye.* (Public Papers of the Presidents of the United States, Lyndon B. Johnson, Book I [1963–64], pp. 704–7)

## What happened next . . .

Soon after the address, fourteen separate task forces began studying nearly every major aspect of U.S. society. The average membership of a task force was nine and each task force was assigned a particular subject: cooperation among government agencies in dealing with financial questions; making the federal government more efficient and less costly; developing policies to prevent economic recessions; developing policies on economic issues related to other countries; and determining how best to help individuals maintain their income. Many specific proposals were included in Johnson's State of the Union address delivered on January 7, 1965.

Johnson stated in the address that the government did not have answers for all the problems facing the United States. However, opponents to government social programs labeled the Great Society a costly attempt to solve all the nation's problems. The amount of money to be spent by the federal government on social programs became a source for debate in all subsequent presidential elections. Meanwhile, Johnson's programs arising from the task forces met with mixed results. Growing social debate over government programs and the war in Vietnam eclipsed Johnson's hope of a united effort to improve American society.

*Johnson shifted the time of the annual State of the Union message to evening so that it could be broadcast to the nation before the largest possible viewing audience.*

## Did you know . . .

- When he made his Great Society speech at the University of Michigan in 1964, Johnson contrasted the tranquility of student life with the turmoil of endless debate in Washington, D.C. However, as the American military presence in Vietnam escalated, college campuses—including the University of Michigan—became the scene of many protests against the war. Sit-ins (where students took possession of a room, hallway, or building and remained there as a sign of protest), marches, and rallies against the war began to overshadow the idealism for social improvement among the young that had been evident earlier in the 1960s. That idealism had led to Johnson's decision to announce his Great Society program at a college graduation.

## Where to Learn More

Bornet, Vaughn Davis. *The Presidency of Lyndon B. Johnson.* Lawrence: University Press of Kansas, 1983.

Foster, Leila M. *The Story of the Great Society.* Chicago: Children's Press, 1991.

Goodwin, Doris Kearns. *Lyndon Johnson and the American Dream.* New York: Harper & Row, 1976. Reprint, New York: St. Martin's Press, 1991.

Grinspan, Mel G., ed. *The Great Society Revisited: Success, Failure, or Remorse?* Memphis: Rhodes College, 1993.

Jordan, Barbara C., and Elspeth D. Rostow, eds. *The Great Society: A Twenty-Year Critique.* Austin, TX: Lyndon B. Johnson School of Public Affairs, 1986.

*Public Papers of the Presidents of the United States, Lyndon B. Johnson, Book I (1963–64)*. Washington, DC: National Archives and Records Service, 1965.

Complete American Presidents Sourcebook

# Richard Nixon

### Thirty-seventh president (1969–1974)

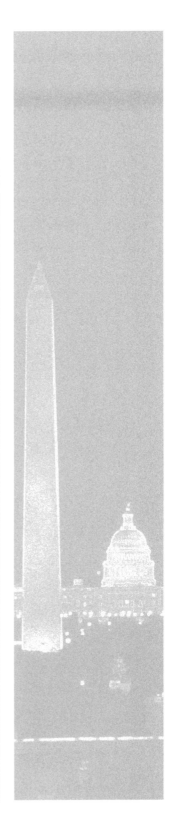

# Richard Nixon

**Born January 9, 1913**
**Yorba Linda, California**
**Died April 22, 1994**
**New York, New York**

**Thirty-seventh president of the United States (1969–1974)**

**Resigned the presidency after his involvement in the Watergate scandal was exposed**

R ichard Nixon is the only president to resign as the nation's chief executive. Facing charges of misconduct in office for his involvement in the Watergate scandal, Nixon chose to resign rather than undergo a lengthy impeachment trial. (Impeachment is the means by which an official is charged with a crime and possibly removed from office). The Watergate scandal arose from the June 1972 break-in of the Democratic Party's national headquarters at the Watergate apartment and office complex in Washington, D.C. The burglars were connected with members of the inner circle of President Nixon's administration.

The scandal brought a shocking downfall to a man who had represented his political party on the national ballot on five occasions—twice (1952 and 1956) as vice president under **Dwight D. Eisenhower** (1890–1969; see entry in volume 4), and three times as the Republican presidential nominee (1960, 1968, and 1972). The scandal also overshadowed President Nixon's accomplishments in foreign relations as well as his attempts to end the Vietnam War (1954–75) and to improve a poor American economy.

"That the way I tried to deal with Watergate was the wrong way is a burden I shall bear for every day of the life that is left to me."

*Richard Nixon*

**Full name:** Richard Milhous Nixon

**Born:** January 9, 1913

**Died:** April 22, 1994

**Burial site:** Nixon Library Grounds, Yorba Linda, California

**Parents:** Francis Anthony and Hannah Milhous Nixon

**Spouse:** Thelma Catherine "Pat" Ryan (1912–1993; m. 1940)

**Children:** Patricia "Tricia" (1946– ); Julie (1948– )

**Religion:** Quaker

**Education:** Whittier College (B.A., 1934); Duke University Law School (LL.B., 1937)

**Occupations:** Lawyer; naval officer

**Government positions:** U.S. Office of Emergency Management attorney; U.S. representative and senator from California; vice president under Dwight D. Eisenhower

**Political party:** Republican

**Dates as president:** January 20, 1969–January 20, 1973 (first term); January 20, 1973–August 9, 1974 (second term)

**Age upon taking office:** 56

Trying to preserve for history his day-to-day conduct in dealing with world issues, President Nixon recorded on audiotapes his discussions with Cabinet officials (presidential advisors) and other counselors. Nixon had hoped those tapes would provide a legacy of his achievements and insight into how his accomplishments came about. Instead, the tapes became the focus of a prolonged legal battle: Suspicion arose that the tapes would reveal the extent of Nixon's knowledge and participation in illegal activities, such as the Watergate break-in. The tapes hastened his downfall.

## Quaker upbringing

Richard Milhous Nixon was born on January 9, 1913, in Yorba Linda, California. He was the second of five sons of Francis Anthony and Hannah Milhous Nixon. The family was part of the Quaker religious sect, also known as the Society of Friends. Quakers believe that each individual can directly feel the presence of God. They value work, community cooperation, spirituality through meditation, and nonviolence.

Nixon worked hard as a young man, including long hours at the family-owned combination gas station and grocery store. After graduating from high school in Whittier, California, Nixon attended Whittier College, a Quaker school. He stayed close to home to help his family: the Nixons faced financial troubles, and one of Nixon's brothers was ill. Nixon majored in history and won a scholarship to Duke University in North Carolina.

He graduated from Duke's well-regarded law school in 1937.

Nixon returned to California and began working with a well-established law firm. He met Thelma Ryan (1913–1993; see entry on **Pat Nixon** in volume 5) soon after his return to Whittier. "Pat" (her father's nickname for her) and Nixon married on June 21, 1940. They would have two daughters, Tricia and Julie.

After America entered World War II (1939–45) in 1941, Nixon worked with a government agency, the Office of Emergency Management, and then joined the U.S. Navy. He earned the rank of lieutenant and spent the war on a Pacific Island serving with the Naval Air Transport Command.

## Aggressive campaigner

After World War II ended, Nixon was in Baltimore, Maryland, awaiting his discharge. He was contacted by a California Republican official and asked to run for the House of Representatives in 1946. Nixon returned to California and entered politics. Although reserved and awkward in crowds, Nixon nevertheless became an effective campaigner by making speeches and attacking the views of his rivals.

## Richard Nixon Timeline

**1913:** Born in California

**1937:** Graduates from Duke University Law School

**1942:** Serves in the U.S. Navy during World War II

**1947–50:** Serves as U.S. representative from California

**1950–53:** Serves as U.S. senator from California

**1953–61:** Serves as vice president under Dwight D. Eisenhower

**1960:** Loses presidential election to John F. Kennedy

**1962:** Loses California gubernatorial election to Edmund G. Brown Sr.

**1969–74:** Serves as thirty-seventh U.S. president

**1973:** Vietnam cease-fire negotiated

**1974:** Resigns as president because of the Watergate scandal

**1994:** Dies in New York

Following the war, the United States and the Soviet Union engaged in tense political conflicts, a situation that came to be known as the Cold War. The United States was especially sensitive to the spread of communism—a system where the government controls the distribution of goods and services and limits individual freedom. In his first campaign, Nixon accused his opponent of being soft on communism,

**Words to Know**

**Communism:** A system where the government controls the distribution of goods and services and limits individual freedom.

**Détente:** A relaxing of tensions between rival nations, marked by increased diplomatic, commercial, and cultural contact.

**Devalued:** An economic situation in which the value of one country's currency (the dollar, for example) is lowered against another international currency.

**Electoral College:** A body officially responsible for electing the president of the United States. In presidential elections, the candidate who receives the most popular votes in a particular state wins all of that state's electoral votes. Votes are distributed among states in ratios based on population. A candidate must win a majority of electoral votes (over fifty percent) in order to win the presidency.

**Impeachment:** A legislative proceeding charging a public official with misconduct. Impeachment consists of the formal accusation of such an official and the trial that follows. It does not refer to removal from office of the accused.

**Indicted:** Officially charged with having committed an illegal act.

**Inflation:** A period of time when money loses some of its value, usually because goods become more expensive.

**Missing in action:** A term that describes military personnel unaccounted for. They might have been captured by the enemy, in which case they become prisoners of war; they might be hiding out and attempting to return to safety; or they might have been killed.

**Racial desegregation:** A policy meant to ensure that people of all racial origins are treated equal.

**Strategic Arms Limitation Treaty (SALT):** Missile reduction program between the United States and the Soviet Union.

**Subpoena:** A formal legal document that commands a certain action or requires a person to appear in court.

**Vietcong:** Vietnamese communists engaged in warfare against the government and people of South Vietnam.

**Watergate scandal:** A scandal that began on June 17, 1972, when five men were caught burglarizing the offices of the Democratic National Committee in the Watergate complex in Washington, D.C. This led to a cover-up, political convictions, and, eventually, the resignation of President Richard Nixon.

and he frequently pursued the issue in debates. He won the election handily.

## Rapid rise in Washington, D.C.

New congressmen generally take a while to learn the skills necessary for political success. But Nixon was a quick learner. He was soon involved in high-profile projects, including the drafting of the Taft-Hartley Act of 1947. The act placed restrictions on union activities and established loyalty oaths for union leaders (oaths that required them to state they were noncommunists). He was also in a special committee that influenced elements of the Marshall Plan (see George C. Marshall box in **Harry S. Truman** entry in volume 4), a program of financial support that helped rebuild European economies devastated by World War II.

Nixon was a member of the Un-American Activities Committee that investigated individuals and organizations that might conspire against the U.S. government. In that capacity, he began the investigation of Alger Hiss (1904–1996), a high-ranking official in the State Department. Writer Whittaker Chambers (1901–1961) testified (acted as a witness) before the Committee that he had been a member of the U.S. Communist Party in the 1920s and 1930s. Chambers charged that Hiss had given him classified (secret) documents to send to the Soviet Union. Hiss denied the charges, but microfilm copies of documents identified as classified and bearing Hiss's handwriting were revealed. Hiss was indicted for (officially charged with) perjury, or lying under oath, by the Department of Justice. The jury failed to reach a verdict (a judgment), but Hiss was convicted (found guilty) after a second trial in January 1950.

The Hiss case, which occurred during Nixon's second term in Congress, brought him national recognition. Nixon ran successfully for a senate seat in 1950. Again, he was able to undermine his opponent on charges of being soft on communism. Fear and suspicion of Communist Party sympathizers was so great during that period that the House Un-American Activities Committee and a senate committee began to misuse the situation. Many Americans accused of being communists by Congress simply held different views or led different lifestyles than did the politicians who investigated them.

*During the 1960 presidential campaign, retiring president Eisenhower became annoyed when candidate Richard Nixon continually stressed how important he had been to the Eisenhower administration as vice president. When asked by a reporter to cite one of the vice president's accomplishments, Eisenhower replied, "Give me a week and I'll think of one."*

Nixon, meanwhile, was concentrating his attention on gaining a higher office. In 1952, he became the running mate of Republican presidential nominee Dwight D. Eisenhower. However, newspapers reported that Nixon had established a secret fund as a senator in which money was donated by individuals seeking political favors. Eisenhower was advised to drop Nixon from the ticket. Nixon responded with an impassioned, nationally televised speech in which he fully disclosed his personal finances. He stated that his wife owned, not a mink coat, but "a respectable Republican cloth coat." And he acknowledged that he did receive a gift: "a little cocker spaniel dog, . . . black and white, spotted, and our little girl Tricia, the six year old, named it Checkers." The address, which came to be known as the "Checkers speech," saved Nixon's place on the ticket.

Eisenhower projected a calm and easy manner as a campaigner and as president, but Nixon was more aggressive. He accused the Democratic Party nominee, Illinois governor Adlai Stevenson (1900–1965; see box in **Dwight D. Eisenhower** entry in volume 4), of being soft on communism. Eisenhower won the election and was a popular president. In the summer of 1955, he suffered a serious heart attack. Nixon held meetings while Eisenhower was ill for three months. Republicans despaired that their most popular candidate might not be well enough to run for a second term. However, by the early spring of 1956, Eisenhower had fully recovered his health and announced he would seek a second term as president. Some advisors wanted him to choose a new vice president, but Eisenhower asked Nixon to run with him a second time.

As vice president, Nixon was quite active. He traveled frequently, spreading American good will to Asia, Africa, and Europe during Eisenhower's second term. He did not fare as well in South America, where rocks were thrown at the Americans. In 1959, Nixon toured the Soviet Union. He and Soviet leader Nikita Khrushchev (1894–1971; see box in **Dwight D. Eisenhower** entry in volume 4) were followed by television cameras as they visited a show on modern households. In a model kitchen, they engaged in a heated debate about their respective forms of government and society. The exchange of views became known as the "kitchen debate."

## Changing fortunes

Nixon quickly emerged as the frontrunner for the 1960 presidential election. He swept through the primaries and locked up the Republican nomination early. His Democratic opponent, Massachusetts senator **John F. Kennedy** (1917–1963; see entry in volume 5), faced a stiffer fight before prevailing as his party's nominee. Always a vigorous campaigner, Nixon crisscrossed the country and established a firm lead in the polls. However, his lead declined during a series of four nationally televised debates. The debates marked the first time that a presidential-campaign debate was broadcast over television, which had only recently reached a majority of American households.

In the debates, Kennedy projected himself as being relaxed, lively, and youthful, showing a sense of humor and idealism. Nixon seemed tired, stiff, and in need of a shave (he refused to wear makeup), and offered a program with few fresh ideas. Neither candidate outshone the other in the quality of their remarks, and neither said anything politically damaging; some commentators, in fact, believe that Nixon had been the more effective debater. Nevertheless, momentum swung to Kennedy during the final few weeks of the campaign and he squeezed out a victory. Kennedy won handily in the Electoral College, 303 to 220, while edging Nixon in the popular vote by less than one percent. (The Electoral College is a body officially responsible for electing the president of the United States. In presidential elections, a candidate must win a majority of electoral votes—over fifty percent—in order to win the presidency. For more information on the Electoral College, see boxes in **George W. Bush** entry in volume 5.)

Disappointed, Nixon returned to California and turned his attention to the position of governor. He was not yet fifty years old. He again waged an aggressive campaign in the California gubernatorial election of 1962. Nixon's tactic of asserting that his opponent was soft on crime and communism failed; Democrat Edmund G. Brown Sr. (1905–1996) defeated him. Believing he had received cool treatment from the California press during the campaign, Nixon addressed his post-election comments to them. He assumed the press was disappointed by the election results because, as he said, "You won't have Nixon to kick around anymore."

**Election Results**

### 1968

| Presidential / Vice presidential candidates | Popular votes | Presidential electoral votes |
|---|---|---|
| Richard M. Nixon / Spiro T. Agnew (Republican) | 31,710,470 | 301 |
| Hubert H. Humphrey / Edmund S. Muskie (Democratic) | 31,209,677 | 191 |
| George C. Wallace / Curtis E. LeMay (American Independent) | 9,893,952 | 46 |

*Democratic vice presidential incumbent Humphrey became presidential nominee only after incumbent president Lyndon B. Johnson dropped out of the race and New York senator Robert F. Kennedy was assassinated. Republican Nixon won the nomination on the second ballot.*

### 1972

| Presidential / Vice presidential candidates | Popular votes | Presidential electoral votes |
|---|---|---|
| Richard M. Nixon / Spiro T. Agnew (Republican) | 47,108,459 | 520 |
| George S. McGovern / R. Sargent Shriver (Democratic) | 29,084,726 | 17 |

*Democrat McGovern won the nomination on the second ballot; Alabama governor George C. Wallace, an early Democratic challenger for the nomination, lost ground after being wounded in an assassination attempt on May 15, 1972.*

The Nixons moved to New York, where the former vice president quickly reestablished himself as a lawyer. He slowly gathered support within his party and campaigned for Republicans throughout the country. As the campaign for the 1968 presidential nomination approached, Nixon was staging a surprise comeback. As a more moderate politician than other hopefuls, including recently elected California governor **Ronald Reagan** (1911– ; see entry in volume 5) and New York governor Nelson Rockefeller (1908–1979; see box in **Gerald R. Ford** entry in volume 5), Nixon enjoyed a smooth ride to the nomination at the Republican Party convention in Miami, Florida, in 1968.

There had been a few confrontations outside of the convention in Miami. Demonstrations in protest of the Vietnam War and for various social causes were met with resistance by local law enforcement authorities. The protests reflected great unrest throughout the nation: People disagreed passionately about the war and civil rights legislation, among other issues. Widespread protests at the Democratic Convention in Chicago later that summer were met with force by Chicago police.

The year 1968 was a violent one. Civil rights leader Martin Luther King Jr. (1929–1968; see box in **John F. Kennedy** entry in volume 5) was assassinated in April. New York senator and former U.S. attorney general Robert F. Kennedy (1925–1968; see box in **John F. Kennedy** entry in volume 5), emerging as the potential Democratic presidential nominee, was assassinated in June.

Vice President Hubert Humphrey (1911–1978; see box in **Lyndon B. Johnson** entry in volume 5) became the Democratic nominee. He had overcome tough challenges by Kennedy and Minnesota senator Eugene McCarthy (1916– ), both of whom had pledged to end the war and had appealed to youthful idealism. Nixon based his campaign on law and order and appealed to what he called the "forgotten Americans"—those who worked hard and were not protesting against their government. Alabama governor George C. Wallace (1919–1998), who had a history of actions *against* racial desegregation, ran on a third-party ticket. (Racial desegregation is the policy of allowing people of different racial origins equal access to their civil liberties.) Wallace won over thirteen percent of the popular vote and carried five southern states in the Electoral College. Nixon and Humphrey each won about forty-three percent of the popular vote, but Nixon won a sure victory in the Electoral College.

## Foreign policy successes

As Nixon took office in January 1969, domestic unrest had increased. Organized protests against the Vietnam War, for greater protection of the natural environment, and for improved civil rights for minorities and women were almost daily occurrences. President Nixon supported the development of the Environmental Protection Agency, an executive-level agency responsible for maintaining environmental quality. On all other issues, the administration carried out conservative policies during Nixon's tenure (time) as president, which included reelection in 1972. Civil rights legislation stalled; Nixon nominated four Supreme Court justices with decidedly conservative backgrounds; and while defense spending increased,

*Richard Nixon was the first president to have visited all fifty states.*

**Richard Nixon Administration**

**Administration Dates**
January 20, 1969–January 20, 1973
January 20, 1973–August 9, 1974

**Vice President**
Spiro T. Agnew (1969–73)
None (1973)
Gerald R. Ford (1973–74)

**Cabinet**

**Secretary of State**
William P. Rogers (1969–73)
Henry A. Kissinger (1973–74)

**Secretary of the Treasury**
David M. Kennedy (1969–71)
John B. Connally (1971–72)
George P. Shultz (1972–74)
William E. Simon (1974)

**Attorney General**
John N. Mitchell (1969–72)
Richard G. Kleindienst (1972–73)
Elliot L. Richardson (1973–74)
William B. Saxbe (1974)

**Postmaster General**
Winton M. Blount (1969–71)

**Secretary of Interior**
Walter J. Hickel (1969–70)
Rogers C. B. Morton (1971–74)

**Secretary of Agriculture**
Clifford M. Hardin (1969–71)
Earl L. Butz (1971–74)

**Secretary of Labor**
George P. Shultz (1969–70)
James D. Hodgson (1970–73)
Peter J. Brennan (1973–74)

**Secretary of Commerce**
Maurice H. Stans (1969–72)
Peter G. Peterson (1972–73)
Frederick B. Dent (1973–74)

**Secretary of Defense**
Melvin R. Laird (1969–73)
Elliot L. Richardson (1973)
James R. Schlesinger (1973–74)

**Secretary of Health, Education and Welfare**
Robert H. Finch (1969–70)
Elliot L. Richardson (1970–73)
Caspar W. Weinberger (1973–74)

**Secretary of Housing and Urban Development**
George W. Romney (1969–73)
James T. Lynn (1973–74)

**Secretary of Transportation**
John A. Volpe (1969–73)
Claude S. Brinegar (1973–74)

funds for education, urban renewal, and antipoverty programs were cut in an effort to reduce government spending.

Nixon faced an economy weakened by inflation (a period of time when money loses some of its value, usually because goods become more expensive). He favored programs

that increased U.S. exports and lowered imports. He imposed wage and price controls. He followed the economic theory that if the cost of goods held steady, workers would not need to have increased pay, thus breaking the momentum of inflation. Inflation slowed by 1972, but in 1973 it picked up again. The Nixon administration then devalued (lowered the value of) the dollar in an attempt to slow inflation.

Domestic issues were handled by his closest aides, Chief of Staff H. R. Haldeman (1926–1993) and campaign advisor John Ehrlichman (1925–1999). Nixon focused most of his direct attention on foreign policy. With his secretary of state, Henry Kissinger (1923– ; see box), President Nixon planned foreign-policy initiatives; many past U.S. presidents had simply reacted to foreign events.

President Nixon made two historic trips in 1972. The former anticommunist champion visited the People's Republic of China in February of that year and signed a trade agreement. It was the first high-level contact between the two nations in over twenty years. In May, he visited the Soviet Union and ini-

**Richard Nixon (left) and Communist Party chief Leonid I. Brezhnev (right) exchange copies of the Strategic Arms Limitation Treaty (SALT). Soviet president Nikolai V. Podgorny (center) looks on.** *Reproduced by permission of the Corbis Corporation.*

# Henry Kissinger

Born Heinz Alfred Kissinger on May 27, 1923, in Furth, Germany, Kissinger was the son of a teacher who lost his job during the 1930s when the Nazi government persecuted Jews in Germany. The family, which included Kissinger's younger brother, Walter Bernhard, left Germany in 1938, moving first to England and then several months later to the United States. They settled in New York City. Kissinger attended high school for a year and then switched to night school so he could work during the day in a factory.

Kissinger served with the U.S. Army Intelligence during World War II (1939–45). After the war, he was a civilian instructor at the European Command Intelligence School in Oberammergau, Germany. He returned to the United States in 1947 to study at Harvard University, where he earned a bachelor's degree in 1950, a master's degree in 1952, and his Ph.D. in 1954. He began teaching in Harvard's government department in 1954 and wrote an acclaimed book, *Nuclear Weapons and Foreign Policy* (1957), that influenced a flexible U.S. foreign policy. He occasionally advised U.S. presidents Dwight D. Eisenhower, John F. Kennedy, and Lyndon B. Johnson. During summers between 1952 and 1969, he directed the Harvard International Seminar, which was attended by many international figures with whom he would later deal as a foreign affairs official.

Kissinger supported New York governor Nelson Rockefeller's unsuccessful bid for the Republican nomination for the presidency in 1968. After Rockefeller was defeated by Richard Nixon, he urged Nixon to appoint Kissinger to head the National Security Council that advises the president on international security issues. Taking on special assignments, Kissinger began pursuing secret negotiations to establish frameworks that were followed up with public diplomacy. Those included agreements on arms limitations (SALT I) with the Soviet Union, the reopening of relations with the People's Republic of China, and "shuttle diplomacy"—where Kissinger traveled back and forth between Middle Eastern nations to establish peace in the region. Other behind-the-scenes developments were not as well received, including the Nixon administration's secret bombing of Cambodia and military operations within that nation during the Vietnam War. Those actions were halted by Congress. Since war had not been officially declared against North Vietnam (and never was), the president had to have approval from Congress to undertake such missions. A high point for Kissinger came when he shared the Nobel Peace Prize with Le Duc Tho (1911–1990), a

**Henry Kissinger.**
*Courtesy of the Library of Congress.*

North Vietnamese negotiator with whom he helped bring an end to American military involvement in Vietnam.

The Strategic Arms Limitations Treaty (SALT) with the Soviet Union followed negotiations that lasted for nearly three years. Kissinger accompanied Nixon to Moscow, where the president and Soviet Communist Party chief Leonid Brezhnev (1906–1982) signed the agreement. Another of Kissinger's successes that began in secret was his organizing of Nixon's renewing relations with China. Working through Pakistani president Agha Muhammad

Yahya Khan (1917–1980), Kissinger flew to China and arranged for an invitation for Nixon to make an official state visit. The Shanghai Communique of 1972 that resulted provided guidelines for the establishment of U.S.-China relations. During his eight years in the National Security Council and State Department, Kissinger flew to China a total of nine times.

After becoming secretary of state—the first to be foreign-born—in 1973, Kissinger conducted what became known as "shuttle diplomacy," where he facilitated negotiations to restore peace among Middle Eastern nations. Kissinger would often fly from Egypt to Israel to Syria or other Middle Eastern nations to develop agreements to secure peace among officials who did not want to meet face to face. After his departure from office following the 1976 electoral defeat of Gerald Ford, Kissinger was self-employed as the director of a consulting firm dealing with international political assessments. In addition to advising a variety of clients on international politics, he wrote several memoirs to explain how history evolved while he was in office. Kissinger joined the faculty of Georgetown University in 1977.

**Nixon and Foreign Relations**

The Cold War, a term that describes tense relations between United States–led democratic nations and Soviet Union–led communist nations, began shortly after the end of World War II. A communist rebellion in China during the late 1940s deposed the democratic government there and further escalated the Cold War. It was during this period that Richard Nixon entered politics and was elected to the House of Representatives based on his strong anticommunist views. Nixon served with the House Un-American Activities Committee that brought communists to trial, had a well-publicized public argument while he was vice president with Soviet leader Nikita Khrushchev, and continued to speak out against communism during his campaign for the presidency in 1968.

It was very surprising, then, that as president, Nixon improved American relations with the Soviet Union and China. His trip to China in 1972 marked the first exchange of diplomatic relations between the leaders of the two nations since shortly after World War II. The stage was set for Nixon's trip to China when he relaxed the U.S. trade embargo (a restriction of trade) and allowed a U.S. table tennis team to play against Chinese counterparts at China's invitation. When Nixon made his trip to China in February 1972, he met with communist chairman Mao Tse-tung (1893–1976) and had lengthy talks with China's premier, Chou En-lai (1898–1976). The talks helped open possibilities for trade and diplomacy. The new era in Chinese-American relations reduced tensions and had a profound impact on world politics. The United States continued

tiated the policy of détente (a relaxing of tensions between rival nations, marked by increased diplomatic, commercial, and cultural contact). Along with securing a new trade agreement with that nation, Nixon began a missile reduction program called the Strategic Arms Limitation Treaty (SALT). He also authorized massive purchases of American wheat by the Soviet government to help it overcome failed agricultural programs.

Nixon defeated South Dakota senator George S. McGovern in a landslide reelection in 1972. The economy had steadied at that point; peace talks between the United States and North Vietnam showed promise of bringing the Vietnam War to an end; and Nixon had improved relations with two longtime enemies of the United States. When a cease-fire in Vietnam was announced in January 1973, Nixon was at the

President Richard Nixon leads a contingent of U.S. and Chinese officials at the Great Wall of China in 1972. *Courtesy of the National Archives and Records Administration.*

to defend the anti-Communist government in Taiwan, an island off the coast of China, but risks of war over that island were reduced and an already weakening relationship between the Soviet Union and China was further tested.

That same year, Nixon held meetings in Russia with Soviet leader Leonid I. Brezhnev that resulted in a treaty to limit strategic nuclear weapons. Those landmark visits that improved relations with old enemies China and the Soviet Union, an accord in January 1973 with North Vietnam to end American involvement in Southeast Asia, and a 1974 agreement between Israel, Egypt, and Syria, negotiated by Nixon's secretary of state, Henry Kissinger, were among the most impressive foreign relations triumphs of any president.

height of his popularity. However, his policies during the war had further inflamed antiwar sentiments. In 1970, four young protesters were killed by National Guard troops at Kent State University in Ohio. Nixon scorned protest demonstrations while praising "average" Americans he called "the silent majority" (see **Richard Nixon** primary source entry in volume 5).

## Vietnam

During the early 1950s, an uprising in a French colony in southeast Asia led the French to abandon the area. Formerly called Indochina, the area was divided into four nations—Cambodia, Laos, and North and South Vietnam—based on historical boundaries. Communists controlled North Vietnam, and South Vietnam was a democracy. In the

The aftermath of a tragic demonstration on the campus of Kent State University on May 4, 1970. Four demonstrators were killed and nine were wounded by the Ohio National Guard after the Guard was called in to restore order following antiwar protests.
*Reproduced by permission of the Corbis Corporation.*

late 1950s, North Vietnamese communist soldiers called the Vietcong invaded South Vietnam to try and overthrow the government and instill a communist system. Under presidents Eisenhower and Kennedy, America sent increasingly larger amounts of supplies and military advisors to help the South Vietnamese. Under President Lyndon B. Johnson, airplane bombing missions against the Vietcong began early in 1965, and American combat troops began arriving by the end of the year. By 1968, around five hundred thousand American servicemen were stationed in Vietnam. When American involvement in the war ended in 1974, over 55,000 American soldiers had died, and more than 150,000 were wounded.

Upon taking office in 1969, President Nixon defined his goal of achieving "peace with honor" in Vietnam. He began a program of withdrawing American troops. By August, twenty-five thousand soldiers left Vietnam; by December, another sixty-five thousand departed. American casualty rates declined noticeably as the policy of Vietnamization—training and equipping South Vietnamese soldiers to fight—was instituted.

Still, the war was expanding. In 1970, American air and ground forces entered neighboring Cambodia to empty Vietcong strongholds. In 1971, American bombers began hitting targets in Laos, a country next to North Vietnam, where the Vietcong established supply lines. After a Vietcong offensive (attack) in March 1972, American planes began bombing North Vietnam for the first time since the Johnson administration. Later that year, mines were placed in important harbors to stop Vietcong supply lines. When peace talks broke down late in 1972, the United States engaged in the largest-ever aerial bombing in history during the month of December 1972.

A cease-fire in January 1973 was greatly welcomed, but it hardly seemed an appropriate time for rejoicing. Lost planes, American soldiers missing in action (unaccounted for) or taken prisoner of war, and the ever increasing protests at home had proven exhausting and dispiriting. All American personnel were finally evacuated from Vietnam in 1974.

## Watergate

In 1973, the Vietnam War was replaced in newspaper headlines by the Watergate scandal. The scandal actually began on June 17, 1972, when five men were caught burglarizing the offices of the Democratic National Committee in the Watergate apartment and office complex in Washington, D.C. Investigations, primarily by newspapers led by the *Washington Post,* uncovered connections between the burglars and members of the Nixon administration.

While the exact nature of the relationship between the burglars and the administration remained unclear, investigators soon discovered other illegal activities connected with the White House. A group called the "plumbers" had been organized to stop "leaks" (unauthorized release of information to the press). The group was involved in a 1971 burglary of a psychiatrist's office; they were seeking information against a patient, Daniel Ellsberg (1931– ). Ellsberg had leaked classified documents (called "the Pentagon Papers") to the press about bombing missions in Vietnam that the Nixon ad-

# The Watergate Hearings

On February 7, 1973, the Senate voted 70 to 0 to establish a seven-man committee, headed by Senator Sam Ervin (1896–1985), a Democrat from North Carolina, to probe the Watergate case. Televised hearings of the Senate Select Committee to Investigate Presidential Campaign Practices (commonly referred to as the Watergate committee, or the Ervin committee) were broadcast daily on national television. The hearings often produced dramatic moments, and they were widely watched. The Ervin committee's televised hearings climaxed in the stunning testimony of White House counsel John Dean, which implicated President Richard Nixon in the Watergate cover-up. Even more damaging was the public testimony of White House aide Alexander Butterfield on July 16, 1973. He revealed the existence of a secret recording system installed in the White House.

An ongoing battle over the tapes ensued: the Senate Committee, special prosecutor Archibald Cox (hired by the Justice Department to conduct an independent investigation), and federal judge John Sirica (who presided over criminal cases related to Watergate) all wanted to review the tapes for evidence of the president's participation in the Watergate scandal.

President Nixon claimed the tapes were private property. He also stated the tapes contained material that might compromise national security, and argued that he had a right to withhold them under the constitutional claim of "executive privilege." Those actions were not well received in the press or the public, where Nixon's popularity plummeted twenty-eight points in the polls; less than forty percent of the people approved of his work as president. When the Ervin committee offered to review the tapes privately, Nixon still refused; when Cox and Sirica subpoenaed seven of the tapes, Nixon challenged their authority to investigate the White House.

The Senate Committee chaired by Senator Ervin was strongly praised. Ervin became nationally acclaimed for his fair management of the hearings. His leadership, visible to millions daily during the televised Watergate proceedings, exemplified honesty, a passion for truth, and a reverence for the Constitution. By the end of the summer of 1973, he had become an American folk hero, and "Uncle Sam" fan clubs, complete with T-shirts and buttons featuring Ervin, appeared around the country.

Ervin's co-chairman was Republican senator Howard H. Baker Jr. (1925– ) of Tennessee. Baker was a close ally of Nixon and was actively involved in Nixon's first successful campaign for the presidency in 1968. Still, Baker remained impartial during

John Dean takes the oath before the Ervin Committee (Senate committee investigating Watergate). *Reproduced by permission of the Corbis Corporation.*

the Watergate investigation and was thorough in delving into the scandal. He won praise from Democrats and Republicans alike. Baker served four terms in the U.S. Senate, including four years as minority leader and four years as majority leader. He retired from the Senate in 1985 and served as White House chief of staff under President Ronald Reagan in 1987 and 1988.

After the Ervin committee concluded its investigation, the evidence and a summary of findings were turned over to the House of Representatives to begin im-peachment hearings against the president. The formal impeachment process begins with the House Judiciary Committee. They call witnesses and discuss the issues relating to impeachable offenses, then vote either to recommend pursuing the case further, or to end legal proceedings. If they vote to approve continuing the case, they draw up charges—called Articles of Impeachment. Those articles are presented to the full House of Representatives. The House then votes on whether or not to impeach the president, which means to formally charge him of "high crimes and misdemeanors." If they vote to impeach the president, a trial is held in the Senate, and the Senate votes whether or not the president is guilty of charges stated in the articles. If found guilty, the president is removed from office.

By the end of July 1974, the House Judiciary committee approved three articles of impeachment. They charged Nixon with misusing his power in order to violate the constitutional rights of U.S. citizens, obstructing justice in the Watergate affair, and defying Judiciary Committee subpoenas. It soon became obvious that the House would approve the articles and the president would have to face a trial in the Senate, where he had little support. Instead, in August 1974, President Nixon resigned from office.

ministration had kept secret. A grand jury (a special jury that meets to decide if an indictment—a formal legal accusation—should be made) indicted White House special assistant on domestic affairs John Ehrlichman, White House special counsel Charles Colson (1931– ), and others for organizing the office break-in.

Meanwhile, investigators discovered that the Committee to Re-Elect the President (a group dubbed "CREEP" by the press) had solicited illegal campaign contributions that were used to finance spying on political opponents; evidence surfaced that more than $500,000 from those funds was paid to the Watergate burglars. Nixon's former attorney general, John Mitchell (1913–1988), White House counsel John Dean (1938– ), White House chief of staff H. R. Haldeman, and Erlichman were implicated in political spying efforts.

On April 30, 1973, Haldeman, Ehrlichman, and Attorney General Richard Kleindienst (1923– ) resigned, and Dean was dismissed. New attorney general Elliot Richardson (1920– ) appointed Harvard Law School professor Archibald Cox (1912– ) as a special prosecutor to investigate the Watergate break-in. (A special prosecutor is an attorney especially appointed to conduct an investigation of government officials on behalf of the government.) A few days later, the Senate Select Committee on Presidential Activities opened hearings. These nationally televised hearings proved riveting: John Dean testified that John Mitchell had ordered the Watergate break-in; he added that a major cover-up was underway (to "cover up" was a term that came into popular use at the time to describe the act of hiding evidence of a crime); and Dean insisted that the president had authorized payments to the burglars to keep them quiet. (The payments were called "hush money," another term that entered the common language.) Nixon fiercely denied the accusations.

The investigation became bogged down in accusations and rebuttals (opposing arguments in response), with no clear sequence of events emerging that directly implicated the president. However, a huge revelation occurred on July 16, 1973. Testifying before the Senate committee, White House aide Alexander Butterfield (1926– ) revealed that Nixon had installed an audiotaping system in the White House to record conversations for history about his day-to-

A political cartoon shows President Nixon tangled in a web of recording tapes. A controversy swirled around Nixon's refusal to turn over White House tapes to the House Judiciary Committee investigating the Watergate affair.
*Drawing by Robert Pryor. Courtesy of the Library of Congress.*

day concerns in the White House. Special Prosecutor Cox immediately authorized a subpoena (a formal legal document that commands a certain action or requires a person to appear in court) for eight tapes, asking for the days and times when John Dean claimed the president had authorized illegal payments. Nixon refused to release the tapes, claiming they were vital to the national security. U.S. District Court judge John Sirica (1905–1992), who presided over the original case involving the Watergate burglars, ruled that Nixon must honor the subpoena; an appeals court upheld the decision.

Instead, on Saturday, October 20, 1973, Nixon ordered Attorney General Richardson to dismiss Cox. Richardson immediately resigned, as did Deputy Attorney General William Ruckelshaus (1934– ). Solicitor General Robert Bork (1927– ) stepped in to discharge Cox. Called "the Saturday Night Massacre," Nixon's actions drew widespread public scorn. To slow criticism, Nixon appointed another special prosecutor, Texas lawyer Leon Jaworski (1905–1982), and gave the subpoenaed tapes to Judge Sirica. However, some conversations were missing, and one tape had a mysterious silence of eighteen minutes' length. Experts determined that portions of the tapes had been erased.

The Watergate scandal dragged on into 1974, sorely testing America's faith in their leaders. By that time, **Gerald R. Ford** (1913– ; see entry in volume 5) had replaced Spiro T. Agnew (1918–1996) as Nixon's vice president. Agnew had been implicated in a separate and personal scandal involving income tax evasion (purposely not paying taxes owed to the government).

In March 1974, a grand jury indicted Mitchell, Haldeman, Ehrlichman, and four other White House officials in the Watergate cover-up; Nixon was named as an "unindicted co-conspirator." With public sentiment clearly against Nixon, the administration eased its defensive tactic of "stonewalling" (the act of obstructing and delaying an investigation, and another term that came into popular usage during the Watergate scandal).

In April, Nixon complied with Jaworski's request for written transcripts of forty-two tapes: They clearly showed the president discussing ways to punish political opponents and to stonewall the Watergate investigation. Nixon refused to submit sixty-four more tapes in May, claiming executive privilege. That practice allows a president to withhold documents from the legislature as a means for maintaining a balance of power (checks and balances) between the president and Congress. However, on July 24, the Supreme Court voted 8 to 0 that Nixon must turn over the tapes.

Meanwhile, impeachment hearings had been underway by the House Judiciary Committee. By the end of July, the committee approved three articles of impeachment: They charged Nixon with misusing his power in order to violate the constitutional rights of U.S. citizens, obstructing justice in the Watergate affair, and defying Judiciary Committee subpoenas. Nixon's last attempts to rally support against a vote of impeachment, which would lead to a Senate trial, were futile. Three tapes he released on August 5, 1974, revealed that he had ordered the Federal Bureau of Investigation (FBI) to stop investigating the Watergate break-in. The tapes (from the

period around June 23, 1972) showed clearly that Nixon had helped direct the cover-up.

Facing certain impeachment and subsequent removal from office, Nixon resigned on August 9. He was the first U.S. president to do so. His successor, Gerald R. Ford, pardoned him for all crimes he might have committed while in office, making Nixon immune (protected) from federal prosecution. (See **Gerald R. Ford** primary source entry in volume 5.) In taking office, Ford exclaimed that "our national nightmare is over" and that the "American system worked." He meant that despite the disruptions caused by the Watergate scandal and the resignation of Nixon, America's government system continued to operate effectively.

Richard and Pat Nixon went into seclusion at their home in San Clemente, California, after leaving Washington, D.C. The former president was disbarred (decertified as a lawyer) in New York after a state court found that he had obstructed justice in connection with Watergate and the Penta-

**Five presidents and first ladies attend the 1994 funeral of former president Richard Nixon. From left to right: Bill and Hillary Clinton, George and Barbara Bush, Ronald and Nancy Reagan, Jimmy and Rosalynn Carter, and Gerald and Betty Ford. U.S. senator Bob Dole and his wife Elizabeth are in the second row.**
*Reproduced by permission of Archive Photos.*

**A Selection of Nixon Landmarks**

**Heritage of San Clemente.** 415 N. El Camino Real, San Clemente, CA (949) 369-1299. Special collections about President Nixon's years in San Clemente are included in this museum. See http://www.sanclemente.com/HeritageCenter/ (accessed on October 10, 2000).

**Nixon Rooms.** Whittier College, Wardman Library, 13406 Philadelphia St., Whittier, CA 90608. (562) 907-4247. Nixon memorabilia, particularly as it pertains to his days as a Whitter student, are contained in this special collection. See http://www.whittier.edu/academic/library/sc.html (accessed on October 10, 2000).

**Richard Nixon Library and Birthplace.** 18001 Yorba Linda Blvd., Yorba Linda, CA 92886. (714) 993-3393. Presidential library, Nixon's 1910 birthplace, the First Lady's Garden, a museum of Nixon artifacts, and the gravesites of the President and Mrs. Nixon make up this nine-acre historic site. The library is one of ten official presidential libraries in the country. See http://www.nixonfoundation.org/ (accessed on October 10, 2000).

gon Papers, and several more court rulings went against him. In 1977, the U.S. Supreme Court upheld a 1974 law giving the government control over Nixon's presidential papers and tape recordings.

Although he wrote several books and traveled abroad on personal diplomatic missions, Nixon was never able to fully return as a respected politician or statesman. The shadow of Watergate remained. He died in New York City on April 22, 1994.

## Legacy

There were plenty of achievements during Richard Nixon's administration. Highlights include détente with the Soviet Union and the reestablishment of relations with China. At home, the administration wrestled with an unstable economy and managed to slow inflation. Government spending was generally lowered, and the founding of the Environmental Protection Agency addressed an area of great concern to many Americans.

The unstable social atmosphere of the Nixon years challenged all national figures. President Nixon achieved a long-desired cease-fire in the Vietnam War. His authorization for bombing campaigns and expansion of the war into neighboring countries, however, increased the outspokenness of the antiwar movement.

Nixon had always taken aggressive approaches to overcoming opponents. When his administration took that philosophy beyond legal limits, the nation was faced with the lawbreaking activities of the executive responsible for carrying out the laws of the land. After a long investigation, the federal system, under the guidelines of the Constitution, followed the process for expelling a chief executive for "high crimes and misdemeanors." Nixon's historic resignation occurred before the official removal of a president could take place. When the Watergate affair was over, relieved Americans could say, "The system worked."

## Where to Learn More

Aitken, Jonathan. *Nixon: A Life*. Washington, DC: Regnery, 1993.

Ambrose, Stephen E. *Nixon*. New York: Simon and Schuster, 1987.

Barr, Roger. *Richard M. Nixon*. San Diego: Lucent, 1992.

Bernstein, Carl, and Bob Woodward. *All the President's Men*. New York: Simon and Schuster, 1974. Reprint, 1999.

Brodie, Fawn M. *Richard Nixon: The Shaping of His Character*. New York: Norton, 1981.

Emery, Fred. *Watergate: The Corruption of American Politics and the Fall of Richard Nixon*. New York: Times Books, 1994.

Fremon, David K. *The Watergate Scandal in American History*. Springfield, NJ: Enslow, 1998.

Hoff, Joan. *Nixon Reconsidered*. New York: BasicBooks, 1994.

Isaacson, Walter. *Kissinger: A Biography*. New York: Simon & Schuster, 1992.

Kissinger, Henry. *White House Years*. Boston: Little, Brown, 1979.

National Archives and Records Administration, Office of Presidential Libraries. *Richard M. Nixon Presidential Materials Staff at Archives II*. [Online] http://www.ibiblio.org/lia/president/nixon.html (accessed on October 31, 2000).

Nixon, Richard. *RN: The Memoirs of Richard Nixon*. New York: Grosset, 1978. Reprint, New York: Simon & Schuster, 1990.

Ripley, C. Peter. *Richard Nixon*. New York: Chelsea House, 1987.

Wicker, Tom. *One of Us: Richard Nixon and the American Dream*. New York: Random House, 1991.

Wills, Garry. *Nixon Agonistes: The Crisis of the Self-Made Man*. Boston: Houghton Mifflin, 1970. Reprint, Atlanta: Cherokee, 1990.

Woodward, Bob, and Carl Bernstein. *The Final Days*. New York: Simon and Schuster, 1976.

# Pat Nixon

**Born March 16, 1912**
**Ely, Nevada**
**Died June 22, 1993**
**Park Ridge, New Jersey**

**Dignified first lady shied away from spotlight, but helped promote volunteerism**

Pat Nixon was never comfortable in the public spotlight that shines on families of political officeholders. She had grown accustomed to it as her husband, **Richard Nixon** (1913–1994; see entry in volume 5), served two terms in Congress and then was elected senator in 1950. In 1952, she was warming to her public position as the wife of the vice presidential candidate. But when the Nixons had to reveal their personal finances to counter charges in the press that Nixon had received secret funds, she strongly disliked the invasion of privacy and became less accessible to the media.

As first lady, Pat Nixon gradually became a more public figure. She traveled to Peru after an earthquake there to help with relief efforts; she made trips to Africa and South America in the diplomat position of personal representative of the president; and she traveled around the United States to meet with volunteer organizations for various causes. After the Watergate scandal began dominating press coverage in 1973, Pat Nixon again sought refuge from the glare of publicity. She had always acted with grace and dignity, but she retreated when the political life became a media circus.

"It takes heart to be in political life."

*Pat Nixon*

**Pat Nixon.**
*Courtesy of the Library of Congress.*

## "St. Patrick's babe"

Born Thelma Catherine Ryan on March 16, 1912, she was nicknamed Pat by her father. Actually, he called her "St. Patrick's babe in the morn" each morning during her infancy when he arrived home from working in a mine. She was born on the eve of St. Patrick's Day, an Irish holiday. Pat's parents, William and Kate Halberstadt Bender Ryan, lived in Ely, Nevada, where William worked as a miner.

The family soon moved to California and operated a small farm. Pat worked regularly on the farm as soon as she was old enough to help pick tomatoes, potatoes, and peppers. She learned to drive a wagon with a team of horses to help gather the Ryans' crops and take them to market. Thirteen years old when her mother died, Pat became the female head of the family for her father and two brothers. She nursed her father through his painful illness of silicosis (a lung disease that afflicts miners from breathing in mineral dust). He died when Pat was seventeen.

Pat looked after her brothers and attended school at Fullerton Junior College. At the age of nineteen, she drove an elderly couple cross-country to New York City. She lived there for three years, working as a stenographer (one who records the spoken word in shorthand, a quick form of writing) and then as an X-ray technician while she took classes at Columbia University. Pat returned to California in 1934 and enrolled at the University of Southern California in Los Angeles.

She was an excellent student, graduating in 1937. To help support her education and herself, Pat worked several jobs: At various times (and some overlapping), she was a store clerk, a dental assistant, an actress for walk-on scenes, and a telephone operator. One teacher claimed to have seen her in class in the morning, working behind a cafeteria counter at lunchtime, studying in a library in the afternoon, and working at a clothing store in the evening—all during the same day.

## The world's a stage

After graduation, Pat became a teacher at Whittier High School in Whittier, California. In addition to teaching typing, she coached cheerleaders and arranged performances of plays. In 1938, she tried out for a part in a drama produced by the Whittier Community Players. Young lawyer Richard Nixon was an amateur actor auditioning for a part. Nixon was immediately fond of Pat and asked her for a date. She replied, "Oh, I'm too busy." He boldly responded, "You shouldn't say that because someday I'm going to marry you."

Pat enjoyed being single and declined her persistent admirer. Nixon tried sending her flowers and poems, but he and Pat remained just friends for awhile. Gradually he won her over. Nixon knew he was succeeding when Pat began helping Nixon's mother at the Nixon family store. They were married in Riverside, California, on June 16, 1940. After a honeymoon in Mexico, the newlyweds returned to Whittier, where Nixon was a rising young lawyer and Pat continued to teach school.

After America entered World War II (1939–45) in 1941, the Nixons each took positions with the Office of Price Administration (OPA), a government agency that helped oversee rationing programs. They worked in Washington, D.C., for six months. Nixon enlisted in the navy and was sent to the Pacific. Pat returned to California, where she worked for an OPA branch in San Francisco.

## Political life begins

Nixon returned to Baltimore, Maryland, after World War II ended in 1945. While awaiting his discharge from the service, he was contacted by a Republican Party official back in Whittier, and asked to run for Congress to represent that district. Pat did not like the public life of a politician, but she helped her husband at his campaign headquarters and often accompanied him to his speeches.

In 1946, the Nixons' first daughter, Tricia, was born. The Nixons moved to Washington, D.C., following Nixon's victory in the 1946 congressional election. Two years later, another daughter, Julie, was born. Nixon was reelected to Congress in 1948, and he was elected to the Senate in 1950. In 1952, he was chosen as the Republican vice presidential candidate on the ticket headed by **Dwight D. Eisenhower** (1890–1969; see entry in volume 4). Just three months before election day, newspapers (beginning with the *New York Post*) reported that Nixon had a secret fund to which donors, in-

Vice presidential candidate Richard Nixon plays piano and sings with his daughters Tricia (left) and Julie, and wife Pat in 1952.
*Reproduced by permission of the Corbis Corporation.*

cluding some who might expect political favors, could contribute. While Nixon denied the accusations, Eisenhower was advised to drop Nixon from the ticket, fearing the scandal might cost Republicans the election.

Although she resented the invasion of their privacy, Pat Nixon approved her husband making the family finances public and going on national television to protect his reputation. The speech helped to lessen the scandal, and Eisenhower coasted to election as president. Pat Nixon traveled extensively with her husband during his time as vice president. The couple visited Asia, Europe, Africa, and the Soviet Union. At home, Pat met regularly with women's groups across the country.

She was disappointed when her husband lost his bid for the presidency in 1960, but she was happy to return to a quiet life in California. She initially resisted her husband's plan to run for governor of California in 1962. After seeing how much he wanted the position, Pat Nixon gave in, but her husband lost a tense and often bitter campaign to Democrat Edmund G. Brown Sr. (1905–1996). The couple moved to New York with their two daughters.

## Back to Washington, D.C.

Nixon maintained a visible role in Republican politics. In 1968, he emerged as the leading contender for the party's nomination for president. He won the nomination and a close election. Nixon had always been somewhat reserved and awkward in crowds. Pat Nixon helped show the warmer, family side of the Nixons.

In her role as first lady, Pat Nixon served as hostess for formal dinner parties involving American and foreign officials. She also arranged informal affairs with more humble folk, often inviting groups of senior citizens or physically challenged people to the White House. Though she preferred not to make public statements or take on great causes, Pat Nixon supported volunteerism and traveled around the country to help showcase the efforts of volunteer groups. She also traveled with her husband to such faraway places as China and the Soviet Union. On her own, she traveled to Peru to help with relief efforts after an earthquake there, and to Africa and South America in the position of personal representative of the president.

During the campaign of 1972, she also grew more at ease in dealing with the press. She even began expressing political opinions, including her hope that her husband would appoint a woman to the Supreme Court. Her interaction with the press stopped shortly after her husband began his second term in 1973. Coverage of the Watergate scandal included much rumor and speculation while the facts were gradually discovered.

## Last years

After the Watergate scandal eventually led to her husband's resignation in 1974, the Nixons returned to California. Pat supported her husband through the ordeal and helped nurse him when he suffered from a life-threatening blood disorder. She enjoyed spending quiet time reading, gardening, and listening to music. In 1976, she suffered a stroke that left her partially paralyzed.

The Nixons moved to New York in 1980 and later to New Jersey to be nearer to their children and their families. Pat Nixon died of lung cancer in June 1993. Her husband died the following year. Both are buried on the grounds of the Richard Nixon Library and Birthplace in Yorba Linda, California.

## Where to Learn More

David, Lester. *The Lonely Lady of San Clemente: The Story of Pat Nixon.* New York: Crowell, 1978.

Eisenhower, Julie Nixon. *Pat Nixon: The Untold Story.* New York: Simon and Schuster, 1986.

Feinberg, Barbara Silberdick. *Patricia Ryan Nixon, 1912–1993.* Chicago: Children's Press, 1998.

# Nixon's "Silent Majority" Speech

**Delivered on November 3, 1969; excerpted from**
***CNN Interactive: Cold War* (Web site)**

*President Nixon describes his plans for ending the Vietnam War
and praises the "silent majority" who are not protesting in the
streets against their government*

During the first year of office for President **Richard Nixon** (1913–1994; see entry in volume 5), the prospects for ending America's involvement in the Vietnam War (1954–75) had not improved. The U.S. military had been engaged in combat in the Vietnam War since 1965; over five hundred thousand troops were stationed there when Nixon took office in January 1969. Protest demonstrations against the war in American cities and on college campuses had become commonplace and were growing larger each month.

In early November 1969, President Nixon addressed the nation on the war in Vietnam. He wanted to ensure that Americans understood the situation there, the progress of peace talks, and the prospects for the withdrawal of American troops; he also wanted to address the growing unrest at home as reflected in antiwar protests. Americans were intensely divided over the war: some wanted an immediate withdrawal of American troops; others believed that the United States could still prevail in Vietnam and viewed withdrawal as an act of surrender and defeat.

"We have faced other crises in our history and have become stronger by rejecting the easy way out and taking the right way in meeting our challenges. Our greatness as a nation has been our capacity to do what had to be done when we knew our course was right."

*Richard Nixon*

President Nixon's speech to the nation on November 3, 1969, roughly consisted of four parts: he reviewed the history of American involvement in Vietnam; he reviewed options for peace and the efforts of his administration to negotiate with North Vietnamese officials; he presented his plan of "Vietnamization"—where troops would be withdrawn gradually while American military personnel trained and prepared South Vietnamese soldiers to continue defending their land; and he concluded by addressing social unrest in the United States over the Vietnam War.

The speech became famous for President Nixon's use of the term "silent majority" to characterize those Americans who were not demonstrating in the streets against the war. In contrast, antiwar demonstrators were called "a vocal minority": "However fervent their cause," Nixon declared bluntly, if that minority "prevails over reason and the will of the majority, this Nation has no future as a free society."

## Things to remember while reading an excerpt from President Nixon's "Silent Majority" speech:

- The excerpt covers the final fourth of President Nixon's speech. In it, the president presented two options for peace—immediate withdrawal of American forces, or a more gradual withdrawal plan. Then, he announced the path he had chosen and explained why he believed it was the right way. The excerpt includes the passage where he contrasted the "vocal minority" (antiwar demonstrators) with the "silent majority."

- Near the end of the speech, President Nixon referred to President **Woodrow Wilson** (1856–1924; see entry in volume 4), who was extremely active in negotiating the armistice and the treaty that ended World War I (1914–18). President Wilson's efforts to establish the League of Nations (see box in **Woodrow Wilson** entry in volume 4)—an international agency that would unite to stop future wars—left him exhausted: he suffered a stroke near the end of his presidency and never again regained his full health.

## *Excerpt from President Nixon's "Silent Majority" speech*

*My fellow Americans, I am sure you can recognize from what I have said that we really only have two choices open to us if we want to end this war.*

*I can order an immediate, **precipitate** withdrawal of all Americans from Vietnam without regard to the effects of that action.*

*Or we can persist in our search for a just peace through a negotiated settlement if possible, or through continued implementation of our plan for **Vietnamization** if necessary—a plan in which we will withdraw all of our forces from Vietnam on a schedule in accordance with our program, as the South Vietnamese become strong enough to defend their own freedom.*

*I have chosen this second course.*

*It is not the easy way.*

*It is the right way.*

*It is a plan which will end the war and serve the cause of peace—not just in Vietnam but in the Pacific and in the world.*

*In speaking of the consequences of a precipitate withdrawal, I mentioned that our **allies** would lose confidence in America.*

*Far more dangerous, we would lose confidence in ourselves. Oh, the immediate reaction would be a sense of relief that our men were coming home. But as we saw the consequences of what we had done, inevitable remorse and divisive **recrimination** would scar our spirit as a people.*

*We have faced other crises in our history and have become stronger by rejecting the easy way out and taking the right way in meeting our challenges. Our greatness as a nation has been our capacity to do what had to be done when we knew our course was right.*

*I recognize that some of my fellow citizens disagree with the plan for peace I have chosen. Honest and patriotic Americans have reached different conclusions as to how peace should be achieved.*

*In San Francisco a few weeks ago, I saw demonstrators carrying signs reading: "Lose in Vietnam, bring the boys home."*

**Precipitate:** Sudden and premature.

**Vietnamization:** A program where American military forces trained South Vietnamese to assume full responsibility for fighting in the Vietnam war.

**Allies:** Partners, specifically a group of nations who act in concert with each other.

**Recrimination:** An accusation that comes after responsibility for an action has been declared.

*Well, one of the strengths of our free society is that any American has a right to reach that conclusion and to advocate that point of view. But as President of the United States, I would be untrue to my oath of office if I allowed the policy of this Nation to be dictated by the minority who hold that point of view and who try to impose it on the Nation by mounting demonstrations in the street.*

*For almost 200 years, the policy of this Nation has been made under our Constitution by those leaders in the Congress and the White House elected by all of the people. If a vocal minority, however fervent its cause, prevails over reason and the will of the majority, this Nation has no future as a free society.*

*And now I would like to address a word, if I may, to the young people of this Nation who are particularly concerned, and I understand why they are concerned, about this war.*

*I respect your **idealism**.*

*I share your concern for peace.*

*I want peace as much as you do.*

*There are powerful personal reasons I want to end this war. This week I will have to sign 83 letters to mothers, fathers, wives, and loved ones of men who have given their lives for America in Vietnam. It is very little satisfaction to me that this is only one-third as many letters as I signed the first week in office. There is nothing I want more than to see the day come when I do not have to write any of those letters.*

*I want to end the war to save the lives of those brave young men in Vietnam.*

*But I want to end it in a way which will increase the chance that their younger brothers and their sons will not have to fight in some future Vietnam someplace in the world.*

*And I want to end the war for another reason. I want to end it so that the energy and dedication of you, our young people, now too often directed into bitter hatred against those responsible for the war, can be turned to the great challenges of peace, a better life for all Americans, a better life for all people on this earth.*

*I have chosen a plan for peace. I believe it will succeed.*

*If it does succeed, what the critics say now won't matter. If it does not succeed, anything I say then won't matter.*

**Idealism:** The belief that ultimate, positive goals can be reached.

I know it may not be fashionable to speak of patriotism or **national destiny** these days. But I feel it is appropriate to do so on this occasion.

Two hundred years ago this Nation was weak and poor. But even then, America was the hope of millions in the world. Today we have become the strongest and richest nation in the world. And the wheel of destiny has turned so that any hope the world has for the survival of peace and freedom will be determined by whether the American people have the moral **stamina** and the courage to meet the challenge of free world leadership.

Let historians not record that when America was the most powerful nation in the world we passed on the other side of the road and allowed the last hopes for peace and freedom of millions of people to be suffocated by the forces of **totalitarianism.**

And so tonight—to you, the great silent majority of my fellow Americans—I ask for your support.

I pledged in my campaign for the Presidency to end the war in a way that we could win the peace. I have initiated a plan of action which will enable me to keep that pledge.

The more support I can have from the American people, the sooner that pledge can be redeemed; for the more divided we are at home, the less likely the enemy is to negotiate at Paris.

Let us be united for peace. Let us also be united against defeat. Because let us understand: North Vietnam cannot defeat or humiliate the United States. Only Americans can do that.

Fifty years ago, in this room and at this very desk, President Woodrow Wilson spoke words which caught the imagination of a war-weary world. He said: "This is the war to end war." His dream for peace after World War I was shattered on the hard realities of great power politics and Woodrow Wilson died a broken man.

Tonight I do not tell you that the war in Vietnam is the war to end wars. But I do say this: I have initiated a plan which will end this war in a way that will bring us closer to that great goal to which Woodrow Wilson and every American President in our history has been dedicated—the goal of a just and lasting peace.

As President I hold the responsibility for choosing the best path to that goal and then leading the Nation along it.

I pledge to you tonight that I shall meet this responsibility with all of the strength and wisdom I can command in accordance with your hopes, mindful of your concerns, sustained by your prayers.

**National destiny:** The ultimate fortune of a nation.

**Stamina:** The energy to endure.

**Totalitarianism:** A system of government where officials maintain complete control over the populace.

*Thank you and goodnight.* (CNN Interactive: Cold War [Web site])

## What happened next . . .

About ninety thousand American troops were withdrawn from Vietnam in 1969. The policy of Vietnamization—training and equipping South Vietnamese soldiers to fight—was instituted. In an earlier part of Nixon's speech, he vowed that the American withdrawal would stop and fighting would intensify if the North Vietnamese tried to take quick advantage of the declining American military presence.

To assist the Vietnamization effort, American forces attempted to wipe out North Vietnamese supply lines and military strongholds in South Vietnam. In 1970, that pursuit led to American air and ground forces entering neighboring Cambodia; in 1971, American bombers began hitting targets in Laos, a country adjacent to North Vietnam; after a North Vietnamese offensive in the South in March 1972, American planes began bombing North Vietnam for the first time in over five years; and late in 1972, the U.S. military hit North Vietnam with the largest-ever aerial bombing in history to that time.

A cease-fire and treaty was agreed to between the United States and North Vietnam in January 1973. All remaining American troops were withdrawn in March of that year. Hostilities between North and South Vietnam began again in 1974, however, and in 1975 South Vietnam fell under communist control.

Meanwhile, antiwar demonstrations intensified from 1970 through 1972. In 1970, at Kent State University in Kent, Ohio, four demonstrators were shot and killed by national guardsmen. More demonstrations followed the 1971 publication of the "Pentagon Papers"—secret American military documents that were leaked to and published by the *New York Times*—revealing that the U.S. military had long been aware that the situation in Vietnam was much bleaker than the

American people had been informed. News of U.S. bombing missions also intensified the antiwar protests.

The scars of the Vietnam War remain deep. Whenever the possibility arises that U.S. military forces might engage in combat, there is an inevitable exclamation, "let's make sure we don't get involved in another Vietnam." Vietnam veterans did not return home to parades or celebrations. Only by the mid-1990s, with the opening of the Vietnam Veterans War Memorial in Washington, D.C., did the nation begin to come to terms with a war that caused great losses and deep dissension.

## Did you know . . .

- In addition to antiwar protests, demonstrators gathered for marches to bring public attention to several other issues. Most notable among them were women who marched to bring attention to the lack of equality in laws regarding men and women. The Feminist Movement would become a political force during the 1970s.

## Where to Learn More

Ambrose, Stephen E. *Nixon.* New York: Simon and Schuster, 1987.

Bochin, Hal. *Richard Nixon: Rhetorical Strategist.* New York: Greenwood Press, 1990.

*CNN Interactive: Cold War.* [Online] http://www.cnn.com/SPECIALS/cold.war/episodes/11/documents/nixon.speech/ (accessed on October 10, 2000).

Genovese, Michael A. *The Nixon Presidency: Power and Politics in Turbulent Times.* New York: Greenwood Press, 1990.

# Gerald R. Ford

**Thirty-eighth president (1974–1977)**

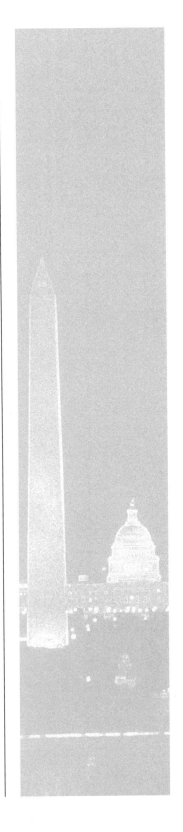

# Gerald R. Ford

**Born July 14, 1913**
**Omaha, Nebraska**

**Thirty-eighth president of the**
**United States (1974–1977)**

**Worked to restore Americans' faith in**
**government, but pardoning Richard Nixon**
**became his undoing**

G erald R. Ford was the first vice president to assume the office of chief executive following the resignation of a president. Ford had served President **Richard Nixon** (1931–1994; see entry in volume 5) as vice president for a mere eight months. A quiet veteran of the national political scene and a former House minority leader (spokesperson for his party in the House of Representatives), Ford was not marked by the scandal that forced Nixon from office.

Sworn in as president in a swift White House ceremony on August 9, 1974, Ford quickly proved himself able. Though he suffered much criticism for granting a full presidential pardon (a release from punishment) to Nixon just a month after taking office, Ford restored honesty and dignity to the nation's highest office after the scandal-ridden Nixon administration.

## Adopted son

Gerald Ford was born on July 14, 1913, in Omaha, Nebraska, and named Leslie Lynch King Jr. His father proved

"My fellow Americans, our long national nightmare is over."

*Gerald R. Ford, upon becoming president*

**Gerald R. Ford.**
*Courtesy of the Library of Congress.*

University of Michigan center Gerald Ford lines up for the Wolverines in the 1930s.
*Reproduced by permission of the Corbis Corporation.*

to be a jealous, difficult husband for Ford's mother, Dorothy Gardner King (1892–1967). By 1915, she had divorced him and returned with her child to her family in Grand Rapids, Michigan. In 1916, she married Gerald R. Ford, the owner of a local paint-and-varnish business. Her boy's name was legally changed to Gerald Rudolph Ford Jr. Ford assumed that his stepfather was his biological parent until he was informed otherwise at age seventeen.

With his three younger brothers, Ford worked in the family business. A standout athlete at Grand Rapids South High School, he won a $100-per-year scholarship—a year's tuition—to the University of Michigan. Ford worked in a hospital to meet his living expenses during college. He played center on the University of Michigan's football team. Ford was offered contracts to play in the National Football League after he graduated in 1935. Instead, he accepted a coaching position at Yale University, hoping to continue his education there. At first, administrators at the Ivy League school allowed him to enroll in their well-known law school only on a part-time basis. Nevertheless, Ford graduated in the top third of his class in 1941. He returned to Grand Rapids and began a private law practice with a college friend.

## Long tenure in Congress

When World War II (1939–45) erupted, Ford enlisted in the U.S. Navy. He served on an aircraft carrier in the Pacific theater (area of military operation). Upon returning home, he joined an eminent Grand Rapids law firm. With the support of his stepfather, who was the county Republican chairman, Ford decided to make a bid for a seat in the U.S. House of Representatives. Ford won the Republican nomination over prominent, archconservative (extremely conservative) Republican Bartel J. Jonkman (1884– 1955), who had represented the Grand Rapids area for nine years.

Joining him on the campaign trail was Ford's new wife, the former Betty Bloomer Warren (1918– ; see **Betty Ford** entry in volume 5). They had dated for just a few months be-

## Fast Facts about Gerald R. Ford

**Full name:** Gerald Rudolph Ford; born Leslie Lynch King Jr.

**Born:** July 14, 1913

**Parents:** Leslie Lynch King and Dorothy Gardner King Ford; Gerald Rudolf Ford (stepfather)

**Spouse:** Elizabeth (Betty) Ann Bloomer Warren (1918– ; m. 1948)

**Children:** Michael Gerald (1950– ); John (Jack) Gardner (1952– ); Steven Meigs (1956– ); Susan Elizabeth (1957– )

**Religion:** Episcopalian

**Education:** University of Michigan (B.A., 1935); Yale University Law School (LL.B., 1941)

**Occupation:** Attorney

**Government positions:** U.S. representative from Michigan; vice president under Richard Nixon

**Political party:** Republican

**Dates as president:** August 9, 1974–January 20, 1977

**Age upon taking office:** 61

## Gerald R. Ford Timeline

**1913:** Born in Nebraska

**1935:** Graduates from the University of Michigan

**1942–46:** Serves in U.S. Navy during World War II

**1948–73:** Serves as U.S. representative from Michigan

**1965–73:** Serves as U.S. House minority leader

**1973:** Appointed vice president by Richard Nixon

**1974–77:** Serves as thirty-eighth U.S. president following resignation of Richard Nixon

**1976:** Loses presidential election to Jimmy Carter

fore Ford proposed, and their wedding was delayed for several months during Ford's campaign for a seat in Congress. He and Betty married on October 18, 1948. They attended a University of Michigan football game the next day as part of their honeymoon trip, which also involved several campaign stops. Ford won the 1948 election by a large margin. He and Betty would have four children, three boys and a girl.

Ford went on to spend the next twenty-four years in the House of Representatives. In Washington, D.C., he quickly learned the art of deal-making on the political scene and won the respect of his colleagues as an honest politician. He joined a number of young House Republicans who called themselves the "Chowder and Marching Society." In that dinner discussion group, Ford first came to know Richard M. Nixon, then a congressman from California.

Ford served on a number of influential committees during his years in the House. For example, he was appointed by President **Lyndon B. Johnson** (1908–1973; see entry in volume 5) to the Warren Commission, the official government inquiry into the 1963 assassination of President **John F. Kennedy** (1917–1963; see entry in volume 5). Two years later, Ford was elected House minority leader by his colleagues. He was one of the nation's most respected and experienced politicians when a political scandal of destructive proportions arose involving the Nixon administration. Richard Nixon had been elected president in 1968.

There were indications that Nixon had wanted Ford as his running mate in 1968. Ford turned down the offer, hoping instead that Republicans would gain a majority of seats in the House. That situation, which did not occur, would have made Ford the Speaker of the House, the person

## Words to Know

**Clemency:** An act of leniency, to show mercy or to lessen punishment.

**House minority leader:** A representative elected by his party colleagues to serve as the leader and spokesperson for the party currently in the minority in the House of Representatives.

**Impeachment:** A legislative proceeding charging a public official with misconduct. Impeachment consists of the formal accusation of such an official and the trial that follows. It does not refer to removal from office of the accused.

**Indictment:** An official charge of having committed a crime.

**Inflation:** A period of time when money loses some of its value, usually because goods become more expensive.

**Midterm elections:** Congressional elections that occur halfway through a president's four-year term are called midterm elections. Representatives are elected every two years and senators every six years.

**Pardon:** A power that allows the president to free an individual or a group from prosecution for a crime.

**Partisan:** Placing the concerns of one's group or political party above all other considerations.

**Speaker of the House:** The person in charge of supervising activity in the House of Representatives. The Speaker is elected by colleagues of the party with a majority in Congress.

**Whip Inflation Now (WIN) program:** An anti-inflation program introduced by President Gerald R. Ford that included a reduction in federal spending and a national volunteer organization that was given the task of finding ways to keep prices down.

overseeing the activities of the House of Representatives. Ford coveted the Speaker position.

## Watergate

In June 1972, several burglars were arrested after they broke into Democratic Party headquarters inside the Watergate apartment and office complex in Washington, D.C. A sustained investigation by news agencies, particularly the *Washington Post,* exposed evidence of a widespread conspiracy that included political espionage (spying) and abuse of power by the Nixon administration. (A conspiracy is an agreement between two or more people to commit a crime.)

As the scandal unfolded, numerous illegal operations were revealed. These illegal actions, intended to harm the reputations of Nixon's political and personal enemies, had been carried out by a group of men surrounding Nixon and had been paid for with campaign funds. The Watergate burglars were associated with the Committee to Re-Elect the President (a group that would come to be called CREEP).

A high-profile congressional investigation was launched, with hearings broadcast daily over national television. The hearings revealed that Nixon had issued certain directives to the Federal Bureau of Investigation (FBI) to cover up the matter. Soon, Nixon's attorney general and members of his staff were facing indictments (formal charges of a crime). (For more on the Watergate scandal, see **Richard Nixon** entry in volume 5).

Meanwhile, in a scandal not related to Watergate, Nixon's vice president, Spiro T. Agnew (1918–1996), was charged with income tax evasion (purposely not paying taxes owed to the government); the scandal forced him to resign from his office on October 10, 1973. Nixon, under the terms of the Twenty-fifth Amendment to the Constitution, was allowed to appoint a successor, depending on congressional confirmation. Ford emerged as his colleagues' leading choice for the job.

Sooner or later, Ford was going to be vice president. "Sooner" might have been in 1968, but he turned down Richard Nixon's offer. Ford was hoping that the Republicans would gain a majority in Congress that year and that he would be elected Speaker of the House—the position Ford really wanted. It did not work out. "Later" might have been in 1980, when Ronald Reagan approached Ford about running as his vice president. Their discussions ended when the press passed word about their talks, and Reagan's offer was never officially made.

Ford was sworn in as vice president on December 6, 1973. At first, he defended the president as more revelations of illegal activities surfaced in the Watergate scandal, but then he began to voice distrust about the men Nixon had appointed and upon whom the president had relied. Ford told an audience in early 1974: "Never again must America allow an arrogant, elite guard of political adolescents like the Committee to Re-Elect the President to bypass the regular party system and dictate the terms of a national election."

Later that summer, a House Judiciary Committee adopted three articles of impeachment (the means by which an official is charged with a crime and possibly removed from office) against Nixon. The House of Representatives was likely to approve the articles of impeachment, which would then be followed by the president facing trial in the Senate. Shock, dismay, and disillusionment with the entire political system was felt across the country. "You're all we've got now, and I mean the country, not the party," one leading Democratic senator told Ford.

*As a teenager, Ford earned money by working in the family paint business, at a concessions stand at an amusement park, and in a restaurant washing dishes and grilling hamburgers.*

## "Our long national nightmare is over"

For a time, it seemed that Nixon might endure a House impeachment vote. But three audiotapes released on August 5, 1974, showed clearly that Nixon had helped direct the cover-up. On August 8, 1974—more than two years after the Watergate break-in—the president informed his second-in-command that he would resign the next day. Nixon said, "Jerry, I know you'll do a good job." Ford took the oath of office the next day in the East Room of the White House and delivered a hurriedly written speech before the assembled crowd and a national television audience. "My fellow Americans," he said, "our long national nightmare is over." The new president concluded by asking the nation to pray for Nixon and his family.

Ford immediately proved himself an upright and relaxed chief executive who did much to restore America's faith in the office. He was vigorous and healthy, had an energetic wife, Betty, and four college-aged children. Ford also had a sense of humor. Among his amusing quirks: Ford stepped outside to fetch his newspaper from the doorstep every morning, and he asked that the Marine band play the University of Michigan fight song ("Hail to the Victors") instead of the traditional presidential tune "Hail to the Chief."

Meanwhile, Nixon still faced charges by a grand jury. Just a month after taking office, Ford surprised the country by

**Ford Becomes President**

On August 9, 1974, Richard Nixon's letter of resignation as thirty-seventh president of the United States was tendered to Secretary of State Henry A. Kissinger by White House chief of staff Alexander M. Haig Jr. (1924– ), at 11:35 A.M. Gerald R. Ford took the oath of office at noon from Supreme Court chief justice Warren E. Burger in the East Room at the White House.

Ford's ascension to the presidency marked the ninth time in U.S. history that a vice president became president after his predecessor was no longer able to serve. The first eight instances were due to the president's death; Ford's rise to the office was the first following a presidential resignation. Ford had become vice president following the 1973 resignation of Spiro T. Agnew. (See Nixon entry for election results from the Nixon/Agnew campaigns.) This marked the first time in U.S. history that a vice president was appointed to the office. Shortly thereafter, Ford chose Nelson A. Rockefeller to be his vice president, the second such appointment. In 1976, Ford attempted to be elected as president on his own, but lost to Democrat Jimmy Carter.

After Ford took the oath of office on that historic August afternoon, the new president's comments were broadcast live on radio and television. Excerpts from his remarks follow:

> Mr. Chief Justice, my dear friends, my fellow Americans:

> The oath that I have taken is the same oath that was taken by George Washington and by every President under the Constitution. But I assume the Presidency under extraordinary circumstances never before experienced by Americans. This is an hour of history that troubles our minds and hurts our hearts.

> Therefore, I feel it is my first duty to make an unprecedented compact with my countrymen. Not an inaugural address, not a fireside chat, not a campaign speech—just a little straight talk among friends. And I intend it to be the first of many.

> I am acutely aware that you have not elected me as your President by your ballots, and so I ask you to confirm me as your President with your prayers. And I hope that such prayers will also be the first of many.

> If you have not chosen me by secret ballot, neither have I gained office by any secret promises. I have not campaigned either for the Presidency or the Vice Presi-

issuing "Proclamation 4311, Granting a Pardon to Richard Nixon." (See **Gerald R. Ford** primary source entry in volume 5.) As Ford observed in a statement to the nation on September 8, 1974, at least a year would pass before a Nixon trial would begin. "Someone must write the end," he said, to "an American tragedy." He added: "In the meantime, the tranquillity to which this nation has been restored by the events

dency. I have not subscribed to any partisan platform. I am indebted to no man, and only to one woman—my dear wife—as I begin this very difficult job.

I have not sought this enormous responsibility, but I will not shirk it. Those who nominated and confirmed me as Vice President were my friends and are my friends. They were of both parties, elected by all the people and acting under the Constitution in their name. It is only fitting then that I should pledge to them and to you that I will be the President of all the people.

Thomas Jefferson said the people are the only sure reliance for the preservation of our liberty. And down the years, Abraham Lincoln renewed this American article of faith asking, "Is there any better way or equal hope in the world. . .?"

To the peoples and the governments of all friendly nations, and I hope that could encompass the whole world, I pledge an uninterrupted and sincere search for peace. America will remain strong and united, but its strength will remain dedicated to the safety and sanity of the entire family of man, as well as to our own precious freedom.

I believe that truth is the glue that holds government together, not only our Government but civilization itself. That bond, though strained, is unbroken at home and abroad.

In all my public and private acts as your President, I expect to follow my instincts of openness and candor with full confidence that honesty is always the best policy in the end.

My fellow Americans, our long national nightmare is over.

Our Constitution works; our great Republic is a government of laws and not of men. Here the people rule. But there is a higher Power, by whatever name we honor Him, who ordains not only righteousness but love, not only justice but mercy.

As we bind up the internal wounds of Watergate, more painful and more poisonous than those of foreign wars, let us restore the golden rule to our political process, and let brotherly love purge our hearts of suspicion and of hate. . . .

I now solemnly reaffirm my promise I made to you last December 6: to uphold the Constitution, to do what is right as God gives me to see the right, and to do the very best I can for America.

God helping me, I will not let you down.

Thank you.

Source: "Gerald R. Ford's Remarks on Taking the Oath of Office as President." Gerald R. Ford Library and Museum (Web site). [Online] http://www.lbjlib. utexas.edu/ford/library/speeches/740001.htm (accessed on October 13, 2000).

of recent weeks could be irreparably lost by the prospects of bringing to trial a former President of the United States. The prospects of such trial will cause prolonged and divisive debate over the propriety of exposing to further punishment and degradation a man who has already paid the unprecedented penalty of relinquishing the highest elective office of the United States."

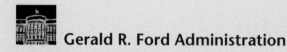

# Gerald R. Ford Administration

**Administration Dates**
August 9, 1974–January 20, 1977

**Vice President**
None (1974)
Nelson A. Rockefeller (1974–77)

**Cabinet**

**Secretary of State**
Henry A. Kissinger (1974–77)

**Secretary of the Treasury**
William E. Simon (1974–77)

**Attorney General**
William B. Saxbe (1974–75)
Edward H. Levi (1975–77)

**Secretary of the Interior**
Rogers C. B. Morton (1974–75)
Stanley K. Hathaway (1975)
Thomas S. Kleppe (1975–77)

**Secretary of Agriculture**
Earl L. Butz (1974–76)
John A. Knebel (1976–77)

**Secretary of Labor**
Peter J. Brennan (1974–75)
John T. Dunlop (1975–76)
William J. Usery Jr. (1976–77)

**Secretary of Commerce**
Frederick B. Dent (1974–75)
Rogers C. B. Morton (1975)
Elliot L. Richardson (1976–77)

**Secretary of Defense**
James R. Schlesinger (1974–75)
Donald H. Rumsfeld (1975–77)

**Secretary of Health, Education and Welfare**
Caspar W. Weinberger (1974–75)
F. David Mathews (1975–77)

**Secretary of Housing and Urban Development**
James T. Lynn (1974–75)
Carla A. Hills (1975–77)

**Secretary of Transportation**
Claude S. Brinegar (1974–75)
William T. Coleman Jr. (1975–77)

## Backlash

Ford's approval rating immediately nosedived. Public opinion and media pundits (experts called upon for their opinions) charged that a Republican "deal" had been made to allow Ford to step up to the presidency in return for an assurance to later absolve Nixon of any wrongdoing (that is, to free him from the consequences of guilt).

Ford had always been an honorable politician. He never risked his integrity—his honesty and his standards of behavior—for political gain. Nevertheless, after the par-

**President Gerald Ford speaks on the telephone in the Oval Office.**
*Reproduced by permission of Archive Photos.*

don, Ford suffered from negative press and took the force of the backlash (hostile reaction) to Watergate. Americans thought that perhaps the office of the president held too much power. Two pieces of significant legislation had already been passed by Congress just before Ford assumed office: The 1973 War Powers Act forced a president to obtain congressional approval before sending troops into battle; and a 1974 reform bill created the congressional Budget Office that limited presidential control over federal spending.

With the midterm elections of 1974, a new group of relatively young Democratic legislators entered Congress; they came to be known as the Watergate babies. Congressional elections occurring halfway through a presidential term can affect the president's dealings with Congress; indeed, after the midterm elections of 1974, new battle lines were drawn between the president and Congress. Those partisan lines were followed through the end of the century: The op-

## Nelson Rockefeller

Nelson Aldrich Rockefeller was born in Bar Harbor, Maine, on July 8, 1908, the third of six children of John B. Rockefeller Jr., and Abby Greene Aldrich. His grandfathers were John D. Rockefeller Sr. (1839–1937), founder of the Standard Oil Company, and U.S. senator Nelson Aldrich (1841–1915) of Rhode Island. Rockefeller attended Dartmouth University, where he majored in economics, taught a Sunday school class, and occasionally worked in the school cafeteria to earn spending money. In 1930, he married Mary Todhunter Clark, a Philadelphia socialite. They had five children.

At age thirty, he was president of the New York Rockefeller Center, a famous grouping of office buildings in central Manhattan. Several trips to Latin America in the late 1930s convinced him of the region's importance to national security. In 1940, Rockefeller accepted his first major governmental position as the head of the Office of Inter-American Affairs. For his effectiveness, he received the government of Chile's Order of Merit in 1945; Brazil made him a member of the National Order of the Southern Cross in 1946; and in 1949, Mexico enrolled him in the Order of the Aztec Eagle.

In 1950, Rockefeller was appointed by President **Harry S. Truman** (1884–1972; see entry in volume 4) as chairman of the International Development Advisory Board. The agency encouraged economic growth in depressed areas in underdeveloped nations. In 1952, President **Dwight D. Eisenhower** (1890–1969; see entry in volume 4) appointed him chairman of the Advisory Committee on Government Organization. Rockefeller organized a new agency, the Department of Health, Education, and Welfare, and then became its first undersecretary, serving until 1954. Then, as a special assistant to President Eisenhower, Rockefeller helped develop the Atoms-for-Peace Plan that publicized and organized safe uses for nuclear power around the world.

Rockefeller was elected governor of New York in 1958. In 1961, he divorced his wife, and in 1963 he married Margaretta Fitler "Happy" Murphy, who was nineteen years younger. Five weeks before marrying

posing party would frequently stall the agenda of the sitting president. Ford was even called before Congress to testify and defend himself over the Nixon pardon.

## Distancing himself from Nixon

Not long after taking office, Ford announced his Vietnam Era Reconciliation Program. This controversial clemency

**Nelson A. Rockefeller.**
*Courtesy of the Library of Congress.*

Rockefeller, "Happy" Murphy had divorced her husband and had given him custody of their children. The remarriage caused so much public disapproval with Rockefeller that he lost the frontrunner status among the 1964 Republican presidential hopefuls.

Rockefeller won four gubernatorial elections in New York, but he lost three attempts for the presidency. On December 11, 1973, more than a year before his fourth term expired, Rockefeller resigned as governor in order to head the National Committee on Critical Choices for Americans and the Commission on Water Quality. He denied that he had resigned in order to plan a fourth presidential attempt. On August 20, 1974, President Gerald Ford nominated Rockefeller to fill the office of vice president that was left vacant after Ford became president. On December 19, Rockefeller was sworn in as vice president.

After his two years as vice president, Rockefeller returned to his interest in art. (In 1930, he became a trustee of the Metropolitan Museum of Art; in 1939, he served as president of the Museum of Modern Art; he founded the Museum of Primitive Art in 1957; and he assembled extensive collections of modern paintings, sculpture, and all types of primitive art). In 1978, he compiled *Masterpieces of Primitive Art,* a book about his art collection. He was contracted to do four more titles, but he died on January 27, 1979.

plan for draft-dodgers—those who had avoided registering for possible military service upon turning eighteen years old—was influenced in part by his draft-aged sons. Intended to help heal the division of national opinion brought on by the Vietnam War (1954–75), the move also distanced Ford from the harsher policies of the Nixon era. However, only about twenty percent of those eligible applied for clemency. Many young men had refused to register for the draft during the unpopular Vietnam War, to which American soldiers were being sent beginning in 1965.

Ford selected former New York governor Nelson Rockefeller (1908–1979; see box) as his vice president and kept Nixon's Cabinet (presidential advisors). During his 865-day term, Ford eventually replaced many officials appointed in the Nixon era. In November 1975, he fired Secretary of Defense James Schlesinger (1929– ) and Central Intelligence Agency (CIA) chief William Colby (1920–1996). Schlesinger was replaced by Donald H. Rumsfeld (1932– ), the youngest defense secretary in history; Colby was replaced by future president **George Bush** (1924– ; see entry in volume 5). The shake-up came to be known as the Sunday Morning Massacre.

Ford was not particularly comfortable as a public speaker, but he communicated sincerity despite a hesitant delivery. Lyndon B. Johnson, president from 1963 to 1969, had once joked that perhaps Ford had played football too long without a helmet. The press picked up on the comment and began writing about his mishaps. Ford was depicted in political cartoons as unlucky, sometimes with a bandage on his forehead. One network newscast replayed footage of him stumbling down airplane steps—eleven times in a single broadcast. Ford was angered by the negative press, but he reacted graciously. Unlike Nixon, he granted the White House correspondents a great deal of access, held monthly press conferences, and gave many one-on-one interviews.

Ford was one of the most athletic, physically fit presidents. The former college football star enjoyed swimming and skiing; he spent much of his vacation time at a residence in Vail, Colorado, that came to be known as the Winter White House. He narrowly avoided two assassination attempts in California in the fall of 1975—one by Lynette "Squeaky" Fromme in Sacramento, the other by Sara Jane Moore in San Francisco.

## Domestic woes

The Ford years were plagued by economic troubles. Inflation (a period of time when money loses some of its value, usually because goods become more expensive) rapidly increased in the second half of 1974. Combined with a jump in unemployment and a slowdown in other economic indicators (such as new-housing construction and overall industrial output), the nation's economy grew steadily worse. Ford called inflation "domestic enemy number one" in his first presidential speech before Congress.

Two months later, he announced an anti-inflation program. The new program included a reduction in federal spending and a national volunteer organization that was given the task of finding ways to keep prices down. The entire program was called "Whip Inflation Now," or WIN, and Ford wore a WIN button when he detailed the program to a joint session of Congress. The program was viewed by media pundits as an ineffective public-relations stunt, and Ford was again ridiculed in the press. To his credit, however, Ford held his ground with Congress to restrain government spending. He vetoed (rejected) over three dozen appropriations bills (legislation authorizing funds for a certain project).

In foreign affairs, Ford presided over the official end of the Vietnam war and the Vietnam era. Some of his decisions angered Henry Kissinger (1923– ; see box in **Richard Nixon** entry in volume 5), who had guided American foreign policy since 1969. American ground troops had officially withdrawn from Vietnam after a 1973 cease-fire, but as a result both South Vietnam and Cambodia fell to communists by 1975. When North Vietnamese communist forces closed in on Saigon, the capital of South Vietnam, Ford gave the order to begin evacuation (removal) of all American personnel. A massive effort, involving helicopters taking off day and night from the roof of the American embassy, helped fourteen hundred Americans and fifty-six hundred Vietnamese flee enemy forces.

Ford also approved several million dollars in aid for a war in Angola, a former Portuguese colony in Africa where Cuban communist guerrillas (persons who fight in an irregular military force, often with the support of the local population) were fighting with local and South African forces. The guerrillas were seeking to establish a Marxist government (an economic system in which a central government oversees the production and distribution of goods). China and the Soviet Union were also providing generous help to opposing factions in what turned out to be an unmanageable civil war.

President Gerald R. Ford (left) and Soviet Communist Party chief Leonid Brezhnev (right) meet for the first time on November 23, 1974, in the Soviet city of Vladivostok.
*Reproduced by permission of the Corbis Corporation.*

The Ford era included an overhaul of foreign intelligence (information about other countries) operations within the CIA. Some agents had been contacted by Nixon administration officials to help cover up Watergate; an internal investigation led by Vice President Rockefeller revealed other abuses of power, including illegal activities against foreign government officials. The CIA had been created in 1947 with a charter that gave it authority to conduct foreign espionage. Involvement with Watergate and subsequent inquiries disclosed that the CIA had conducted domestic (within the United States) spying activities against American anti-Vietnam War protesters. Furthermore, the agency had been involved in unsuccessful assassination attempts of foreign leaders during prior administrations, most famously upon Cuba's Fidel Castro (1926– ). Ford eventually fired CIA chief William Colby.

In early 1976, Ford issued the first executive order concerning intelligence services. The decree stated that the agency's goals should originate inside the president's National Security Council. The order also established several boards and committees designed to keep an eye on the CIA, restricted some forms of surveillance, and, for the record, stated that involvement in political assassination attempts on foreign leaders was prohibited.

Elsewhere in his foreign-policy strategy, Ford approved aid to both Israel and Egypt. The somewhat controversial measure helped convince leaders of the warring nations to agree to interim peace proposals that eventually led to the historic 1978 Camp David Agreement (see box in **Jimmy Carter** entry in volume 5). The Ford administration negotiated an arms-reduction agreement with the Soviet Union. President Ford authorized a dramatic and successful military response to the seizing of an American merchant ship, the *Mayaguez*, by Khmer Rouge forces (of Cambodia) in the Gulf of Siam in May 1975.

## Bid for a full term

The 1976 presidential campaign was well underway when the nation celebrated the two hundredth anniversary of the signing of the Declaration of Independence. A massive outpouring of national sentiment known as the Bicentennial Celebration peaked on July 4. Americans hoped it signaled an end to a recent era marred by a disastrous war, economic and energy woes, an unprecedented presidential scandal, and political assassinations.

Ford was opposed within the Republican Party by former California governor and conservative Republican **Ronald Reagan** (1911–  ; see entry in volume 5). Reagan found support with his criticism of Ford's moderate Republican politics and positioned himself as the genuine inheritor to Republican conservatism as well as an outsider who would clean up Washington.

Reagan nearly took the Republican nomination from Ford at the national convention in August 1976, in part because of a split in the Republican Party over Nelson Rockefeller. Ford was urged to drop his vice president from the ticket. When he did—in favor of Kansas senator Bob Dole (1923– ), who would later be his party's presidential nominee in 1996— it was widely viewed as a disloyal gesture. Meanwhile, the De-

**A Selection of Ford Landmarks**

**Gerald R. Ford Library.** 1000 Beal Ave., Ann Arbor, MI 48109. (734) 741-2218. The Ford Library and Museum make up one institution, despite being located in two different cities. The library contains materials from the Cold War era and from the political career of Gerald Ford. It is one of ten official presidential libraries in the country. See http://www.lbjlib.utexas.edu/ford/homepage.htm (accessed on October 13, 2000).

**Gerald R. Ford Museum.** 303 Pearl St., NW, Grand Rapids, MI 49504-5353. (616) 451-9263. The Ford Library and Museum make up one institution, despite being located in two different cities. Artifacts surrounding President Ford's childhood, congressional career, and vice presidential and presidential years are featured, along with many interactive exhibits. See http://www.lbjlib.utexas.edu/ford/homepage.htm (accessed on October 13, 2000).

**President Gerald R. Ford Birthsite and Gardens.** 3202 Woolworth Ave., Omaha, NE 68103. (402) 444-5962. A memorial park sits on the site of the birthplace of President Ford. The house he lived in as an infant was destroyed by a fire in 1971. A rose garden in honor of first lady Betty Ford and a kiosk containing Ford memorabilia are featured in the park. See http://www.nebraskahistory.org/conserve/brthsite.htm (accessed on October 13, 2000).

mocrats nominated plain-speaking Georgia governor **Jimmy Carter** (1924– ; see entry in volume 5), who campaigned with the promise, "I will never lie to you." Ford lost ground in a televised debate on foreign policy when he mistakenly downplayed the Soviet Union's dominance of Eastern Europe.

The 1976 election was notable for the lowest voter turnout since 1948. Ford lost to Carter by a narrow margin. After the election, Ford retired from politics. He was considered for vice president by Ronald Reagan in 1980, but Reagan eventually dropped the idea, which included a plan to broaden the role of the vice president. Ford has spent his post-presidential years in good health, making many speeches and taking pride in his presidential library established in Grand Rapids, Michigan. During the Republican National Convention of 2000, he suffered a mild stroke. Typically, he emerged from the challenge with good spirits and optimism.

# Legacy

In his inauguration speech in January 1977, Jimmy Carter opened with the words, "For myself and for our Nation, I want to thank my predecessor for all he has done to heal our land," and he reached over to shake Gerald Ford's hand. The thirty-eighth president has suffered from historical and political analysis that views him an interim (temporary) president with little leadership ability. Yet Ford acted decisively at several critical moments, such as the *Mayaguez* incident, and offered significant legislation that helped shape American politics in an era of change. His handling of the CIA, for instance, established far more congressional authority over the agency.

Ford's use of his deal-making abilities—a talent that had earned him respect in Washington years before he became even vice president—meant that he was willing to pardon Nixon and build agreements with foreign powers like the Soviet Union. He faced considerable opposition, however, from the Democratic-controlled Congress. He lost support among some Republicans as well for failing to apply stronger conservative values in policy areas. The more conservative members of his Republican Party became energized and gradually asserted a more aggressive form of Republican politics that Ronald Reagan came to represent. Reagan narrowly lost the Republican nomination for president to Ford in 1976, then won the nomination and the presidency in 1980 and 1984.

Ford led the country through a transitional period in which Congress gained more control over public policy and lawmaking than it had previously enjoyed. That change endured through the rest of the century, with the opposing party in Congress continually frustrating the sitting president. A certain national affection remained for the Midwestern ordinariness that Ford personified. Ford told biographer John Robert Greene, as recounted in *The Presidency of Gerald R. Ford,* "I want to be remembered as a . . . nice person, who worked at the job, and who left the White House in better shape than when I took over."

# Where to Learn More

Cannon, James. *Time and Chance: Gerald Ford's Appointment with History.* New York: HarperCollins, 1994. Reprint, Ann Arbor: University of Michigan Press, 1998.

Collins, David R. *Gerald R. Ford: 38th President of the United States.* Ada, OK: Garrett Educational, 1990.

Ford, Gerald R. *A Time to Heal: The Autobiography of Gerald R. Ford.* New York: Harper & Row, 1979.

*Gerald R. Ford Library and Museum.* [Online] http://www.lbjlib.utexas. edu/ford/homepage.htm (accessed on October 13, 2000).

Greene, John Robert. *The Limits of Power: The Nixon and Ford Administrations.* Bloomington: Indiana University Press, 1992.

Greene, John Robert. *The Presidency of Gerald R. Ford.* Lawrence: University Press of Kansas, 1995.

Persico, Joseph E. *The Imperial Rockefeller: A Biography of Nelson A. Rockefeller.* New York: Simon and Schuster, 1982.

Simon, William E. *A Time for Truth.* New York: Reader's Digest Press, 1978.

Sipiera, Paul P. *Gerald Ford: Thirty-eighth president of the United States.* Chicago: Childrens Press, 1989.

TerHorst, Jerald F. *Gerald Ford and the Future of the Presidency.* New York: Third Press, 1974.

Turner, Michael. *The Vice President as Policy Maker: Rockefeller in the Ford White House.* Westport, CT: Greenwood Press, 1982.

# Betty Ford

**Born April 8, 1918**
**Chicago, Illinois**

**One of the most candid of first ladies on political as well as personal issues**

**B**etty Ford became one of the most admired American women of her era. After many years in Washington, D.C., where her husband served as a congressman, she landed rather suddenly in the public eye in 1973. Her husband, **Gerald Ford** (1913– ; see entry in volume 5), was appointed vice president. The following year, the Fords moved to the White House when President **Richard Nixon** (1913–1994; see entry in volume 5) resigned from office.

The Fords worked to bring a refreshing air of normality to the White House. A former dancer and fashion model with a graceful bearing and forthright manner, Betty Ford was an immediately popular first lady known for her candidness and humor. Her battle with breast cancer and her later admission of a substance-abuse problem further endeared her to the public.

## Dancer

Born Elizabeth Ann Bloomer on April 8, 1918, in Chicago, Illinois, "Betty" moved to Grand Rapids, Michigan, as a very young child with her family. Her father, William

"Maybe if I as first lady could talk about [breast cancer] candidly and without embarrassment, many other people would be able to as well."

*Betty Ford*

**Betty Ford.**
*Courtesy of the Library of Congress.*

Bloomer, was a sales representative whose work took him away from home for long periods of time. As a young girl, Betty vowed never to marry a man whose job would make him an absent husband and father. Enrolled in a dance school by the age of eight, Betty subsequently studied many varieties of dance. By the time she was in her teens, she was teaching dance to younger students.

When she graduated from Grand Rapids Central High School in 1936, Betty planned to move to New York City to pursue a career in dance. Her recently widowed mother objected. A compromise was reached: Betty spent two summers at Bennington College, a progressive liberal arts school in Vermont that offered special sessions with Martha Graham (1894–1991), one of the most celebrated figures in modern dance. In 1939, Betty moved to New York City. She took classes and won a place in Graham's auxiliary concert troupe (group of performers); she also worked as a model and enjoyed the fast-paced life of the city.

By her own admission, Betty possessed neither the discipline nor the dedication to succeed in dance. After a time, she moved back to Grand Rapids and founded her own dance troupe. In 1942, she married William G. Warren, a man she had known for several years, but the marriage turned out to be an unwise decision. "My friends were getting married, and I thought I ought to get married too," she later wrote in *The Times of My Life* (1978). The two were divorced after five years of marriage.

## An engaging campaign

After her divorce, Betty was employed as the fashion coordinator at a department store in Grand Rapids. Through some mutual friends, she met Gerald Ford, a handsome Grand Rapids lawyer, World War II veteran, and former University of Michigan football star. The two dated for just a few months before Ford proposed.

Their wedding was delayed for several months while Ford campaigned for a seat in Congress. Betty knew little about politics and did not think her fiancé had a chance of winning, but she was energetic during his campaign. After he won the Republican nomination, the couple married on October 18, 1948. They attended a University of Michigan football game the next day as part of their honeymoon trip, which also involved several campaign stops.

Ford won the election, and several more after that—making him the often absent partner Betty Ford had once vowed to avoid. During his two and a half decades representing Michigan's Fifth Congressional District in the U.S. House of Representatives, Betty Ford raised four children— Michael, John, Steven, and Susan, born between 1950 and 1957—at their home in Alexandria, Virginia. She was also active in a number of organizations, from the Cub Scouts to the National Federation of Republican Women.

The demands of her active life eventually caught up with her; by the time her husband was elected House minority leader in 1965, she had begun to suffer from a number of physical problems. She also experienced a minor breakdown that led to visits with a psychotherapist. The therapy helped, but the pain medication her other doctors prescribed did not. For the next several years, Betty Ford became increasingly dependent on a variety of tranquilizers and sedatives (calming drugs); their effects were dangerously heightened by her social drinking habits.

## Delayed retirement

The Fords planned to retire to Michigan soon, where they could enjoy a calmer life. Instead, they were suddenly thrust into the national spotlight in the fall of 1973, when Ford was named vice president, following the resignation of Spiro T. Agnew (1918–1996).

Betty Ford found that she liked the responsibilities of her new role. Much more was required of her than during her rather uneventful years as a congressional wife and suburban mother. She rose to the challenge. Like her husband, she traveled extensively during his eight-month term, overcoming a fear of public speaking to address large crowds who were charmed by her warm, forthright style.

When President Nixon resigned and her husband was sworn in as president on August 9, 1974, Betty Ford held the Bible upon which his hand rested. Afterward, he said in a speech that "I am indebted to no man and only to one woman—my dear wife." Ford and his family were instant

**President Ford with Betty Ford after her surgery for breast cancer in 1974.**

*Reproduced by permission of the Corbis Corporation.*

celebrities, beloved by the news media. Their family seemed much like any other American one, with three college-age sons and a long-haired, blue-jean-wearing daughter in her final year of high school. As the new first lady, Ford was a tremendous hit. "She seems to have just what it takes to make people feel at home in the world again," media observer Marshall McLuhan (1911–1980) told the *New York Times Magazine* late in 1974. "Something about her makes us feel rooted and secure—a feeling we haven't had in a while."

## Early advocate for breast-cancer awareness

Several weeks after her husband took office, Betty Ford underwent a radical mastectomy, surgical removal of the breasts, after she was suddenly diagnosed with breast cancer. News of the surgery shocked the country. The disease in that part of the body was still somewhat of an unmentionable subject during this era. Thousands of letters of support poured in to the White House that wished the first lady well; many women recounted their own breast-cancer scares and thanked Betty Ford for speaking so openly about her condition. She compelled many women to visit their doctors for a check-up.

After a speedy recovery, Betty Ford was back at her White House desk and on the road with her husband. One of the most public presidential wives in American history, she gave an extraordinary number of interviews and was not shy about publicly stating her opinion on issues of the day. She affirmed her support for the Equal Rights Amendment (ERA), a proposal that would have prohibited discrimination on the basis of gender. During the Ford administration, the ERA was in the ratification process at the state level, but was eventually defeated (an amendment to the Constitution must be approved by at least three-fourths of the states). The first lady also called the 1973 Supreme Court decision to legalize abortion "the best thing in the world . . . a great, great decision."

Such attitudes were quite in tune with the changing times, but for a first lady to support them was a dramatic break with the past. When reporters asked about the president's reaction to his wife's well-publicized opinions, White House press secretary Ron Nessen dryly noted that "the President has long since ceased to be perturbed or surprised by his wife's remarks." The Fords enjoyed what appeared to be a spirited modern marriage. Photographers once caught Betty Ford pushing her husband, fully clothed, into a swimming pool. She told Jane Howard in a 1974 interview for the *New York Times Magazine,* "I don't feel that because I'm First Lady I'm any different from what I was before. It can happen to anyone. After all, it has happened to anyone."

Invitations to the Fords' Washington social events became highly desirable. Betty Ford was active in a number of causes, including the National Endowment for the Arts and organizations that helped disabled children. She conveyed a personal warmth, sincerity, and ordinariness that regularly landed her on "Most Admired Women" polls and other honors and tributes.

## A legacy of help

Betty Ford campaigned intensely on behalf of her husband when he made his bid for the presidency in 1976.

She was bitter about her husband's election loss, and after the couple officially retired to Palm Springs, California, her problems with drugs and alcohol worsened. After her family sat her down and confessed how worried they were about her behavior, Ford checked herself into the Long Beach Naval Hospital Alcohol and Drug Rehabilitation Service for a detoxification program. Such a program is designed to free a person from a dependence on addictive substances.

Again, Betty Ford's public admission of a problem once considered a secretive affliction resulted in massive amounts of support mail. Inspired by many heartbreaking stories and pleas for help, Betty Ford dedicated herself to a new, dual role as someone raising awareness about substance-abuse problems and improving the availability of treatment. In 1982, the Betty Ford Center, an inpatient clinic for drug and alcohol dependency associated with a Palm Springs hospital, was opened. Betty Ford remained its chairperson for many years and continued to be closely affiliated with it into the twenty-first century.

## Where to Learn More

Cassiday, Bruce. *Betty Ford: Woman of Courage.* New York: Dale Books, 1978.

Ford, Betty, with Chris Chase. *The Times of My Life.* New York: Harper & Row, 1978.

Ford, Betty, with Chris Chase. *Betty, A Glad Awakening.* Garden City, NY: Doubleday, 1987.

# Ford's Pardon of Richard Nixon

**Delivered September 8, 1974; excerpted from**
*The History Place: Great Speeches Collection* **(Web site)**

*President Ford expresses his reasons for pardoning
former president Nixon*

**P**resident **Gerald Ford** (1913– ; see entry in volume 5) was in office for slightly less than a month when he granted a pardon to former president **Richard Nixon** (1913–1994; see entry in volume 5). The pardon protected Nixon against prosecution for any crimes he committed during his presidency. Ford intended the gesture to help the nation move ahead following the Watergate scandal that had led to the first resignation by a president in office in the nation's history.

After taking the oath of office a month earlier, Ford proclaimed that "our national nightmare is over" and "the Constitution worked" (through a peaceful transfer of power from one president to another). The pardon a month later was welcomed by many as an end to the scandal—a view shared as well by many historians.

At the time, however, the pardon was extremely controversial. Some believed that a corrupt bargain had been struck between Nixon and Ford—where Ford was nominated as vice president by Nixon in exchange for future protection. Others believed that the pardon indicated that some Americans are above the law; they argued that former president

"My conscience tells me clearly and certainly that I cannot prolong the bad dreams that continue to reopen a chapter that is closed. My conscience tells me that only I, as President, have the constitutional power to firmly shut and seal this book."

*Gerald R. Ford*

Nixon should face the same form of justice that any other American would encounter.

## Things to remember while reading President Ford's comments regarding the pardon of Richard Nixon:

- At the beginning of the speech and at its conclusion, Ford took personal responsibility for his controversial decision to pardon ex-president Nixon. Near the end, he used the term "The buck stops here." The saying was popularized by President **Harry S. Truman** (1884–1972; see entry in volume 4): "passing the buck" refers to those who allow others to make decisions and attempt to avoid responsibility.

- After noting that there were no historic or legal precedents (previous actions or decisions) for granting such a pardon, President Ford cited his obligation as president to ensure "domestic tranquility" (peace within the nation). He argued that the Watergate scandal had already caused divisiveness within the nation (the scandal began more than two years earlier); legal proceedings against ex-president Nixon could continue for several more years. "My concern (in granting the pardon) is the immediate future of this great country," Ford declared.

- Public opinion weighed heavily against Nixon: in January 1974, as many as 79% of Americans polled favored his impeachment. Ford described his pardon as an act of mercy for Nixon. He also argued that continuing legal proceedings might not conclusively end the effects of the scandal.

### *President Ford's comments regarding the pardon of Richard Nixon*

*Ladies and gentlemen: I have come to a decision which I felt I should tell you and all of my fellow American citizens, as soon as I was certain in my own mind and in my own conscience that it is the right thing to do. I have learned already in this office that the difficult decisions always come to this desk. I must admit that many of them do not look at all the same as the hypothetical questions that I have answered freely and perhaps too fast on previous occasions. My customary policy is to try and get all the facts and to consider the opinions of my countrymen and to take counsel with my most valued friends. But these seldom agree, and in the end, the decision is mine.*

*To **procrastinate**, to agonize, and to wait for a more favorable turn of events that may never come or more compelling external pressures that may as well be wrong as right, is itself a decision of sorts and a weak and potentially dangerous course for a President to follow.*

*I have promised to uphold the Constitution, to do what is right as God gives me to see the right, and to do the very best that I can for America. I have asked your*

**President Gerald R. Ford tells the nation that he is giving former president Richard Nixon a "full, free and absolute pardon."** *Reproduced by permission of the Corbis Corporation.*

*help and your prayers, not only when I became President but many times since. The Constitution is the supreme law of our land and it governs our actions as citizens. Only the laws of God, which govern our consciences, are superior to it.*

*As we are a nation under God, so I am sworn to uphold our laws with the help of God. And I have sought such guidance and searched my own conscience with special **diligence** to determine the right thing for me to do with respect to my predecessor in this place, Richard Nixon, and his loyal wife and family. Theirs is an American tragedy in which we all have played a part. It could go on and on and on, or someone must write the end to it. I have concluded that only I can do that, and if I can, I must.*

*There are no historic or legal precedents to which I can turn in this matter, none that precisely fit the circumstances of a private citizen who has resigned the Presidency of the United States. But it is common knowledge that serious allegations and accusations hang like a sword over our former President's head, threatening his health*

**Procrastinate:** Delay, leave unfinished.

**Diligence:** Care, concern.

*as he tries to reshape his life, a great part of which was spent in the service of this country and by the **mandate** of its people. After years of bitter controversy and **divisive** national debate, I have been advised, and I am compelled to conclude that many months and perhaps more years will have to pass before Richard Nixon could obtain a fair trial by jury in any jurisdiction of the United States under governing decisions of the Supreme Court.*

*I deeply believe in equal justice for all Americans, whatever their station or former station. The law, whether human or divine, is no **respecter** of persons; but the law is a respecter of reality. The facts, as I see them, are that a former President of the United States, instead of enjoying equal treatment with any other citizen accused of violating the law, would be cruelly and excessively penalized either in preserving the presumption of his innocence or in obtaining a speedy determination of his guilt in order to repay a legal debt to society.*

*During this long period of delay and potential **litigation**, ugly passions would again be aroused. And our people would again be **polarized** in their opinions. And the credibility of our free institutions of government would again be challenged at home and abroad. In the end, the courts might well hold that Richard Nixon had been denied due process, and the verdict of history would even more be inconclusive with respect to those charges arising out of the period of his Presidency, of which I am presently aware.*

*But it is not the ultimate fate of Richard Nixon that most concerns me, though surely it deeply troubles every decent and every compassionate person. My concern is the immediate future of this great country. In this, I dare not depend upon my personal sympathy as a long-time friend of the former President, nor my professional judgment as a lawyer, and I do not.*

*As President, my primary concern must always be the greatest good of all the people of the United States whose servant I am. As a man, my first consideration is to be true to my own convictions and my own conscience.*

*My conscience tells me clearly and certainly that I cannot prolong the bad dreams that continue to reopen a chapter that is closed. My conscience tells me that only I, as President, have the constitutional power to firmly shut and seal this book. My conscience tells me it is my duty, not merely to proclaim domestic tranquillity but to use every means that I have to insure it.*

*I do believe that the buck stops here, that I cannot rely upon public opinion polls to tell me what is right.*

**Mandate:** Power to act on another's behalf.

**Divisive:** Causing disagreement.

**Respecter:** One who gives special attention to.

**Litigation:** Legal proceedings.

**Polarized:** Broken into opposing factions.

Complete American Presidents Sourcebook

*I do believe that right makes might and that if I am wrong, 10 angels swearing I was right would make no difference.*

*I do believe, with all my heart and mind and spirit, that I, not as President but as a humble servant of God, will receive justice without mercy if I fail to show mercy.*

*Finally, I feel that Richard Nixon and his loved ones have suffered enough and will continue to suffer, no matter what I do, no matter what we, as a great and good nation, can do together to make his goal of peace come true.*

*[At this point, Ford began reading from the proclamation granting the pardon.] "Now, therefore, I, Gerald R. Ford, President of the United States, pursuant to the pardon power conferred upon me by Article II, Section 2, of the Constitution, have granted and by these presents do grant a full, free, and absolute pardon unto Richard Nixon for all offenses against the United States which he, Richard Nixon, has committed or may have committed or taken part in during the period from [January] 20, 1969 through August 9, 1974."*

*[President Ford signed the proclamation and then resumed reading.] "In witness whereof, I have hereunto set my hand this eighth day of September, in the year of our Lord nineteen hundred and seventy-four, and of the Independence of the United States of America the one hundred and ninety-ninth."* (The History Place: Great Speeches Collection *[Web site]*)

## What happened next . . .

Although many people welcomed the pardon as an act that could help the nation address other problems that had been overwhelmed by attention to Watergate, Ford's action drew a fierce public backlash. The response affected Ford's ability to carry out his administration's agenda. He had to appear before the U.S. House Committee on the Judiciary to explain that there were no deals connected with the pardon. Meanwhile, politicians increasingly found themselves having to promise not to lie to or mislead the public. The outcry gradually died down, but Americans' faith in their political leaders suffered.

A long legal battle over the public release of tapes of Nixon's White House conversations continued into the 1990s. Had the pardon not been issued, the case against ex-president Nixon would have been at least as time-consuming and complicated. The tapes, meanwhile, confirmed that public opinion against the president had been correct. He was involved in the Watergate scandal.

## Did you know . . .

- Ford's decision to pardon Nixon likely ended his chances for victory in the presidential election of 1976. The pardon was announced by Ford on a Sunday morning, when news reporting around Washington, D.C., was generally slow. It did not work out that way. Ford's popularity plummeted, and instead of being viewed as an act of mercy that could help heal the nation, the pardon further divided many Americans. By election time in 1976, the American economy showed signs of improvement and there were no foreign affairs crises. Still, voters turned to Democrat **Jimmy Carter** (1924– ; see entry in volume 5), who had far less political experience than Ford.

## Where to Learn More

Ford, Gerald R. *A Time to Heal: The Autobiography of Gerald R. Ford.* New York: Harper & Row, 1979.

The History Place: Great Speeches Collection. "Gerald R. Ford Pardoning Richard Nixon." [Online] http://www.historyplace.com/speeches/ford.htm (accessed on October 13, 2000).

Mollenhoff, Clark R. *The Man Who Pardoned Nixon.* New York: St. Martin's Press, 1976.

Sidey, Hugh. *Portrait of a President.* New York: Harper & Row, 1975.

# Jimmy Carter

**Thirty-ninth president (1977–1981)**

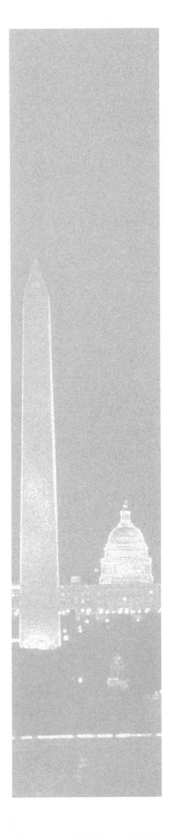

# Jimmy Carter

**Born October 1, 1924**
**Plains, Georgia**

**Thirty-ninth president of the United States
(1977–1981)**

**Washington outsider had foreign relations
successes but was hampered by weak
economy and Iran hostage crisis**

W hen Jimmy Carter was elected the thirty-ninth president in 1976, public faith in elected officials was very low. The long Vietnam War (1954–75) and the Watergate scandal (1972–74), which ultimately resulted in the resignation of President **Richard Nixon** (1913–1994; see entry in volume 5) from office, dispirited many Americans about their leaders. Inflation (a decline in the value of money) and fuel prices were on the rise; American industries faced increasingly stronger international competition and were responding slowly; and the Cold War, a tense period of strained diplomatic relations, military buildup, and the constant threat of war between the United States and the Soviet Union and their respective allies, was raging. Many people had come to distrust "Washington insiders." Carter, a soft-spoken peanut farmer and former state legislator from Georgia, offered a refreshing alternative to the federal power brokers (influential politicians) in the capital.

Over a remarkable two-year period beginning in 1974, Carter emerged from being a virtually unknown candidate to become president. Carter campaigned as an outsider, vowing to make the government "competent and compassionate"

"Our American values are not luxuries, but necessities—not the salt in our bread but the bread itself."

*Jimmy Carter*

**Jimmy Carter.**
*Courtesy of the Library of Congress.*

## Fast Facts about Jimmy Carter

**Full name:** James Earl Carter Jr.

**Born:** October 1, 1924

**Parents:** James Earl and Lillian Gordy Carter

**Spouse:** Eleanor Rosalynn Smith (1928– ; m. 1946)

**Children:** John William (Jack) (1947– ); James Earl (Chip) III (1950– ); Donnel Jeffrey (1952– ); Amy Lynn (1967– )

**Religion:** Southern Baptist

**Education:** U.S. Naval Academy (B.S., 1947)

**Occupations:** Farmer; warehouseman; navy lieutenant

**Government positions:** Georgia state senator and governor

**Political party:** Democratic

**Dates as president:** January 20, 1977– January 20, 1981

**Age upon taking office:** 52

again. As it turned out, however, he proved unable to stimulate the sagging economy. His foreign policy successes—most notably in the Middle East, China, and Panama—were offset by the Soviet Union's invasion of Afghanistan and troubles with Iran. A revolution there in 1977 against a leader supported by the United States flamed anti-American sentiments and culminated when fifty-two Americans were held hostage for 444 days, from November 1979 to January 1981.

Although compassionate and principled, Carter was unable to instill confidence, and he served only one term in office. The very quality that voters found appealing in Carter—his outsider's status in Washington—weighed heavily against him when he tried to push his agenda through Congress. Both the Senate and the House held Democratic majorities during his administration, but Carter still found himself fighting for much of his legislation and accepted compromises that weakened his policies. By the third year of his presidency, Carter suffered some of the lowest approval ratings of any twentieth-century president.

Carter became more popular and more respected *after* he left the White House. He embarked on a career as an international human rights mediator; a founder of and spokesman for Habitat for Humanity, an organization that helps build homes for poor families; and a founder of the Atlanta-based Carter Center that brings attention to international problems. He was among the most active ex-presidents.

## Boyhood on a farm

James Earl Carter Jr. was born on October 1, 1924, in Plains, Georgia. His father, James Earl, was a farmer and the proprietor of a small store in Archery, Georgia, three miles west of Plains. His mother, known as "Miss Lillian," was a registered nurse. Jimmy grew up with numerous duties on his father's farm. He "mopped" the family's cotton with a mixture of poisonous arsenic, molasses, and water to deter boll weevils, small beetles that damage cotton plants. He helped pick the cotton when it ripened. He picked peanuts, too, boiling them and then selling bags of them in Plains for a dollar. This early money-making venture earned him the nickname "Hot," short for "Hotshot."

Eventually, the Carter family would include two sisters, Gloria and Ruth, and a brother, Billy, who was thirteen years younger than Jimmy. All of them were encouraged by their mother to excel in school and to prepare for college. At his segregated (whites only) public school, Jimmy was singled out by a teacher, Julia Coleman, who encouraged him to undertake difficult assignments. He was equally captivated by an uncle, Tom Gordy, who was in the navy. To a young boy rising before dawn to perform tiring farm chores, life in the navy—with its travel to exotic ports— seemed like an ideal career. Not surprisingly, Jimmy Carter set his sights on the U.S. Naval Academy at a very young age, writing to the elite college for information while he was still in elementary school.

When it became clear that Carter would be the valedictorian (the student with the highest academic rank) of his high school class, he sought the required recommendation from his congressman to attend the Naval Academy in Annapolis, Maryland. He was accepted, but he did not go to Annapolis right out of high school. Concerned that he was not

## Jimmy Carter Timeline

**1924:** Born in Georgia

**1946:** Graduates from U.S. Naval Academy

**1953:** Leaves the navy nuclear-powered submarine program to take over the family peanut farm

**1963–67:** Serves as Georgia state senator

**1971–75:** Serves as Georgia governor

**1977–81:** Serves as thirty-ninth U.S. president

**1979:** Iran takes fifty-two American embassy officials hostage; Soviet Union invades Afghanistan (United States responds by boycotting 1980 Olympics in Moscow)

**1980:** Loses presidential election to Ronald Reagan

**1982:** Founds the Carter Center, a nonprofit organization that promotes human rights, improved public health, and advances in agriculture

## Words to Know

**Camp David Accords:** An agreement of peace following negotiations led by President Carter, signed by Israeli prime minister Menachem Begin and Egyptian president Anwar el-Sadat on March 26, 1979.

**Cold War:** A term that describes a period from 1945 to the late 1980s characterized by tense conflicts and failed diplomacy between the Soviet Union and the United States and their respective allies.

**Freeze:** Legally disallow access to money belonging to a party accused of illegal acts. The financial institution that stores the money is not allowed to transact business with the party during such a freeze. Billions of dollars deposited by the Iranian government in U.S. banks was frozen during the Iran hostage crisis.

**Habitat for Humanity:** An organization that helps build homes for poor families. The Jimmy Carter Work Project is part of the organization.

**Human rights:** Principles based on the belief that human beings are born free and equal; governments must respect those rights or they can be accused of human rights violations.

**Incumbent:** The elected official currently holding a particular office.

**Inflation:** A period of time when money loses some of its value, usually because goods become more expensive.

**Interest rates:** The percentage of a loan that a person agrees to pay for borrowing money.

**Iran hostage crisis:** A 444-day period from November 4, 1979, to Inauguration Day 1981 when Iran held fifty-two American embassy officials hostage following the toppling of the American-backed Shah of Iran.

**Populist:** Appealing to small farmers, laborers, and other workers with modest incomes.

prepared academically for the rigorous science and mathematics at the Naval Academy, he attended Southwestern Junior College for a year and Georgia Tech University for another year, sharpening his skills in math and physics. He entered the U.S. Naval Academy in 1943.

## Submarine specialist

The extra preparation in science paid off handsomely for Carter. He was an excellent student at Annapolis, graduating in the top ten percent of his class in June 1946. One month later, he married Rosalynn Smith (1928– ; see entry on Rosalynn Carter in volume 5)—another native of Plains—and the newlyweds moved to Norfolk, Virginia. There, Carter became a systems tester on two experimental gunnery ships, the *Wyoming* and the *Mississippi.*

Carter liked to be challenged. Soon after his first son was born in July 1947, he decided to move into the submarine branch of the navy. More schooling followed as he prepared for demanding tasks aboard a submarine. After finishing his studies in December 1948, he was assigned to the U.S.S. *Pomfret,* based in Pearl Harbor, Hawaii. He had not been on the ship long when it encountered bad weather in the Pacific Ocean. One night while he was standing watch on the bridge, Carter was swept overboard by a wave. As he struggled against the storm surge, another wave tossed him onto the submarine's gun barrel. He was able to crawl along the gun barrel and back onto the deck, narrowly escaping death.

Naval lieutentant commander Jimmy Carter in 1948, two years after his graduation from the U.S. Naval Academy.
*Reproduced by permission of Archive Photos.*

When the Korean War (1950–54) began, Carter was reassigned to an experimental submarine, the U.S.S. *K–1,* still under construction. First in San Diego, California, and then in New London, Connecticut, Carter supervised engineering of quiet diving-and-surfacing mechanisms and techniques. He was aboard the *K–1* when it made its maiden (first) voyage.

Another challenge loomed. The navy was beginning to build nuclear-powered submarines under the supervision of Admiral Hyman Rickover (1900–1986). Carter applied to Rickover to be part of that program. Assigned to the new atomic submarine U.S.S. *Seawolf* as a senior officer, Carter spent long days helping to design the ship and educate its crew. Meanwhile, he continued his own graduate studies in nuclear physics at New York's Union College. The young lieutenant seemed destined for the highest ranks in the U.S. Navy.

## A return to Plains

When Carter's father died of cancer in 1953, he made a decision that shocked not only his superiors in the navy but his wife as well: He chose to move back to Plains and take over the family business. Carter felt that he would not be able to spend enough time with Rosalynn and his three sons if he stayed in the navy. He was also concerned about his mother's well-being. Although the idea of entering politics did not at first factor in his decision, it later became an important reason for returning to his roots.

Upon their return, Jimmy and Rosalynn Carter discovered that the peanut warehouse and other Carter interests were financially troubled. By combining hard work and more scientific farming methods, they were able to reverse the losses and make the farm and warehouse profitable again. Jimmy also followed his father's example of civic service, gaining election to the county board of education and serving as president of the Georgia Planning Association. A move into state politics was the next logical step; in 1962, he ran for a seat in the Georgia state senate.

Carter became a state senator only after he proved that his opponent's victory was based on illegal voting practices. After an initial period of ill-will in which he and his family received threats, he quickly became a popular and well-liked state senator within his district and in the state capital. He was particularly dedicated to improving public education in Georgia.

By 1966, Carter had decided to run for governor, even though he was not well known and faced several well-established Democratic opponents. The Carter family traveled tirelessly throughout the state campaigning, but Carter failed to win the Democratic nomination. Disappointed and depressed, he returned to Plains, and there he found peace and hope in his religious faith. After that, Carter always referred to himself as a "born again" Christian. His respect for Christian principles remained an important part of his life.

In 1970, Carter ran again for Georgia governor. This time, he won. A conservative Democrat, he reorganized Georgia's state bureaucracy to make it run more efficiently on less money. He also made public his support of the civil rights

Former state senator Jimmy Carter shovels peanuts in a warehouse on the family peanut farm in Plains, Georgia, in 1969.
*Reproduced by permission of Archive Photos.*

movement and integration, expressing hope that race relations would improve not only in Georgia but throughout the South.

After his single term as Georgia's governor, Carter decided to run in the 1976 election for president. He met people in streets, diners, and town meetings, often with the greeting, "Hello, I'm Jimmy Carter, and I'm going to be your next president." Often wearing blue jeans and work shirts, and staying in private homes rather than in hotels when he

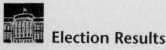

## Election Results

### 1976

| Presidential / Vice presidential candidates | Popular votes | Presidential electoral votes |
| --- | --- | --- |
| Jimmy Carter / Walter Mondale (Democratic) | 40,977,147 | 297 |
| Gerald R. Ford / Robert Dole (Republican) | 39,422,671 | 240 |

*Incumbent president Ford narrowly defeated former California governor Ronald Reagan on the first ballot, 1,187 to 1,070. An interesting footnote in the election occurred when two former Georgia governors were on the national ballot: Jimmy Carter, as the Democratic nominee, and Lester G. Maddox, as the obscure American Independent Party nominee. Maddox had also served as Carter's lieutenant governor.*

traveled, Carter projected a refreshingly populist image. (Populist ideas appeal to small farmers, laborers, and other workers with modest incomes.)

Carter and his wife began his vigorous campaign for the Democratic nomination in 1974. He stressed the need to bring a more people-oriented, more virtuous government back to Washington. He was hardly known at all outside his state, and he could not match the financial resources of some of the better-known Democratic candidates for the office. During a time of political scandal, he was not marked by accusations of corruption, nor had he ever held a previous position in national government. That "outsider" status became a major asset in his campaign.

By promising a new style of government, he emerged on top in a large field of Democratic candidates. In the 1976 general election, Carter scored a narrow victory over his Republican opponent, incumbent president **Gerald R. Ford** (1913– ; see entry in volume 5). Contributing to Carter's win was the negative fallout from President Ford's pardon of former President Richard Nixon following the Watergate scandal.

## Challenges of the presidency

At his inauguration (swearing-in ceremony) on January 20, 1977, Carter made a symbolic point by walking to the site of his speech with his wife and family. The message was

#  Jimmy Carter Administration

**Administration Dates**
January 20, 1977–January 20, 1981

**Vice President**
Walter F. Mondale (1977–81)

**Cabinet**

**Secretary of State**
Cyrus R. Vance (1977–80)
Edmund S. Muskie (1980–81)

**Secretary of the Treasury**
W. Michael Blumenthal (1977–79)
G. William Miller (1979–81)

**Attorney General**
Griffin B. Bell (1977–79)
Benjamin R. Civiletti (1979–81)

**Secretary of the Interior**
Cecil D. Andrus (1977–81)

**Secretary of Agriculture**
Robert S. Bergland (1977–81)

**Secretary of Labor**
F. Ray Marshall (1977–81)

**Secretary of Commerce**
Juanita M. Kreps (1977–79)

Philip M. Klutznick (1980–81)

**Secretary of Defense**
Harold Brown (1977–81)

**Secretary of Health, Education and Welfare**
Joseph A. Califano Jr. (1977–79)
Patricia R. Harris (1979–80)

**Secretary of Housing and Urban Development**
Patricia R. Harris (1977–79)
Maurice E. "Moon" Landrieu (1979–81)

**Secretary of Transportation**
Brockman "Brock" Adams (1977–79)
Neil E. Goldschmidt (1979–81)

**Secretary of Energy**
James R. Schlesinger (1977–79)
Charles W. Duncan Jr. (1979–81)

**Secretary of Health and Human Services**
Patricia R. Harris (1980–81)

**Secretary of Education**
Shirley M. Hufstedler (1979–81)

clear: Jimmy Carter intended to restore confidence in government by proving himself to be one of the people, an ordinary Christian farmer who happened to be running the nation.

Carter was intelligent and ambitious. Realizing he had scant experience in national politics, he filled his Cabinet (board of presidential advisors) with competent political veterans, prominent businesspeople, and academics (scholarly thinkers). His vice president, Walter Mondale (1928– ), had

*Jimmy Carter's mother, Miss Lillian, was a popular figure during his administration. She had been a Peace Corps Volunteer in her fifties, and in her sixties she became the first mother of a president to serve on a diplomatic mission.*

had a distinguished record as a longtime U.S. senator from Minnesota. African American voters had supported Carter overwhelmingly, and he recognized their confidence in him by recruiting two African American women for his Cabinet and by naming Andrew Young (1932– ) as U.S. ambassador to the United Nations.

Carter's honeymoon (in political terms, a period when a newly elected official is given the chance to begin work without conflicts, like a newlywed person) as president was very brief. His appointee to head the Office of Management and Budget, Georgia banker Bert Lance (1931– ), came under close observation for his banking practices back in Georgia. Seizing on the Lance issue as proof that Carter was no different from his presidential predecessors, journalists and politicians demanded that Carter fire Lance. Carter stood by his friend until Lance himself resigned in the early autumn of 1977. Lance was later acquitted (cleared) of all charges that had been filed against him. However, the Lance affair—as well as continuing troubles with inflation and high prices for gas and oil (which became known as the energy crisis)—eroded Carter's approval rating within a matter of months after he had taken office.

Carter also lost effectiveness by not making strong allies in Congress. He believed he could rally people and thereby inspire Congress to action. In 1977, for example, he made an impressive, nationally televised speech on the need for an energy policy to counter high costs and dwindling supplies. Legislation in Congress faltered, however, and the eventual energy policy that emerged was only modestly successful.

## Foreign policy successes

Carter held firm beliefs about human rights and was not afraid to criticize foreign governments that violated the rights of their citizens. (Human rights refers to ideas based on the belief that human beings are born free and equal and that governments must respect those ideas.) Nevertheless, he did not press the issue when his criticisms created tension in foreign policy. Under his administration, several important events occurred that have had a lasting impact on world history. Facing stiff opposition in Congress, Carter pushed for ratification of a treaty that would turn the Panama Canal over to the government of Panama on December 31, 1999. The treaty was subsequently implemented without incident. Carter's administration formally recognized the People's Republic as the sole government of China. That led to the establishment of normal diplomatic relations with Communist China.

The president's successful attempt to secure peace between the warring nations of Israel and Egypt was the single most important achievement of his administration. After meeting separately with Israeli prime minister Menachem Begin (1913–1992) and Egyptian president Anwar el-Sadat (1918–1981), Carter invited both men to Camp David, Maryland, and urged them to negotiate a treaty (see box). Very significant issues divided the two governments, but over a period of thirteen days in September 1978, Carter was able to help them bridge differences. A peace treaty (the Camp David Accords) was drafted and signed in Washington, D.C., on March 26, 1979.

Deeply concerned about nuclear weapons and their destructive potential, Carter attempted to negotiate a strategic arms limitation treaty (referred to as SALT-II) with the Soviet Union. Months of talks between U.S. and Soviet diplomats produced a treaty, but some members of Congress felt it threatened America's powers of defense. When the Soviet Union invaded Afghanistan in December 1979, all talk of ratifying the SALT-II treaty was tabled. The following year, Carter withdrew American participation in the Summer Olympics being held in Moscow.

## Troubles at home and abroad

Despite efforts to stimulate the economy, Carter was not able to stem the tides of domestic inflation and unemployment. In fact, by the end of his term, interest rates (the amount charged in order to borrow money) severely depressed the home-mortgage market and discouraged economic expansion. An energy crisis fueled by an increase in prices by the oil-producing nations of the Middle East created high prices and shortages of gasoline and fuel oil. The image of long lines of cars leading into gas stations became commonplace. Carter campaigned hard for conservation of fuel and

# Camp David Principals: Anwar Sadat and Menachem Begin

For thirteen days in September 1978, President Jimmy Carter met with Israeli prime minister Menachem Begin and Egyptian president Anwar el-Sadat in an attempt to forge together an agreement of peace between the two countries. On March 26, 1979, the two Middle East leaders signed the Camp David Accords.

Anwar Sadat (ON-wahr suh-DOT) was born on December 25, 1918, in a village near Cairo. He graduated from a military academy in 1938 and was stationed in Upper Egypt. He was jailed twice for contacts with Germans in World War II (1939–45) and was later tried and acquitted on charges of conspiring to assassinate a pro-British politician in 1946.

Sadat took part in the takeover of 1952 in which Gamal Abdel Nasser (1918–1970) overthrew Egypt's King Faruk (1920–1965). Sadat held several government posts and served as vice president from 1964 to 1966 and again from 1969 to 1970. After Nasser's death in 1970, Sadat was elected president. In a show of strength, he sought revenge for Egypt's humiliating defeat by Israel in the Six-Day War of 1967. In October 1973, he launched the so-called Yom Kippur War, timed to begin around that Jewish holiday. Egyptian forces advanced and then a

cease-fire agreement was negotiated before full-scale battles began.

Menachem Begin (men-AH-kim BAY-ginn) was born on August 16, 1913, in Brest Litovsk, Poland (now Belarus) and trained in law at the University of Warsaw. He was active in Zionism—an international movement that began late in the nineteenth century to create a Jewish community in Palestine. (Its followers completed their goal when the state of Israel was established in 1948.) When Nazis invaded Poland in 1939, Begin fled to Lithuania. He was arrested in 1940 by Soviet authorities for Zionist activity and sentenced to eight years of hard labor. He was held in Siberia in 1940 and 1941.

In 1942, Begin arrived in Palestine when Polish army units joined Allied forces in the Middle East and North Africa. He soon became commander of a guerrilla group seeking to expel the British from Palestine. After Israel became independent, Begin founded the Herut (Freedom) Party and represented it in Israel's parliament beginning in 1949. He served as Herut's leader for over thirty years. Begin became Israel's prime minister in 1977.

Begin became the first Israeli prime minister to meet officially and publicly with an Arab head of state when he welcomed

Egyptian president Sadat to Jerusalem in November 1977. Sadat's surprise visit to Israel was the first for an Arab leader. President Carter brought the two together at Camp David, Maryland, in September 1978. They signed two agreements: one provided for an Israeli-Egyptian peace treaty within three months; the other began a five-year transition toward self-government for Palestinians, a group of Arabs who were displaced when the nation of Israel was established. Begin and Sadat shared the Nobel Peace Prize for 1978 and signed the final treaty in March 1979. The Palestinian part of the agreement, however, still remained in negotiation stages over twenty years later.

The Camp David Accords were rejected by other Arab nations. Together with Sadat's program for modernizing Egypt, the president lost support within his country. His economic policies created a new class of entrepreneurs who made quick fortunes. Sadat's "open-door" policy encouraged foreign business, especially in Egypt's oil-rich Arab neighboring countries. But there was little investment in productive industries. Riots broke out in January 1977 when the government reduced food subsidies (assistance) for the average Egyptian.

In Sadat's last years, many Islamic religious groups disapproved of the Westernization and corruption in Egypt, as well as the treaty with Israel. Violence between Christians and Muslims broke out. In September 1981, Sadat struck back by arresting hundreds of politicians, banning journals, and expelling the Soviet ambassador. On October 6, 1981, Muslim religious radicals shot him to death as he reviewed a military parade. The shocked West paid tribute to Sadat: Three former U.S. presidents (Nixon, Ford, and Carter), as well as Israeli prime minister Begin attended Sadat's funeral. Egyptians and Arabs reacted differently. The streets of Cairo, which millions of mourners had jammed when Nasser died, remained eerily silent. Sudan's president was the only Arab head of state to attend the funeral.

After the Camp David Accords, Begin won a new term in office, and in 1982 he authorized an Israeli invasion of southern Lebanon. But in September 1983, Begin suddenly resigned as prime minister. Begin apparently believed that he could no longer perform his tasks satisfactorily. He seemed to be severely affected by the death of his wife the previous year and by the continuing casualties suffered by Israelis in Lebanon. Begin spent most of his remaining years in seclusion. He died in 1992.

Egyptian president Anwar Sadat, U.S. president Jimmy Carter, and Israeli prime minister Menachem Begin.
*Reproduced by permission of AP/Wide World Photos.*

use of alternative energy sources, including nuclear power plants. He called America's need to conserve energy and to find alternative sources "the moral equivalent of war."

His administration created the Department of Energy, but Carter's attempts to encourage the use of alternate sources of fuel were dealt blows by a coal miners' strike and a nuclear reactor accident at the Three Mile Island nuclear power plant near Harrisburg, Pennsylvania. (A small amount of radioactive gas escaped, which threatened public health. No lasting health problems were recorded, however, but people demanded better safety precautions from energy companies as a result.) Conservation proved unpopular with voters who needed their cars to commute to work, as well as those who heated their homes with oil and natural gas.

The final blow to the Carter administration occurred on November 4, 1979. An Islamic revolution had occurred in oil-rich Iran. The American-allied Shah of Iran, Mohammad Reza Pahlavi (1919–1980), was forced to flee the country. Gravely ill

with cancer, the Shah entered a New York hospital for treatment. To Iranians, the Shah's presence in America suggested that he would use the United States as a base from which to return and reclaim Iran, with America's backing. Shortly after the Shah was hospitalized, an angry mob advanced on the American embassy in Tehran, Iran. They took the staff as hostages and demanded the Shah's return to Iran for trial as ransom.

The hostage crisis was Carter's greatest test as president. As the days turned into months, the image of Americans being held captive seemed to many a symbol of Carter's ineffectiveness as a leader. Diplomatic efforts to free the hostages proved useless, even after Carter froze all Iranian assets in the United States. (During the freeze, the financial institutions where the assets were stored were not allowed to transact business with those who deposited the assets.) Worse, a military rescue operation failed: Almost half of the helicopters involved developed mechanical problems, and another crashed into a transport plane, killing eight American soldiers.

President Jimmy Carter (right) meets with Mohammad Reza Pahlavi—the Shah of Iran—in November 1977. The Shah was forced out of the country in 1979; his presence in the United States for cancer treatment led to the kidnapping of fifty-two American embassy officials in Iran.
*Reproduced by permission of Archive Photos.*

**The Iran Hostage Crisis**

What became known as the Iran hostage crisis began on November 4, 1979. A group of anti-American demonstrators in Tehran, the capital city of Iran, stormed the American embassy, trapped fifty-two American workers there, and held them hostage for 444 days.

Carter was a symbol of hatred for revolutionary Iranians because his administration showed support for Mohammad Reza Pahlavi (1919–1980), the Shah (sovereign leader) of Iran. The conflict between the Shah and Islamic fundamentalists in Iran dated back to the 1950s. (A fundamentalist is someone who believes all social systems and interaction should be based strictly on religious teachings; a fundamentalist Christian follows the Bible as law, and an Islamic fundamentalist uses the Koran.) The Shah had ruled since 1941, when he was twenty-one years old. With help from the United States, he modernized his nation after World War II and accumulated wealth by exporting oil.

However, the disparity in wealth between a small minority of Iranians—many with connections to the Shah—and a larger, poorer class led to social tension. The Shah continued to have support from the United States as he pursued reforms during the 1960s and 1970s. However, many Iranians believed the reforms were a sham and began mistrusting the United States. Special military forces employed by the Shah cracked down on his opponents.

Ayatollah Ruhollah Khomeini (1902–1989) was a vocal opponent of the Shah because traditional Islamic values were being forsaken as Iran was being modernized. (An ayatollah is a supreme religious leader of Islam.) The Ayatollah Khomeini attracted a growing group of followers by the 1950s. He was exiled from Iran in 1963 after publicly criticizing the Shah.

An economic downturn in Iran during the mid-1970s increased public outcries against him, and his crackdowns against opponents became more widespread. Anti-American sentiment spread. As the Shah's forces and revolutionaries clashed in a series of violent and bloody demonstrations, the Carter administration's continued support for the Shah fueled anti-American sentiment among the Islamic revolutionaries. The Shah eventually fled Iran in 1979. The revolutionaries were further incensed against the United States when the deposed Shah was allowed refuge in New York. He was receiving medical treatment for cancer, but the rebels believed he was courting American sympathy to help him return to power. Meanwhile, the Ayatollah Khomeini returned triumphantly to Iran in February 1979. He became the nation's leader and proclaimed Iran an Islamic Republic.

The takeover of the American embassy and the holding of hostages was praised by the Ayatollah. As anti-American sentiment crystallized, the Ayatollah became more powerful as the ultimate authority in a government based on the religious laws of Islam and run by Islamic clergy. He called for religious revolutions in surrounding countries. He opposed the culture of the United States.

After being held in the embassy for twenty days, the hostages were bound, blindfolded, covered with blankets, and taken to a series of makeshift prisons. During a series of seemingly endless interrogations, they were beaten and humiliated by their captors. An hour of running in place each morning was the only exercise they were permitted. After three months, the hostages were placed in small cells and not allowed to communicate. Hostages who violated the rules were locked in cold, dark cubicles for as long as three days. Toward the end of their confinement, they were forced to stand before a mock firing squad.

The taking of hostages immediately received worldwide attention. Most of the nations of the world joined the United States in condemning the actions of the Iranian revolutionaries. However, the success with which the Iranians used hostages to humiliate a superpower inspired terrorists in other nations to try similar tactics. Meanwhile, militants pieced together shredded documents they found in the embassy to try and prove the building held a "nest of spies." They produced documents that showed, they claimed, the United States and the Soviet Union had joined forces to oppose the revolution.

The hostage crisis was humiliating for the United States and harmed the Carter administration, which had underestimated the growing Islamic revival in Iran. A rescue mission in April 1980, known as Eagle Claw, failed when helicopters malfunctioned during a desert sandstorm. The mission was abandoned, but eight men died when a helicopter collided with a plane during the retreat. The failure of the operation further angered military and civilian leaders in the United States.

Economic sanctions by President Carter against Iran caused hardships for that nation but increased the determination of the hostage takers. President Carter's unflagging support of the Shah and his inability to resolve the hostage crisis contributed to his landslide defeat by Ronald Reagan in 1980. The hostages' long ordeal finally ended after 444 days in captivity: their release was timed for January 20, 1981—the day Ronald Reagan became president, replacing Jimmy Carter.

The Carter administration eventually secured the release of the American hostages. However, that did not occur until after the presidential election of 1980. The level of public disappointment with Carter was clearly evident at election time. Although he secured the Democratic nomination for a second term, Carter was soundly defeated by Republican **Ronald Reagan** (1911– ; see entry in volume 5), who won 489 electoral votes to Carter's 49 votes. In a final insult directed at the outgoing U.S. president, the Iranians did not give the American hostages their freedom—after 444 days of captivity—until after Reagan had been sworn in as president on January 20, 1981.

## Life after the presidency

In his fifties when he left office, Carter realized that he had many more productive years ahead of him. Free to pursue his interest in human rights, he became a private citi-

Jimmy and Rosalynn Carter help build a house in Atlanta, Georgia, as part of their work for Habitat for Humanity.
*Reproduced by permission of the Corbis Corporation.*

zen of international stature. Carter served as an arbitrator in international disputes, supervised elections in other countries, and formed coalitions to find private solutions to social problems. In 1982, he and his wife founded the Carter Center in Atlanta, a nonprofit organization that promotes human rights, democracy, improved public health, and advances in agriculture. In 1984, the Carters also became involved with Habitat for Humanity International, a nonprofit organization dedicated to building new homes for the poor. (The Jimmy Carter Work Project is a part of the organization.) Carter became a respected elder statesman frequently honored for his tireless work on behalf of humanity.

In October 2000, the former president announced that he was splitting from the Southern Baptist Convention because of "increasingly rigid" views that run against "the basic premises of my Christian faith." Carter pointed to the Baptist group's opposition to women as pastors and its call for

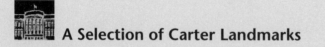

## A Selection of Carter Landmarks

**Jimmy Carter Library and Museum.** 441 Freedom Parkway, Atlanta, GA 30307–1498. (404) 331-3942. On the grounds of the thirty-seven-acre Carter Presidential Center, the library holds approximately 27 million pages of President Carter's White House material, including photographs, and audio and video tape. A museum includes hands-on exhibits relating to Carter's political career. The library is one of ten official presidential libraries in the country. See http://www.cartercenter.org/ and http://carterlibrary.galileo.peachnet.edu/index.htm (accessed on October 24, 2000).

**Jimmy Carter National Historic Site.** 300 N. Bond St., Plains, GA 31780. (229) 824-4104. The site—in Plains and Archery—includes President Carter's boyhood farm, school, and the railroad depot that served as his campaign headquarters during the 1976 election. A museum and visitor center is located in Plains High School. See http://www.nps.gov/jica/ (accessed on October 24, 2000).

wives to be submissive to their husbands as key factors for leaving the denominational group.

## Legacy

Jimmy Carter's administration never established momentum. The president moved cautiously and supported moderate programs that rallied few Democrats in Congress and were opposed by Republicans. A steadily worsening economy and problems overseas drained his attempts to build support. He had appealed to voters as a Washington outsider, but once inside Washington, D.C., Carter did not build the support he needed. Opinion polls showed that the public liked Carter as a person, but he consistently lost favor for his leadership abilities.

Among his successes, Carter substantially increased the percentage of minorities and women in high-level bureaucratic and judicial positions. He confronted the energy shortage by establishing a national energy policy. He created the Department of Education to improve public schools. In foreign affairs, the Camp David Accords in 1978 formally ended hostilities between Israel and Egypt. Carter fortified positive relations with China in 1979 when the United States formally recognized the Chinese communist government. Carter condemned the Soviet Union's invasion of Afghanistan and promoted human rights as a policy.

A weak economy and a setback in foreign affairs can undermine any president. High inflation and high unemployment at the same time, and the ongoing hostage crisis in Iran were in the daily news as Carter ran for reelection in 1980. Americans turned away from Carter when they went to the polls that year. Despite a resounding election defeat, Carter quickly reemerged as an independent statesman, showing that he had not lost trust and respect during the difficult years of his presidency.

## Where to Learn More

Abernathy, M. Glenn, Dilys M. Hill, and Phil Williams, eds. *The Carter Years: The President and Policy Making.* New York: St. Martin's Press, 1984.

Bourne, Peter G. *Jimmy Carter: A Comprehensive Biography from Plains to Post-Presidency.* New York: Scribner, 1997.

Brinkley, Douglas. *The Unfinished Presidency: Jimmy Carter's Journey Beyond the White House.* New York: Viking, 1998.

Carter, Jimmy. *Keeping Faith: Memoirs of a President.* New York: Bantam, 1982.

Carter, Jimmy. *Why Not the Best?* Nashville: Broadman Press, 1975. Reprint, Fayetteville: University of Arkansas Press, 1996.

Finklestone, Joseph. *Anwar Sadat: Visionary Who Dared.* Portland, OR: Frank Cass, 1996.

Hargrove, Erwin C. *Jimmy Carter as President: Leadership and the Politics of the Public Good.* Baton Rouge: Louisiana State University Press, 1988.

*Jimmy Carter Library.* [Online] http://carterlibrary.galileo.peachnet.edu/ (accessed on October 24, 2000).

Perlmutter, Amos. *The Life and Times of Menachem Begin.* Garden City, NY: Doubleday, 1987.

Richman, Daniel A. *James E. Carter: 39th President of the United States.* Ada, OK: Garrett Educational Corp., 1989.

Slavin, Ed. *Jimmy Carter.* New York: Chelsea House, 1989.

Thompson, Kenneth W., ed. *The Carter Presidency: Fourteen Intimate Perspectives of Jimmy Carter.* Lanham, MD: University Press of America, 1990.

Wells, Tim. *444 Days: The Hostages Remember.* San Diego: Harcourt Brace Jovanovich, 1985.

# Rosalynn Carter

**Born August 18, 1927**
**Plains, Georgia**

**Spoke out for causes that she believed in—delivering speeches, testifying before Congress, and even attending Cabinet meetings**

A ttractive and poised, Rosalynn Carter was a serious contributor to the political campaigns of her husband, **Jimmy Carter** (1924– ; see entry in volume 5), and an extremely busy and well-respected first lady. Mrs. Carter had no fears about traveling alone as a representative of the Carter administration. She attended Cabinet meetings (meetings of presidential advisors) and kept a full schedule of activities. Through her work as honorary chairman of the President's Commission on Mental Health, she helped raise national consciousness about the treatment and rights of mental health patients. As she had been for most of her adult life, Mrs. Carter was a strong partner for her husband and a significant spokesperson for the causes in which she believed.

## Her best friend's older brother

Rosalynn Carter was born in Plains, Georgia, on August 18, 1927, the oldest of four children of Wilburn Edgar and Allethea Murray Smith. Her father, a farmer and a mechanic, died of leukemia when Rosalynn was thirteen. Her

"I had already learned from more than a decade of political life that I was going to be criticized no matter what I did so I might as well be criticized for something I wanted to do, attending Cabinet meetings. If I had spent all day 'pouring tea,' I would have been criticized for that too."

*Rosalynn Carter*

**Rosalynn Carter.**
*Courtesy of the Library of Congress.*

1457

mother worked as a seamstress, and later in the local post office, to support the family, but it was always a struggle to make ends meet. Rosalynn helped with sewing, housework, and child care while still doing the best she could in school. What little spare time she had was spent with her best friend, Ruth Carter (1929–1983), Jimmy Carter's younger sister.

Rosalynn was three years younger than Jimmy; they did not socialize during their high school years. They began to date after her freshman year at Georgia Southwestern College, while Carter was a midshipman at the U.S. Naval Academy. After a six-month courtship, carried on mostly by letter-writing, Jimmy Carter proposed marriage. At first, Rosalynn turned him down because she wanted to finish her college education. When he proposed a second time, however, she accepted. They were married a month after he graduated from the U.S. Naval Academy in 1946.

## Navy wife

Having spent her entire life in Georgia—most of it in Plains—Rosalynn Carter welcomed the opportunity to be a navy wife. Her three sons were all born in different states: John William (1947– ) in Virginia, James Earl III (1950– ) in Hawaii, and Donnel Jeffrey (1952– ) in Connecticut. The family also lived briefly in California and New York. Rosalynn enjoyed the independence she had achieved living away from home. She was stunned when her husband told her he wanted to move back to Plains and run his deceased father's business. In her autobiography, *First Lady from Plains,* she recalled: "I argued. I cried. I even screamed at him." She did not want to return to Plains because of memories of tough times there.

Rosalynn finally agreed to her husband's plan and the couple returned to Plains. Rosalynn performed accounting work for the Carter peanut warehouse and supervised other family interests. She supported her husband completely when he entered state politics; she spent many long hours campaigning for him as he ran first for state senator and later for governor of Georgia. During his presidential campaign, she traveled independently to forty-one states to give speeches on his behalf, and her enthusiasm greatly contributed to his election bid. Jimmy Carter narrowly defeated President **Gerald R. Ford** (1913– ; see entry in volume 5) in the 1976 election.

## Active first lady

Once established as first lady, Mrs. Carter worked hard to further her husband's policies, while simultaneously emerging as a woman with missions of her own. She was a vocal supporter of the Equal Rights Amendment (ERA), a proposed Constitutional amendment, to specifically recognize the rights of women. (The ERA was not ratified.) She was a proponent of patients' rights for the mentally ill and a supporter of the performing arts. She represented her husband on formal occasions and traveled to Latin America as his personal emissary (representative). All these tasks were accomplished while she was also raising her daughter Amy (1967– ), who was only nine years old when Jimmy Carter became president.

By her own admission, Mrs. Carter was quite bitter when her husband failed to win reelection in 1980. She felt betrayed by the press, which had attacked President Carter for the hostage situation in Iran, the ongoing energy crisis, and inflation. She felt strongly that Carter would have had a successful second term, and she thought she would have trouble readjusting to a quiet life in Plains after being so busy and so famous for four years. Her bitterness soon faded, however, when she discovered that the American people still valued her opinions and watched her with admiration.

## Respected private citizen

As a private citizen, Rosalynn Carter worked with her husband to promote international human rights through the Atlanta-based Carter Center. She helped increase public awareness of Habitat for Humanity, a private program that builds homes for needy Americans. She continued her work on behalf of the mentally ill. In 1991, Rosalynn Carter co-founded a program called "Every Child by Two," with the goal of early childhood immunization against diseases. Her humanitarian work earned her numerous honors, awards, and citations, including several honorary degrees.

In her autobiography, Mrs. Carter wrote: "I would be out there campaigning right now if Jimmy would run again. I miss the world of politics." This sentiment was penned soon after she had left the White House, before she discovered that she and her husband could continue to make a serious impact on international affairs. Although Rosalynn Carter remained far from the political limelight, her contributions to improving the quality of life did not diminish, nor did she lose the independent spirit that endeared her to so many during her years as first lady.

## Where to Learn More

Carter, Rosalynn. *First Lady from Plains*. Boston: Houghton Mifflin, 1984. Reprint, Fayetteville: University of Arkansas Press, 1994.

Sandak, Cass R. *The Carters*. New York: Crestwood House, 1993.

Turk, Ruth. *Rosalynn Carter: Steel Magnolia*. New York: Franklin Watts, 1997.

# Carter's "Human Rights and Foreign Policy" Speech

**Delivered in June 1977; excerpted from *Civnet* (Web site)**

*President Carter describes a foreign policy based on respect for human rights*

In his speeches, President **Jimmy Carter** (1924– ; see entry in volume 5) often invoked ideals of American democracy as guides to explaining his policies. He had difficulty during his presidency, however, in translating those principles into action. He succeeded in restoring faith and trust in the presidency—as reflected in consistently high ratings in polls for his trustworthiness. However, his effectiveness as a leader rated much lower in opinion polls. He was unable to rally support in Congress or among voters for many of his programs.

Carter applied to American foreign policy his belief that political actions should reflect the nation's highest moral ideals. That standard emphasized human rights—that all individuals should be free and equal. His most profound statement of that belief occurred at a commencement (graduation) address at the University of Notre Dame in South Bend, Indiana, in June 1977—less than six months after he took office.

"I have a quiet confidence in our own political system. Because we know that democracy works, we can reject the arguments of those rulers who deny human rights to their people."

*Jimmy Carter*

## Things to remember while reading an excerpt from President Carter's "Human Rights and Foreign Policy" speech:

- Carter insisted that the expectations Americans have regarding their government and leaders should apply as well to the government's practices in foreign policy. During the 1970s, the United States had several international successes in foreign policy. At the same time, there were revelations that the United States had engaged in illegal acts since the 1950s while attempting to stop the spread of communism abroad. The communist system, as practiced in the Soviet Union and the People's Republic of China, restricted the freedom of individuals while pursuing policies where the state (government) controlled business, industry, agriculture, and the distribution of goods.

- Reviewing in his speech the recent history of American foreign policy, Carter noted that many actions were motivated by two primary goals: stopping the spread of Soviet-style communism, and banding together "in an almost exclusive alliance" with non-communist nations of Europe. Together with America's long and ultimately unsuccessful involvement in the Vietnam War (1954–75), Carter argued, the United States lost prestige among many nations in the world outside of Europe. Carter suggested that a different world had emerged in the mid-1970s—one in which the U.S. could reemerge as a leader by maintaining the principles of democracy.

- Carter insisted that the United States became the wealthiest and most powerful nation on Earth after World War II (1939–45) because of the freedom enjoyed by its people. That was the essence of his "human rights" doctrine: freedom breeds prosperity. That doctrine went against programs in those countries where human rights were curtailed by governments hoping to achieve economic development through government controls.

## *Excerpt from President Carter's "Human Rights and Foreign Policy" speech*

*I want to speak to you today about the strands that connect our actions overseas with our essential character as a nation. I believe we can have a foreign policy that is democratic, that is based on fundamental values, and that uses power and influence, which we have, for humane purposes. We can also have a foreign policy that the American people both support and, for a change, know about and understand.*

*I have a quiet confidence in our own political system. Because we know that democracy works, we can reject the arguments of those rulers who deny **human rights** to their people.*

*We are confident that democracy's example will be compelling, and so we seek to bring that example closer to those from whom in the past few years we have been separated and who are not yet convinced about the advantages of our kind of life.*

*We are confident that the democratic methods are the most effective, and so we are not tempted to employ **improper tactics** here at home or abroad.*

*We are confident of our own strength, so we can seek substantial **mutual reductions** in the nuclear arms race.*

*And we are confident of the good sense of American people, and so we let them share in the process of making foreign policy decisions. We can thus speak with the voices of 215 million, and not just of an isolated handful. . . .*

*For too many years, we've been willing to adopt the flawed and erroneous principles and tactics of our **adversaries**, sometimes abandoning our own values for theirs. We've fought fire with fire, never thinking that fire is better quenched with water. This approach failed, with **Vietnam** the best example of its intellectual and moral poverty. But through failure we have now found our way back to our own principles and values, and we have regained our lost confidence.*

*By the measure of history, our Nation's **200 years** are very brief, and our rise to world eminence is briefer still. It dates from **1945**, when Europe and the old international order lay in ruins. Before*

**Human rights:** Principles based on the belief that human beings are born free and equal; governments must respect those rights or they can be accused of human rights violations.

**Improper tactics:** Illegal activities used to bring favorable results.

**Mutual reductions:** When two parties reduce their supplies at equal rates.

**Adversaries:** Enemies.

**Vietnam:** A reference to the Vietnam War.

**200 years:** A reference to the age of the United States.

**1945:** A reference to the end of World War II.

*then, America was largely on the periphery of world affairs. But since then, we have inescapably been at the center of world affairs.*

*Our policy during this period was guided by two principles: a belief that **Soviet expansion** was almost inevitable but that it must be contained, and the corresponding belief in the importance of an almost exclusive alliance among non-Communist nations on both sides of the Atlantic. That system could not last forever unchanged. Historical trends have weakened its foundation. The unifying threat of conflict with the Soviet Union has become less intensive, even though the competition has become more extensive.*

*The Vietnamese war produced a profound moral crisis, sapping worldwide faith in our own policy and our system of life, a crisis of confidence made even more grave by the **covert pessimism** of some of our leaders.*

*In less than a generation, we've seen the world change dramatically. The daily lives and aspirations of most human beings have been transformed. **Colonialism** is nearly gone. A new sense of national identity now exists in almost 100 new countries that have been formed in the last generation. Knowledge has become more widespread. **Aspirations** are higher. As more people have been freed from traditional constraints, more have been determined to achieve, for the first time in their lives, social justice.*

*The world is still divided by ideological disputes, dominated by regional conflicts, and threatened by danger that we will not resolve the differences of race and wealth without violence or without drawing into combat the major military powers. We can no longer separate the traditional issues of war and peace from the new global questions of justice, equity, and human rights.*

*It is a new world, but America should not fear it. It is a new world, and we should help to shape it. It is a new world that calls for a new American foreign policy—a policy based on constant decency in its values and on optimism in our historical vision. . . .*

*Our policy must reflect our belief that the world can hope for more than simple survival and our belief that dignity and freedom are fundamental spiritual requirements. Our policy must shape an international system that will last longer than secret deals.*

*We cannot make this kind of policy by manipulation. Our policy must be open; it must be candid; it must be one of constructive global involvement, resting on five **cardinal** principles.*

**Soviet expansion:** The spread of communism backed by the resources and military force of the Soviet Union.

**Covert pessimism:** Hidden gloom.

**Colonialism:** When one nation controls the people of another area.

**Aspirations:** Hopes.

**Cardinal:** Central.

**Complete American Presidents Sourcebook**

I've tried to make these premises clear to the American people since last January. Let me review what we have been doing and discuss what we intend to do.

First, we have reaffirmed America's commitment to human rights as a fundamental **tenet** of our foreign policy. In ancestry, religion, color, place of origin, and cultural background, we Americans are as diverse a nation as the world has even seen. No common mystique of blood or soil unites us. What draws us together, perhaps more than anything else, is a belief in human freedom. We want the world to know that our Nation stands for more than financial prosperity. . . .

Throughout the world today, in free nations and in **totalitarian** countries as well, there is a preoccupation with the subject of human freedom, human rights. And I believe it is **incumbent** on us in this country to keep that discussion, that debate, that contention alive. No other country is as well-qualified as we to set an example. We have our own shortcomings and faults, and we should strive constantly and with courage to make sure that we are legitimately proud of what we have.

Second, we've moved deliberately to reinforce the bonds among our democracies. In our **recent meetings in London**, we agreed to widen our economic cooperation, to promote free trade, to strengthen the world's monetary system, to seek ways of avoiding **nuclear proliferation**. We prepared constructive proposals for the forthcoming meetings on **North-South problems** of poverty, development, and global well-being. And we agreed on joint efforts to reinforce and to modernize our common defense. . . .

Third, we've moved to engage the Soviet Union in a joint effort to halt the **strategic arms** race. This race is not only dangerous, it's morally deplorable. We must put an end to it. I know it will not be easy to reach agreements. Our goal is to be fair to both sides, to produce **reciprocal** stability, parity, and security. We desire a **freeze** on further modernization and production of weapons and a continuing, substantial reduction of strategic nuclear weapons as well. We want a comprehensive ban on all nuclear testing, a prohibition against all chemical warfare, no attack capability against space satellites, and arms limitations in the **Indian Ocean**. We hope that we can take joint steps with all nations toward a final agreement eliminating nuclear weapons completely from our arsenals of death. We will persist in this effort.

**Tenet:** Belief.

**Totalitarian:** A form of government in which one group maintains absolute control over citizens and all individual considerations are deemed as less important than the will of the state.

**Incumbent:** An obligation.

**Recent meetings in London:** A discussion among leaders from the United States and its European allies, including Great Britain, France, and West Germany.

**Nuclear proliferation:** An increase in the manufacturing of nuclear weapons.

**North-South problems:** Economic differences between more wealthy countries north of the equator (in Europe, Asia, and North America) and poorer countries south of the equator (nations in Africa, Asia, and South America).

**Strategic arms:** Missiles and other weapons aimed at strategic targets.

**Reciprocal:** Shared.

**Freeze:** Legally disallow access to money belonging to a party accused of illegal acts.

**Indian Ocean:** A reference to increased military build-up in areas around the Indian Ocean, including India, the Middle East, and Southeast Asia.

*Now, I believe in **detente** with the Soviet Union. To me it means progress toward peace. But the effects of detente should not be limited to our own two countries alone. We hope to persuade the Soviet Union that one country cannot impose its system of society upon another, either through direct military intervention or through the use of a client state's military force, as was the case with Cuban intervention in **Angola**.*

*Cooperation also implies obligation. We hope that the Soviet Union will join with us and other nations in playing a larger role in aiding the developing world, for common aid efforts will help us build a bridge of mutual confidence in one another.*

*Fourth, we are taking deliberate steps to improve the chances of lasting peace in the Middle East. Through wide-ranging consultation with leaders of the countries involved—Israel, Syria, Jordan, and Egypt—we have found some areas of agreement and some movement toward **consensus**. The negotiations must continue. . . .*

*And fifth, we are attempting, even at the risk of some friction with our friends, to reduce the danger of nuclear proliferation and the worldwide spread of conventional weapons. . . .*

*Let me conclude by summarizing: Our policy is based on an historical vision of America's role. Our policy is derived from a larger view of global change. Our policy is rooted in our moral values, which never change. Our policy is reinforced by our material wealth and by our military power. Our policy is designed to serve mankind. And it is a policy that I hope will make you proud to be Americans.* (Civnet [Web site])

## What happened next . . .

The Carter administration had mixed results in foreign policy. In 1977, the United States agreed to treaties that gave Panama sovereignty over the Panama Canal Zone (beginning on December 31, 1999), a strip of land that has a canal linking the Atlantic and Pacific oceans. Some Americans objected to relinquishing power over that important zone. In 1978, Carter helped bring the nations of Israel and Egypt into a peace agreement (signed in 1979) called the Camp David Accords

**Detente:** A relaxing of tensions between rival nations. A period of detente is marked by increased diplomatic, commercial, and cultural contact.

**Angola:** An African nation that was the site of a civil war. A commmunist faction was backed by the Soviet Union and Cuba.

**Consensus:** General agreement.

(Camp David is the Maryland site where Carter met with the leaders of those nations.) In 1979, Carter formally recognized the government of communist China, helping ease world tensions among large and powerful nations.

However, the 1979 Soviet Union invasion of Afghanistan led to tensions between the two nations. A pact reducing nuclear weapons was delayed. Among actions the Carter administration took against the Soviet Union was a boycott of American participation in the 1980 Summer Olympic Games held in Moscow in 1980. The Soviet Union and its allies responded by boycotting the 1984 Summer Olympic games in Los Angeles, California. And in 1979, a revolution in Iran toppled the leadership of the Shah of Iran, Mohammad Reza Pahlavi (1919–1980), who had been backed by the American government. After the United States allowed the Shah to enter a New York hospital for cancer treatment, fifty-two Americans were captured in Iran and held hostage for over a year.

After his presidency, Jimmy Carter became a more successful and respected international statesman in his pursuit of human rights. In addition to publicizing human rights through an organization he founded called the Carter Center, he helped negotiate treaties and agreements among foreign nations and supervised free elections in nations that only recently embraced democracy.

## Did you know . . .

- Jimmy Carter was able to pursue human rights issues far more effectively as an independent political figure through the Carter Center, established in 1982. The Carter Center, in partnership with Emory University in Atlanta, "is guided by a commitment to human rights and the alleviation of human suffering; it seeks to prevent and resolve conflicts, enhance freedom and democracy, and improve health." In 2000, for example, delegations from the Carter Center observed elections in such nations as Mexico, Peru, the Dominican Republic, and Mozambique. The delegation withdrew from Peru when it determined that fair elections were not possible under the conditions with which ballots would be counted.

## Where to Learn More

International Resource for Civic Education. "Human Rights and Foreign Policy (1977)." *Civnet.* [Online] http://www.civnet.org/resoures/teach/basic/part8/55.htm (accessed on October 31, 2000).

Muravchik, Joshua. *The Uncertain Crusade: Jimmy Carter and the Dilemmas of Human Rights Policy.* Lanham, MD: Hamilton Press, 1986.

Smith, Gaddis. *Morality, Reason, and Power: American Diplomacy in the Carter Years.* New York: Hill and Wang, 1986.

Thornton, Richard C. *The Carter Years: Toward a New Global Order.* New York: Paragon House, 1991.

# Ronald Reagan

### Fortieth president (1981–1989)

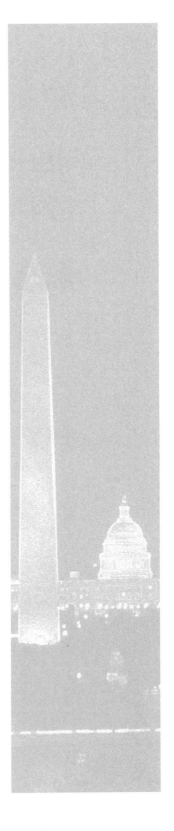

# Ronald Reagan

**Born February 6, 1911**
**Tampico, Illinois**

**Fortieth president of the United States**
**(1981–1989)**

**Changed the direction of government—**
**moved to decrease taxes and government**
**regulation and took a strong stand on**
**foreign relations**

From the time American colonists first began to consider breaking from England to form their own system of government, lively discussion has occurred among Americans over the extent of powers their government should have. When ratification (formal approval) of the Constitution was debated in the late 1780s, some notable patriots argued that the federal government it described would wield too much authority over individual states. States' rights versus federal power has remained a heated issue since the earliest days of the nation.

In the twentieth century, federal powers expanded in such areas as government regulation of business and banking and in the enactment of social welfare programs (government programs, supported by tax money, that provide financial assistance, training, and jobs). The New Deal program of **Franklin D. Roosevelt** (1882–1945; see entry in volume 4) during the 1930s, the Fair Deal program of **Harry S. Truman** (1884–1972; see entry in volume 4) during the 1940s, and the Great Society program of **Lyndon B. Johnson** (1908–1973; see entry in volume 5) during the 1960s—all were designed to confront social and economic problems.

"Government is not the solution to our problem, government is the problem."

*Ronald Reagan*

**Ronald Reagan.**
*Courtesy of the Library of Congress.*

## Fast Facts about Ronald Reagan

**Full name:** Ronald Wilson Reagan

**Born:** February 6, 1911

**Parents:** John Edward and Nelle Wilson Reagan

**Spouses:** Jane Wyman (1914– ; m. 1940, divorced 1948); Nancy Davis (1921– ; m. 1952)

**Children:** Maureen Elizabeth (1941– ); Christina (1947–1947); Michael Edward (adopted; 1945– ); Patricia Ann (1952– ); Ronald Prescott (1958– )

**Religion:** Disciples of Christ

**Education:** Eureka College (B.A., 1932)

**Occupations:** Rancher; army captain; radio sports commentator; actor

**Government positions:** California governor

**Political party:** Republican

**Dates as president:** January 20, 1981–January 20, 1985 (first term); January 20, 1985–January 20, 1989 (second term)

**Age upon taking office:** 69

In 1980, Ronald Reagan campaigned on the theme "Government is not the solution to our problem, government is the problem." By cutting taxes, ending several social welfare programs, and reducing government regulations on business, he reversed major political trends of the federal government in the twentieth century. His policies helped revive a sluggish American economy.

Reagan's policies and his speech-making skills inspired tremendous enthusiasm from his supporters that resulted in two landslide election victories. His opponents, meanwhile, pointed to enormous federal budget deficits (shortages; debts) during his administration. They also cited examples of business and administration officials who engaged in unlawful practices in the absence of federal supervision. Nevertheless, the nation's oldest president emerged vigorous and still popular after two terms. "I am the same man I was when I came to Washington," he said upon leaving office. "I believe the same things I believed when I came to Washington."

## Multimedia man

Ronald Wilson Reagan was born February 6, 1911, in Tampico, Illinois. He was the younger of two sons of Nelle and John Reagan. His father, a traveling shoe salesman, fell on hard times during the Great Depression (1929–41) and was an alcoholic. Reagan's mother provided a stable home life and taught her sons to read. The family lived in Dixon, Illinois, from the time Reagan was nine.

Reagan attended Eureka College near Peoria, Illinois. His leadership skills, athletic ability, and interest in acting were already in evidence. While majoring in economics, Reagan served as student body president, captained the swim team, played football, and was an actor in the school's theater. He became a local radio sportscaster in 1932 and moved on to a larger station, WHO, in Des Moines, Iowa, in 1936. One of his tasks was to "describe" Chicago Cubs baseball games; often that meant recreating the action from reports and making his broadcast sound as if it came live from the ballpark.

In 1937, while covering baseball spring training in California, Reagan took a screen test (a filmed audition). Signed to a contract, he went on to act in over fifty films—from *Boy Meets Girl* (1938) to *The Killers* (1964). His films included *King's Row* (1941), several westerns, and films in which he costarred with a chimpanzee named Bonzo (including *Bedtime for Bonzo,* 1951). Perhaps his best known film was *Knute Rockne: All American* (1940), in which he played Notre Dame football star George Gipp (1895–1920) and earned the nickname "the Gipper."

In 1941, Reagan married actress Jane Wyman (1914–  ). They had three children—Maureen, Michael, who was adopted, and Christina, who died three days after she was born. Reagan and Wyman divorced in 1949. During World War II (1939–45), Reagan served in the U.S. army and attained the rank of captain. Based in the states, Reagan was responsible for creating and editing films produced by the army.

In 1952, Reagan married actress Nancy Davis (1921–  ; see entry on **Nancy Reagan** in volume 5). They would have two children. The couple acted together in a movie, *Hellcats of the Navy* (1957)—Nancy's last film. Reagan's acting career

Ronald Reagan, in a scene from *Knute Rockne: All American,* in which he played college football star George Gipp. That role earned him the nickname "the Gipper."

*Reproduced by permission of Archive Photos.*

## Ronald Reagan Timeline

**1911:** Born in Illinois

**1938:** Appears in first motion picture

**1947–52, 1959:** Serves as president of the Screen Actors Guild

**1954:** Becomes television spokesman for the General Electric Company and makes speeches around the country promoting the American way

**1967–75:** Serves as California governor

**1976:** Falls eighty votes shy of becoming the Republican nominee for president

**1981–89:** Serves as fortieth U.S. president

**1981:** Wounded in assassination attempt

**1985:** The first of several summits with Soviet leader Mikhail Gorbachev takes place

**1986:** Iran-Contra scandal breaks

**1994:** Announces he has Alzheimer's disease

was less important to him by then as well. He had served six one-year terms as president of the Screen Actors Guild (a union for actors) from 1947 to 1952. (He was asked to serve again in 1959 to lead the Guild through a strike and negotiations with major movie corporations.) During his early terms as the Guild's president, Reagan testified before the House Committee on Un-American Activities, helping to uncover communist activities within the movie industry.

Reagan accepted a position as spokesperson for the General Electric Company in 1954. In addition to hosting a weekly television series, he traveled the country as a guest speaker promoting the virtues of the American social and political system. Reagan was officially a Democrat through the 1950s but his political views aligned closely with conservative Republicans of the era. Their pro-business agenda, support for increased military spending, and desire to limit federal programs would later be revived in the 1980s, when Reagan served as president.

## Political action

Reagan became an active Republican in 1962. A relaxed and persuasive speaker before the camera, he made a spirited television campaign speech in 1964 for Republican presidential nominee Barry Goldwater (1909–1998). Reagan's performance and belief in the conservative Republican cause led a group of California businessmen to suggest that he run for office.

Reagan triumphed soundly in the 1966 California gubernatorial (governor's) election over Edmund G. "Pat" Brown Sr. (1905–1996), a fairly popular incumbent (official currently holding office). The victory by nearly one million

## Words to Know

**Counterculture:** Behavior and values that reject conventional manners.

**Détente:** A relaxing of tensions between rival nations. A period of détente is marked by increased diplomatic, commercial, and cultural contact.

**Gubernatorial:** Relating to the office of governor.

**Incumbent:** The elected official currently holding office.

**Iran-Contra scandal:** A scandal during the Reagan administration during which government officials made illegal sales of weapons to Iran. Money made from those sales were diverted to secret funds provided to the Contras in the civil war in El Salvador. This was illegal, since Congress must authorize foreign aid.

**Permissive:** Tolerant of behavior and values that go against conventional manners.

**Presidential primaries:** Elections held in states to help determine the nominees of political parties for the general election. Each party disperses a certain number of delegates to each state. A candidate must win support of a majority of those delegates to win the party's presidential nomination. In states that hold primary elections, delegates are generally awarded to candidates based on the percentage of votes they accumulate; in some states, the leading vote-getter wins all of those state's delegates.

**Satellite nations:** Countries politically and economically dominated by a larger, more powerful nation.

**Social welfare:** A term that encompasses government programs that provide assistance, training, and jobs to people.

**Strategic Defense Initiative (SDI):** A proposed—but never approved—technological system (nicknamed "Star Wars," after the popular movie) that combined several advanced technology systems that could, in theory, detect and intercept missiles fired by enemies of the United States.

**Terrorist:** A person who uses acts of violence in an attempt to coerce by terror.

votes was at the time the largest ever over an incumbent governor in the history of the United States.

California had become a haven for counterculture youth who were rejecting the values of their parents' generation. California also had become a hotbed of protest over growing American involvement in the Vietnam War (1954–75). Reagan criticized such activities, finding them es-

*Reagan was a swimmer and a football player in college, and his early jobs included work as a sportscaster and a lifeguard.*

pecially improper on college campuses. He appealed to a broad spectrum of voters, from the wealthy to many working-class Democrats—a feat of coalition building (bringing people together) that Reagan would duplicate during his later presidential elections.

Facing a Democrat-led state legislature, Reagan acted gradually on his campaign pledges to slow the growth of state government and to lower property taxes. He tied those initiatives (legislative proposals) to balancing the state budget. In his program, some taxes were raised in order to provide the state with more money to balance the budget. At the same time, government programs were reduced. The state then dispersed much of the tax money it collected to local communities. Those communities took control of programs that had been previously administered by the state; leftover funds allowed local communities to lower property taxes.

Continuing to challenge protests on college campuses, Reagan reduced funding for the vast University of California system. Those funds were later increased as demonstrations became less common. Reagan's stance against the protest movement and his conservative values were drawing attention around the country. He was mentioned as a possible presidential candidate in 1968. However, former vice president and 1960 presidential candidate **Richard Nixon** (1913–1994; see entry in volume 5) began campaigning early and aggressively, and he locked up the party's nomination.

Reelected governor of California in 1970, Reagan confronted welfare (government assistance to poor people), another area of government spending. Citing vast fraud (cheating) in the system, Reagan introduced a program in which the number of people who qualified for welfare was greatly reduced. Those who did qualify generally received more financial assistance over a limited period of time. Reagan cut taxes further and restricted the state government's power to regulate business.

## Riding a wave

Reagan was appealing to Republicans who believed that their party should take stands on social issues as well as

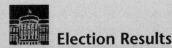

# Election Results

## 1980

| Presidential / Vice presidential candidates | Popular votes | Presidential electoral votes |
|---|---|---|
| Ronald Reagan / George Bush (Republican) | 43,904,153 | 483 |
| Jimmy Carter / Walter Mondale (Democratic) | 35,483,883 | 49 |
| John Anderson / VP nominee was not chosen (National Unity) | 5,720,060 | 0 |

*Incumbent president Carter shook off a challenge by Massachusetts senator Edward Kennedy to win the Democratic nomination; Republican Reagan's main competition was from former CIA director and ambassador to China Bush (whom he chose as his running mate) and Illinois congressman John Anderson (who ran in the general election as an independent).*

## 1984

| Presidential / Vice presidential candidates | Popular votes | Presidential electoral votes |
|---|---|---|
| Ronald Reagan / George Bush (Republican) | 54,455,075 | 525 |
| Walter Mondale / Geraldine Ferraro (Democratic) | 37,577,185 | 13 |

*This election was most notable for former vice president Mondale's selection of New York representative Ferraro as his running mate, the first female from a major party to run on a national ticket.*

limit government programs. They were upset that America had become a more permissive (tolerant; thoughtlessly relaxed about moral values) society beginning in the 1960s. Increasingly, conservative religious groups were gaining political strength. They wanted to contest Supreme Court rulings that disallowed prayer in public schools and the 1973 *Roe v. Wade* ruling that overturned most state laws banning abortion (the purposeful ending of a pregnancy). Conservative religious groups found a champion in Reagan, who entered the race for president in 1976.

Reagan challenged the sitting president, **Gerald R. Ford** (1913– ; see entry in volume 5), who had assumed office following the resignation of President Richard Nixon in 1974. Ford battled a Democrat-controlled Congress over cuts he wanted in social programs and taxes. Reagan promised more aggressive action in those areas. Ford was more moderate as well on social issues. During a closely fought campaign for the Republican nomination, Reagan won support in several southern and western states. He lost the nomination to Ford by a mere eighty votes. When Ford failed to win the presidential election of 1976, Reagan emerged as a frontrunner for the Republican nomination in 1980.

Reagan prevailed in the 1980 Republican presidential primaries (elections held in states to help determine the nominees of political parties for the general election). His main two opponents were **George Bush** (1924– ; see entry in volume 5), who eventually agreed to be Reagan's running mate, and John Anderson (1922– ), who went on to run as an independent in the general election. Incumbent president **Jimmy Carter** (1924– ; see entry in volume 5) was beset by difficulties and low approval ratings. The U.S. economy was stagnant, people were upset over continued high fuel costs, and an October 1979 raid on the American embassy in Iran resulted in fifty-two Americans being taken hostage—an action supported by the Iranian government. Negotiations failed to win their release, as did a risky rescue mission. As election day in 1980 approached, the hostages were still held captive. (See box in **Jimmy Carter** entry in volume 5.)

Reagan promised to stimulate the economy by providing tax cuts. He planned to downsize government programs while greatly increasing military spending. During televised debates between the two candidates, Reagan appeared polished and relaxed while dismissing Carter's policies (often saying, "There you go again") for conserving natural resources, reducing energy consumption, and pursuing détente (better relations) with the Soviet Union. Promising to take a hard-line foreign policy, reduce regulations on business, and dismantle many government-sponsored programs, Reagan was able to inspire the electorate (voters). Along with the coalition he had developed of big business and religious conservative supporters, Reagan attracted a fair portion of working-class Democrats. He won fifty-one percent of the popular vote and a landslide (489 to 49 votes) in the Electoral College (For more information in the Electoral College, see boxes in **George W. Bush** entry in volume 5.) Riding along his wave of popularity, Republicans gained a majority in the Senate for the first time since 1954.

## Reaganomics

 In his inaugural address (see **Ronald Reagan** primary source entry in volume 5), Reagan announced "an era of national renewal." The release of American hostages by Iran occurred on that day, raising national spirits. Just two months into office, however, Reagan was shot by John Hinckley Jr. (1955– ), who was later judged insane. Concern for the president soon turned to relief as Reagan made limited public appearances and displayed his usual cheery nature during a recovery period of several weeks. (Ever the humorist, he was quoted as saying to his wife, "Honey, I forgot to duck." Just before being treated, he reportedly said to a doctor, "I hope you are a Republican.")

 The period of national economic recovery took much longer. At a low point in October 1982, eleven percent of Americans were unemployed. Battling with a Democrat-controlled House of Representatives to initiate his cuts of government social programs, Reagan was able to push through the

President Reagan waves to onlookers just moments before being shot on March 30, 1981. Press secretary James Brady (bald man behind and to the left of Reagan); Washington, D.C., police officer Thomas Delahanty (first policeman from right); and Secret Service agent Timothy McCarthy (far right, looking at Reagan) were also wounded.
*Reproduced by permission of the Corbis Corporation.*

# Ronald Reagan Administration

**Administration Dates**
January 20, 1981–January 20, 1985
January 20, 1985–January 20, 1989

**Vice President**
George Bush (1981–89)

**Cabinet**

**Secretary of State**
Alexander M. Haig Jr. (1981–82)
George P. Shultz (1982–89)

**Secretary of the Treasury**
Donald T. Regan (1981–85)
James A. Baker III (1985–88)
Nicholas F. Brady (1988–89)

**Attorney General**
William F. Smith (1981–85)
Edwin Meese III (1985–88)
Richard L. Thornburgh (1988–89)

**Secretary of the Interior**
James G. Watt (1981–83)
William P. Clark (1983–85)
Donald P. Hodel (1985–89)

**Secretary of Agriculture**
John R. Block (1981–86)
Richard E. Lyng (1986–89)

**Secretary of Labor**
Raymond J. Donovan (1981–85)

William E. Brock III (1985–87)
Ann Dore McLaughlin (1987–89)

**Secretary of Commerce**
Malcolm Baldrige (1981–87)
C. William Verity (1987–89)

**Secretary of Defense**
Caspar W. Weinberger (1981–87)
Frank G. Carlucci (1987–89)

**Secretary of Housing and Urban Development**
Samuel R. Pierce Jr. (1981–89)

**Secretary of Transportation**
Andrew L. Lewis Jr. (1981–83)
Elizabeth H. Dole (1983–87)
James H. Burnley IV (1987–89)

**Secretary of Energy**
James B. Edwards (1981–82)
Donald P. Hodel (1982–85)
John S. Herrington (1985–89)

**Secretary of Health and Human Services**
Richard S. Schweiker (1981–83)
Margaret M. Heckler (1983–85)
Otis R. Bowen (1985–89)

**Secretary of Education**
Terrel H. Bell (1981–85)
William J. Bennett (1985–88)
Lauro F. Cavazos (1988–89)

Economic Recovery Tax Act of 1981. Along with lowering taxes, he cut federal spending for a variety of programs, from job training, to college student loans, to Medicare coverage (medical insurance for senior citizens). Many government restrictions on business were eased, while organized labor was dealt a blow when Reagan fired 11,800 air traffic controllers who went on strike. Calling the strike illegal because it endangered public safety, Reagan took away the strikers' union certification. Very few strikers ever returned to work.

The government deregulation of business placed fewer restrictions on business expansion. Many large companies began merging or were bought by larger corporations, which helped fuel a stock market surge: Investors were rewarded when stocks they owned in such corporations increased in value.

The president's pro-business policies, dubbed "Reaganomics," were based on "supply-side" theories developed by such economists as Milton Friedman (1912– ). (In supply-side economics, tax cuts provide consumers with more money to spend, and businesses are encouraged to increase production of goods.) By 1983, the American economy recovered and continued growing for the next six years. There were some difficulties, however. For example, less economically advantaged people generally missed out on the growing prosperity, having little money with which to invest. Fewer restrictions on investing money led some stockbrokers to make risky investments or to take advantage of relaxed government monitoring of their activities. As investors consistently bought and sold stocks at ever increasing prices, many stocks became overvalued. That reality struck hard on October 19, 1987, when the stock market plummeted (fell quickly).

As a whole, stocks lost a whopping thirty-six percent in value during that month. Many people lost money, but the downturn soon balanced out as stocks returned to more realistic values. The economy continued to grow through 1988, Reagan's final full year in office.

## Peace through strength

Military spending increased dramatically during the Reagan years. The spending helped encourage the expansion of military-based industries. That spending also increased the national debt: reductions in taxes, a growing trade deficit (imports of goods far outnumbered exports), and military spending combined to place the government in debt, to which the

*Reagan was known as a pro-business president, but he had plenty of experience on the other side of the negotiating table. As student body president of Eureka College, he led a student strike against tuition hikes, and he later served as president of the Screen Actors Guild, a union representing film actors.*

*While Reagan was in office, two elderly leaders of the Soviet Union died within a year. When asked at a press conference why he did not pursue stronger diplomatic ties with the Soviet Union, Reagan once remarked that he wanted to meet with Soviet leaders "but they keep dying on me."*

Reagan administration responded by cutting more government social programs.

The largest amount of defense spending was targeted for the Strategic Defense Initiative (SDI), a proposed technological system popularly called "Star Wars" after the 1977 movie. The SDI system combined several advanced technology systems that could, at least in theory, detect and intercept missiles fired by enemies of the United States. The entire proposal was never approved by Congress. Opponents cited extreme costs and uncertainty over the practical use of the system.

Increased military spending reflected Reagan's foreign policy approach of "peace through strength"—the belief that superior military power would make American foes (defined as those who undermined freedom) reluctant to try to expand their power over their own people or other nations. Reagan was specifically targeting the Soviet Union, which he called an "evil empire" in speeches during 1982 and 1983 before small groups and Great Britain's Parliament. Reagan moved the United States away from the policy of détente with the Soviet Union to be consistent in its demands that the Soviet Union extend freedom to people under its domination. A series of summits between the Reagan administration and Soviet leaders eventually resulted in a 1987 treaty scaling back nuclear weapons.

Meanwhile, the Soviet Union's grip on its satellite nations—countries politically and economically dominated by the larger, more powerful Soviet Union—was weakening. Tired of Soviet domination, groups of people within such nations as Poland, Czechoslovakia, and East Germany were rallying fellow citizens to demand more democratic systems. The Soviet Union itself became more reform-minded through its leader, Mikhail Gorbachev (1931– ; see box). Between 1985 and 1990, he introduced *perestroika* ("restructuring") of the economy and *glasnost* ("openness") in political and cultural affairs. By the end of the decade, communist states allied with the Soviet Union began transforming into democracies.

Meanwhile, the United States was involved in a series of military actions. A revolution in the Central American nation of Nicaragua in 1979 had brought a Marxist regime into power. (Marxists believe in the political and economic theories of German philosopher Karl Marx [1818–1883], who promoted socialism, which advocates the government control of property and production.) Reagan cut aid to that nation and began supporting a group (called Contras) fighting a similar rebellion (against a group called the Sandinistas) in El Salvador, a neighbor to Nicaragua. The president sent U.S. marines into the Middle East nation of Lebanon to stem the tide of international terrorist activities. Over two hundred marines stationed there were killed in a subsequent terrorist attack. Days later, the president ordered marines to the Caribbean island of Grenada to restore the government there that had been overthrown by rebels.

The north African nation of Libya was accused of encouraging terrorist activities that included a takeover of an Italian ocean liner in 1985 in which an American was killed; hijacking an airplane, redirecting it to Beirut, Lebanon, and holding hostages there for thirty-nine days; bombings in airports in Rome, Italy, and Vienna, Austria, that killed several people, including five American tourists; and a bomb that exploded in a German dance club frequented by American servicemen. The Reagan administration ordered retaliatory (revenge-like) bombing of sites in several Libyan locales.

## "The Great Communicator"

Reagan's popularity remained steadily high following his inauguration. Opponents were concerned with the loss of social programs that had helped those less fortunate, with the easing of government regulations that protected the environment, and with the continued buildup of the military. Reagan was increasingly seen as a spokesperson for powerful conservative groups.

Reagan's conservatism was demonstrated in his selection of judges to fill vacancies across the country. He influenced federal court decisions by appointing three conservative Supreme Court justices—Sandra Day O'Connor (1930– ; see box), the first female to serve on the court; Antonin Scalia (1936– ); and William Rehnquist (1924– ) as chief justice in 1986. Scalia was named after two previous appointments failed to pass Congress.

The growth of the economy, firm support by his backers, continued appeal to working-class Americans, and Reagan's upbeat speeches (he was nicknamed "the Great Com-

*Jelly beans, Ronald Reagan's favorite snack, were always in plentiful supply for the president's meetings.*

**Mikhail Gorbachev**

Mikhail Gorbachev (pronounced mih-KILE GOR-buh-choff) was born on March 2, 1931, in the tiny Russian farm village of Privolnoe. He was two years old when Communist dictator Joseph Stalin (1879–1953) ordered all private farms seized and placed under government control. Peasant farmers were forced to work on collective farms (a group of small farms). The government dictated what would be grown, how much of it, and what the farmers would be paid. Many members of Gorbachev's family worked on the collective farms.

In 1950, Gorbachev entered the distinguished Moscow State University, where he received a broad education. While in school, he met and married a philosophy student, Raisa Maksimovna Titorenko (1932–1999). He also joined the Communist Party. After graduating in 1955, he went to the city of Stavropol to work for the Party. He rose through the leadership ranks during the next fifteen years to become the Party leader in Stavropol in 1970. At the same time, he was elected to the Supreme Soviet, the highest legislative body in the Soviet Union.

Yuri Andropov (1914–1984), head of the KGB (secret police), was from Stavropol. He took Gorbachev under his wing and named him agricultural secretary of the Communist Party in 1978. Just two years later, Gorbachev joined the Politburo, the ruling body of the Party. His high standing among the Communists at this time was unusual because of his age. While most lead-

ers were in their seventies, Gorbachev was under fifty. Andropov became general secretary (leader) of the Party in 1982 following the death of Leonid Brezhnev (1906–1982). As Andropov's key assistant, Gorbachev took control of the running of the economy.

When Andropov died in 1984, Konstantin Chernenko (1911–1985) was chosen instead of Gorbachev to become the new leader. But when Chernenko died in early 1985, Gorbachev was finally appointed general secretary of the Communist Party, making him the leader of his country. Gorbachev immediately began a campaign of reforms in the Soviet Union. He forced many conservative Communist leaders out of government and replaced them with younger members who shared his views. He began policies called *perestroika* ("restructuring") and *glasnost* ("openness") that removed government controls over the economy and allowed the Soviet people to discuss openly the problems facing their country.

Seeking peace abroad and at home, Gorbachev and American president Ronald Reagan signed a treaty in 1987 limiting the number of nuclear weapons each country could have. Gorbachev decided to end the war in Afghanistan, which had pitted anticommunist Afghans against their government and the Soviet Union since 1978. By 1989, all Soviet troops were removed from that country. For all of his peace efforts, Gorbachev was awarded the Nobel Peace Prize in 1990.

**Mikhail Gorbachev and Ronald Reagan in December 1987.** *Reproduced by permission of Archive Photos.*

Gorbachev's most important change in the Soviet Union came in 1989 when he allowed other political parties to run against the Communists in general elections. Communists had controlled the Soviet Union since the Russian Revolution in 1917. The Communists lost their power and Gorbachev separated himself from them by taking the position of Soviet president. The Communist dictatorship had ended.

With the weakening of communism in Eastern Europe, many countries and ethnic groups wanted their independence. In 1989, East and West Germany were reunited. In 1990, Lithuania became the first of the Baltic states to declare its independence from the Soviet Union. In the Soviet-controlled republics of Armenia and Georgia, ethnic wars broke out. Gorbachev

sought to maintain some control over these areas, but his own position at home was in trouble. His plan to gradually release government control of farms and industry was not happening fast enough for the Soviet people. Because they had suffered in poverty for many years, they wanted quicker reforms. Boris Yeltsin (1931– ), a chief critic of Gorbachev, was elected president of the Russian Republic in June 1991.

Conservative Politburo members thought Gorbachev was giving away too much power. In August 1991, they kidnapped him in hopes of regaining government control. But the coup (overthrow of the government) failed after four days when Yeltsin rallied the Russian people against the Communist leaders. Gorbachev returned to Moscow, though Yeltsin now had the support of the majority of people. Gorbachev then dissolved the Communist Party, admitting later that the defeat of communism was a victory for common sense, reason, democracy, and common human values.

Gorbachev granted independence to the remaining republics that had been controlled by the Soviet Union. On December 8, 1991, a new economic federation—the Commonwealth of Independent States—was formed among those republics. Gorbachev resigned the office of president, becoming a private citizen. At midnight on December 31, 1991, the red Communist flag with its gold hammer and sickle was lowered in Moscow and the Union of Soviet Socialist Republics came to an end.

## Sandra Day O'Connor

Sandra Day O'Connor was born on March 26, 1930, in El Paso, Texas. The oldest of three daughters of Harry and Ada Mae Day, she was raised on the family ranch in southeastern Arizona. Educational opportunities in the area were limited, so O'Connor was sent to live with her maternal grandmother in El Paso. There, she attended a private school for girls before studying at Austin High School. After graduating in 1946, she studied economics at Stanford University in Stanford, California. After taking a law course in her senior year, O'Connor entered Stanford Law School in 1950, graduating third in her class two years later. While at Stanford, she met John Jay O'Connor III, whom she married soon after graduation.

Although qualified as a lawyer, O'Connor had difficulty finding a job. She worked as a deputy county attorney in San Mateo, California, while waiting for her husband to graduate from law school. When he was drafted for military service as an army lawyer in Frankfurt, West Germany, O'Connor followed him. She worked in Frankfurt as a civilian lawyer for the U.S. Army Quartermaster Corps. Returning to

Phoenix, Arizona, in 1957, she opened her own law practice. Between 1960 and 1965, O'Connor devoted herself to raising her three sons, doing volunteer work, and serving on the Maricopa County Board of Adjustments and Appeals and the Governor's Committee on Marriage and Family.

O'Connor returned to the legal profession as assistant attorney general for Arizona before being elected to the state senate in 1969 on the Republican ticket. While serving three terms in the senate, she became concerned with sex discrimination and the problems of families living in poverty. As state senator, she pushed for revision of discriminatory Arizona laws, developing legislation that allowed women to jointly manage property held with their husbands. When O'Connor became the majority leader of the Arizona senate in 1972, she was the first woman to hold that office in any state senate. In 1974, after serving five years in the senate, she decided to return to the courts of law.

After winning election to the Superior Court of Maricopa County, she served for four years as a trial judge, earning a reputation for toughness combined with gen-

municator") were reflected in the 1984 presidential election. Reagan was reelected with the largest total of electoral votes ever, 525. He won forty-nine states, compared with one state (Massachusetts) and the District of Columbia for the Democratic candidate, former vice president Walter Mondale (1928– ), who won only thirteen electoral votes.

**Sandra Day O'Connor.**
*Courtesy of the Library of Congress.*

uine concern. In 1979, Arizona governor Bruce Babbitt (1938– ) named O'Connor to the Arizona Court of Appeals.

When campaigning for the presidency in 1980, Ronald Reagan pledged that he would appoint a woman to fill one of the first vacated Supreme Court seats. When Associate Justice Potter Stewart (1915–1985) announced his retirement in June 1981, the search for a successor began. It ended with President Reagan's nomination of O'Connor on July 7, 1981. After her nomination was confirmed by the Senate Judiciary Committee, she became the first woman in history to serve on the Supreme Court. At the time of her appointment, O'Connor was praised for her understanding of women's issues, an area of knowledge that many felt the Supreme Court was lacking. Since her appointment, she has won a reputation as a judicial conservative who upholds the law rather than rewrites it.

O'Connor worked hard to try to eliminate legal impediments that challenged the progress of women to meet their career goals. She credited the rise of women's demands for equal opportunity since the 1960s for helping bring about social changes that made it possible for her to become a Supreme Court justice. O'-Connor continues to be recognized as an accomplished leader and a fair-minded, highly competent judge. In 1993, the *American Bar Association Journal* called her arguably the most influential woman official in the United States. In August 1997, the American Bar Association (ABA) awarded O'Connor its ABA Medal.

A highlight of his second term was the passage in 1986 of a sweeping tax law that, among other effects, allowed millions of low-income families to forego paying taxes. In 1987, Reagan and Soviet president Mikhail Gorbachev signed a treaty limiting the number of nuclear weapons each country could have.

**Ronald Reagan speaks at his State of the Union address on February 4, 1986. Behind him are Vice President George Bush (left) and Speaker of the House Tip O'Neill.**
*Reproduced by permission of the Corbis Corporation.*

Still, opponents of Reagan's policies became increasingly vocal. The 1986 midterm elections brought more Democrats into the House, and the party recaptured the majority of seats in the Senate. Congress hampered many of the president's attempts at further legislation. A result was often bitter ill will between the nation's two major parties that would continue on through the end of the century.

In 1986, newspapers began reporting that Reagan's administration had made illegal sales of weapons to Iran. Additional stories traced money from those sales to secret funds provided to the Contras in the civil war in El Salvador. Reagan angrily denied both charges. But a congressional investigation in 1987 revealed that Reagan administration officials had arranged arms sales to Iran. Since 1979, when Americans were taken hostage in Iran, Congress had prohibited diplomatic and trade efforts with that country. It was discovered that the sale was made to help influence a political group based in Iran that had ties with another group in Lebanon holding Americans hostage. Providing funds to Contra leaders constituted another illegal act, since Congress must authorize such foreign aid.

The nationally televised Iran-Contra hearings revealed an administration in which some officials were acting without supervision. Despite claims that he did not remember participating in the events, evidence suggested that Reagan had authorized the arms sales. Even if he did not know about the diversion of funds, opponents charged, the president had been misinformed or was unaware about events in his own administration. Two Reagan officials were found guilty of illegal activities. Reagan, the committee concluded, "clearly failed to take care that the laws be faithfully executed."

Reagan's last year in office was unremarkable. His administration weathered the stock market crash of 1987 and the Iran-Contra scandal. His support remained steady, even as Americans grew increasingly frustrated with partisanship in Congress. Reagan, meanwhile, left office after two terms as, he later noted, "the same man I was when I came to Washington." During the time in between, the United States had regained economic strength. His vice president, George Bush, was elected president in 1988.

In 1990, Reagan published his autobiography, *An American Life*. He opened the Ronald Reagan Presidential Library in California in 1991. Only in 1994 did he begin to slow down. He was discovered to be suffering from Alzheimer's disease, a degenerative affliction that affects the brain. The Reagans immediately helped found the Ronald and Nancy Reagan Research Institute as part of the National Alzheimer's Association. In 2000, the House of Representatives voted to award the Congressional Gold Medal to Reagan and his wife.

**Former president Ronald Reagan hammers away at remnants of the Berlin Wall in September 1990, less than a year after Germans began to dismantle the famous symbol of communism.**
*Reproduced by permission of Archive Photos.*

## Legacy

During the administration of Ronald Reagan, fifty years of progressive social legislation that began with Franklin Roosevelt's New Deal programs was turned aside. Government spending—except for defense—was curtailed, and taxes were cut. The deregulation of business encouraged a rush of corporate mergers and buyouts that continued through the end of the century. Having selected one third of the Supreme Court justices in place when he left office, Reagan ensured that conservative views would be influential in that body into the new century.

Large increases in military spending and imbalanced trade created a huge national debt that became an issue in the 1988 and 1992 presidential elections. As the country prospered at the end of the century and vastly increased trade, the national debt finally began to decrease. Some of the more harmful effects of deregulation—those that had fueled the stock market crash of 1987 (and another in 1989)—were later addressed.

During the Reagan years, the Cold War, which had dominated American foreign policy since the end of World War II, began to wane. Supporters credit his hard-line stances with the Soviet Union and his support for American military buildup as major factors. A more general historical assessment emphasizes actions and events within the Soviet Union and surrounding nations it had dominated as key reasons for the thawing of the Cold War.

The issue of the extent of influence the federal government should wield continued to be a major source of debate in subsequent presidential elections. The Reagan administration clearly pursued policies that deemphasized the role of the federal government. Republican presidential candidates in the next four elections campaigned on that theme with moderate variations.

## A Selection of Reagan Landmarks

**Ronald Reagan Birthplace.** 111 Main St., Tampico, IL 61283. (815) 438–2815. President Reagan was born in the bedroom of this small apartment. A museum can be found on the first floor.

**Ronald Reagan Boyhood Home.** 816 S. Hennepin Ave., Dixon, IL 61021. (815) 288-3404. The Reagan family lived here in the 1920s. Reagan memorabilia is on display in the visitors center. See http://dixonillinois.com/ (accessed on November 1, 2000).

**Ronald Reagan Presidential Library and Museum.** 40 Presidential Drive, Simi Valley, CA 93065. (800) 410-8354. The library and museum contain presidential documents and photographs, as well as artifacts of the former president from childhood through the presidency. The library is one of ten official presidential libraries in the country. See http://www.reaganfoundation.org/ and http://www.reagan.utexas.edu/ (accessed on October 24, 2000).

## Where to Learn More

Blumenthal, Sidney, and Thomas Byrne Edsall. *The Reagan Legacy*. New York: Pantheon Books, 1988.

Cannon, Lou. *President Reagan: The Role of a Lifetime*. New York: Simon & Schuster, 1991. Reprint, New York: Public Affairs, 2000.

Eureka College. *Ronald "Dutch" Reagan and Eureka College: The Foundations of Leadership*. [Online] http://Reagan.Eureka.edu/ (accessed on October 24, 2000).

Gorbachev, Mikhail. *Gorbachev: On My Country and the World*. New York: Columbia University Press, 2000.

Herda, D. J. *Sandra Day O'Connor: Independent Thinker*. Springfield, NJ: Enslow, 1995.

Huber, Peter W. *Sandra Day O'Connor*. New York: Chelsea House, 1990.

Judson, Karen. *Ronald Reagan*. Springfield, NJ: Enslow, 1997.

Pemberton, William E. *Exit with Honor: The Life and Presidency of Ronald Reagan*. Armonk, NY: M. E. Sharpe, 1997.

Reagan, Ronald. *An American Life*. New York: Simon and Schuster, 1990.

*Ronald Reagan Home Page*. [Online] http://reagan.webteamone.com/ (accessed on November 1, 2000).

*Ronald Reagan Presidential Foundation*. [Online] http://www.reaganfoundation.org/ (accessed on October 24, 2000).

*Ronald Reagan Presidential Library*. [Online] http://www.reagan.utexas.edu/ (accessed on October 24, 2000).

*Ronald Reagan . . . The Official Site.* [Online] http://www.ronaldreagan. com/ (accessed on November 1, 2000).

Schwartzberg, Renée. *Ronald Reagan.* New York: Chelsea House, 1991.

Sullivan, George. *Mikhail Gorbachev.* New York: J. Messner, 1988.

Wills, Gary. *Reagan's America: Innocents at Home.* Garden City, NY: Doubleday, 1987.

# Nancy Reagan

**Born July 6, 1921**
**New York, New York**

**Enjoyed being in the limelight and used her influence to promote the "Just Say No" antidrug campaign**

N ancy Reagan's eight years as first lady passed through three distinct stages: an initial period of serving as hostess at elegant parties, refurbishing the White House living quarters, and expanding the White House fine dinnerware collection; a second phase in which she became more active in social causes, such as the "Just Say No!" antidrug campaign; and a final phase in which she became protective of her husband **Ronald Reagan** (1911– ; see entry in volume 5) during the controversies of the Iran-Contra investigation.

A devoted couple, the Reagans helped each other through the best and worst of times. Nancy helped inspire her husband's fighting spirit as he recovered from a gunshot wound in 1981 following a failed assassination attempt. She was at his side as he recovered from surgeries in July 1985 and January 1987.

After riding off together into the sunset—the two former actors returned to their California ranch—the Reagans enjoyed a peaceful retirement. That time was made difficult as the former president was diagnosed with Alzheimer's disease, a degenerative affliction of the brain. The Reagans immediate-

"My life really began when I married my husband."

*Nancy Reagan*

**Nancy Reagan.**
*Courtesy of the Library of Congress.*

ly helped found the Ronald and Nancy Reagan Research Institute in 1994 as part of the National Alzheimer's Association.

## The theater life

Nancy Reagan was born Anne Frances Robbins in New York City on July 6, 1921. She was nicknamed Nancy by her mother, Edith Luckett, a theater actress. Nancy's parents separated when she was two. After that, Nancy saw little of her father, Kenneth Robbins, a New Jersey automobile dealer. Her mother often toured the country with acting companies, and Nancy came under the care of an aunt and uncle who lived in Bethesda, Maryland.

Edith Luckett would visit her daughter as often as possible, especially when she was acting in plays on Broadway (New York City's theater district). As a child, Nancy enjoyed dressing in costumes and pretending to be an actress, but not until after she learned an important lesson about the illusion of theater. She attended a play in which her mother's character died. Nancy began weeping in the audience, and her mother waved to her from the stage to show that she was simply pretending.

In May 1929, Edith Luckett married Loyal Davis, a neurosurgeon and chairman of the Department of Surgery at Northwestern University near Chicago, Illinois. Luckett gave up acting, and Nancy was adopted by her stepfather, from whom she got the name Davis. Nancy lived with her parents in a large Chicago apartment on Lakeside Drive. The Davises enjoyed a strong family life.

Growing up in wealthy surroundings, Nancy learned to like fine clothes and dining out with her parents. They were often joined by socialites and theater people. She attended a private school, where she was president of the drama club, and went on to Smith College in Northampton, Massachusetts, beginning in 1939. Majoring in drama, she graduated in 1943 and returned to Chicago.

While her stepfather served in the U.S. Army medical corps, Nancy worked briefly as a nurse's aide with her mother and acted in local theater. Offered a small part in a play called *Ramshackle Inn* that opened on Broadway in January 1944, Nancy moved to New York.

The play ran for six months. Nancy remained in New York, continuing to act in small parts, working as a model, and meeting many of her mother's friends, including actor Clark Gable (1901–1960). When she was invited west to California in 1949 to take a screen test (a filmed audition), she arranged through her mother's friend, actor Spencer Tracy (1900–1967), to have a well-respected, professional director, George Cukor (1899–1983), prepare her screen test. She went on to act in eleven films.

## Nancy and Ronnie

In the fall of 1949, she met actor Ronald Reagan, who had recently been divorced from actress Jane Wyman (1914– ). Nancy knew him from his films and they began a friendship. When Nancy learned that her name had appeared on a list of movie industry people suspected of being communist, she had a mutual acquaintance call Reagan, then head of the Screen Actors Guild, to investigate. Reagan checked into the matter and reported through the friend that Nancy was not a suspect. When Nancy insisted that Reagan call her directly, their phone conversation led to a date.

Their romance developed gradually. Reagan was still upset over his divorce, but he found a companion in Nancy. He was extremely talkative and she enjoyed listening to him. They became engaged in February 1952. After postponing marriage twice because they both were working on films, the couple was married on March 4, 1952, with actor William Holden (1918–1981) serving as best man. Later that year, their first child, Patricia Ann ("Patti"; 1952– ), was born. A son, Ronald Prescott (1958– ), was born in 1958. Reagan had had three children during his first marriage (one was adopted and one died in infancy).

The film careers of the Reagans were both winding down in the 1950s. Reagan took a position as spokesperson for the General Electric Company. He hosted a popular television program sponsored by the company, and he traveled around the country making speeches on behalf of business and the American way. The Reagans bought a ranch and moved among a wealthy circle of friends in southern California. They costarred together in a film, *Hellcats of the Navy,* in 1957. It was Nancy's last film work.

Reagan became more politically active during the 1960s. His last film, *The Killers,* was released in 1964. That same year, he made a campaign speech on television for Republican presidential candidate Barry Goldwater (1909–1998). Goldwater lost the election, but Reagan impressed California Republicans enough to become their candidate for governor in 1966. He won the election.

## Governor's wife

Nancy was never deeply interested in politics. She traveled with her husband to campaign appearances and speeches. Her adoring gaze upon her husband as he spoke was often noted by political commentators, and Reagan's advisors asked her to tone it down. The Reagans were a good match: He loved to talk, and she loved to listen.

As California's first lady, Nancy Reagan oversaw the renovation of the state capitol in Sacramento. She visited state hospitals, particularly as wounded servicemen were returning from the Vietnam War (1954–75). During the war, she wrote a syndicated column, donating her salary to the National League of Families of American Prisoners and Missing in Action in Southeast Asia. Mrs. Reagan made regular visits to hospitals and homes for the elderly as well as to schools for physically and emotionally handicapped children.

After observing participants in the Foster Grandparent Program, which brought together senior citizens and handicapped children, she soon became a spokesperson for the cause. Later, as first lady of the United States, Mrs. Reagan continued to help expand the program on a national level.

She provided advice to the governor on the people he selected for his staff and helped arrange his schedule. The Reagans hosted many festive events in Sacramento in the north and in the Los Angeles area of southern California.

## In Washington, D.C.

After Ronald Reagan won the presidential election of 1980, Nancy arranged glittering social occasions where men wore tuxedos and women long, floor-length gowns. Her expensive tastes in parties, White House dinnerware, gowns,

jewelry, and furnishings met with some criticism. President Reagan was trimming the federal budget, while White House social spending was growing larger. Nancy Reagan countered by claiming her gowns were on loan from designers and were donated to museums after she wore them. Early press troubles with extravagance were not helped by her publishing an autobiography, *Nancy* (1980), *before* she became first lady.

Those initial concerns soon passed. Her involvement with the foster grandparents program and the fight against drug abuse were praised. She became a spokesperson for the "Just Say No!" campaign that advised young people against drugs through television and press campaigns. She supported private efforts, as opposed to government programs, to help combat drug abuse. In April 1985, Mrs. Reagan expanded her drug awareness campaign to an international level by inviting first ladies from around the world to talks on drug abuse among youths. During the fortieth anniversary of the United Nations in 1985, Mrs. Reagan hosted thirty first ladies for a second international drug conference.

Ronald and Nancy Reagan
enjoy horseback riding at
their ranch in Santa Barbara,
California.
*Reproduced by permission of
Archive Photos.*

## Tough times

Nancy Reagan also helped her husband through recovery of serious medical problems: He was wounded in an assassination attempt in 1981 and had colon surgery in 1985
and prostate surgery in 1987. The first lady herself underwent
surgery to treat breast cancer in 1987. She became increasingly involved in helping direct her husband's administration
during his second term. She preferred a more relaxed schedule
for the president, particularly after his surgeries, that concentrated on the most significant issues to address. As the Iran-
Contra scandal entangled the Reagan administration, she became angry with staff members whom she felt had not helped
better prepare him for answering questions from the press.

Nancy Reagan enjoyed being first lady but welcomed
retirement following the end of the president's second term
early in 1989. She quickly established the Nancy Reagan Foundation to continue her campaign to educate people about the

dangers of substance abuse. In 1994, the Nancy Reagan Foundation joined forces with the BEST Foundation For A Drug-Free Tomorrow. The groups developed the Nancy Reagan Afterschool Program to promote drug prevention for youth. Mrs. Reagan's memoir, *My Turn,* was published in 1989.

The Reagans returned to their California ranch, where the former president remained active before beginning to suffer the effects of Alzheimer's disease. The couple remained devoted to each other as Reagan began suffering more profound effects of the disease. The Reagans founded the Ronald and Nancy Reagan Research Institute as part of the National Alzheimer's Association in 1994. The institute helps focus attention on the disease and provide information about the disease.

The Ronald Reagan Presidential Library in Simi Valley, California, opened in 1991. Nancy Reagan served on the board of the Ronald Reagan Presidential Foundation, which pursues Reagan's Four Pillars of Freedom—preserving individual liberty, promoting economic opportunity, advancing democracy around the world, and instilling pride in America's national heritage.

## Where to Learn More

Reagan, Nancy. *My Turn: The Memoirs of Nancy Reagan.* New York: Random House, 1989.

Reagan, Nancy. *Nancy.* New York: Morrow, 1980.

Reagan, Nancy, and Ronald Reagan. *I Love You, Ronnie.* New York: Random House, 2000.

Sandak, Cass R. *The Reagans.* New York: Crestwood House, 1993.

# Reagan's First Inaugural Address

**Delivered on January 18, 1981; excerpted from *Bartleby.com: Great Books Online* (Web site)**

*Expressing optimism in troubled times, President Reagan envisions a period of national renewal*

The inauguration of **Ronald Reagan** (1911– ; see entry in volume 5) in 1981 promised a new start for the nation. The 1970s had begun with U.S. soldiers fighting in the Vietnam War (1954–75) and ended with American hostages being held in Iran after over four hundred days. The resignation of President **Richard Nixon** (1913–1994; see entry in volume 5), soaring fuel costs, and diminishing international prestige were other problems of the 1970s that Americans were anxious to put behind them.

Reagan had capitalized on that sense of discontent during his campaign for the presidency. Always speaking with optimism, he declared that the federal government had grown too large and too intrusive in the lives of its citizens. Promising to scale back government programs to promote only those that created opportunity, Reagan hoped to begin a period of national renewal.

There was a sense of freshness surrounding his inaugural. For the first time, an inauguration ceremony was held on the terrace of the West Front of the Capitol. And on that day, the American hostages held by the revolutionary govern-

> "I do not believe in a fate that will fall on us no matter what we do. I do believe in a fate that will fall on us if we do nothing."
>
> *Ronald Reagan*

ment of Iran were finally released (see box in **Jimmy Carter** entry in volume 5).

## Things to remember while reading an excerpt from President Reagan's first inaugural address:

- In his opening statements (not included in the following excerpt), President Reagan acknowledged outgoing president **Jimmy Carter** (1924– ; see entry in volume 5) and remarked on the uniqueness of the peaceful transition of power that occurs when each new U.S. president is sworn into office. President Reagan then launched into the main body of his speech, which can be divided into three parts: he identified problems the nation faced; he announced his theme—"government is not the solution to our problems"; and he stated his objective, "a healthy, vigorous, growing economy that provides opportunities for all Americans."

- During the middle portion of the address (starting with "So as we begin"), Reagan related his plan of action. He placed that plan within the context of reiterating a basic truth about the American government—"the Federal government did not create the States; the States created the Federal Government"—to help persuade Americans about the rightness of his cause.

- Throughout the speech, Reagan made references to common Americans. Often he presented their ordinary jobs and concerns as being heroic. Reagan used that viewpoint often in his speeches, helping to relate to and inspire his listeners. It was among several qualities that made him an engaging and persuasive speaker who was dubbed, "The Great Communicator." In the conclusion of his speech, he used the example of one American to help express his overall, optimistic outlook.

## *Excerpt from President Reagan's first inaugural address*

*The business of our nation goes forward. These United States are confronted with an economic affliction of great proportions. We suffer from the longest and one of the worst sustained **inflations** in our national history. It distorts our economic decisions, penalizes thrift, and crushes the struggling young and the **fixed-income** elderly alike. It threatens to shatter the lives of millions of our people.*

*Idle industries have cast workers into unemployment, causing human misery and personal **indignity**. Those who do work are denied a fair return for their labor by a tax system which penalizes successful achievement and keeps us from maintaining full productivity.*

*But great as our tax burden is, it has not kept pace with public spending. For decades, we have piled deficit upon deficit, **mortgaging** our future and our children's future for the temporary convenience of the present. To continue this long trend is to guarantee tremendous social, cultural, political, and economic upheavals.*

*You and I, as individuals, can, by borrowing, live beyond our means, but for only a limited period of time. Why, then, should we think that collectively, as a nation, we are not bound by that same limitation?*

*We must act today in order to preserve tomorrow. And let there be no misunderstanding—we are going to begin to act, beginning today.*

*The economic ills we suffer have come upon us over several decades. They will not go away in days, weeks, or months, but they will go away. They will go away because we, as Americans, have the capacity now, as we have had in the past, to do whatever needs to be done to preserve this last and greatest **bastion** of freedom.*

*In this present crisis, government is not the solution to our problem.*

*From time to time, we have been tempted to believe that society has become too complex to be managed by self-rule, that government by an elite group is superior to government for, by, and of the people. But if no one among us is capable of governing himself, then*

**Inflations:** Periods of time when money loses some of its value, usually because goods become more expensive.

**Fixed-income:** Limited, but regular income. Reagan is specifically mentioning retirees, who receive regular pension and social security payments and who face economic troubles when the prices of goods continually rise.

**Indignity:** Insult.

**Mortgaging:** Paying off a loan over the course of several years.

**Bastion:** Stronghold.

who among us has the capacity to govern someone else? All of us together, in and out of government, must bear the burden. The solutions we seek must be **equitable,** with no one group singled out to pay a higher price.

We hear much of **special interest groups.** Our concern must be for a special interest group that has been too long neglected. It knows no sectional boundaries or ethnic and racial divisions, and it crosses political party lines. It is made up of men and women who raise our food, patrol our streets, man our mines and our factories, teach our children, keep our homes, and heal us when we are sick—professionals, industrialists, shopkeepers, clerks, cabbies, and truck drivers. They are, in short, "We the people," this breed called Americans.

Well, this administration's objective will be a healthy, vigorous, growing economy that provides equal opportunity for all Americans, with no barriers born of bigotry or discrimination. Putting America back to work means putting all Americans back to work. Ending inflation means freeing all Americans from the terror of runaway living costs. All must share in the productive work of this "new beginning" and all must share in the bounty of a revived economy. With the idealism and fair play which are the core of our system and our strength, we can have a strong and prosperous America at peace with itself and the world.

So, as we begin, let us take inventory. We are a nation that has a government—not the other way around. And this makes us special among the nations of the Earth. Our Government has no power except that granted it by the people. It is time to check and reverse the growth of government which shows signs of having grown beyond the consent of the governed.

It is my intention to **curb** the size and influence of the Federal establishment and to demand recognition of the distinction between the powers granted to the Federal Government and those reserved to the States or to the people. All of us need to be reminded that the Federal Government did not create the States; the States created the Federal Government.

Now, so there will be no misunderstanding, it is not my intention to do away with government. It is, rather, to make it work—work with us, not over us; to stand by our side, not ride on our back. Government can and must provide opportunity, not smother it; foster productivity, not stifle it.

If we look to the answer as to why, for so many years, we achieved so much, prospered as no other people on Earth, it was because here,

**Equitable:** Equal.

**Special interest groups:** Groups that lobby for legislation that will specifically benefit their group.

**Curb:** Restrain.

in this land, we unleashed the energy and individual genius of man to a greater extent than has ever been done before. Freedom and the dignity of the individual have been more available and assured here than in any other place on Earth. The price for this freedom at times has been high, but we have never been unwilling to pay that price.

It is no coincidence that our present troubles parallel and are proportionate to the intervention and intrusion in our lives that result from unnecessary and excessive growth of government. It is time for us to realize that we are too great a nation to limit ourselves to small dreams. We are not, as some would have us believe, doomed to an inevitable decline. I do not believe in a fate that will fall on us no matter what we do. I do believe in a fate that will fall on us if we do nothing. So, with all the creative energy at our command, let us begin an era of national renewal. Let us renew our determination, our courage, and our strength. And let us renew our faith and our hope.

We have every right to dream heroic dreams. Those who say that we are in a time when there are no heroes just don't know where to look. You can see heroes every day going in and out of factory gates. Others, a handful in number, produce enough food to feed all of us and then the world beyond. You meet heroes across a counter—and they are on both sides of that counter. There are **entrepreneurs** with faith in themselves and faith in an idea who create new jobs, new wealth and opportunity. They are individuals and families whose taxes support the Government and whose voluntary gifts support church, charity, culture, art, and education. Their patriotism is quiet but deep. Their values sustain our national life. . . .

In the days ahead I will propose removing the roadblocks that have slowed our economy and reduced productivity. Steps will be taken aimed at restoring the balance between the various levels of government. Progress may be slow—measured in inches and feet, not miles—but we will progress. It is time to reawaken this industrial giant, to get government back within its means, and to lighten our **punitive** tax burden. And these will be our first priorities, and on these principles, there will be no compromise. . . .

And as we renew ourselves here in our own land, we will be seen as having greater strength throughout the world. We will again be the **exemplar** of freedom and a beacon of hope for those who do not now have freedom. . . .

This is the first time in history that this ceremony has been held, as you have been told, on this West Front of the Capitol. Standing

**Entrepreneurs:** People who start or invest in new business ventures.

**Punitive:** Punishing.

**Exemplar:** Model.

*here, one faces a magnificent vista, opening up on this city's special beauty and history. At the end of this open mall are those shrines to the giants on whose shoulders we stand. . . .*

*Beyond those monuments to heroism is the Potomac River, and on the far shore the sloping hills of Arlington National Cemetery with its row on row of simple white markers bearing crosses or Stars of David. They add up to only a tiny fraction of the price that has been paid for our freedom. . . .*

*Under one such marker lies a young man—Martin Treptow— who left his job in a small town barber shop in 1917 to go to France with the famed Rainbow Division. There, on the western front, he was killed trying to carry a message between battalions under heavy artillery fire.*

*We are told that on his body was found a diary. On the **flyleaf** under the heading, "My Pledge," he had written these words: "America must win this war. Therefore, I will work, I will save, I will sacrifice, I will endure, I will fight cheerfully and do my utmost, as if the issue of the whole struggle depended on me alone."*

*The crisis we are facing today does not require of us the kind of sacrifice that Martin Treptow and so many thousands of others were called upon to make. It does require, however, our best effort, and our willingness to believe in ourselves and to believe in our capacity to perform great deeds; to believe that together, with God's help, we can and will resolve the problems which now confront us.*

**Flyleaf:** Blank endpaper of a book.

*And, after all, why shouldn't we believe that? We are Americans. God bless you, and thank you.* (Bartleby.com: Great Books Online [Web site])

## What happened next . . .

In his speech, Reagan observed that "progress may be slow—measured in inches and feet, not miles—but we will progress." Small progress in overcoming the economic crisis he identified in the address was made during the first two years of his presidency. Beginning in 1983, the American economy improved and expanded consistently over the next six years—through the end of Reagan's second term in office.

Tax reduction acts passed in 1981 and 1986 helped relieve the tax burden that Reagan blamed for having stifled growth. Government programs, which Reagan identified as another form of burden, were cut back during his administration with mixed results. Businesses were able to act with less restraint, but some took advantage of reduced government supervision. The government deficit that Reagan targeted for reduction in his inaugural address actually grew during his presidency, partly from increased military spending and a trade imbalance where imports far outbalanced exports and partly from resistance by Congress to further cuts in government programs.

The economy improved. Some government regulations were later enacted to help maintain order and stability in business. One of the results of the Reagan presidency has been the more careful consideration and debate, as well as resistance, that greets each potential new regulation. To his supporters, that reality is an example of what they call "the Reagan Revolution"—an administration that turned away from a fifty-year trend of large government social programs and brought renewed emphasis to the question of how powerful Americans want their government to be.

## Did you know . . .

- Ronald Reagan's policies are often compared with those of conservative Republicans during the 1950s who were strongly anticommunist and wanted to reduce the influence of government at home. When Reagan first came to occupy the White House, he ordered some of the memorabilia and pictures of President **Harry S. Truman** (1884–1972; see entry in volume 4) removed. Truman had served from 1945 to 1953 and often battled with congressional Republicans over federal programs he wanted to initiate to improve social and economic situations at home.

## Where to Learn More

Dallek, Robert. *Ronald Reagan: The Politics of Symbolism.* Cambridge, MA: Harvard University Press, 1984. Reprint, 1999.

Hagstrom, Jerry. *Beyond Reagan: The New Landscape of American Politics.* New York: Norton, 1988.

"Ronald Reagan: First Inaugural Address." *Bartleby.com: Great Books Online.* [Online] http://www.bartleby.com/124/pres61.html (accessed on October 25, 2000).

Schaller, Michael. *Reckoning with Reagan: America and Its President in the 1980s.* New York: Oxford University Press, 1992.

Sloan, John W. *The Reagan Effect: Economics and Presidential Leadership.* Lawrence: University Press of Kansas, 1999.

# George Bush

**Forty-first president (1989–1993)**

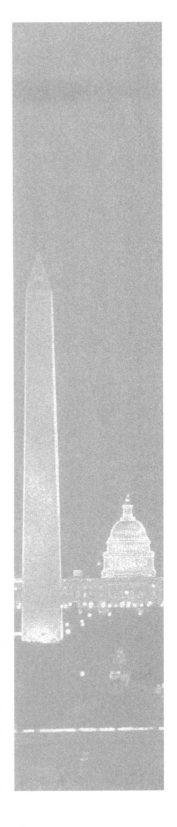

# George Bush

**Born June 12, 1924**
**Milton, Massachusetts**

**Forty-first president of the United States**
**(1989–1993)**

**Lifelong political team player finally achieved the top office and presided during the Gulf War and the end of the Cold War**

K nown as a team player, George Bush was skilled at establishing defined goals for programs and then rallying support. That talent was displayed during his presidency in his international leadership during the Gulf War (1991). Leading at home, in the highly partisan political environment (where the concerns of one's party are placed above all other considerations) of Washington, D.C., proved more difficult.

Bush's presidency was challenged on two fronts—a Democratic-controlled Congress and an increasingly hostile conservative group within Bush's own Republican Party. (Conservative political philosophy is characterized by limited government influence and support for conventional social values.) Bush came to office with a distinguished record of public service. After being vice president to the popular **Ronald Reagan** (1911– ; see entry in volume 5), Bush became the first sitting vice president in 150 years to be elected president. Conservative Republicans wanted Bush to continue Reagan's policies of tax cuts, increased military spending, and reduction of all other government spending. When Bush concentrated instead on reducing the huge federal budget

"A government that remembers that the people are its master is a good and needed thing."

*George Bush*

**George Bush.** *Courtesy of the Library of Congress.*

## Fast Facts about George Bush

**Full name:** George Herbert Walker Bush

**Born:** June 12, 1924

**Parents:** Prescott Sheldon and Dorothy Walker Bush

**Spouse:** Barbara Pierce (1925– ; m. 1945)

**Children:** George Walker (1946– ); Pauline Robinson (Robin) (1949–1953); John (Jeb) Ellis (1953– ); Neil Mallon (1955– ); Marvin Pierce (1956– ); Dorothy Walker (1959– )

**Religion:** Methodist

**Education:** Yale University (B.A., 1948)

**Occupations:** Oilman

**Government positions:** U.S. representative from Texas; U.S. ambassador to the United Nations; CIA director; vice president under Ronald Reagan

**Political party:** Republican

**Dates as president:** January 20, 1989– January 20, 1993

**Age upon taking office:** 64

deficit (created when government spending exceeded income), supporting business reforms, and restoring education and environmental programs, Bush faced resentment within his own party. Democrats, meanwhile, claimed his policies were too modest.

Bush was more effective with his foreign policy. He was president during a period of remarkable international developments. The Soviet Union's dominance over eastern European nations ended, and former republics within the Union of Soviet Socialist Republics (USSR), including Russia, became independent. The Cold War that had exerted tremendous influence on American life and politics for forty years was over.

In 1991, an international coalition (alliance) spearheaded by the Bush administration swiftly expelled the invading military of Iraq from the nation of Kuwait in the Gulf War. Bush's popularity soared over his handling of the Gulf War and foreign affairs. That support wore away the following year as the nation's economy gradually worsened. Bush failed to be reelected in 1992.

## Early accomplishments

George Herbert Walker Bush was born on June 12, 1924, in Milton, Massachusetts. Bush, his three brothers, and a sister grew up primarily in Greenwich, Connecticut. His father, Prescott Bush (1895–1972), was a wealthy investment banker who also served as a Republican senator from Connecticut from 1952 to 1963. A moderate, he supported the policies of President **Dwight D. Eisenhower** (1890–1969; see entry in volume 4) and distanced himself from more stridently conservative Republicans. George Bush would follow the same political principles as his father. Interestingly, Ronald Reagan's principles were often compared by commentators with the more conservative Republicans of the 1950s.

Bush's mother, Dorothy (1901–1992), came from the wealthy family of a leading Missouri industrialist. She is credited with establishing a sense of humbleness in her children, a trait later seen in Bush's interest in team-building over individual accomplishment. After graduating from the private Phillips Academy in Massachusetts, Bush enlisted in the U.S. Navy during World War II (1939–45). He became an ensign and then the Navy's youngest pilot. Bush flew fifty-eight combat missions in the Pacific theater (scene of military operations) during World War II. During one mission, his plane was shot down over the ocean, killing two crew members. Bush clung to wreckage until being rescued by a submarine. He was awarded the Distinguished Flying Cross for bravery in action.

## George Bush Timeline

**1924:** Born in Massachusetts

**1967–71:** Serves as U.S. representative from Texas

**1971–73:** Serves as U.S. ambassador to the United Nations

**1974–75:** Serves as U.S. envoy to China

**1975–77:** Serves as director of the Central Intelligence Agency (CIA)

**1981–89:** Serves as vice president under Ronald Reagan

**1989–93:** Serves as forty-first U.S. president

**1989:** Cold War ends

**1991:** Gulf War takes place

**1992:** Loses reelection bid to Bill Clinton

Upon returning home from military service, Bush married Barbara Pierce (1925– ; see entry on **Barbara Bush** in volume 5), daughter of a New York magazine publisher. They would have six children: two of them—**George W. Bush** (1946– ; see entry in volume 5), the forty-third president of the United States, and John (1953– ), known as Jeb, who later became governor of Florida in the 1990s—would follow their father into politics. A daughter, Robin, died of leukemia (a disease caused by an abnormal increase of white blood cells) at age three.

Bush enrolled at Yale University and graduated in 1948 after three years. He majored in economics, captained the school's baseball team, and was a member of Yale's most exclusive group, the Skull and Bones Society. After graduation,

Words to Know

**Apartheid:** A policy of racial segregation and economic and social discrimination against non-European peoples in the Republic of South Africa.

**Caucus:** An organized vote by registered and designated members of a political party to determine the amount of support within a state for the party's presidential candidates.

**Central Intelligence Agency (CIA):** A U.S. government agency charged with accumulating information on foreign countries.

**Cold War:** An era (1946–89) of tense conflicts and failed diplomacy between the Soviet Union and its allies and the United States and its allies.

**Conservative:** A political philosophy of limited government influence and support for conventional social values.

**Coup:** A sudden overthrow of a government, often by the country's military.

**Covert operations:** Secret, undercover acts used to help influence the outcome of events.

**Federal budget deficit:** When government spending exceeds income (from taxes and other revenue).

**National Security Council:** A group of military advisors assisting the president.

**Partisan:** Placing the concerns of one's group or political party above all other considerations.

**Peacekeeping force:** A military force sponsored by the United Nations that polices areas that have been attacked by another group clearly defined as aggressors.

**Presidential primaries:** Elections held in states to help determine the nominees of political parties for the general election. Each party disperses a certain number of delegates to each state. A candidate must win support of a majority of those delegates to win the party's presidential nomination. In states that hold primary elections, delegates are generally awarded to candidates based on the percentage of votes they accumulate; in some states, the leading vote-getter wins all of those states' delegates.

**Rapprochement:** Reestablishment of relations with a country after it has undergone a dramatic change in government.

**Recession:** A situation of increasing unemployment and decreasing value of money.

**Sanctions:** Measures taken to restrict trade or diplomatic relations in protest of another country's policies.

he moved his family to Texas, where Bush took an administrative position at an oil-field supply company. In 1953, he and a friend cofounded the Zapata Petroleum Company. Bush became president in 1954 of a subsidiary (a company owned or controlled by another company), the Zapata Off-Shore Company. The company was headquartered in Houston in 1958. By the mid-1960s, Bush sold his stake in the company and became a self-made millionaire at age forty-one.

## Enters politics

Bush became active in Republican politics during the early 1960s, helping to organize local and state groups. In 1964, he won the Republican nomination for a U.S. Senate seat but lost to Democrat Ralph W. Yarborough (1903–1996) during a landslide election year for that party. In 1966, Bush ran successfully for the House of Representatives, becoming the first Republican ever to represent the Houston area in Congress. Former vice president and 1960 presidential candidate **Richard Nixon** (1913–1994; see entry in volume 5) campaigned on Bush's behalf.

During his two terms in the House, Bush was a practical, business-oriented legislator. After Nixon was elected president in 1968, Bush supported the administration's policy of gradual troop reduction during the Vietnam War (1954–75). In 1970, Bush ran for the Senate. He was defeated by Lloyd Bentsen (1921– ), a moderate Democrat whose views were not that dissimilar to those of Bush: Both represented the more business-oriented agenda of the changing South that would be called the "New South" in the 1970s. (Later, in 1988, Bentsen and Bush would again vie for office when Bush was the Republican presidential candidate and Bentsen the Democratic vice presidential candidate.)

Bush was not out of political work for long. President Nixon nominated him to be U.S. representative to the United Nations. Despite concern over his lack of foreign-policy experience, Bush was confirmed by the Senate for the position in February 1971. His strong administrative and communication skills helped him in efforts to establish a peacekeeping force (a military force sponsored by the United Nations) in the Middle East and to reduce U.S. financial support for the United Nations. (The United States had been by far the largest financial supporter of the international agency.)

In 1973, Bush became chairman of the Republican National Committee at the urging of President Nixon. In that position, Bush directed the party's national activities. Within weeks, the Watergate scandal began dominating the news. The scandal, which centered on a 1972 burglary of Democratic National Headquarters, involved members of the Nixon administration. Bush managed to hold his party together during the scandal that forced the resignation of President Nixon in August 1974. Bush remained supportive of the president until evidence firmly showed that Nixon was involved in the scandal. Bush sent Nixon a letter recommending his resignation shortly before the president officially stepped down.

**Gerald R. Ford** (1913– ; see entry in volume 5), Nixon's successor, offered Bush the opportunity to select a position in Ford's administration. Bush opted to become envoy to China. (An envoy is a government representative sent on a special mission.) President Nixon had reestablished U.S. relations with China in 1972 after a twenty-year period without diplomatic contact. During 1974 and 1975, Bush helped to further diplomatic activities between the two nations.

He was called back home in 1975 to become director of the Central Intelligence Agency (CIA), the U.S. government department charged with collecting information about other countries. The agency had been wracked by investigations that uncovered abuses of power and illegal, covert operations (secret acts intended to influence events) in foreign countries. Bush succeeded in lifting the morale of the agency through his professionalism while carrying out an executive order (a presidential proclamation that immediately becomes law) that forced the agency to work within its defined, legal mission.

Following Ford's defeat in the 1976 presidential election, Bush returned to private life. He took care of business, served as chairman of a Houston bank, and began gathering support for a run at the White House in 1980.

## Team player

Bush's major opponent for the Republican presidential nomination of 1980 was former California governor

Ronald Reagan, who was very nearly the party's candidate in 1976. Reagan appealed to religious conservatives who favored prayer in public schools (known as school prayer) and a ban on abortion (the purposeful ending of a pregnancy). Additionally, Reagan planned to enact a program of tax cuts, reduced government spending on social programs, and vastly increased military spending. Through tax cuts, Reagan reasoned, consumers would have more spending power to help stimulate a sluggish U.S. economy. During the campaign for the Republican nomination, Bush called the Reagan program "voodoo economics"—a magic plan. Bush represented a more moderate faction of the Republican Party.

Bush won the early Iowa caucus (an organized vote by registered members of a political party to determine the amount of support for a potential presidential candidate in a particular state). In February 1980, however, he lost to Reagan in the New Hampshire presidential primary (an election held in a state to help determine who will be the party's presiden-

**CIA director George Bush (left, leaning over table) makes a point at a June 1976 meeting with President Gerald R. Ford (far right) and members of the National Security Council.** *Reproduced by permission of the Corbis Corporation.*

*Vice President Bush was a reassuring presence to the nation in March 1981 after President Reagan was wounded in an assassination attempt. Less reassuring was Reagan's secretary of state, Alexander Haig, who blurted out, "I'm in charge here," following the shooting of the president. Haig was out of the administration the following year.*

tial candidate in the general presidential election). Despite a few primary wins by Bush, Reagan gathered enough support to win the party's presidential nomination. Reagan first offered the vice presidency to Gerald Ford, who envisioned a kind of co-presidency. Reagan decided against that kind of arrangement and asked Bush instead. Bush became a team player, supporting Reagan's economic policies while appealing to more moderate voters. He brought foreign-policy experience to the ticket as well. The Republicans won convincingly, defeating President **Jimmy Carter** (1924– ; see entry in volume 5) and Vice President Walter Mondale (1928– ).

Bush's foreign policy expertise was put to use as vice president. He traveled to sixty countries over the next eight years, often in ceremonial roles, but also making valuable contacts and representing administration policies. At home, he headed task forces on crime, terrorism, and drug smuggling. Bush was a reassuring presence to the nation following an assassination attempt on the president after less than three months in office. Bush helped run the country while Reagan recovered from a gunshot wound. In a more official capacity, Bush served as acting president for eight hours in 1985. President Reagan arranged the transfer of power to occur as he underwent an operation for cancer. The event, which spanned from 11:30 A.M. to 7:30 P.M. on July 13, 1985, was the first such temporary transfer of power in the nation's history.

## From landslide to scandal

In 1984, Reagan was reelected in a landslide, this time defeating former vice president Mondale. Reagan remained popular through his second term despite a controversy involving the illegal sale of arms to Iran known as the Iran-Contra scandal. Since the scandal involved members of the president's National Security Council of military advisors, of which Bush was a member, the vice president was indirectly implicated as well.

The Iran-Contra scandal revealed careless supervision within the Reagan White House, where some officials were making illegal deals with and without the president's knowledge. Bush denied any involvement in illegal activities. Like Reagan, he was never officially charged with wrongdoing, although the president admitted guilt in authorizing illegal contact with members of the Iranian government.


## A kinder, gentler nation

Bush had to overcome questions about the Iran-Contra scandal when he ran for president in 1988. Reagan's popularity among conservatives was another issue. Reaganomics, the economic policies that Bush had once called "voodoo economics," had revived the American economy. Conservatives wanted Bush to maintain Reagan's policies, but Bush recognized the need to confront an increasing budget deficit, prosperity that primarily benefited the wealthiest people, and problems that arose from Reagan's deep cuts in government programs. Some of Reagan's policies were regularly attacked by Democrats. Calling for a "kinder, gentler nation," Bush proposed a more moderate approach as well as cuts in military spending that would not compromise the nation's military capabilities.

To help satisfy conservatives, Bush made a pledge early in his campaign—"Read my lips: no new taxes"—he would later come to regret. He ran a hard-hitting campaign against Democratic candidate Michael Dukakis (1933– ), making accusations that the Massachusetts governor was weak on crime and environmental issues. With the support of the popular, outgoing president, Bush won a clear victory, taking fifty-three percent of the popular vote and winning forty

**George Bush Administration**

*Administration Dates*
January 20, 1989–January 20, 1993

*Vice President*
Dan Quayle (1989–93)

*Cabinet*

**Secretary of State**
James A. Baker III (1989–92)
Lawrence S. Eagleburger (1992–93)

**Secretary of the Treasury**
Nicholas F. Brady (1988–93)

**Attorney General**
Richard L. Thornburgh (1989–91)
William P. Barr (1991–93)

**Secretary of the Interior**
Manuel Lujan Jr. (1989–93)

**Secretary of Agriculture**
Clayton Yeutter (1989–91)
Edward Madigan (1991–93)

**Secretary of Labor**
Elizabeth H. Dole (1989–90)
Lynn Morley Martin (1991–93)

**Secretary of Commerce**
Robert A. Mosbacher (1989–92)
Barbara H. Franklin (1992–93)

**Secretary of Defense**
Richard Cheney (1989–93)

**Secretary of Housing and Urban Development**
Jack Kemp (1989–93)

**Secretary of Transportation**
Samuel K. Skinner (1989–91)
Andrew H. Card Jr. (1992–93)

**Secretary of Energy**
James Watkins (1989–93)

**Secretary of Health and Human Services**
Louis Sullivan (1989–93)

**Secretary of Education**
Lauro F. Cavazos (1989–90)
Lamar Alexander (1991–93)

**Secretary of Veterans Affairs**
Edward J. Derwinski (1989–92)
Anthony J. Principi (1992–93)

states in the Electoral College for a 426- to 111-vote victory. (The Electoral College is a body officially responsible for electing the president of the United States. In presidential elections, a candidate must win a majority of electoral votes— over fifty percent—in order to win the presidency. For more information on the Electoral College, see boxes in **George W. Bush** entry in volume 5.)

Politics in Washington, D.C., however, was neither kind nor gentle. Long battles over the annual budget with

Congress occurred, as Democrats wanted to increase Bush's proposed spending plans and Republicans wanted to further decrease spending. Budgets have to be authorized by Congress and the president in order for federal workers to receive their pay; that funding was threatened in 1990 over a budget impasse. To help complete the budget process, Bush compromised with Democrats on a federal deficit reduction plan that included increases in taxes. Conservatives were outraged and blocked the plan, but a different version that included higher taxes and Bush's tax reform ideas passed. Conservatives began to abandon Bush.

Bush supported several other actions that countered policies of the Reagan administration. Government regulations on unfair business and financial practices were introduced; a social and civil rights program, the Americans with Disabilities Act, which lowered legal and physical obstacles to the physically challenged, was approved in 1990; additional money was targeted for improvement of education and the nation's highways; and the Clean Air Act set new antipollution standards for fuel burning.

Meanwhile, the economy stopped growing, and a recession (a period of increasing unemployment and decreasing value of money) hit in 1990. Despite the financial growth of the 1980s, more than fourteen percent of Americans still lived in poverty. In his battles with Congress, Bush vetoed (rejected) thirty-five pieces of legislation. The nation began viewing Washington, D.C., as a place where nothing was being accomplished because of struggles between the two political parties.

During his term in office, Bush appointed two Supreme Court justices. His nomination of David Souter (1939– ) passed Congress, but an uproar developed over Bush's nomination of Clarence Thomas (1948– ). Anita Hill (1956– ), a former member of Thomas's staff, accused him of sexual harassment, resulting in a tense Senate confirmation hearing that was nationally televised. Thomas was eventually approved by the Senate by a narrow, 52-to-48 vote, mostly along partisan lines—a true reflection of the times.

The Bush White House, meanwhile, brought a refreshing sense of calm to the nation. Bush held regular press conferences, went jogging around Washington, D.C., and

*When Bush was elected president in 1988, it marked the first time in over 150 years (since 1836) that the sitting vice president was elected president. Theodore Roosevelt, Calvin Coolidge, Harry S. Truman, and Lyndon B. Johnson were vice presidents who assumed the highest office upon the death of the president. They were each sitting presidents when elected to a full term.*

held more informal White House gatherings. First lady Barbara Bush was a soothing, grandmotherlike presence.

## World of change

Bush's experience in foreign policy proved to be a real strength. Through his support of sanctions against the government of the Republic of South Africa, he helped pressure reform that put an end to apartheid. (Sanctions are measures taken to restrict trade or diplomatic relations in protest of another country's policies. Apartheid is a policy of racial segregation and economic and social discrimination against non-European peoples in South Africa.) In December 1989, Bush authorized an American invasion of Panama to bring about the fall and arrest of the nation's leader, General Manuel Noriega (1936– ). Noriega had nullified (overturned) a national election that he was clearly losing, and he supported the international drug trade. Twenty-four hundred American troops assisted Panamanian rebels to overthrow the Noriega government. Noriega was brought to the United States to face trial for drug trafficking (the selling of illegal drugs). He was later convicted. Twenty-three Americans died in the fighting in Panama.

Meanwhile, Eastern European nations (including Poland, Czechoslovakia, and East Germany) began liberating themselves from years of communist domination by the Soviet Union. During this time, Soviet president Mikhail Gorbachev (1931– ; see box in **Ronald Reagan** entry in volume 5) introduced reforms in his nation that weakened the exclusive power wielded by the Soviet communist party. The reforms hastened the collapse of the Soviet Union, freeing former Soviet states to form independent nations. Russia was the largest and most powerful of those independent nations.

Bush and Gorbachev signed a strategic arms reduction pact in August 1991. (Strategic arms are the weapons required to wage a war.) Shortly after, Gorbachev faced a coup (a sudden overthrow of a government, often by the country's military). He was saved through the efforts of Boris Yeltsin (1931– ). Yeltsin was subsequently voted the new president of Russia in 1992.

Bush encouraged the fall of the communist state in the Soviet Union, recognized the resulting governments of the new nations that were formerly Soviet republics, and began rapprochement (reestablishment of friendly relations) in 1992 with the new Russian government led by Yeltsin. Another missile reduction pact between the United States and Russia was signed in 1992.

## Operation Desert Storm

In August 1990, the small, oil-rich nation of Kuwait was attacked by its Middle East neighbor, Iraq. Iraq also positioned armies near the borders of Saudi Arabia and Iran, threatening to dominate the world's oil supply (at the time, Kuwait held ten percent of the world's oil reserves, Iran held ten percent, and Saudi Arabia held twenty-five percent).

President Bush helped forge a broad international coalition against Iraq that included support from most United Nations (U.N.) members, includ-

ing Arab nations often reluctant to challenge their neighbors. Citing Iraq's unprovoked attack and its threat to the world's oil reserve, Bush ordered the largest deployment of American forces (425,000 soldiers) since the Vietnam War. He called it Operation Desert Shield. In January 1991, Bush asked Congress for and was granted the authority to use all necessary means to expel Iraqi forces from Kuwait. Operation Desert Storm, as the mission to liberate Kuwait was now called, was launched on January 17, 1991. Nine different nations participated in massive bombing missions on strategic sites within Iraq.

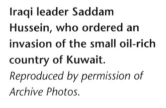

**Iraqi leader Saddam Hussein, who ordered an invasion of the small oil-rich country of Kuwait.**
*Reproduced by permission of Archive Photos.*

While Bush was achieving his goals of minimizing U.S. casualties and returning control of Kuwait to its government, Iraqi leader Saddam Hussein (1937– ) ordered a missile attack on Israel. He hoped to draw that nation into the conflict, which might inspire other Middle Eastern countries to withdraw from the war. Bush managed to keep the Israeli government from retaliating (returning the attack) while offering military protection.

An Iraqi tank, destroyed in the Gulf War, rests near a series of oil well fires started by Saddam Hussein's forces in northern Kuwait.
*Reproduced by permission of AP/Wide World Photos.*

As Iraqi forces were being overwhelmed, Saddam Hussein offered to withdraw from part of Kuwait, but Bush, supported by U.N. resolutions against Iraq, remained firm on complete withdrawal. In February 1991, ground forces hastened the Iraqi withdrawal from Kuwait in less than one hundred hours. The brief Gulf War was over in less than two months; 149 Americans died in action, while at least 10,000 Iraqi soldiers were killed.

With his handling of the Gulf War, Bush's popularity skyrocketed. He received some criticism by those who felt the ground forces should have gone on to remove Saddam Hussein from power. But the defined mission, legally sanctioned by the U.N., had been accomplished. When the Iraqi leader began crushing revolts within his own nation, Bush helped establish a "no fly" zone patrolled by the U.S. Air Force where Iraqi aircraft were not allowed. That zone protected ethnic regions within Iraq from being assaulted.

Two more noteworthy foreign policy events took place during Bush's term in office. To help support peace talks in the Middle East, he convinced Israel to stop building settlements on land outside Israel's border that was occupied by their military. To help encourage international trade, Bush aides began negotiating the North American Free Trade Agreement (NAFTA) with Canada and Mexico. The agreement, which eliminated almost all trade barriers between the three nations, was later ratified in November 1993, after Bush left office.

## Dramatic fade

With the Gulf War triumph and Bush's soaring popularity in 1991, his reelection the following year seemed a sure thing. But the continued sluggishness of the American economy eroded Bush's support. He was attacked by conservatives within his own party over taxes and government spending. At the 1992 Republican convention, outspoken conservatives were able to influence the party's platform away from Bush's more moderate beliefs.

Bush had been unable to break through in struggles with Congress. His attacks on his Democratic opponent, **Bill Clinton** (1946– ; see entry in volume 5), on issues of character and trust accomplished little. A relaxed and polished speaker, Clinton excelled in a new type of presidential debate—the town meeting. In that setting, candidates are free to walk around a stage area instead of standing behind lecterns (reading stands) on podiums (raised platforms). In the town meeting forum, candidates are asked questions by members of the audience.

Meanwhile, Bush's appeal to moderate conservatives was affected by the emergence of a third-party candidate, H. Ross Perot (pronounced puh-ROH, 1930– ; see box), a Texas billionaire. Perot gained support for his stand on two key issues: He wanted a more aggressive approach to attacking the federal budget deficit; and, as an outsider not associated with either of the nation's two major parties, he could break through the gridlock (a term he popularized) between the parties that hampered legislation in Washington, D.C. ("Gridlock" generally refers to a traffic jam so complete that no vehicle can move.)

# H. Ross Perot

Henry Ross Perot was born on June 27, 1930 in Texarkana, Texas. He grew up in Texarkana and spent one year at the local junior college. He then attended the U.S. Naval Academy, graduating in 1953 as class president. After graduation, he spent four years at sea.

At the Naval Academy, Perot received a basic education in engineering. He had no special training in electronics or computing, but his personal qualities impressed a representative from IBM, a leading company in the relatively new computer industry. When Perot left the navy, he was hired by IBM to sell computers in Dallas. In 1962, after he could not convince IBM that it could make money by leasing unused computer time to clients who needed it, Perot started his own business, Electronic Data Systems (EDS). In the years that followed, EDS expanded to run entire data-processing departments for insurance companies, banks, and state and national governments. By the end of the 1960s, Perot sold a small fraction of his shares in the business for $5 million.

As he grew extremely wealthy in the 1970s and 1980s, Perot became known for his international and philanthropic concerns. During the Vietnam War, he tried to improve the treatment of American prisoners of war in North Vietnam. In December 1969, Perot sent two planeloads of food, gifts, and medical supplies to prisoners, but the North Vietnamese refused to accept delivery of the goods. The publicity surrounding the episode, however, may have led to improved conditions in prison camps.

In the early 1970s, EDS attempted to improve data processing on Wall Street by purchasing a subsidiary of a stock brokerage firm. Unfortunately, the firm was in serious financial difficulties, and Perot ended up losing $60 million. In the late 1970s, EDS expanded internationally, obtaining contracts in Saudi Arabia and Iran. In 1978, after a financial dispute with the Iranian government, two leading EDS officers were arrested and imprisoned. Perot set out to win their release, even paying a quiet visit to Iran himself. An EDS rescue team was formed and trained but did not penetrate the prison where the men were held. Reportedly at the urging of an Iranian employee of EDS, an Iranian mob broke into the prison and released the prisoners. The EDS officials escaped and, with the rescue team, fled the country on foot. This episode was later recounted in a bestselling novel, *On the Wings of Eagles.*

In 1984, General Motors (GM) purchased EDS. The automaker looked to EDS to unify the data processing system in its diverse operations. For the forty-five percent of EDS stock that Perot owned, he received nearly $1 billion in cash and 5.5 million shares of stock in a new company called GME. Tensions between EDS and

**Ross Perot.** *Reproduced by permission of Archive Photos.*

GM mounted, however, and Perot criticized GM's way of doing business. In the fall of 1986, GM bought out Perot's GME shares, ending his connection with EDS. Perot agreed not to open a new profit-making data-processing business for three years. By 1989, GM and Perot were in court over the question of whether Perot had held to this agreement in forming a new company, Perot Systems.

In 1992, Perot's career switched gears when he spearheaded a campaign to have himself elected president of the United States under the Independent Party. Perot appeared on the *Larry King Live* television show on February 20, 1992, and said he would run for president if a grass-roots effort was successful in placing his name on the ballot in all fifty states. Public reaction was phenomenal. Perot sounded like a candidate eager to be elected, and his supporters saw in him the country's economic and social salvation. "If [elected], we'll be working night and day to fix all these problems," he said in May on the People's Radio Network. He told the *New York Times* he favored a congressional act to limit federal spending and claimed he could cut waste in the federal budget. He vowed to balance the federal budget and erase the budget deficit. He also said he would finance his own presidential campaign, instead of relying on donations.

As the summer unfolded, Perot began encountering criticisms. He was increasingly painted as an arrogant, paranoid man unwilling to take a stand on any given issue. On July 19, Perot abruptly dropped out of the race. As presidential candidates George Bush and Bill Clinton began scrambling to lure the abandoned Perot supporters to their sides, the media sought to expose the Texas billionaire as just another quitter. Perot proved them wrong. He reentered the race, performed fairly well in presidential debates, and won eighteen percent of the popular vote. Perot ran again in 1996, on the Reform Party ticket, receiving eight percent of the vote. After the 1996 election, Perot continued to dabble in business and politics. His Reform Party, however, became deeply divided over candidates for the 2000 election.

Perot abruptly dropped from the race in August, only to reemerge just as suddenly in October. Meanwhile, Bush's support continued to fade. He won only thirty-seven percent of the popular vote to Clinton's forty-three percent. Perot ran a strong third with nineteen percent.

After the election, Bush returned to Houston. He wrote his memoir, enjoyed his grandchildren, and continued to lead an active life. The physically fit ex-president even made a parachute jump in 1997—this time, though, he did it willingly; fifty-three years earlier, he had been forced to bail out of his Navy plane in a parachute. He dedicated his jump to the two pilots who did not survive when their plane was shot down.

On January 20, 2001, Bush became only the second president to be the father of a president, when George W. Bush was inaugurated as the nation's forty-third president. **John Adams** (1735–1826; see entry in volume 1) and **John Quincy Adams** (1767–1848; see entry in volume 1) were the first father-son combination.

## Legacy

Governing in the highly partisan environment that had come to distinguish the nation's capital during the late twentieth century was frustrating. That ongoing struggle and Bush's limited-government approach during weak economic times contributed to his dramatic downfall. Ronald Reagan had won reelection in 1984 by asking Americans whether they were better off after his first term than when he first ran for election. In 1992, Bush could not ask that same question with confidence. Still, Bush's limited government policies and his careful reductions in military spending were practiced by his successor, Bill Clinton, as the economy surged in the mid-1990s.

Moderates and conservatives within Bush' Republican Party continued to struggle. In 1994, conservatives won surprisingly large election victories to help Republicans take both houses of Congress. By the late 1990s, however, Republicans saw their presidential candidate, Bob Dole (1923– ), lose the 1996 election and their congressional majorities drop off.

Bush's handling of the Gulf War was his finest accomplishment: the goals were well defined, support was carefully

**Complete American Presidents Sourcebook**

## A Selection of Bush Landmarks

**George Bush Gallery of the National Museum of the Pacific War.** Admiral Nimitz Museum and Historical Center, 340 E. Main St., Fredericksburg TX 78624. (830) 997-4379. Bush's military career is the focus of this exhibit. See http://www.tpwd.state.tx.us/park/nimitz/bush.htm (accessed on October 26, 2000).

**George Bush Presidential Library and Museum.** 1000 George Bush Drive West, College Station, TX 77845. (979) 260-9552. The library contains the vast holdings of the official papers, photographs, and other documents related to the career of George Bush. Artifacts of the Bush family are displayed in the museum. The library is one of ten official presidential libraries in the country. See http://bushlibrary.tamu.edu/ (accessed on October 26, 2000).

gathered, and the results were swift. His leadership and diplomacy in the changing world of the 1990s provided an example for future presidents to follow.

## Where to Learn More

Boyd, Aaron. *Ross Perot: Businessman Politician.* Greensboro, NC: M. Reynolds, 1994.

Bush, George. *All the Best, George Bush: My Life in Letters and Other Writings.* New York: Scribner, 1999.

Follett, Ken. *On Wings of Eagles.* New York: W. Morrow, 1983.

*George Bush Presidential Library and Museum.* [Online] http://bushlibrary.tamu.edu/ (accessed on October 26, 2000).

*The George Bush Web Site.* http://www.chez.com/georgebush/english/ (accessed on October 26, 2000).

Green, Fitzhugh. *George Bush: An Intimate Portrait.* New York: Hippocrene, 1989.

Greene, John Robert. *The Presidency of George Bush.* Lawrence: University Press of Kansas, 2000.

Hill, Dilys M., and Phil Williams, eds. *The Bush Presidency: Triumphs and Adversities.* New York: St. Martin's Press, 1994.

Joseph, Paul. *George Bush.* Minneapolis: Abdo, 1999.

Levy, Peter B. *Encyclopedia of the Reagan-Bush Years.* Westport, CT: Greenwood Press, 1996.

Mason, Todd. *Perot: An Unauthorized Biography.* Homewood, IL: Business One Irwin, 1990.

Parmet, Herbert S. *George Bush: The Life of a Lone Star Yankee.* New York: Scribner, 1997.

Sufrin, Mark. *The Story of George Bush: The Forty-First President of the United States.* Milwaukee: Gareth Stevens, 1997.

# Barbara Bush

**Born June 8, 1925**
**Rye, New York**

**Wrote about the family dog for children and was a strong advocate of literacy**

Nicknamed "everybody's grandmother," first lady Barbara Bush projected a friendly, unassuming, and witty presence to the nation. With five grown children and more than twice as many grandchildren, she was the center of a large extended family. That family-rootedness showed in her work for family literacy, the idea of involving the whole family to help both parent and child learn to read and write. She became a public spokesperson for the cause after her husband **George Bush** (1924– ; see entry in volume 5) became vice president in 1981. During her time as first lady, she founded the Barbara Bush Foundation for Family Literacy. In 2001, she became only the second woman—and the first since **Abigail Adams** (1744–1818; see entry in volume 1)—to be the wife and the mother of U.S. presidents.

"The home is the child's first school, the parent is the child's first teacher, and reading is the child's first subject," Barbara Bush noted in describing the foundation. "Parents who lack basic literacy skills cannot experience the pleasure of reading a story to their children. The children, in turn, will not reap the educational benefits of being read to. And ac-

> "The home is the child's first school, the parent is the child's first teacher, and reading is the child's first subject"
>
> *Barbara Bush*

cording to the experts, reading to children early and often is the single most important thing parents can do to prepare them to start school ready to learn. If no one intervenes, this pattern is repeated in each new generation."

Barbara Bush intervened. More appropriately, she volunteered. The social responsibility and satisfaction of such volunteer work was championed by the Bushes throughout their lives.

## Young love

Born Barbara Pierce on June 8, 1925, she was the daughter of Pauline and Marvin Pierce. Her father was a magazine publisher (and president of *McCall's,* one of the leading magazines of the time) headquartered in New York. Pauline was the daughter of an Ohio supreme court justice. Barbara enjoyed a happy childhood in Rye, a suburb of New York City. In her teens, she went to Ashley Hall, a boarding school in South Carolina. Back home for Christmas vacation in 1941, she met George Bush at a dance. She was sixteen and he was seventeen. They were engaged within six months, just as Barbara turned seventeen on June 8, 1942. Four days later, George Bush enlisted in the U.S. Navy on his eighteenth birthday.

Bush became a pilot with the navy, flying bombing missions in the Pacific Ocean during World War II (1939–45). Shot down on one mission in the Pacific, his plane plunged into the ocean and two crew members died. Bush was rescued by an American submarine. While on leave from the military, George and Barbara married on January 6, 1945.

After the war, Bush entered Yale University in the fall of 1945 and graduated in 1948. He and Barbara and their young son, **George W. Bush** (1946– ; see entry in volume 5), moved to Texas, where Bush took a job in the oil industry. The Bushes would have five more children. A daughter, Robin, died at age three from leukemia (a disease caused by an abnormal increase of white blood cells). Barbara later remarked, "because of Robin I love every living human more."

Bush became wealthy during the 1950s, and he turned to politics in the 1960s. He was twice elected to represent the Houston area in the U.S. Congress. Beginning in 1970, he held a variety of important government jobs, crowning his political career with becoming vice president in 1981 and president in 1989. All the while, Barbara focused on raising her children and establishing homes. From 1945, when they were married, to 1993, when the Bushes retired to Houston, Barbara moved the family twenty-nine times.

## Family literacy

Barbara Bush first became a national spokesperson for family literacy while her husband was vice president. She consistently expanded on that role during the 1980s and her time as first lady, from 1989 to 1993. She hosted a weekly radio program called "Mrs. Bush's Story Time," where she read aloud stories and promoted family reading. She wrote a best-selling children's story, *Millie's Book,* based on the Bush family's dog. Profits from the book went to literacy programs. In 1989, she founded the Barbara Bush Foundation for Family Literacy and served as its honorary chairperson. The foundation supports family literacy programs and promotes the value of literacy. Barbara Bush traveled to literacy centers throughout the country to help with the cause. Her spirit of volunteerism was also evident in her work on behalf of the elderly and patients suffering from the AIDS virus. She supported school volunteer programs as well.

As first lady, Barbara Bush selected her causes carefully and maintained a low political profile. Yet, she influenced President Bush's priorities and his appointments in the areas of health, housing, and drug enforcement. She raised money for the United Negro College Fund, assisted with a major fund raising campaign for the Morehouse College School of Medicine, and worked on behalf of Sloan-Kettering and other hospitals, nursing homes, and hospices.

Mrs. Bush was one of the most popular presidential wives. In her 1994 bestseller, *Barbara Bush: A Memoir,* she described a conversation she had with Raisa Gorbachev (1932–1999), wife of the Russian leader, in which she explained her appeal: "I told [Raisa], as honestly as I could, that I felt it was because I threatened no one—I was old, whiteheaded and large. I also told her that I stayed out of my husband's affairs." However, Barbara Bush was "intense, irreverent, funny, a lot tougher and more combative than her public

Barbara Bush reads to a group of children in Washington, D.C., on January 31, 1989. Literacy was a chief concern of hers as first lady. *Reproduced by permission of the Corbis Corporation.*

image suggests," noted Bill Minutaglio in *First Son: George W. Bush and the Bush Family Dynasty.*

## Active retirement

Barbara Bush remained active after the Bushes retired to Houston in 1993. She hosted events at the George Bush Library at Texas A&M University and occasionally gave speeches to represent her favorite causes. She continued to be involved with health improvement programs and the Barbara Bush Foundation. She also worked on behalf of the Leukemia Society of America and the Boys & Girls Clubs of America.

Mostly, though, the former first lady focused her time on family matters, including the fourteen grandchildren who regularly joined their grandparents at their Kennebunkport, Maine, vacation home. Twelve grandchildren joined them there after the 2000 Republican National Convention, where her son, George W. Bush, was nominated for president. Barbara Bush generally kept a low profile during the campaign, but selective stops she made to support her son were always well attended. When George W. Bush was inaugurated in 2001 as the forty-third president, Barbara Bush became only the second woman to be both the wife and the mother of U.S. presidents.

## Where to Learn More

Bush, Barbara. *Barbara Bush: A Memoir.* New York: Scribner's Sons, 1994.

Bush, Barbara. *Millie's Book: As Dictated to Barbara Bush.* New York: William Morrow, 1990.

Greenberg, Judith E. *Barbara Pierce Bush, 1925–.* New York: Children's Press, 1999.

Kilian, Pamela. *Barbara Bush: A Biography.* New York: St. Martin's Press, 1992.

Minutaglio, Bill. *First Son: George W. Bush and the Bush Family Dynasty.* New York: Times Books, 1999.

# Bush's Address to Congress on the Crisis in Kuwait

**Delivered on September 11, 1990; excerpted from *Speech Communication @ Texas A&M University* (Web site)**

*President Bush discusses the "new world order," reflected in the international condemnation of the invasion of Kuwait by Iraq*

On August 2, 1990, the army of Iraq invaded the neighboring nation of Kuwait. The Iraqi military also established a stronghold near the border of Saudi Arabia. Those actions were condemned through a series of resolutions passed by the United Nations (U.N.). The resolutions and subsequent diplomatic efforts on the part of the United States and other nations failed to convince Iraqi leader Saddam Hussein (1937– ) to relinquish control of Kuwait.

President **George Bush** (1924– ; see entry in volume 5) received solid support from Americans as he mobilized the American military and exerted diplomatic pressure on Iraq. A month after the invasion, he spoke before a joint session of Congress and a national audience to reinforce support and to demonstrate American resolve to the Iraqis.

While carefully defining America's stand on Iraqi aggression against Kuwait, Bush discussed "the new world order"—the beginning of a profoundly different relationship among nations since the fall of the Soviet Union, which began disintegrating in 1989. That new world order was ex-

"Vital issues of principle are at stake. Saddam Hussein is literally trying to wipe a country off the face of the earth. We do not exaggerate. Nor do we exaggerate when we say: Saddam Hussein will fail."

*George Bush*

emplified by the cooperation among countries through the U.N. in its condemnation of Iraqi aggression.

At the same time as these events, Congress and the president were locked in a serious budget dispute. Turning to that budget dispute in the address, Bush called for cooperation that could overcome the profoundly serious economic and political problems within the United States.

## Things to remember while reading an excerpt from President Bush's address to Congress on the crisis in Kuwait:

- President Bush wanted to present clear goals to Americans about the nation's response to Iraqi aggression against Kuwait. Since the Vietnam War (1954–75), Americans had grown particularly sensitive to military actions where the United States was not directly threatened.

- The president made reference to a "new world order." The collapse of the Soviet Union during this period changed the world's balance of power. The Soviet Union and the United States had been the world's two "superpowers." In the new world order, according to Bush, cooperation among many nations was vital to maintain peace and to check aggression by one nation against another.

- Throughout the period from Iraq's invasion of Kuwait in August 1990 to the Gulf War of January and February 1991, President Bush worked closely with the U.N. to forge worldwide unity against Iraq's aggressive action. Bush spoke of the important role the U.N. played in the new world order. The Persian Gulf crisis was identified as the first test of that new world order.

- President Bush likened international cooperation to the kind of unity the United States had to show in addressing a major financial crisis at home. Congress and the president were engaged in a struggle over the federal budget; as the struggle continued, the government's power to operate was being compromised. In a section of the speech not included in the following excerpt, Bush defined four courses of action Congress should follow: 1) pass the president's proposed budget with tax reductions; 2) include modest decreases in military spending without threatening "our vital margin of safety"; 3) increase domestic energy production and conservation to reduce dependence on foreign oil; and 4) enact a five-year plan to reduce the federal deficit.

## *Excerpt from President Bush's address to Congress on the crisis in Kuwait*

*We gather tonight, witness to events in the **Persian Gulf** as significant as they are tragic. In the early morning hours of August 2nd, following negotiations and promises by Iraq's dictator, Saddam Hussein, not to use force, a powerful Iraqi army invaded its trusting and much weaker neighbor, Kuwait. Within three days, 120,000 Iraqi troops with 850 tanks had poured into Kuwait, and moved south to threaten Saudi Arabia. It was then I decided to check that aggression.*

*At this moment, our brave servicemen and women stand watch in that distant desert and on distant seas, side by side with the forces of more than 20 other nations. . . .*

*So if ever there was a time to put country before self and patriotism before party, that time is now. Let me thank all Americans, especially those in this chamber, for your support for our forces and their mission.*

*That support will be even more important in the days to come.*

*So tonight, I want to talk to you about what is at stake—what we must do together to defend civilized values around the world, and maintain our economic strength at home.*

*Our objectives in the Persian Gulf are clear, our goals defined and familiar: Iraq must withdraw from Kuwait completely, immediately and without condition. Kuwait's legitimate government must be restored. The security and stability of the Persian Gulf must be assured. Americans citizens abroad must be protected.*

*These goals are not ours alone. They have been endorsed by the **U.N. Security Council** five times in as many weeks. Most countries share our concern for principle. And many have a stake in the stabil-*

**Persian Gulf:** A gulf that lies between the Arabian peninsula and southern Iran, with parts of Kuwait and Iraq situated at the northernmost point.

**U.N. Security Council:** A group of powerful nations within the United Nations empowered to decide on military actions the U.N. should pursue.

*ity of the Persian Gulf. This is not, as Saddam Hussein would have it, the United States against Iraq. It is Iraq against the world. . . .*

*We stand today at a unique and extraordinary moment. The crisis in the Persian Gulf, as grave as it is, also offers a rare opportunity to move toward an historic period of cooperation. Out of these troubled times, our fifth objective—a new world order—can emerge: a new era, freer from the threat of terror, stronger in the pursuit of justice, and more secure in the quest for peace. An era in which the nations of the world, east and west, north and south, can prosper and live in harmony.*

*A hundred generations have searched for this elusive path to peace, while a thousand wars raged across the span of human endeavor. Today that new world is struggling to be born. A world quite different from the one we've known. A world where the rule of law* **supplants** *the rule of the jungle. A world in which nations recognize the shared responsibility for freedom and justice. A world where the strong respect the rights of the weak.*

*This is the vision I shared with* **President Gorbachev in Helsinki.** *He, and other leaders from Europe, the gulf, and around the world, understand that how we manage this crisis today could shape the future for generations to come.*

*The test we face is great—and so are the stakes. This is the first assault on the new world we seek, the first test of our* **mettle.** *Had we not responded to this first* **provocation** *with clarity of purpose; if we do not continue to demonstrate our determination; it would be a signal to actual and potential* **despots** *around the world.*

*America and the world must defend common vital interests. And we will.*

*America and the world must support the rule of law. And we will.*

*America and the world must stand up to aggression. And we will.*

*And one thing more. In pursuit of these goals America will not be intimidated.*

*Vital issues of principle are at stake. Saddam Hussein is literally trying to wipe a country off the face of the earth.*

*We do not exaggerate.*

*Nor do we exaggerate when we say: Saddam Hussein will fail.*

**Supplants:** Replaces.

**President Gorbachev in Helsinki:** A reference to a conversation between President Bush and Soviet president Mikhail Gorbachev during their arms reduction talks in Helsinki, Finland, just a few days prior to this speech.

**Mettle:** Courage.

**Provocation:** Taunting.

**Despots:** Dictators; rulers with total power.

Vital economic interests are at risk as well. Iraq itself controls some 10 percent of the world's proven oil reserves. Iraq plus Kuwait controls twice that. An Iraq permitted to swallow Kuwait would have the economic and military power, as well as the arrogance, to intimidate and coerce its neighbors—neighbors who control the lion's share of the world's remaining oil reserves. We cannot permit a resource so vital to be dominated by one so ruthless. And we won't. Recent events have surely proven that there is no substitute for American leadership. In the face of tyranny, let no one doubt American credibility and reliability.

Let no one doubt our staying power. We will stand by our friends.

One way or another, the leader of Iraq must learn this fundamental truth.

From the outset, acting hand in hand with others, we've sought to fashion the broadest possible international response to Iraq's aggression. The level of world cooperation and condemnation of Iraq is unprecedented.

Armed forces from countries spanning four continents are there at the request of King Fahd of Saudi Arabia to deter and if need be to defend against attack. Muslims and non-Muslims, Arabs and non-Arabs, soldiers from many nations, stand shoulder to shoulder, resolute against Saddam Hussein's ambitions.

We can now point to five United Nations Security Council resolutions that condemn Iraq's aggression. They call for Iraq's immediate and unconditional withdrawal, the restoration of Kuwait's legitimate Government, and categorically reject Iraq's cynical and self-serving attempt to annex Kuwait. . . .

We are now in sight of a United Nations that performs as envisioned by its founders. We owe much to the outstanding leadership of Secretary General Perez de Cuellar. The U.N. is backing up its words with action. The Security Council has imposed mandatory **economic sanctions** on Iraq, designed to force Iraq to relinquish the spoils of its illegal conquest. The Security Council has also taken the decisive step of authorizing the use of all means necessary to ensure compliance with these sanctions.

Together with our friends and allies, ships of the United States Navy are today patrolling Mideast waters. They have already intercepted more than 700 ships to enforce the sanctions. Three regional

**Economic sanctions:**
Punishment by one nation or a group of nations against another in the form of a suspension of trade or other economic activities. The punishment is meant as a form of pressure, since the sanctioned nation suffers economic hardships.

leaders I spoke with just yesterday told me that these sanctions are working. Iraq is feeling the heat.

We continue to hope that Iraq's leaders will recalculate just what their aggression has cost them. They are cut off from world trade, unable to sell their oil. And only a tiny fraction of goods gets through.

The communique with President Gorbachev makes mention of what happens when the **embargo** is so effective that the children of Iraq literally need milk or the sick truly need medicine. Then, under strict international supervision that guarantees the proper destination, food will be permitted.

At home, the material cost of our leadership can be steep. That's why Secretary of State [James A.] Baker and Treasury Secretary [Nicholas F.] Brady have met with many world leaders to underscore that the burden of this collective effort must be shared. We are prepared to do our share and more to help carry that load; we insist others do their share as well. . . .

I cannot predict just how long it will take to convince Iraq to withdraw from Kuwait. Sanctions will take time to have their full intended effect. We will continue to review all options with our allies, but let it be clear: We will not let this aggression stand.

Our interest, our involvement in the gulf, is not **transitory**. It predated Saddam Hussein's aggression and will survive it. Long after all our troops come home, and we all hope it's soon, there will be a lasting role for the United States in assisting the nations of the Persian Gulf. Our role, with others, is to deter future aggression. Our role is to help our friends in their own self-defense. And something else: to **curb the proliferation** of chemical, biological, ballistic missile, and above all, nuclear technologies.

Let me also make clear that the United States has no quarrel with the Iraqi people. Our quarrel is with Iraq's dictator, and with his aggression. Iraq will not be permitted to annex Kuwait. That's not a threat, or a boast, that's just the way it's going to be.

Our ability to function effectively as a great power abroad depends on how we conduct ourselves here at home. Our economy, our armed forces, our energy dependence, and our cohesion all determine whether we can help our friends and stand up to our foes.

For America to lead, America must remain strong and vital. Our world leadership and domestic strength are mutual and reinforcing; a woven piece, as strongly bound as **Old Glory.**

**Embargo:** A complete suspension of trade by one nation against another.

**Transitory:** Momentary.

**Curb the proliferation:** Restrain the growth.

**Old Glory:** The U.S. flag.

Complete American Presidents Sourcebook

*To revitalize our leadership capacity, we must address our budget deficit—not after Election Day, or next year, but now.*

*Higher oil prices slow our growth, and higher defense costs would only make our fiscal deficit problem worse. That deficit was already greater than it should have been—a projected $232 billion for the coming year. It must—it will—be reduced. To my friends in Congress, together we must act this very month, before the next **fiscal year** begins October 1, to get America's economic house in order. The gulf situation helps us realize we are more economically vulnerable than we ever should be. Americans must never again enter any crisis, economic or military, with an excessive dependence on foreign oil and an excessive burden of Federal debt. Most Americans are sick and tired of endless battles in the Congress and between the branches over budget matters. It is high time we pulled together, and get the job done right. It is up to us to straighten this out.* (Speech Communication @ Texas A&M University [Web site])

**Fiscal year:** A standard accounting period of twelve months. Many organizations have fiscal years other than the January-to-December period.

## What happened next . . .

When Iraq failed to honor the U.N. resolutions, the U.N. decided on a date (January 15, 1991) by which Iraqi forces were to abandon Kuwait. When that date passed, a massive, coordinated air strike of strategic targets in Iraq was launched by several nations. The air strikes were followed a month later by land forces that quickly forced Iraqi occupiers into retreat and liberated Kuwait within one hundred hours.

When the clearly defined mission of removing the Iraqi army from Kuwait was completed, the Gulf War was over. There were some Americans who felt that U.S. forces should have continued fighting until Saddam Hussein was ousted from power. Such an action would have been illegal under international law. Saddam Hussein continued to pose a threat for the next decade, but his powers for aggression were closely checked.

The new world order that Bush described continued to act through the United Nations against aggression in the world's trouble spots. The United States was successful in getting other nations to cooperate in such events. However, such alliances remain fragile. Other nations face the same concerns Americans have about the danger and human cost of sending young men and women to patrol foreign lands to stand against aggression.

The speech, in many ways, reflected Bush's presidency. He was successful in rallying Americans and other nations to support the U.N. effort against Iraqi aggression. For that action, he was immensely popular. He was less successful in rallying Congress to agree on a legislative package that would reduce the federal deficit and stimulate the sluggish economy. Largely because of that failure, Bush was not reelected president in 1992.

## Did you know . . .

- The Gulf War was virtually a televised war. Some cable networks, especially CNN (the Cable News Network), devoted hours of nonstop coverage to show bombing raids, computer-aided tracking of missiles as they hit specific targets, and news conferences that provided updates. Three American officials became familiar spokespersons and particularly popular public figures during the war: they were General Colin Powell (1937– ), head of the Joint Chiefs of Staff (the group of leaders representing each branch of the U.S. military); Dick Cheney (1941- ; see box in **George W. Bush** entry in volume 5), secretary of defense (who became vice president in 2001); and General H. Norman Schwarzkopf (1934- ), head of U.S. Central Command (commander of U.S. forces) in the Persian Gulf.

## Where to Learn More

Bush, George, and Brent Scowcroft. *A World Transformed.* New York: Knopf, 1998.

Hurst, Steven. *The Foreign Policy of the Bush Administration: In Search of a New World Order.* New York: Pinter, 1999.

Mervin, David. *George Bush and the Guardianship Presidency.* New York: St. Martin's Press, 1996.

Texas A&M University, Department of Speech Communication. "Iraqi Aggression in the Persian Gulf." *Speech Communication @ Texas A&M University.* [Online] http://www.tamu.edu/scom/pres/speeches/gbaggress.html (accessed on November 2, 2000).

# Bill Clinton

**Forty-second president (1993–2001)**

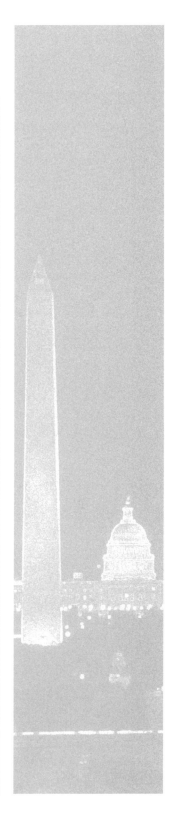

# Bill Clinton

**Born August 19, 1946**
**Hope, Arkansas**

**Forty-second president of the United States**
**(1993–2001)**

**Possessed a remarkable ability to**
**survive crushing political defeats and**
**personal scandals**

**B**ill Clinton experienced heights and depths as president: He presided during the longest-ever sustained growth of the American economy, and he faced an impeachment trial. (An impeachment process involves charging an elected official with having committed a crime; a trial is conducted to determine whether or not the misconduct requires removal from office.) President Clinton's impeachment trial nearly resulted in his removal from office. The American public gave the clearest assessment of his presidency: Low marks for his personal conduct, and increasing support for his performance as president.

Clinton took office in 1993 during an unstable period: The American economy was weak because of a huge federal budget deficit (the nation was spending more than it was taking in as income); war and strained relations threatened several parts of the world; and the partisanship (the placing of one's own political party's interests above all other considerations) that had plagued the federal government for twenty years had grown worse. Having achieved only mixed success during his first two years in office, the Democratic president

"I like the job of president. . . . The bad days are part of it. I didn't run to have a pleasant time. I ran to have a chance to change the country and if the bad days come with it, that's part of life, and it's humbling and educational. It keeps you in your place."

*Bill Clinton*

**Bill Clinton.** *Courtesy of the White House.*

## Fast Facts
## about Bill Clinton

**Full name:** William Jefferson Clinton; born William Jefferson Blythe IV

**Born:** August 19, 1946

**Parents:** William Jefferson Blythe III and Virginia Dell Cassidy Blythe Clinton Dwire Kelley; Roger Clinton (stepfather)

**Spouse:** Hillary Diane Rodham (1947– ; m. 1975)

**Children:** Chelsea Victoria (1980– )

**Religion:** Baptist

**Education:** Georgetown University (B.S., 1968); attended Oxford University; Yale Law School (J.D., 1973)

**Occupations:** Attorney; law professor

**Government positions:** Arkansas attorney general and governor

**Political party:** Democratic

**Dates as president:** January 20, 1993– January 20, 1997 (first term); January 20, 1997–January 20, 2001 (second term)

**Age upon taking office:** 46

faced greater challenges when Republicans made large gains in Congress during the 1994 midterm elections (congressional elections that occur midway through a president's term). Midterm congressional elections sometimes dramatically change the balance of power in Congress, and the 1994 elections did just that: For the first time in forty years, Republicans had majorities in both houses of Congress.

Clinton seemed to thrive after the setbacks, as he had during his entire political career. While continuing to increase American trade, the president pursued more moderate economic policies at home. The economy began booming. Meanwhile, Clinton enjoyed foreign policy successes when he helped bring together warring factions in Europe and in the Middle East.

In 1999, Clinton faced a trial of impeachment in the U.S. Senate following improper relations with a White House intern and evidence of perjury (the voluntary violation of an oath or vow) and obstruction of justice. While the nation debated whether his misdeeds were the "high crimes and misdemeanors" the Constitution cites as impeachable offenses, Congress pushed ahead on the impeachment process. True to the partisan spirit of the times, impeachment votes almost strictly followed party lines. Clinton was impeached on two counts in the House of Representatives. A Senate trial did not result in the two-thirds majority vote required to remove the president. After the trial, Americans were at least reassured that the Constitutional process had worked. The entire episode reinforced the public's general opinion: they agreed that the president's personal conduct was shameful, but generally approved of his performance as president.

## Overcomes troubled home life

Bill Clinton was born William Jefferson Blythe IV on August 19, 1946, in Hope, Arkansas. His father, William Jefferson Blythe III (1918–1946), a traveling salesman, died in an automobile accident three months before Clinton was born. Only much later in life did Clinton learn that his father had been married to two other women prior to his mother, Virginia (1923–1994); Clinton also discovered that he had relatives—a half-brother and a half-sister—from those other marriages. When he was two years old, Clinton was left in the care of his maternal grandparents. His mother went to New Orleans, Louisiana, to study nursing. She married Roger Clinton (1909–1967) and returned to Hope, Arkansas, when Bill was four.

The family settled in Hot Springs, Arkansas, when Clinton was seven, and he began attending school. Clinton was a strong student even though he grew up in a troubled household. His stepfather was an alcoholic and a gambler who physically abused the family. At age fourteen, Clinton stood up to him to defend his mother. The family became close enough again that Clinton was adopted by his stepfather at age sixteen and took his surname.

Clinton learned to play saxophone and was especially interested in studying government. At age sixteen, he was selected to take part in the American Legion Boy's Nation Program, a government study series sponsored by the American Legion, a military veterans' group. He traveled with other members of the program to Washington, D.C., where the boys met **President John F. Kennedy** (1917–1963; see entry in volume 5). That meeting inspired Clinton to want to become a politician.

Clinton went on to study international affairs at Georgetown University in Washington, D.C. While at

 **Bill Clinton Timeline**

**1946:** Born in Arkansas

**1963:** Meets President John F. Kennedy as part of the American Legion Boy's Nation government study program

**1977–79:** Serves as Arkansas attorney general

**1979–81, 1983–93:** Serves as Arkansas governor

**1993–2001:** Serves as forty-second U.S. president

**1998:** Impeached on two counts in the U.S. House of Representatives

**1999:** Remains in office after a Senate trial does not result in the two-thirds majority needed to remove him from office

# Words to Know

**Electoral College:** A body officially responsible for electing the president of the United States. In presidential elections, the candidate who receives the most popular votes in a particular state wins all of that state's electoral votes. Votes are distributed among states in ratios based on population. A candidate must win a majority of electoral votes (over fifty percent) in order to win the presidency.

**Ethnic cleansing:** Actions intended to rid an area of a particular ethnic group either through deportation, intimidation, or acts of genocide (mass murder).

**Federal deficit:** When government spending exceeds income (from taxes and other revenue).

**Grand jury:** A group empowered to decide whether a government investigation can provide enough evidence to make criminal charges against a citizen.

**Impeachment:** A legislative proceeding charging a public official with misconduct. Impeachment consists of the formal accusation of such an official and the trial that follows. It does not refer to removal from office of the accused.

**Incumbent:** Refers to the elected official currently holding office during an election period.

**Independent counsel:** A federal position established during the 1970s to investigate federal officials accused of crimes. The Independent Counsel Act, intended to perform in a nonpartisan manner in rare occasions, was not renewed in 1999.

**Medicare:** A government program that provides financial assistance to older people to help cover medical costs.

**Midterm elections:** Congressional elections that occur midway through a president's term. The elections change the

Georgetown, he served as an intern for Arkansas senator J. William Fulbright (1905–1995) and was active in public demonstrations for civil rights and against the Vietnam War (1954–1975). After graduating from the university in 1968, Clinton won a Rhodes scholarship, a competitive scholarship program that funds study for two or three years at Oxford University in England.

During that period, Clinton was subject to the lottery system through which young men were drafted into the army. He signed a letter of intent to join the Reserve Army

balance of power in Congress, bringing in more supporters for or challengers to the president.

**National health insurance:** A proposed government program that would offer assistance and medical coverage to all Americans to help pay for the increasing costs of medical care.

**North Atlantic Treaty Organization (NATO):** An alliance for collective security created by the North Atlantic Treaty in 1949 and originally involving Belgium, Canada, Denmark, France, Great Britain, Iceland, Italy, Luxembourg, the Netherlands, Norway, Portugal, and the United States.

**Partisanship:** Placing the concerns of one's group or political party above all other considerations.

**Peacekeeping force:** A military group authorized through an international agreement to maintain peace in a troubled area. Peacekeeping forces police an area and enforce laws and treaties; they do not take military action unless provoked.

**Perjury:** The voluntary violation of an oath or a vow; answering falsely while under oath (having previously sworn to tell the truth).

**Rhodes scholarship:** A competitive scholarship program established through the estate of Cecil J. Rhodes that funds study for two or three years at Oxford University in England.

**Sanctions:** Punishment against a nation involved in activities considered illegal under international law; such punishment usually denies trade, supplies, or access to other forms of international assistance to the nation.

**Social Security:** A government program that provides pensions (a regular sum of money) to American workers after they reach age sixty-five.

**Welfare:** Government assistance to impoverished people.

Training Corps at the University of Arkansas but did not follow through after his lottery number made him extremely unlikely to be drafted. His actions to avoid military service were later publicized by his political opponents in an attempt to discredit him.

After completing his studies in England, Clinton moved on to the law school at Yale University, from which he graduated in 1973. He returned to his home state to teach at the University of Arkansas law school.

A teenaged Bill Clinton (left) shakes hands with President John Kennedy in 1963; this meeting inspired Clinton to become a politician.
*Photography by Arnold Sachs. Reproduced by permission of Archive Photos.*

## Learning from defeat

Clinton was already politically active by then. In 1972, he had worked in the presidential campaign of South Dakota senator George McGovern (1922– ), serving as the campaign's coordinator in Texas. Hillary Rodham (1947– ; see entry on **Hillary Rodham Clinton** in volume 5), a fellow law student at Yale with whom he fell in love, also worked for the McGovern campaign. She came to teach at the University of Arkansas in

1974 after having served as a legal assistant to the U.S. House of Representatives committee that considered impeachment of President **Richard Nixon** (1913–1994; see entry in volume 5). Clinton and Rodham were married on October 11, 1975. Their daughter, Chelsea, was born on February 27, 1980.

Clinton ran for the U.S. House of Representatives in 1974. He lost the election against the popular Republican incumbent (the elected official holding office at that time), John Paul Hammerschmidt (1922– ), but gained valuable recognition and experience from his strong showing. Two years later, Clinton was elected attorney general of Arkansas. In that position, he worked on behalf of consumers and the environment against large utility (power, light, and water) companies. In 1978, he was elected the state's governor at age thirty-two. With a group of young and idealistic supporters, Clinton took an aggressive approach to improving the state's education system and roads. He suffered a backlash when he raised driver's license fees to help pay for his program. In addition, he angered the state's powerful timber, poultry, and energy industries by challenging their pricing practices and land use. Clinton was defeated in a reelection bid in 1980 by Republican Frank White (1933– ).

The defeat made him a more cautious politician. He learned to build support and estimate public opinion rather than attempt to lead by force of his authority. He won the governorship again in 1982 and was reelected to four consecutive two-year terms. In 1990, he was reelected to a four-year term. (While he was governor, the state law on governor's tenure changed from two-year to four-year terms.)

Clinton was successful as governor in tackling the state's education problems. Following a study coordinated by Hillary Rodham Clinton, the governor instituted a program that raised teacher salaries and set up testing programs for teachers and students. Students had to pass a basic skills exam in order to move on to high school. By 1992, Arkansas had the best high-school graduation rate in the nation. Clinton also improved health care in the state and initiated a job training program that was mandatory for all welfare recipients (people of working age who receive financial assistance from the government). He attracted businesses to the state that led to the creation of over two hundred thousand jobs.

## National reputation

His national reputation grew with these successes and other activities. In 1985 and 1986, Clinton was chairman of the Southern Growth Policies Board, which recommended new areas for economic development for the region. In 1988, Clinton gave the nominating speech for the Democratic presidential candidate, Massachusetts governor Michael Dukakis (1933– ), at the party's national convention. The national exposure was a mixed blessing: often, the person giving the nominating speech is being presented to the public as someone to watch for in future elections; but many believed Clinton overstayed his welcome by making a long speech.

In 1990, Clinton was named chairman of the Democratic Leadership Council. Through that position, he convinced Democratic officials to take more moderate stands on policies than the party's New England faction did; that group favored large government programs to address the nation's problems. Working with other southern leaders, including Al Gore (1948– ; see box), a U.S. senator from Tennessee, Clinton forged a group called the New Democrats. They brought a more business-oriented approach to issues than did their party colleagues. In 1991, Clinton was voted most effective governor by his peers in a poll conducted by *Newsweek* magazine.

## "It's the economy, stupid"

That year, Clinton announced his candidacy for president. Most leading Democrats were reluctant to enter the race at that time because Republican president **George Bush** (1924– ; see entry in volume 5) was enormously popular. Bush's support gradually eroded, however, as the American economy weakened. Clinton's early start helped him stay ahead of leading Democratic challengers as they entered the race. He recovered quickly from setbacks and was widely visible in town meetings and television talk shows. He proposed programs to improve the economy, create jobs, provide national health insurance, and reduce the federal budget deficit. (National health insurance refers to a proposed government program that would ensure that all Americans would have medical insurance coverage to help pay for medical expenses; the federal budget deficit is a shortage that occurs when the government spends more money than it collects.)

## Election Results

### 1992

| Presidential / Vice presidential candidates | Popular votes | Presidential electoral votes |
|---|---|---|
| Bill Clinton / Al Gore (Democratic) | 44,908,233 | 370 |
| George Bush / Dan Quayle (Republican) | 39,102,282 | 168 |
| H. Ross Perot / James B. Stockdale (Independent Ticket) | 19,221,433 | 0 |

*Texas businessman Perot's strong third-party presence in the race resulted in the first time in history that a presidential candidate (Clinton) won with less than half of the popular vote.*

### 1996

| Presidential / Vice presidential candidates | Popular votes | Presidential electoral votes |
|---|---|---|
| Bill Clinton / Al Gore (Democratic) | 45,590,703 | 379 |
| Robert Dole / Jack Kemp (Republican) | 37,816,307 | 159 |
| H. Ross Perot / Pat Choate (Reform) | 7,866,284 | 0 |

During the campaign, Clinton was confronted with several public revelations about his behavior—from avoidance of the draft to marital infidelities. By early summer of 1992, he trailed not only President George Bush, but a third-party candidate, Texas businessman H. Ross Perot (1930– ; see box in **George Bush** entry in volume 5), as well. Perot's main campaign issue—reducing the federal deficit—was embraced by Clinton. Perot quit the race for personal reasons on the same day that Clinton was officially nominated as the Democratic candidate for president.

Clinton's selection of Tennessee senator Al Gore, an experienced Washington, D.C., politician, gave energy to the campaign. The two idealistic and moderate Democrats formed the youngest-ever presidential ticket in combined years of age.

Campaigning on the theme that government should take a more active role in improving the economy, Clinton generated support over Bush's policy of limited government.

# Al Gore

After having been among the most active and influential vice presidents in American history, Al Gore narrowly lost the presidential election of 2000 to **George W. Bush** (1946– ; see entry in volume 5). Gore became the third Democratic Party candidate to win the popular vote but lose in the Electoral College. The other two Democrats were Samuel J. Tilden (1814–1886; see box in **Rutherford B. Hayes** entry in volume 3) in 1876 and **Grover Cleveland** (1837–1908; see entry in volume 3) in 1888. When Gore left office in 2001 as vice president, it was the first time in twenty-five years that Gore did not hold an elected position in Washington, D.C.

Born in 1948 in Carthage, Tennessee, Albert Gore Jr. spent part of his childhood living on the family farm and in Washington, D.C., while his father served in the U.S. Senate. While his parents made the rounds of speeches and meetings, young Al was left in the care of Alota and William Thompson, tenant farmers who ran the Gore family farm. Gore's father, Albert Gore Sr. (1907–1998), was a three-term senator from Tennessee. His mother, Pauline (1913– ), was among the first women graduates from Vanderbilt University's law school.

After graduating from Harvard University in 1969, Gore served in the U.S. Army as a reporter during the Vietnam War. Like his father, who lost reelection in 1970 in part for his opposition to the war, Gore

did not support continued American military involvement in Vietnam. Gore remarked that his father's experience through the Vietnam era taught him the importance of standing up for one's beliefs. Following his military service, Gore worked as a reporter for a Nashville newspaper while attending law school at Vanderbilt. He married his longtime sweetheart, Mary Elizabeth (Tipper) Aitcheson (1948– ); they would eventually have four children.

Covering local government as a reporter reawakened Gore's interest in politics. He ran for U.S. Congress in 1976 and won the election. During a distinguished congressional career, Gore served four terms in the House and was elected to two terms in the Senate. Gore became known for his intense attention to research and detail—a result of his days as an investigative reporter. In 1980, he was assigned to the House Intelligence Committee studying nuclear arms. Committing himself to eight hours a week of study on the subject, Gore eventually published a comprehensive security plan in the February 1982 issue of *Congressional Quarterly.* Three weeks later, a group of American diplomats visiting Moscow to talk with Soviet arms control experts first learned of the "Gore Plan" from the Soviets' copies of Gore's article.

Gore announced his presidential candidacy in 1988. He won presidential primaries in five southern states, but

**Al Gore.** *Reproduced by permission of Archive Photos.*

Massachusetts governor Michael Dukakis won his party's nomination. The following year, Gore experienced a life-changing moment. While leaving a baseball stadium in April 1989 with his six-year old son, Albert III, Gore watched helplessly as the boy darted away from him and was hit by a car. The child was dragged a total of fifty feet. He showed no sign of life by the time his father reached him. The child was rushed to Johns Hopkins Hospital in Baltimore, Maryland. Following surgery and months of rehabilitation, he made a full recovery. But the trauma changed Gore's outlook on life. During this time, Gore began writing *Earth in the Balance,* an examination of how mismanagement of the environment leaves children with what he called a degraded earth and a diminished future.

In 1992, Democratic presidential nominee Bill Clinton selected Gore as his running mate. Although both were southerners who shared many of the same views, Gore balanced the ticket in two important ways: He had served in Vietnam and he had experience in foreign relations. With unemployment high and issues such as health care prominent, Clinton and Gore were effective in campaigning on improving the economy. They won the election, and Gore became one of the most active, high-profile vice presidents in history. During the following eight years, Gore supervised fourteen major policy areas, including the environment, telecommunications, urban policy, government efficiency, and technology.

In 1996, the Clinton-Gore team won reelection. Gore remained loyal to Clinton while the president faced an impeachment trial. In 2000, Gore took on a new challenge: he attempted to become only the second sitting vice president in 150 years to be elected president. In one of the closest and most dramatic elections in U.S. history, Gore won the popular vote but fell short in electoral votes to George W. Bush, son of the former president. (For more information on the close 2000 election, see the **George W. Bush** entry in volume 5.)

*Bill Clinton was the first president born after World War II.*

The Clinton campaign staff was inspired by a slogan they used among themselves, "It's the economy, stupid," to constantly remind them that the economy was the major issue. Publicly, Clinton spoke for "the forgotten middle class"—working Americans who were most harmed by the effects of budget deficits and the sluggish economy.

Clinton took the lead in polls and maintained it when the Republican national convention became bogged down in debate among religious conservatives and a more moderate faction represented by Bush. When Perot suddenly reentered the race a few weeks before election day, none of the three candidates was able to draw more support. Clinton won a sound victory in the Electoral College—370 votes to 168—over Bush, but he won only forty-three percent of the popular vote. (The Electoral College is a body officially responsible for electing the president of the United States. In presidential elections, a candidate must win a majority of electoral votes—over fifty percent—in order to win the presidency. For more information on the Electoral College, see boxes in **George W. Bush** entry in volume 5.) Bush won thirty-seven percent, and Perot, in the best third-party showing since former president **Theodore Roosevelt** (1858–1919; see entry in volume 3) placed second in 1912, won nineteen percent.

## Slow start

President Clinton had very mixed results during his first two years in office. He appointed a record number of women and minorities to government positions, but several of his choices were not approved by Congress. Clinton moved quickly on a controversial issue—whether or not homosexuals should be allowed in the military—before Congress, the military, and the general public had a chance to debate the issue. He promoted a "don't ask, don't tell" policy. This expression means that military officials are discouraged from questioning new military recruits about their sexual preference, and military personnel are not required to answer questions about it. The policy was generally considered a failure and did not resolve debates concerning sexual orientation and the military.

Meanwhile, the president changed his mind on a campaign pledge to restrict trade with China because of that

# Bill Clinton Administration

**Administration Dates**
January 20, 1993–January 20, 1997
January 20, 1997–January 20, 2001

**Vice President**
Al Gore (1993–2001)

## Cabinet

**Secretary of State**
Warren M. Christopher (1993–97)
Madeleine Albright (1997–2001)

**Secretary of the Treasury**
Lloyd M. Bentsen (1993–94)
Robert E. Rubin (1995–99)
Lawrence H. Summers (1999–2001)

**Secretary of Defense**
Les Aspin (1993–94)
William J. Perry (1994–97)
William S. Cohen (1997–2001)

**Attorney General**
Janet Reno (1993–2001)

**Secretary of the Interior**
Bruce Babbitt (1993–2001)

**Secretary of Agriculture**
Mike Espy (1993–94)
Daniel Glickman (1994–2001)

**Secretary of Commerce**
Ronald H. Brown (1993–96)

Mickey Kantor (1996–97)
William M. Daley (1997–2000)
Norman Y. Mineta (2000–2001)

**Secretary of Labor**
Robert B. Reich (1993–97)
Alexis M. Herman (1997–2001)

**Secretary of Health and Human Services**
Donna E. Shalala (1993–2001)

**Secretary of Housing and Urban Development**
Henry G. Cisneros (1993–97)
Andrew M. Cuomo (1997–2001)

**Secretary of Transportation**
Federico Peña (1993–97)
Rodney Slater (1997–2001)

**Secretary of Energy**
Hazel R. O'Leary (1993–97)
Federico Peña (1997–98)
Bill Richardson (1998–2001)

**Secretary of Education**
Richard W. Riley (1993–2001)

**Secretary of Veteran Affairs**
Jesse Brown (1993–97)
Togo D. West Jr. (1997–2000)
Hershel W. Gober (2000–2001)

country's human-rights violations. He decided that open trade might encourage China to become a more democratic government.

Clinton experienced his biggest policy failure in his administration's pursuit of a national health insurance program. He appointed his wife, Hillary, to investigate various options and make proposals. She had handled a similar task on education issues when Clinton was governor of Arkansas. The Clinton health plan faced resistance from the massive health insurance industry. Many in Congress and the general public found the program Clinton eventually proposed too complicated and believed that too much government supervision was required.

Clinton enjoyed several successes. The Family and Medical Leave Act of 1993 allowed parents of newborns and people with medical problems to take up to twelve weeks of unpaid leave from their jobs. Clinton helped push through Congress the North American Free Trade Agreement (NAFTA), which the Bush administration had negotiated with Canada and Mexico. The agreement lifted virtually all restrictions in trade between the three nations. The more sweeping General Agreement on Tariffs and Trade (GATT) followed and further strengthened international trade. Another agreement opened up more American trade with Asian nations on the Pacific Rim (nations with access to the Pacific Ocean).

Through the efforts of Vice President Gore, the Clinton administration was able to trim the number of federal employees and make the government more efficient. A sweeping crime bill in 1994 provided federal money to states to hire an additional one hundred thousand police officers nationwide.

Clinton's early troubles, however, and a well-organized Republican national campaign, led to large gains by Republicans in midterm congressional elections of 1994. Republicans rallied around a "Contract with America," whereby party candidates promised to move quickly on a wide variety of legislative programs within one hundred days. When Republicans won majorities in both houses of Congress, they were able to fulfill the contract. A sweeping welfare reform package was soon passed as part of the contract, and President Clinton signed it into law. Both sides claimed credit for the program. For President Clinton to support and then sign a bill reforming and reducing government involvement in a major social program was a significant break from his Democratic presidential predecessors.

A stalemate over the president's budget in 1995, however, proved disastrous for congressional Republicans. They wanted to cut many of Clinton's proposed expenditures in order to fund a tax break. Clinton refused. The federal budget must be approved in order for the government to pay federal workers and fund programs. When Republicans refused to enact temporary funding measures, the government literally shut down. National parks and museums, as well as many government agencies, were closed. The public backlash over this costly political showdown hurt Republicans more than the president. Clinton gained further public support by defending such programs as Social Security and Medicare. (Social Security is a government program that provides pensions—a regular sum of money—to Americans after age sixty-five; Medicare provides financial aid to cover the cost of older Americans' medical expenses.

By the election year of 1996, momentum was clearly on the president's side. Clinton was helped by a booming economy. Increases in jobs and wages led to increased tax revenue; the huge federal deficit was cut in half by 1996. Crime was down as well.

Clinton remained ahead of his rivals during the presidential campaign of 1996. Winning six percent more of the popular vote than he had in 1992, Clinton easily outdistanced Republican nominee Robert Dole (1923– ), who won thirty-seven percent of the vote, and third-party candidate H. Ross Perot, who received eight percent of the vote.

## Assertive militarism

Internationally, the world had changed in the early 1990s. After World War II (1939–45), many nations of the world allied either with the United States or with the Soviet Union. With the collapse of the Soviet Union in 1991, the United States began working more closely with the United Nations for international cooperation against acts of aggression by one nation or one ethnic group against another. For the important post of U.S. ambassador to the United Nations, he chose Madeleine Albright (1937– ; see box). She had previously advised several Democratic leaders on international affairs.

The first test faced by the United States and other nations occurred in the African country of Somalia. A civil war there left thousands suffering from starvation and abuse. The

# Madeleine Albright

When Madeleine Albright was named U.S. ambassador to the United Nations (U.N.) in 1993, she completed a circle of family involvement with the organization. Her father, Josef Korbel, had been a Czechoslovakian diplomat and became chairman of a special U.N. commission shortly after World War II. When he completed his work, he asked the U.S. government for political asylum (protection against political oppression) following a communist takeover of his country.

Born Maria Jana Korbel in 1937 in Prague, Czechoslovakia, Albright was rechristened Madeleine when her family settled in America. Describing her early life to the *Los Angeles Times,* she said she was "the little blond girl in the newsreels who would be handing flowers to arriving diplomats." After her family was granted political asylum in the United States, her father became a professor at the University of Denver.

Albright graduated with honors from Wellesley College in 1959. Three days later, she married Joseph Albright, a descendent of a family of newspaper publishers. Albright worked with the *Rolla Daily News* in Missouri before moving to Chicago with her husband. In the mid-1970s, Albright

and her family moved to Washington, D.C. While raising her three young children, she earned a doctorate by commuting to Columbia University in New York. She became a legislative assistant to U.S. senator Edmund S. Muskie (1914–1996) of Maine in 1976. In 1978, she served on the national security staff of President Jimmy Carter (1924– ; see entry in volume 5) as a legislative liaison for her former Columbia University professor, national security advisor Zbigniew Brzezinski (1928– ).

Albright joined the faculty of Georgetown University in 1982 and served as an advisor to two Democratic presidential candidates, Walter F. Mondale (1928– ) in 1984 and Michael Dukakis in 1988. After Dukakis's defeat, Albright became president of the Center for National Policy, a Democratic think tank (a group that discusses policies and issues). Specializing in Eastern Europe and the Soviet Union, Albright consistently advocated a more active U.S. role in promoting democracy in those countries. Upon her appointment to the United Nations by President Clinton in 1993, Albright was thrust immediately into pressing issues, including the administration's response to the civil war in the former nation of Yugoslavia, which had divided into five

United States sent a military force to protect food and medical supplies. The mission proved unpopular at home when American military personnel were shot at. The American force was withdrawn and replaced by a U.N. force.

**Madeleine Albright.** *Photography by Rick Wilking. Reproduced by permission of Archive Photos.*

independent nations. During the next four years, she supported policies involving economic sanctions against Iraq (which were initially put in place after the conclusion of the Persian Gulf War), relief efforts for the African nations of Somalia and Rwanda, and the movement toward democracy in the Caribbean country of Haiti.

Following President Clinton's re-election in 1996, several changes were made to his Cabinet, including the resignation of the secretary of state, Warren Christopher (1925– ). Clinton nominated Albright to be the country's first female secretary of state, and the U.S. Senate quickly confirmed her nomination. She took office at the beginning of 1997. Albright had numerous issues and conflicts to confront. She helped convince Clinton to keep U.S. troops stationed in Bosnia (one of the five nations formed from Yugoslavia) past a June 1998 deadline in order to protect a peace agreement. She was a forceful advocate for the improvement of the human rights situation in China, and she helped ease Russian opposition to an expansion of the North Atlantic Treaty Organization (NATO) with nations formerly dominated by the Soviet Union. Perhaps her most important mission as secretary of state was helping further Israeli-Palestinian peace negotiations.

According to the *U.S. News and World Report,* Albright believed that there were some advantages to being a female secretary of state. "I can maybe be less formal or can sit down with children or hold a baby or something like that." She added, "It doesn't matter what gender the secretary of state of the United States is. The most important advantage is that I am representing the United States."

In other trouble spots, the United States worked through such organizations as the North Atlantic Treaty Organization (NATO), an alliance of nations created by the North Atlantic Treaty in 1949. Fighting between ethnic groups in the nation of Bosnia was fierce, but West European countries were reluctant to enter the dangerous situation. (Bosnia and Herzegovina, which together became one of five nations formed after the dissolution of Yugoslavia, is often referred to simply as Bosnia.) American air strikes against Bosnian Serbs, a group that was engaged in the genocidal practice of "ethnic cleansing," helped begin peace negotiations. (Genocide means the deliberate destruction of a group of people because of race, ethnic background, or political or religious beliefs. Ethnic cleansing is the continual mistreatment, forceful removal from an area, imprisonment, and killing, sometimes in great numbers, of an ethnic minority by a more powerful ethnic majority.) In 1995, a multi-ethnic government was formed and a NATO peacekeeping force (a military group authorized by international agreement to maintain the peace in a troubled area) that included twenty thousand U.S. soldiers enforced the ceasefire.

When the Kosovo region of Serbia attempted to gain independence, a brutal ethnic-cleansing campaign against citizens of Albanian descent in Kosovo was launched by Serbian president Slobodan Milosevic (1941– ). His army entered Kosovo early in 1999. NATO began bombing raids in the spring. A peace agreement that granted self-rule for Kosovo was approved by the Serbian parliament, and the air strikes ended in June 1999. Milosevic was voted out of power in Serbia in 2000. Meanwhile, beginning in late 1998, the United States and Great Britain launched air strikes against Iraq after that nation violated the terms of its surrender in the Gulf War of 1991.

The strategy of "assertive militarism," as Madeleine Albright called it, was a new form of international cooperation against acts of aggression. The United Nations, often influenced by forceful leadership from the United States, became a stronger body through which international coalitions (partnerships) could be formed to police troubled areas.

President Clinton faced difficulties with the communist nations of Cuba and North Korea. The president ordered sanctions against Cuba when that government encouraged thousands of refugees, many emptied out of Cuban prisons, to flee to the United States. (Sanctions are forms of punishment, often economic in nature, against a nation involved in activities considered illegal under international law.) Mean-

while, evidence mounted that North Korea was building a nuclear weapons program. After pressuring North Korea, the
Clinton administration agreed to help that nation develop
safe forms of nuclear energy; in exchange, North Korea shut
down factories suspected of nuclear weapons research. In
2000, Madeleine Albright became the highest-ranking American official ever to visit North Korea. The United States established more normal relations with Communist China and the
independent nation of Russia, opening up trade while apply-
ing pressure privately for those nations to embrace democratic reform.

President Clinton's most successful foreign policy initiative involved Mexico, after it fell dangerously close to economic collapse in 1994. Clinton offered over $12 billion in
loans over the objections of Congress. He demanded that
Mexico follow strict economic policies that would invite foreign investment. The plan worked, as Mexico paid off a majority of the loans ahead of schedule.

*Israeli prime minister
Yitzhak Rabin (left),
President Clinton (center),
and Palestine Liberation
Organization (PLO)
chairman Yasser Arafat
(right) at the White House
after signing a peace accord
in 1993. Reproduced by
permission of Archive Photos.*

# Alan Greenspan

Born in New York City on March 6, 1926, Alan Greenspan was the only child of Herman H. and Rose G. Greenspan. Greenspan attended public schools in New York City and enrolled in the famous Juilliard School of Music. He left after a year to play tenor saxophone and clarinet in a swing band. At New York University, he received bachelor's and master's degrees in economics in 1948 and 1950.

In the early 1950s, Greenspan came under the intellectual influence of novelist Ayn Rand (1905–1982). According to *U.S. News and World Report,* Greenspan said that Rand made "me see that capitalism is not only efficient and practical, but also moral." Greenspan virtually invented the business of providing economic analyses specifically for senior business executives. He and bond trader William Townsend founded an economic consulting firm that provided industrial and financial institutions with forecasts and other business-related services. The firm was immediately successful and Greenspan became a wealthy man. He was named to the boards of such prestigious companies as Alcoa, Capital Cities/ABC, J.P. Morgan & Co., and Mobil Corporation. He was also elected chairman of the Conference of Business Economists, president of the National Association of Business Economists, and director of the National Economists Club.

Greenspan's career in the private sector (private industry) was interrupted by calls to public service. He served as chairman of the Council of Economic Advisors (1974–77), as chairman of the Commission on Social Security Reform (1981–83), and as a consultant to the Congressional Budget Office. Greenspan assumed his most important public position on August 11, 1987, replacing Paul A. Volcker (1927– ) as chairman of the Board of Governors of the Federal Reserve System (the Fed). The Fed controls the creation of money and influences key interest rates, thereby controlling fluctuations in prices of financial market assets, such as stocks and bonds. The Fed also provides temporary loans (through the so-called discount window) to banks and other financial institutions in times of need. This "lender of last resort" function was the primary reason the Fed was created by Congress in 1913. It was intended to combat a trend that when an individual bank failed it often affected other banks and led to a general financial market collapse.

Less than two months after assuming office, Greenspan was faced with such a financial market crisis. On "Black Monday," October 19, 1987, the stock market collapsed as terrified sellers dumped millions of shares. Falling stock prices automatically triggered millions of additional sale orders. Buyers who had previously bought stocks "on margin"—borrowing some portion of the purchase price—were forced to provide additional collateral (money or other items of value) when

**Alan Greenspan.** *Photography by Gary Hershorn. Reproduced by permission of Archive Photos.*

these stock prices fell. The financial system neared collapse from a lack of ready cash. Acting quickly, Greenspan met with top Fed officials and mapped a strategy for easing the cash crunch, using the Fed's financial power to strengthen the troubled financial institutions. Before the market opened on Tuesday, October 20, Greenspan announced the Fed's "readiness to serve." With the full force and power of the Fed backing, the fear of a general collapse receded and stocks soon rebounded.

Greenspan's worries were far from over. The federal budget deficit had swollen to $221 billion by 1986 and was exerting a powerful inflationary effect on the economy. Having weathered the financial market panic of 1987, Greenspan

sought to send a clear signal that the fight against inflation was now his top priority. His four-year term as chairman expired in 1991. However, President Bush reappointed Greenspan. In 1996 and 2000, President Clinton reappointed Greenspan to additional four-year terms.

Greenspan calmed uncertain domestic and global economic markets. From 1989 to 1992, he tightened lending practices, and he refused to inflate the money supply in reaction to a temporary worldwide price hike for oil. By 1992, the economy was on an upward trend. In 1994, Greenspan raised interest rates several times in a successful effort to thwart possible inflation. Over the next few years, the Fed gradually decreased the prime lending rate. As a result, the economy boomed at an historic pace, the federal budget balanced, and the nation's inflation rate fell below two percent.

In 1998, a Louis Harris survey of four hundred senior executives gave Greenspan a favorable rating of ninety-seven percent. Greenspan, who married television reporter Andrea Mitchell, has sometimes been described as the second most powerful person in the world, after the American president. The 1990s, as a period marked by peace and prosperity in the United States, could easily be called the Age of Greenspan.

*Clinton was the first elected president ever to face an impeachment trial in the Senate. President Andrew Johnson faced a trial in 1868, but he was not an elected president; he had assumed office following the assassination of President Abraham Lincoln. In 1974, President Richard Nixon resigned before facing a vote of impeachment.*

The Clinton administration encouraged notable but fragile achievements in peace talks between Great Britain and Northern Ireland, and with Israel and its Middle East neighbors. Those areas, long in conflict, had the framework for peaceful coexistence. In 1993, Clinton helped arrange a peace accord between Israeli prime minister Yitzhak Rabin and Palestine Liberation Organization (PLO) chairman Yasser Arafat. Rabin was later assassinated by an Israeli extremist upset with the accord. Further cooperation between Israel and Palestine led to the 1998 Wye River Accord (named after the negotiation site in Maryland). That sense of cooperation remained fragile. In the autumn of 2000, daily violence erupted in areas where Israelis and Palestinians share neighborhoods.

## Economic heights

At home, the economy continued to boom. In 1997, the level of unemployment in the nation reached a thirty-year low. In 1998, the federal budget showed a surplus (more money collected than spent). By 2000, the nation continued the longest sustained economic growth in its history. The economic conditions were closely monitored by Alan Greenspan (1926– ; see box), chairman of the Federal Reserve.

Clinton had campaigned in 1992 on behalf of the "forgotten middle class" and had promised tax relief (a reduction in taxes) for that group. Greenspan impressed on Clinton the need to concentrate instead on reducing the federal deficit. Clinton's 1993 deficit reduction plan included tax increases of $250 billion, largely gathered from the nation's wealthiest individuals and through a tax on gasoline. Greenspan, meanwhile, used his power as Federal Reserve chairman to encourage investment and spending. Those actions helped fuel a return to prosperity. In addition, the Clinton administration's energetic expansion of international trade opened new markets for American products in the global economy (a term that reflects interrelationships among businesses in several countries).

As his presidency drew to a close, Clinton began introducing social, environmental, and education programs. He called for an end to the "digital divide"—an expression that describes how wealthier school districts have better access to the Internet than poorer ones.

Clinton's presidency began with questions concerning how best to attack the nation's economic problems. It ended with the question of how best to use the government surplus. Clinton, however, was fortunate to still be president at the end of the century. In 1999, he became the second president ever to face an impeachment trial in the Senate. **Andrew Johnson** (1808–1875; see entry in volume 2) was the first; Johnson had escaped removal from office by the slimmest of margins: one vote.

With first lady Hillary Rodham Clinton looking on, President Bill Clinton denies on January 26, 1998, that he had sexual relations with former White House intern Monica Lewinsky. Seven months later, he admitted that he did. *Reproduced by permission of Archive Photos.*

## Personal lows

What became known as the Whitewater scandal began with a 1978 real estate deal involving Bill and Hillary Clinton while he was governor of Arkansas. The Clintons' partner in the deal used profits to open up a bank that later failed and was bailed out by the federal government. Improprieties in the deal and the question of whether Clinton had

# Janet Reno

The seventy-eighth attorney general of the United States and the first woman to hold the position, Janet Reno had a high profile and often controversial tenure. Born on July 21, 1938, in Miami, Florida, Reno was the eldest of the four children of journalists Henry and Jane Reno. Reno's father, a Danish immigrant, was a police reporter for the *Miami Herald,* and Reno's mother was an investigative reporter for the now defunct *Miami News.*

After graduating from local public schools, Reno attended Cornell University. She graduated with a degree in chemistry in 1960, then entered the Harvard University Law School, from which she graduated in 1963. In 1962, she had been denied a summer job by a prominent Miami law firm because she was a woman; later, in the mid-1970s, she became a partner (part of a group that directs a firm's activities) of that same firm. She worked with private law firms from 1963 to 1971, then began serving as a lawyer for the state of Florida. Working with the Florida House of Representatives during 1971 and 1972, Reno helped revise the state constitution to allow for a reorganization of the state's court system. She held other important positions with the state before returning to private practice in 1976. Reno was appointed the top prosecutor for Dade County, Florida, in 1978 and held the position until 1993.

After some early setbacks, she won a strong reputation as a tough prosecutor.

Reno's successes in prosecuting violent crimes won approval from opponents, and she received praise from some minority communities for her efforts to use the prosecutor's office to tackle social ills affecting society. Reno tried alternatives to the incarceration of youth, stressing the link between a nurturing childhood and the prevention of crime. She aggressively prosecuted child abuse cases; pursued delinquent fathers for child support; and established a domestic crime unit. By 1993, when she was nominated as attorney general by President Bill Clinton, her reputation was such that she was confirmed unanimously by the Senate after smooth hearings.

Reno barely had time to settle into the job when controversy erupted. The Branch Davidians, a religious cult with ties to private militia movements (military-styled groups) opposed to taxes and gun control, refused to allow government law officials into its compound (a group of buildings) in Waco, Texas, to investigate alleged illegal activities, including stockpiling weapons and abusing children. Four federal agents died in an attempted raid in March 1993. Cult members barricaded themselves in the compound. After six weeks, federal agents stormed the compound, using tear gas. A raging fire ensued, and eighty of eighty-nine members of the cult were killed in the blaze. Arguments over the cause of the fire eventually

**Janet Reno.** *Reproduced by permission of the Corbis Corporation.*

led to a trial in 2000 to determine if government officials were responsible. A five-person jury advised the judge of the case that the fire was likely started by cult members, and the judge cleared the government of wrongdoing.

Scandals involving President Clinton and members of his administration also brought controversy to Reno. She had to rule whether or not there was sufficient grounds to pursue several cases. In the partisan atmosphere of Washington, D.C., Reno faced criticism whether she approved or denied such investigations. She did allow a special prosecutor of the Whitewater scandal to broaden his case, which eventually led to the impeachment trial of President Clinton.

In 2000, Reno's department became involved in an international case surrounding Elian Gonzalez, a six-year-old boy who was part of a group of ten people fleeing Cuba. The boat of the ten refugees (which included his mother) sank off the coast of Florida, and only the boy survived a rescue attempt. Relatives of the boy in Florida fought against judicial orders that he be returned to his father in Cuba. The event dragged on for several months before the boy was forcibly removed from the custody of relatives during a government raid and returned to his father. Outrage followed on the part of those who wanted the boy to remain in the United States. Some congressional Republicans called for an investigation, but the action was quickly halted when it was obvious that most Americans agreed that court rulings should be upheld and the boy should be returned to his father.

Reno weathered such controversies and sustained criticism by political opponents to become the longest-serving U.S. attorney general. She disclosed in 1995 that she was suffering from early stages of Parkinson's disease, a degenerative nerve disorder. That cut down on her ability to pursue her hobbies of hiking and canoeing, but she remained dedicated to public service.

# "High Crimes and Misdemeanors"

Article II, section 4, of the U.S. Constitution states: "The President, Vice President, and all civil Officers of the United States, shall be removed from Office on Impeachment for, and Conviction of, Treason, Bribery, or other High Crimes and Misdemeanors."

The Framers of the Constitution deliberately used, but did not define, "high crimes and misdemeanors." Congress was left to decide the definition, and, thus, impeachment is a matter of political judgment. When the Constitution was being written, George Mason (1725–1792; see box in **James Madison** entry in volume 1) and **James Madison** (1751–1836; see entry in volume 1) argued that there were other "great and dangerous offenses" than treason and bribery, and Mason proposed adding

"high crimes and misdemeanors." In eighteenth-century English language, a "misdemeanor" meant bad behavior (corruption, for example), and "high crimes" was similar to "great and dangerous offenses." Politicians, lawyers, and historians have been arguing about the exact meaning of "high crimes and misdemeanors" ever since.

That debate was prominent during the impeachment trial of President Bill Clinton. Most Americans and U.S. senators agreed that Clinton had committed personal offenses, and some argued that those wrongs had compromised the office of the president. However, many agreed that those acts did not jeopardize the nation as "great and dangerous offenses." The president survived the Senate impeachment trial based primarily on that view.

misused his authority as governor became the focus of an investigation beginning in 1994. An independent counsel began examining evidence; the independent counsel—an investigative lawyer—was a federal position established during the 1970s to investigate federal officials accused of crimes in a nonpartisan manner.

During the investigation, questions arose about several possibly related actions during Clinton's presidency, including misuse of Federal Bureau of Investigation (FBI) files, the firing of officials in the White House travel office, and campaign fund-raising activities. The taint of scandal seemed everywhere. However, after a five-year, $50 million investigation, the president was not charged with wrongdoing when the Whitewater investigation ended in 2000.

Newspaper headlines following the impeachment of President Clinton by the U.S. House of Representatives on December 19, 1998. *Reproduced by permission of AP/Wide World Photos.*

Meanwhile, the president had been sued for sexual harassment by Paula Jones, a former Arkansas state government employee. She asserted that then-Governor Clinton had made sexual advances and, when rebuffed, had created a hostile work environment for her. Other claims of extramarital affairs involving Clinton had already surfaced. The sexual harassment case was eventually dismissed in federal court in 1998. During the proceedings, however, the president was

# The Impeachment of Bill Clinton

The House Judiciary Committee originally drew up four articles of impeachment against President Bill Clinton, but the House of Representatives only approved (by majority vote) two of the Articles: Article I charged the president with having committed perjury; and Article II charged him with obstruction of justice.

Several incidents led to the Clinton impeachment trial:

- The Whitewater investigation: President Clinton had been accused of illegal activities involving a real estate deal dating back to 1978 in Arkansas. In January 1994, after continuous pressure by opponents, the Clinton administration appointed a special prosecutor to investigate the accusations. Formed during the 1970s Watergate scandal, the office of special prosecutor is a temporary position convened by the U.S. attorney general to conduct an independent investigation of officials in the Executive branch accused of wrongdoing. Kenneth Starr assumed the position of special prosecutor in August 1994 after the original appointee resigned.

- The Paula Jones sexual harassment case: In May 1994, former Arkansas state worker Paula Jones filed suit claiming sexual harassment by Bill Clinton while he was governor of Arkansas. The question of whether a sitting president can be the subject of a civil (nongovernmental) suit was argued in several courts until May 1997, when the Supreme Court made a historic ruling that Jones's lawsuit could continue while Clinton was president.

- Improper conduct by the president: Clinton and White House intern Monica Lewinsky engaged in an improper sexual relationship during the winter of 1995–96. The affair was brought to the attention of Kenneth Starr, who obtained proof by having Lewinsky's friend, Linda Tripp, audiotape conversations she had with Lewinsky during January 1998. Lewinsky had denied the affair just a few days earlier while testifying in writing (an affadavit) under oath in the Jones lawsuit case. Tripp first began recording on audiotape her conversations with Lewinsky during the summer of 1997. That action was later declared illegal. The taping in January 1998, on the other hand, was a legal act since it was part of a criminal investigation.

Key dates, from January 1998 through 2000:

**January 1998:** January 7—As part of the Paula Jones case, Monica Lewinsky signs an affadavit (legal claim) denying her affair with Clinton. January 16—Lewinsky is privately confronted with evidence of the affair by Starr. January 17—Clinton gives a deposition in the Jones suit, denying an affair with Lewinsky. January 19—Rumors spread over the Internet about an article being planned by *Newsweek* magazine that would publicly expose the Clinton-Lewinsky affair for the first time; *Newsweek* had planned to delay the article until more evidence was presented. January 22 and 26—Clinton emphatically denies having had an affair with Lewinsky to television reporters; the denials are broadcast repeatedly on news shows.

**February 1998:** Starr is accused of pressuring Lewinsky to make false statements, and the Clinton administration files a complaint over leaks of information from Starr's team. Meanwhile, Clinton is accused of having coached and influenced aides to testify in his favor before Starr's grand jury (a group empowered to decide whether a government investigation can provide enough evidence to make criminal charges against a citizen). Clinton and several of his friends are accused of trying to help Lewinsky land a job in return for denying the affair.

**Spring 1998:** April 1—A U.S. district judge in Arkansas dismisses the Jones lawsuit against Clinton for lack of evidence. May 4—A U.S. district court in Washington, D.C., denies Clinton's claim of executive privilege to limit grand jury questioning of him and his aides.

**Summer 1998:** July 17—A judge refuses an attempt by the Clinton administration to shield secret service agents from testifying. Clinton is subpoenaed to testify before the grand jury. August 17—Clinton testifies for four hours before the grand jury. He admits to having had an inappropriate relationship with Lewinsky. September 3—Senator Joseph Lieberman (1942– ) of Connecticut becomes the first Democrat in Congress to publicly rebuke the President. (Lieberman would later become the Democratic vice presidential candidate in 2000). September 11—Clinton publicly apologizes to Lewinsky and her family for the first time.

**Fall 1998:** September 21—The Starr Report, which includes all of Lewinsky's grand jury testimony, is released to the public. October 8—The U.S. House votes to conduct an inquiry on Starr's allegations that Clinton was guilty of perjury and obstruction of justice. November 3—Despite the scandal, Democrats make gains in national elections; over sixty-five percent of voters polled do not want Clinton impeached. November 13—Clinton and Jones settle the lawsuit for $850,000, but with no apology or admission of guilt. November 20—The House Judiciary committee begins an inquiry on whether to impeach Clinton. December 11—The Judiciary Committee, voting strictly on partisan lines, approves four articles of impeachment

→

## The Impeachment of Bill Clinton (contd.)

against President Clinton. December 19—The House votes to impeach Clinton on two of the articles.

**1999:** January 7: Impeachment trial begins in the Senate. February 12: Impeachment trial ends. A two-thirds majority (67 of 100 votes) was necessary to convict the president and remove him from office. The vote on Article I (perjury) was

54 not guilty, and 45 guilty. The vote on Article II (obstruction of justice) was 50 not guilty, 50 guilty.

**Fall 2000:** Independent Prosecutor Act is not renewed by Congress. Whitewater investigation concludes with no official charges of wrongdoing on the part of President and Mrs. Clinton.

forced to testify. A historic Supreme Court ruling in 1997 determined that a sitting president could be called to testify in a civil (non-governmental) court case. Meanwhile, the Whitewater special prosecutor, Kenneth Starr (1946– ), received permission from Attorney General Janet Reno (1938– ; see box) to examine claims that some of the president's testimony in the Jones case was perjurious (false, or marked by perjury).

Perjury came to light when it was discovered that the president had had an inappropriate relationship with a young White House intern, Monica Lewinsky (1973– ), in 1997. Clinton denied the relationship in January 1998, but taped phone conversations by a coworker of Lewinsky's, Linda Tripp (1946– ), revealed her talking candidly about the relationship. Other evidence was uncovered to involve the president. In August 1998, after months of denial, Clinton admitted to an "improper relationship" with the intern.

Independent counsel Kenneth Starr released a long and detailed report in September 1998 that accused the president of having committed perjury and obstruction of justice. In November 1998, the House Judiciary committee began debate on whether the charges were grounds for impeachment. Voting strictly on party lines, the Republican-led majority of the committee voted on four articles of impeachment. The entire House of Representatives then voted by majority (again virtually on party lines) to impeach the president on two of the articles.

The Senate trial began on January 7, 1999, and ended on February 6. Little changed in the accusations or evidence to convince the necessary two-thirds majority in the Senate to vote for impeachment. The president, meanwhile, was shamed before his family and the nation. However, the Constitutional process worked its course, and the president was able to govern effectively again.

When the impeachment trial ended, Senate leaders of the two parties shook hands—a hopeful sign that partisanship might be easing. Despite President Clinton's many confrontations with the Republican Congress, the two groups had managed to pass bills that helped to improve the economy and to reform welfare. Whereas the impeachment of Andrew Johnson in 1868 resulted in a weakened presidency, no significant change in power resulted from Clinton's impeachment. Meanwhile, the legislation that created the office of the independent counsel came up for renewal before Congress in 1999 and was allowed to expire.

Americans turned their attention to the question of what to do with budget surpluses being generated by the booming economy. Some favored returning the money to the people through tax cuts. Others, like President Clinton, wanted to use the money to support Social Security, because many more Americans would be retiring in the near future. That debate, and the ongoing concern of how deeply America should be involved in keeping the peace in foreign conflicts, were significant issues to ponder as America entered the twenty-first century.

## Legacy

During the presidential election of 2000, President Bill Clinton made only a few appearances on behalf of the Democratic nominee, Vice President Al Gore. The president's personal conduct had remained an issue, and there was concern that voters might react against Gore for his association with Clinton. On the other hand, Clinton remained very popular among groups of Americans who prospered during his presidency and who believe that the federal government

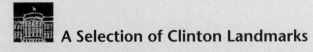

## A Selection of Clinton Landmarks

**Hope, Arkansas, Sites.** Hempstead County Economic Development Corporation, P.O. Box 971, Hope, AR 71802-0971. (800) HOPE-USA. Markers show various sites associated with a young Bill Clinton. As of early 2001, none of the sites other than his birthplace home are open to the public. See http://www.hopeusa.com/clinton/believe.html (accessed on November 6, 2000).

**Hot Springs, Arkansas, Sites.** Hot Springs Convention and Visitors Bureau, 134 Convention Blvd., Box K, Hot Springs National Park, AR 71902. (800) 543-2284. Seven-year-old Bill Clinton moved here with his family in 1953. This tour has markers of sites important to Clinton when he lived in Hot Springs. As of early 2001, none of the sites are open to the public. See http://www.hotsprings.org/things/hometown/default.asp (accessed on November 6, 2000).

**President Clinton's First Home.** P.O. Box 1925, Hope, AR 71802-1925. (800) 338-1384. The home in which Bill Clinton lived during his first four years has been restored. See http://www.hopeusa.com/clinton/house.html and http://www.clintonbirthplace.com/ (accessed on November 6, 2000).

should take an active role in addressing the nation's problems. His rousing campaign appearances on behalf of his wife, Hillary, who was elected U.S. senator from New York in 2000, reflected his continued popularity among a core group of supporters.

Clinton's approach to government was more moderate than those of previous Democratic presidents of the twentieth century. He demonstrated more concern for business growth, pursued trade policies that increased the role of American business in the global economy, and had success in reforming or restructuring some government programs. The economy boomed, trade increased, and waste in government spending was reduced, all of which helped fuel the longest sustained economic growth in American history.

Sustained success in foreign policy proved more elusive. The Clinton administration worked hard in peace efforts between Israel and Palestinian officials, including two important agreements (in 1993 and 1998) for cooperation. Those agreements did not lead to treaties, however, and daily violence erupted between the sides again in 2000. The president's continual pursuit of expanded trade helped improve U.S. relations with many countries.

Clinton proved able to rebound from setbacks and personal scandals. The president's problems and a general climate of partisan politics, however, clouded a time of relative peace and sustained prosperity. The accomplishments of the Clinton administration, especially the president's handling of the economy and his leadership in reforming or expanding government programs, reflected a more moderate approach to government than his Democratic predecessors.

## Where to Learn More

Anderson, Paul. *Janet Reno: Doing the Right Thing*. New York: Wiley, 1994.

Burford, Betty M. *Al Gore: United States Vice President*. Hillside, NJ: Enslow, 1994.

Burns, James MacGregor, and Georgia J. Sorenson. *Dead Center: Clinton-Gore Leadership and the Perils of Moderation*. New York: Scribner, 1999.

Clinton, Bill. *Between Hope and History: Meeting America's Challenges for the 21st Century*. New York: Times Books, 1996.

Cohen, Daniel. *The Impeachment of William Jefferson Clinton*. Brookfield, CT: Twenty-First Century Books, 2000.

Cwiklik, Robert. *Bill Clinton: President of the 90s*. Brookfield, CT: Millbrook Press, 1997.

Dobbs, Michael. *Madeleine Albright: A Twentieth-century Odyssey*. New York: Henry Holt, 1999.

Gore, Albert. *Earth in the Balance: Ecology and the Human Spirit*. Boston: Houghton Mifflin, 1992. Reprint, 2000.

Kelly, Michael. *Bill Clinton*. New York: Chelsea House, 1998.

Kramer, Barbara. *Madeleine Albright: First Woman Secretary of State*. Springfield, NJ: Enslow, 2000.

Maraniss, David. *First in His Class: A Biography of Bill Clinton*. New York: Simon & Schuster, 1995.

Martin, Justin. *Greenspan: The Man Behind the Money*. Cambridge, MA: Perseus Publishing, 2000.

McLoughlin, Merrill, ed. *The Impeachment and Trial of President Clinton: The Official Transcripts, from the House Judiciary Committee Hearings to the Senate Trial*. New York: Times Books, 1999.

Meachum, Virginia. *Janet Reno: United States Attorney General.* Springfield, NJ: Enslow, 1995.

Renshon, Stanley A. *High Hopes: The Clinton Presidency and the Politics of Ambition.* New York: New York University Press, 1998.

Schier, Steven E., ed. *The Postmodern Presidency: Bill Clinton's Legacy in U.S. Politics.* Pittsburgh: University of Pittsburgh Press, 2000.

Stephanopoulos, George. *All Too Human: A Political Education.* New York: Little Brown & Company, 1999.

University of Michigan. Documents Center. *Impeachment of President William Jefferson Clinton.* [Online] http://www.lib.umich.edu/lib-home/Documents.center/impeach.html (accessed on November 14, 2000).

Woodward, Bob. *Maestro: Greenspan's Fed and the American Boom.* New York: Simon & Schuster, 2000.

# Hillary Rodham Clinton

**Born October 26, 1947**
**Chicago, Illinois**

**Politically active lawyer championed children's issues as first lady**

The most politically active first lady since **Eleanor Roosevelt** (1884–1962; see entry in volume 4), Hillary Rodham Clinton spoke out effectively on issues relating to education and children. Before coming to the White House, she chaired an Arkansas state commission on education, served on dozens of corporate and civic boards, and made a career as one of America's leading attorneys. She was named one of the nation's top one hundred lawyers by the *National Law Review* in 1988 and 1991. In 2000, as the first first lady to run for public office, she defeated her opponent in the U.S. senate race in New York.

## Social work

The oldest of three children of Hugh and Dorothy Rodham, Hillary was born on October 26, 1947. Her father owned a fabric store and her mother was a homemaker. Hillary grew up in the Chicago suburb of Park Ridge, Illinois, where she was active in ballet, swimming, tennis, the Girl Scouts, and a church group. Led by Reverend Don Jones, the church group would babysit children of parents who had to

"It is time to break our silence. It is time for us to say . . ., and the world to hear, that it is no longer acceptable to discuss women's rights as separate from human rights."

*Hillary Rodham Clinton*

**Hillary Rodham Clinton.**
*Courtesy of the Library of Congress.*

travel in order to work. The group also raised funds through sporting events and a small circus for poverty-stricken children in urban areas.

Hillary was her high-school class president and a member of the student council and the debate team. She attended Wellesley College in Massachusetts. The assassination in 1968 of civil rights leader Martin Luther King Jr. (1929–1968; see box in **John F. Kennedy** entry in volume 5), whom she had once met through Jones after hearing King preach in 1962, further increased her interest in social justice. Graduating from Wellesley with honors, Clinton became the college's first student commencement speaker, an honor usually reserved for a distinguished professional. She polled her classmates on what she should say and solicited from them poems and ideas. Her goal was to communicate the turmoil of America at a time of an unpopular war, political assassinations, and rioting in cities. The speech was discussed in an article in *Life* magazine, giving Hillary her first national media exposure.

She went on to Yale Law School, where she wrote what became a well-known paper on the rights of children. Hillary worked with impoverished youths at the Yale–New Haven Hospital. At Yale, she met Marian Wright Edelman (1939– ), founder of the Children's Defense Fund (CDF), a Washington-based lobbying group. She would later work for the group as a staff lawyer and board chairperson.

Hillary also met **Bill Clinton** (1946– ; see entry in volume 5) at Yale. Their paths had already crossed briefly when she met him again while registering for classes. He talked with her for an hour as the registration line moved slowly forward. When they reached the front of the line, an official cried out, "Bill, what are you doing here? You already registered."

## Busy professional career

After graduation in 1973, Bill Clinton returned to Arkansas to teach, and Hillary went to Cambridge, Massachusetts, to work at CDF. Soon afterward, she went to Washington, D.C., to serve as a legal assistant to the congressional committee that was considering whether or not to recommend the impeachment of President **Richard Nixon** (1913–1994; see entry in volume 5). After it was shown that the president was involved in the Watergate scandal, Nixon chose to resign instead, rather than face an impeachment trial.

Hillary joined Bill Clinton in Arkansas when she took a teaching position at the University of Arkansas Law School. The Clintons were married in 1975. Hillary continued to teach and headed the legal aid clinic at the school. In 1977, she joined the Rose Law Firm in Little Rock, Arkansas.

Bill Clinton was elected governor of Arkansas in 1978, but he lost his bid for reelection two years later. That same year, the couple's daughter, Chelsea, was born. Clinton was reelected in 1982. Hillary Rodham Clinton became chairperson of the Arkansas Education Standards Committee, an unpaid public position. Traveling throughout the state, she held meetings and visited schools as part of her preparation to recommend improvements in education to state legislators. She supervised a study that led to new standards for public schools, including teacher testing and smaller class sizes. Many of her recommendations became law, and the Arkansas education system showed measurable improvement over the next decade.

Throughout her husband's twelve years as governor, Hillary Rodham Clinton continued her efforts to help children. She initiated the Home Instruction Program for Preschool Youth and became a board member of the state's Children's Hospital. She served on the Southern Governors' Association Task Force on Infant Mortality.

## Going national

At the onset of the 1992 presidential campaign, many Democratic presidential hopefuls believed President **George Bush** (1924– ; see entry in volume 5) was unbeatable because of his popularity after the Gulf War (1991). Clinton began campaigning early for the nomination and established himself as a strong candidate. However, the campaign turned stormy as critics tried to discredit both of the Clintons. After charges of infidelity were made against her husband, Hillary felt obligated to defend her marriage on the television program *60 Minutes*.

Hillary Rodham Clinton's outspokenness sometimes made her a campaign issue. She was often quoted as saying,

**The Clinton family in November 1997.** *Photograph by Ira Schwartz. Reproduced by permission of Archive Photos.*

"If you vote for him, you get me." When asked by the press if her career as a lawyer conflicted with the responsibilities of first lady, Clinton replied, "I suppose I could have stayed home and baked cookies and had teas, but what I decided to do is fulfill my profession." The media zeroed in on the cookie comment, fueling a new controversy. The press also focused attention on Clinton's legal writings, some of them twenty years old and dating from law school. She had once written that the rights of children are often ignored by courts and that at one time in history women, like slaves, had no rights. As a result, her critics accused her of encouraging children to sue their parents over trivial matters and equating marriage with slavery.

Soon after President Clinton's inauguration, he announced that his wife would take the unpaid position as chairperson of a task force charged with producing a health care reform plan. No first lady had ever been given such an important assignment. The goal of the task force was to produce a health care system that would insure all Americans, but the plan was not accepted by Congress.

In the spring of 1995, Hillary Rodham Clinton, accompanied by her daughter, completed a twelve-day goodwill tour of southern Asia, where they met with heads of state and everyday citizens. In September 1995, she served as honorary chairperson of the American delegation to the United Nations Fourth World Conference on Women, held in Beijing, China. At the conference, the first lady delivered an impassioned speech in which, according to *Time* magazine reporter Karen Tumulty, she unleashed the most stinging human rights rebuke ever by a prominent American representing the government on Chinese soil. To great cheers, Clinton declared, "It is time to break our silence. It is time for us to say here in Beijing, and the world to hear, that it is no longer acceptable to discuss women's rights as separate from human rights."

Around the same time, Hillary Rodham Clinton was in the process of writing *It Takes a Village: And Other Lessons Children Teach Us,* which was published in 1996. The book is based on an African proverb: "It takes a village to raise a child." The book became a bestseller.

## Her own career

During her husband's scandal-plagued second term in office, Hillary Rodham Clinton continued to travel the globe, in the process becoming the most traveled first lady in history. She often met with women who ran clinics and small businesses and delivered her usual strong message for better schooling, health care, and empowerment of women. In late

1997, she chaired a White House conference on the issue of child care.

She defended her husband during the impeachment proceedings of late 1998 and early 1999. Even in the 1990s, many in the general public did not know what to make of such an independent and politically active first lady. She won a measure of sympathy after revelations concerning her husband's infidelities became public, but she kept her own feelings private.

In February 2000, after months of speculation, Hillary Rodham Clinton officially announced her candidacy for the U.S. senate position in New York that would be vacated by the retiring Daniel Patrick Moynihan (1927– ). On September 13, she won the Democratic primary, and on November 7, she defeated her Republican opponent, Rick Lazio (1958– ), to become New York's first female U.S. senator.

## Where to Learn More

Clinton, Hillary Rodham. *An Invitation to the White House: At Home with History*. New York: Simon & Schuster, 2000.

Clinton, Hillary Rodham. *It Takes a Village, and Other Lessons Children Teach Us*. New York: Simon & Schuster, 1996.

Kent, Deborah. *Hillary Rodham Clinton*. New York: Children's Press, 1998.

King, Norman. *The Woman in the White House: The Remarkable Story of Hillary Rodham Clinton*. New York: Carol Publishing Group, 1996.

Milton, Joyce. *The First Partner: Hillary Rodham Clinton*. New York: William Morrow, 1999.

# Clinton's Final
# State of the Union Address

**Delivered on January 27, 2000; excerpted from**
*The White House* **(Web site)**

*A once beleaguered leader gushes with optimism as he begins his*
*final year as president*

**W**hen President **Bill Clinton** (1946– ; see entry in volume 5) delivered his final State of the Union address on January 27, 2000, the United States was enjoying its longest ever period of sustained economic growth. Accordingly, his speech was upbeat about the state of the nation, and optimistic on future prospects.

The speech came less than a year after he survived an impeachment trial. That the president could speak boldly of the nation's well-being, and that he proposed more aggressive government programs, showed that the presidency had not been weakened by the impeachment ordeal. However, his speech did not inspire or rally Congress into swift action, either.

Clinton's final State of the Union address was important as a reflection of optimism expressed during a time of prosperity. He envisioned great achievements to come. That view contrasted with the state of the nation at the time he took office in 1992, when America was beset by a sluggish economy. His call in 2000 for increases in government investment in social and educational programs contrasted with his exclamation three years earlier that "the era of big government

"My fellow Americans, we have crossed the bridge we built to the 21st century. Now, we must shape a 21st century American revolution—of opportunity, responsibility and community."

*Bill Clinton*

is over." His optimism contrasted as well with the image a year earlier of a beleaguered leader fighting to save his presidency.

## Things to remember while reading an excerpt from President Clinton's final State of the Union address:

- After a rousing opening statement, the president reviewed some of the nation's recent accomplishments. He then envisioned a better world, made pledges to help bring that world about, and suggested several courses of action.

- All presidents have their personal "defining issues"—beliefs on which they stand with conviction. President Clinton's defining issues appear in the following excerpt: he wanted to continue to reduce the federal deficit, protect Social Security and Medicare, and improve education. The prosperity of the nation created a government surplus (more money collected than spent). President Clinton wanted that money used to invest in his defining issues.

- The largest portion of the president's proposals concerned education (included in the excerpt). Not excerpted are comments he made on such issues as health care and the environment.

## *Excerpt from President Clinton's final State of the Union address*

*We are fortunate to be alive at this moment in history. Never before has our nation enjoyed, at once, so much prosperity and social progress with so little internal crisis and so few external threats. Never before have we had such a blessed opportunity—and, therefore, such a profound obligation—to build the more perfect union of our founders' dreams.*

*We begin the new century with over 20 million new jobs; the fastest economic growth in more than 30 years; the lowest unemployment rates in 30 years; the lowest poverty rates in 20 years; the lowest African American and Hispanic unemployment rates on* record; the first back-to-back **budget surpluses** in 42 years. And next month, America will achieve the longest period of economic growth in our entire history.

We have built a new economy.

And our economic revolution has been matched by a revival of the American spirit: crime down by 20 percent, to its lowest level in 25 years; teen births down seven years in a row; adoptions up by 30 percent; welfare rolls cut in half to their lowest levels in 30 years.

My fellow Americans, the state of our union is the strongest it has ever been.

As always, the real credit belongs to the American people. My gratitude also goes to those of you in this chamber who have worked with us to put progress over **partisanship**.

Eight years ago, it was not so clear to most Americans there would be much to celebrate in the year 2000. Then our nation was gripped by economic distress, social decline, political **gridlock**.

The title of a best-selling book asked: "America: What Went Wrong?" . . .

In 1992, we just had a road map; today, we have results.

But even more important, America again has the confidence to dream big dreams. But we must not let this confidence drift into complacency. For we, all of us, will be judged by the dreams and deeds we pass on to our children. And on that score, we will be held to a high standard, indeed, because our chance to do good is so great.

My fellow Americans, we have crossed the bridge we built to the 21st century. Now, we must shape a 21st century American revolution—of opportunity, responsibility and community. We must be now, as we were in the beginning, a new nation.

At the dawn of the last century, Theodore Roosevelt said, "the one characteristic more essential than any other is foresight . . . it should be the growing nation with a future that takes the long look ahead." So, tonight, let us take our long look ahead—and set great goals for our nation.

To 21st century America, let us pledge these things: Every child will begin school ready to learn and graduate ready to succeed. Every family will be able to succeed at home and at work, and no child will be raised in poverty. We will meet the challenge of the

**Budget surpluses:** A situation in which income exceeds spending.

**Partisanship:** Placing the concerns of one's group or political party above all other concerns.

**Gridlock:** In political terms, a situation where politicians are unable to find areas of agreement while legislation stalls.

*aging of America. We will assure quality, affordable health care, at last, for all Americans.*

*We will make America the safest big country on Earth. We will pay off our national debt for the first time since 1835. We will bring prosperity to every American community. We will reverse the course of **climate change** and leave a safer, cleaner planet. America will lead the world toward shared peace and prosperity, and the far frontiers of science and technology. And we will become at last what our founders pledged us to be so long ago—one nation, under God, indivisible, with liberty and justice for all. . . .*

*[Two] years ago, as we reached across party lines to reach our first balanced budget, I asked that we meet our responsibility to the next generation by maintaining our fiscal discipline. Because we refused to stray from that path, we are doing something that would have seemed unimaginable seven years ago. We are actually paying down the national debt. . . .*

*Beyond paying off the debt, we must ensure that the benefits of debt reduction go to preserving two of the most important guarantees we make to every American—Social Security and **Medicare**. Tonight, I ask you to work with me to make a bipartisan down payment on Social Security reform by crediting the **interest savings** from debt reduction to the Social Security Trust Fund so that it will be strong and sound for the next 50 years.*

*But this is just the start of our journey. We must also take the right steps toward reaching our great goals. First and foremost, we need a 21st century revolution in education, guided by our faith that every single child can learn. Because education is more important than ever, more than ever the key to our children's future, we must make sure all our children have that key. That means quality preschool and after-school, the best trained teachers in the classroom, and college opportunities for all our children.*

*For seven years now, we've worked hard to improve our schools, with opportunity and responsibility—investing more, but demanding more in turn. Reading, math, college entrance scores are up. Some of the most impressive gains are in schools in very poor neighborhoods.*

*But all successful schools have followed the same proven formula: higher standards, more accountability, and extra help so children who need it can get it to reach those standards. I have sent Congress a reform plan based on that formula. It holds states and*

**Climate change:** A reference to "global warming"—where the amount of pollution in the air has an effect on climate, leading to unexpected and dangerous changes.

**Medicare:** A program of government assistance to older people to help them pay medical bills.

**Interest savings:** In banking, "interest" is a charge for borrowing money. Since the government had been spending more money than it was earning, it was borrowing against future earnings, creating debt. The government then had to pay off the debt plus interest on that debt. By paying off the debt, the amount of interest owed decreases. The government had budgeted to pay off the debt at a certain figure, but that figure decreased as the debt was paid off sooner. President Clinton proposes that the money left over (interest savings) should be used to support Social Security.

school districts accountable for progress, and rewards them for results. Each year, our national government invests more than $15 billion in our schools. It is time to support what works and stop supporting what doesn't.

Now, as we demand more from our schools, we should also invest more in our schools. Let's double our investment to help states and districts turn around their worst-performing schools, or shut them down. Let's double our investments in after-school and summer school programs, which boost achievement and keep people off the streets and out of trouble. If we do this, we can give every single child in every failing school in America—everyone—the chance to meet high standards.

Since 1993, we've nearly doubled our investment in **Head Start** and improved its quality. Tonight, I ask you for another $1 billion for Head Start, the largest increase in the history of the program.

We know that children learn best in smaller classes with good teachers. For two years in a row, Congress has supported my plan to hire 100,000 new qualified teachers to lower class size in the early grades. I thank you for that, and I ask you to make it three in a row.

And to make sure all teachers know the subjects they teach, tonight I propose a new teacher quality initiative—to recruit more talented people into the classroom, reward good teachers for staying there, and give all teachers the training they need.

We know **charter schools** provide real public school choice. When I became President, there was just one independent public charter school in all America. Today, thanks to you, there are 1,700. I ask you now to help us meet our goal of 3,000 charter schools by next year.

We know we must connect all our classrooms to the Internet, and we're getting there. In 1994, only 3 percent of our classrooms were connected. Today, with the help of the Vice President's **E-rate program**, more than half of them are. And 90 percent of our schools have at least one Internet connection.

But we cannot finish the job when a third of all our schools are in serious disrepair. Many of them have walls and wires so old, they're too old for the Internet. So tonight, I propose to help 5,000 schools a year make immediate and urgent repairs; and again, to help build or modernize 6,000 more, to get students out of trailers and into high-tech classrooms. . . . (The White House [Web site])

**Head Start:** A pre-school program in which children receive care and begin learning.

**Charter schools:** Schools in which attendance is based on demonstrated ability (good grades), rather than where one lives.

**E-rate program:** A government program that assists schools to gain access to the Internet.

## What happened next . . .

Most of the items proposed in President Clinton's State of the Union address were approved by Congress as part of the annual budget. Since 2000 was a presidential election year and economic prosperity was continuing, many in Congress did not feel obliged to move swiftly to enact new programs proposed by the president. The two legislative branches continued to struggle in many battles to gain hard won settlements.

President Clinton's speech began a new decade with a bold vision. What happened next would be determined by new leaders, and a new generation coming of age.

## Did you know . . .

- Like other presidents, Bill Clinton faced several instances when he had to choose whether to strictly follow courses of action he had outlined during his campaign for the presidency, or whether he should show flexibility. For example, in 1992, he believed that more government programs and actions were necessary to address social and economic issues. During his administration, however, the size of government was reduced and some departments were either combined or discontinued to create more efficiency. The government program of welfare was among those reformed and reduced.

- Clinton proclaimed near the end of his first term that "the era of big government was over." He meant that many programs had been reduced or ended. Clinton still continued to support new programs to combat social and economic problems (as reflected in his final State of the Union address), but his more limited approach to government marked a new era of Democratic policies.

## Where to Learn More

Clinton, Bill. *The Clinton Foreign Policy Reader: Presidential Speeches with Commentary.* Edited by Alvin Z. Rubinstein, Albina Shayevich, and Boris Zlotnikov. Armonk, NY: M. E. Sharpe, 2000.

Shull, Steven A. *American Civil Rights Policy from Truman to Clinton: The Role of Presidential Leadership.* Armonk, NY: M. E. Sharpe, 1999.

Waldman, Michael. *POTUS Speaks: Finding the Words that Defined the Clinton Presidency.* New York: Simon & Schuster, 2000.

White House. "2000 State of the Union Address: Transcript." *The White House.* [Online] http://www1.whitehouse.gov/WH/SOTU00/sotu-text.html (accessed on November 13, 2000).

# George W. Bush

**Forty-third president (2001– )**

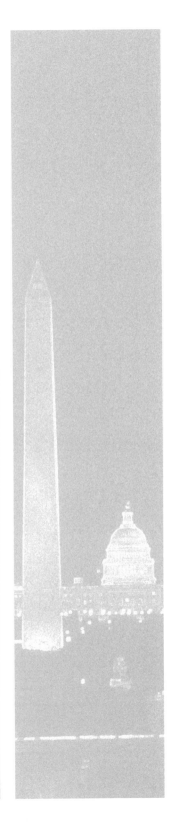

# George W. Bush

**Born July 6, 1946**
**New Haven, Connecticut**

**Forty-third president of the United States
(2001– )**

**After winning one of the most contested
presidential elections in U.S. history,
"Dubya" became the second son of a
president to become president himself**

ive weeks after the presidential election of 2000, George
W. Bush could finally be assured that he had won one of
the closest of presidential contests in one of the most contested of presidential elections. Bush secured a slim Electoral College majority over his Democratic challenger, Vice President
Al Gore (1948– ; see box in **Bill Clinton** entry in volume 5),
271–266. The historic 2000 election marked the first time
that the U.S. Supreme Court made a ruling on a presidential
election. In a divided judgment (with five justices supporting,
and four dissenting), the Court's ruling stopped a recounting
of ballots in Florida, ending weeks of dramatic twists and
turns of legal wrangling.

Bush became the fourth president to win in the Electoral College (see boxes), but not the popular vote. He was
also the second president's son to be elected president of the
United States. His father, **George Bush** (1924– ; see entry in
volume 5), served as president from 1989 to 1993. The other
father-son combination was **John Adams** (1735–1826; see
entry in volume 1) and **John Quincy Adams** (1767–1848; see
entry in volume 1).

"It seemed to me that
elite central planners
were determining the
course of our nation. I
wanted to do something
about it."

*George W. Bush, on his decision
to enter politics*

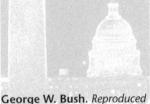

**George W. Bush**. *Reproduced
by permission of Archive
Photos.*

## Fast Facts about George W. Bush

**Full name:** George Walker Bush

**Born:** July 6, 1946

**Parents:** George Herbert Walker and Barbara Pierce Bush

**Spouse:** Laura Welch (1946– ; m. 1977)

**Children:** Jenna Welch (1981– ); Barbara Pierce (1981– )

**Religion:** Methodist

**Education:** Yale University (B.A., 1968); Harvard University (M.B.A., 1975)

**Occupations:** Pilot; oilman; owner, Texas Rangers baseball team

**Government positions:** Texas governor

**Political party:** Republican

**Dates as president:** January 20, 2001–

**Age upon taking office:** 54

Taking office at a time of prosperity, Bush hoped to introduce several bold policies and to de-emphasize federal government programs. But helping unite a nation and political factions deeply divided over the election was Bush's major task: the popular and electoral votes had been very close; Democrats and Republicans each had fifty U.S. senators, and Republicans had only a small majority in the House; and election controversies led many to doubt the impartiality of courts and some election officials.

The main controversy of election 2000 centered on the state of Florida. The state's twenty-five electoral votes were in dispute, and the winner of the state would win the presidency. Less than one thousand votes separated Bush and Gore, but thousands of votes were questioned: some were not tabulated by vote-counting machines, while other votes had been validated by questionable practices allowed by some voting officials. Some voters claimed they had been denied the opportunity to vote by election officials who were using incomplete information. Future reform of voting practices might well prove to be the legacy of election 2000.

After a U.S. Supreme Court ruling on Tuesday, December 12, ended attempts by Gore to have disputed Florida votes recounted by people, rather than machines, Bush became president-elect. Bush and Gore made efforts toward harmony in speeches to the nation on December 13, and Bush pledged to follow the same kind of consensus-building he had pursued as governor of Texas.

Bush had an opportunity when taking office to maintain an unprecedented (never seen before) period of prosperity in America and to use the abundance of wealth to further improve the nation. He hoped to pursue a more limited role for the federal government, and intended to focus on legislation regarding tax relief, education, and retirement benefits. All of those initiatives, however, were dependent on the ability of Bush to lead effectively following a hotly contested election; politicians of both parties to put aside the partisanship that had been especially prominent in Washington, D.C., during the final three decades of the twentieth century; and American voters to feel confident in the voting process.

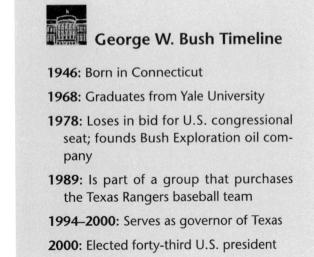

## George W. Bush Timeline

**1946:** Born in Connecticut

**1968:** Graduates from Yale University

**1978:** Loses in bid for U.S. congressional seat; founds Bush Exploration oil company

**1989:** Is part of a group that purchases the Texas Rangers baseball team

**1994–2000:** Serves as governor of Texas

**2000:** Elected forty-third U.S. president

## Follows family traditions

George Walker Bush was born on July 6, 1946, in New Haven, Connecticut, where his father was enrolled at Yale University after having served in World War II (1939–45). After his father, **George Bush** (1924– ; see entry in volume 5) graduated in 1948, the family moved to Texas, where the senior Bush took an administrative position at a company that provided supplies for oil drilling. The Bush family lived in Midland, Texas, and then in Houston as the oil business thrived. While in the seventh grade, George W. Bush attended the same junior high school in Midland as Laura Welch (1946– ; see entry on **Laura Bush** in volume 5); they did not meet then, but years later they would be husband and wife.

Like his father, Bush attended Phillips Academy (an academy is a private school that prepares students for college) in Andover, Massachusetts, and went on to Yale University. He was an average student, president of his fraternity, and a member of an exclusive group, the Skull and Bones Society. While still at Yale in 1966, his father was elected as a U.S. representative from Texas, continuing a Bush tradition of public service; George W. Bush's grandfather, Prescott Bush (1895–1972), had been a Republican U.S. senator from Connecticut from 1952 to 1963. After serving in Congress, George Bush went on to hold positions in the presidential administrations of **Richard Nixon** (1913–1994; see entry in volume 5) and **Gerald R. Ford** (1913– ;

**Words to Know**

**Absentee ballot:** A vote cast by a citizen of a state who cannot be present at a polling place on election day. It is generally reserved for senior citizens and those who work out of state or out of the country, including people serving in the military.

**Autonomy:** The freedom of an individual or group to make decisions.

**Chad:** The tiny piece of a ballot that is punched out after a voter uses a stylus to push in and leave a hole to represent his or her choice. In voting districts that use a punch card system, ballots have perforations; when punched with a stylus, the chad is supposed to fall away, leaving a hole that indicates the voter's choice. A machine then recognizes the hole and counts the vote. When a chad does not fall completely off a ballot, machines do not count the vote. A "hanging chad" is a piece that remains attached at a corner or side of a perforation. A "dimpled chad" indicates that a stylus was used to push at the perforation but did not punch through.

**Compassionate conservative:** President Bush's description of someone who believes in the principles of limited government and local control but also supports public education and some social programs.

**Delegate:** A member of a party or organization who has a vote that represents a larger group and helps determine the leader of that party or organization.

**Electoral College:** A body officially responsible for electing the president of

see entry in volume 5) during the 1970s, before being elected vice president and president in the 1980s.

George W. Bush returned to Texas after graduating from Yale in 1968 with a degree in history. He became involved in the oil business. Restless in his mid-twenties, Bush completed a fifty-three-week program with the Texas Air National Guard, learning to fly planes and earning the rank of lieutenant. At the time, he lived in the same Houston apartment complex as Laura Welch, but, again, their paths did not cross. When he was not called to fight in the Vietnam War (1959–75), Bush worked at several jobs, including a program called Pull for Youth for underprivileged children.

Bush continued to be restless, spending most of his time driving sports cars and enjoying an active social life. "I

the United States. In presidential elections, the candidate who receives the most popular votes in a particular state wins all of that state's electoral votes. Votes are distributed among states in ratios based on population. A candidate must win a majority of electoral votes (over fifty percent) in order to win the presidency.

**Exit poll:** A statistical analysis conducted in each state during an election by independent agencies for news services that combine statistics from past voting trends, recent polls, and actual surveys of voters after they leave polling places. Exit polls are generally accurate in predicting election outcomes.

**Exploratory committee:** A group established by a potential political candidate to examine whether enough party, public, and financial support exists for the potential candidate to officially announce that he or she is running for an elected position.

**Partisan:** Placing the concerns of one's group or political party above all other considerations.

**Primaries:** Elections held to determine candidates for a general election. Presidential primaries are a means used by some state political parties to determine whom their party delegates will support. Each state is allotted a certain number of delegates based on the number of party members in that state. Delegates are assigned to candidates based on the results of a primary election.

wasn't interested in taking root," he told *Time* magazine in 1994 about his early adulthood. "I was having fun."

Bush returned east to attend the Harvard Business School, graduating with a master's degree in business administration (an M.B.A., an advanced degree) in 1975. Then, he went back to Texas to become an oilman. In 1977, at an outdoor barbecue party in Midland, Texas, he finally met Laura Welch officially. A whirlwind romance followed, and they were married within three months. Their twin daughters, Jenna and Barbara (named after their grandmothers), were born in 1981.

## Successful oilman

Bush ran for a seat in Congress from Texas in 1978. He explained years later in his autobiography, *A Charge to*

*Keep,* why he wanted to enter politics. He was angered by federal legislation that placed price controls on gas that was drilled and processed in the United States and angered by government monitoring that determined which industries could use natural gas. "It seemed to me that elite central planners were determining the course of our nation. I wanted to do something about it."

After losing the election to Democrat Kent R. Hance (1942– ), Bush focused on his small, thriving company called Bush Exploration. The business specialized in finding and evaluating new areas to drill for oil. In 1983, he merged his outfit with Spectrum 7; three years later, Spectrum 7 was bought by a large company, Harken Energy. Bush received $600,000 worth of Harken stock and won a lucrative consulting contract. In 1990, Bush sold two-thirds of his Harken stake for nearly $850,000.

Meanwhile, his father served two terms as vice president under **Ronald Reagan** (1911– ; see entry in volume 5) and won the Republican nomination for president in 1988. George W. Bush helped manage his father's presidential campaign, moving with his wife and twin daughters to Washington, D.C. He gained respect from campaign insiders and Republicans in general by rallying the campaign team through the ups and downs of a tight race that eventually turned into a solid victory for his father.

Back in Texas after the election, Bush served from 1990 to 1994 as head of Hearts and Hammers, a volunteer group dedicated to repairing homes. He also organized a group of wealthy investors to buy the Texas Rangers, a major league baseball team. He assumed a role as managing partner and helped the team build a fan-friendly new stadium called The Ballpark in Arlington. Riding a wave of popularity from his success with the Rangers, Bush decided it was an ideal time to make another try for elected office.

## "I might run for governor"

"I vividly remember the night I first thought I might run for governor," recalled Bush years later in his autobiography, *A Charge to Keep*. On May 1, 1993, Texas voters turned down a proposal for redistributing school funds, a program favored by Governor Ann Richards (1933– ). Bush watched a press conference at which a disappointed Richards challenged voters to come forward if they had a better idea for the school finance system. Bush turned to his wife, Laura, and said, "I have a suggestion. I might run for governor."

Bush ran for governor of Texas in 1994 against Richards, a popular Democratic incumbent. Drawing on deep support among Republicans (including the man who defeated Bush in 1978, Kent Hance, who had switched to the Republican Party in 1985) and having experienced organizers, including some from his father's national campaigns of 1988 and 1992, Bush ran a positive, issue-oriented campaign. Focusing on welfare reform, a crackdown on crime (especially concerning juveniles), and autonomy (freedom to make decisions) for local school districts, Bush, to the surprise of many, won with 53.5 percent of the vote. Twenty thousand people attended Bush's inauguration in Austin, including famous preacher Billy Graham (1918– ), legendary baseball pitcher and former Texas Ranger Nolan Ryan (1947– ), and, of course, his father George Bush and his mother **Barbara Bush** (1925– ; see entry in volume 5), who were now in retirement.

After only a year in office, Bush was hailed as the most popular big-state governor in the country. He earned a reputation as a "compassionate conservative"—someone who believes in the principles of limited government and local control but also supports public education and some social programs. He worked to improve public schools, cut taxes, put welfare recipients to work, and encouraged new business and job growth. Bush won reelection in 1998 with sixty-eight percent of the vote.

That whopping reelection triumph brought him more national attention. But even before he was reelected governor in 1998, Bush finished first in a 1997 poll among Republicans concerning potential presidential candidates for the 2000 election. On the day of his inaugural for his second term as governor, Bush attended a church service he described in his autobiography as one of his life-defining moments. The reverend of the First United Methodist Church in Austin said that America was starved for honest leaders who have "ethical and moral courage." After the service, Bush's mother, Barbara, turned to him and said, "He [the reverend] was talking to you."

The 2000 Republican presidential ticket and their wives: (From left to right) Laura Bush, George W. Bush, Dick Cheney, and Lynne Cheney. *Reproduced by permission of the Corbis Corporation.*

With the backing of his family, Bush began courting support and raising funds for a run for the presidency. Even before he officially announced an exploratory committee to examine his chances and organize support, groups of legislators from several states visited Austin to encourage him to run. (An exploratory committee is a group established by a potential political candidate to examine whether enough party, public, and financial support exists for the candidate to announce officially that he or she is running for an elected position.)

By January 2000, before states begin holding caucuses (meetings of members of a political party) or primaries, or elections through which political parties choose their presidential candidates, Bush was the frontrunner of a large field of Republican candidates. He established clear momentum early, and all of the other candidates gradually dropped from the race. By March 2000, Bush was endorsed by 41 U.S. senators, 175 U.S. representatives, and 27 governors. Bush secured enough delegate support to be the Republican nominee long

Complete American Presidents Sourcebook

before the party's summer national convention. (A delegate is a member of a party or an organization who has a vote that represents the votes of a larger group.)

As Bush became more widely known, he was often called by the nickname "W." and "Dubya" to distinguish him from his father and to show a more personable side of the candidate. Questions persisted among the press and voters, however, about Bush's grasp of national issues and foreign affairs. His first major decision as the likely nominee (a candidate does not become a party's official nominee until winning a majority of votes during the party's national convention) was selecting Dick Cheney (1941– ; see box) as his running mate. Cheney had a long and distinguished political career and offered the kind of federal government experience Bush lacked.

Bush's pledge to build a team approach to his prospective presidential administration, his selection of Cheney, and his solid performances in debates and speeches reassured voters that he could handle the job of being president. His plans for large cuts in taxes and allowing young workers to invest part of their Social Security savings proved popular. His policies that promised more individual and local control (and less federal supervision) in the areas of medical insurance and education struck the right chord among voters.

Bush solidified support with a strong, nationally televised speech when he accepted the Republican nomination for president (see **George W. Bush** primary source entry in volume 5). Mixing a folksy approach ("Our founders first defined [the purpose of the federal government] here in Philadelphia. . . . Ben Franklin was here. Thomas Jefferson. And, of course, George Washington—or, as his friends called him, 'George W.'") with clear policy measures, Bush took the lead in voter polls during the summer of 2000. Bush maintained a slight lead in most polls, but by election day most news agencies declared the presidential race "too close to call." Indeed, Election Day 2000 proved to be a great drama, and the historical drama continued on for several weeks.

## Tally hassle, Florida

The presidential election of 2000 marked the third time in American history that the winner had a majority of

# Dick Cheney

As vice president to George W. Bush, Dick Cheney was serving his fourth Republican president, in addition to having been a strong congressional ally of President Ronald Reagan during the 1980s. Born Richard Bruce Cheney on January 30, 1941, in Lincoln, Nebraska, Cheney grew up in Casper, Wyoming, where his father, Richard, worked for the U.S. Department of Agriculture. Cheney enjoyed hunting and fishing, captained his high school football team, and excelled academically. He did not fare so well when he went to college at Yale University. Feeling uncomfortable in New England, he left during his sophomore year and returned home.

Cheney worked for two years as a lineman for an electrical company before continuing college in 1963, this time at the University of Wyoming. He was partly motivated to return to school to keep up with his sweetheart, Lynne Vincent, who was showing great promise as a student writer. They were married in 1964. Lynn Cheney subsequently distinguished herself as an author, as editor of the *Washingtonian* magazine, as a university professor, and as head of the National Endowment for the Arts. The Cheneys raised two daughters, Mary and Elizabeth.

Cheney graduated from the University of Wyoming with a bachelor's degree in political science in 1965 and a master's degree the following year. Meanwhile, he served internships in the state legislature and the governor's office. He began coursework at the University of Wisconsin in 1967, but left for Washington, D.C., to be an assistant for a Wisconsin senator. Cheney moved on in 1969 to a position as special assistant to the director of the Office of Opportunity, a program initiated by newly inaugurated president Richard Nixon. Over the next few years, Cheney rose steadily to more prominent positions, including deputy White House counsel and assistant director of the Cost of Living Council. Cheney left Washington, D.C., in 1973 for a position as an investment advisor in Wyoming while the nation was in turmoil over the Watergate scandal.

In August 1974, after President Nixon resigned from office, Cheney was asked to join President Gerald Ford's transition staff (a staff that supervises the change of power from one president to another). Cheney was soon promoted to assistant to the president and then to chief of staff. He advised on political matters, scheduled meetings for the president, and supervised the White House staff. After Ford was defeated by **Jimmy Carter** (1924– ; see entry in volume 5) in the 1976 election, Cheney returned to Wyoming and worked with a banking firm. In 1978, he won the Republican nomination for the state's single seat in the House of Representatives, despite having suffered a heart attack during the campaign. He went on to easily beat his Democratic rival, and was reelected to Congress five more times.

**Dick Cheney.** *Reproduced by permission of the Corbis Corporation.*

Cheney served as chairman of the Republican House Policy Committee and strongly supported the policies of the administration of Ronald Reagan. In April 1989, after new president George Bush failed to win the approval for his first choice as secretary of defense, John Tower (1925–1991), he nominated Cheney for the post. The Senate quickly confirmed the nomination. Cheney had no military experience, but he possessed excellent organizational skills needed during a time of change and international turmoil. After the fall of the Soviet Union in 1989, the United States began cutting back on military spending—an area supervised by Cheney.

Cheney helped organize American military operations. Troops were sent to Panama to arrest the country's military dictator, Manuel Noriega (1936– ), who had nullified (made void; overturned) a national election he was losing and was wanted on international drug charges. When the Iraqi army invaded Kuwait in August 1990, Cheney had to oversee massive troop, supply, and ship movements to the Persian Gulf. He helped direct the Gulf War, which began on January 16, 1991. The war was over by the end of February with the primary goal—pushing the Iraqi army out of Kuwait—quickly accomplished. Following the war, Cheney resumed his role in cutting military costs, closing unnecessary military bases, and helping build American peacekeeping forces (units that assist with actions taken by the United Nations). Cheney's Cabinet stint ended when **Bill Clinton** (1946– ; see entry in volume 5) was inaugurated president in January 1993.

In 1995, Cheney became chief executive at the Halliburton Company, the largest oil drilling and construction services provider in the world. In 2000, he left the firm when George W. Bush asked Cheney to be his vice presidential running mate. Cheney's vast experience in Washington, D.C., his forthrightness, and his calm, assured manner were excellent compliments to the more lively, yet less-experienced, Bush. Following the Bush-Cheney victory in the controversial 2000 election, Cheney became vice president on Inauguration Day 2001.

electoral votes, but received fewer popular votes. In 1888, **Benjamin Harrison** (1833–1901; see entry in volume 3) had a clear majority of electoral votes, and the outcome was not contested. In 1876, on the other hand, electoral votes in four states were disputed. Those electoral votes proved decisive for **Rutherford B. Hayes** (1822–1893; see entry in volume 3), who had lost in the popular vote. A similar situation developed in 2000 concerning the twenty-five electoral votes of one state, Florida. The winner of those electoral votes would be the new president.

On election day (Tuesday, November 7, 2000), most news agencies predicted a close vote that would hinge on Pennsylvania, Michigan, and Florida, three key states with large numbers of electoral votes. Shortly after 8:00 P.M., news agencies began projecting, based on exit polls (surveys of people after they voted), that Democratic challenger Al Gore won the vote in all three states and seemed headed for an Electoral College victory.

When actual vote tallies from Florida showed different trends, however, news agencies, around 10:00 P.M., took back their projection and began referring to Florida as "too close to call." The race for the presidency was so close that at 1:30 A.M. (Wednesday morning, November 8), both candidates, based on actual vote tallies, had secured 242 electoral votes, with 54 still to be decided (and 270 needed to win). Then, at 2:15 A.M., news agencies projected Bush would win Florida. Since tallies in most other states also favored Bush, some news agencies declared him the winner.

**Republican presidential candidate George W. Bush speaks at a rally in Lafayette, Louisiana, in September 2000.** *Reproduced by permission of the Corbis Corporation.*

At 2:30 A.M., Gore phoned Bush to congratulate him and to concede. At 3:15 A.M., Gore was in a limousine en route

## Election Results

### 2000

| Presidential / Vice presidential candidates | Popular votes | Presidential electoral votes |
|---|---|---|
| George W. Bush / Richard Cheney (Republican) | 50,456,167 | 271 |
| Al Gore / Joseph Lieberman (Democratic) | 50,996,064 | 266 |

*After nineteen days of manual vote recounts in Florida and legal wrangling, Bush was formally certified as that state's winner. This led to Gore officially contesting the Florida results. Following key decisions in Bush's favor from the Florida Supreme Court and the U.S. Supreme Court, Gore conceded the election, thereby giving Bush the twenty-five electoral votes from Florida needed to declare him president-elect. Gore's electoral vote total wound up at 266, rather than 267, when a voter from the District of Columbia (which Gore had won) decided not to cast a vote for either candidate.*

to make a concession speech before supporters gathered at the Nashville War Memorial in Tennessee. Along the way, Gore received word about voting irregularities in Florida. The car turned around, and Gore returned to his home. At 3:45 A.M., Gore called Bush to retract his concession: "As you may have noticed," he said, "things have changed," pointing to reports of voting irregularities in Florida. The two had a tense exchange.

When daylight came on Wednesday morning, there was still no new president-elect. NBC news anchorman Tom Brokaw (1940– ) noted that news agencies had confused the electorate with their projections: "We don't just have egg on our face," he stated. "We have omelet all over our suits." Vote tallies completed in Florida later in the day showed that Bush edged Gore by 1,784 votes. Under Florida law, such a close vote total automatically generates a recount.

Meanwhile, voting problems in the state were widely publicized. Some voters in Palm Beach County complained about a confusing ballot; more than nineteen thousand votes were disqualified in that county, which has a system where voters use a stylus to punch a hole in a card beside the name of the candidate of their choice. The cards have perforations; when punched with a stylus, the perforation is supposed to fall away (a punched perforation is called a "chad"). The nineteen thousand ballots disqualified had more than one candidate se-

# How the Electoral College Works

The election of 2000 renewed debate over whether the Electoral College should be abolished in favor of using the popular vote to determine who becomes president.

When the U.S. Constitution was being drafted, delegates devised the Electoral College as a way to entrust the responsibility to the people for electing presidents. The delegates agreed that an election based on the popular vote could easily be influenced by partisan politics. They were also concerned that voters in one state might not be well informed about a candidate from another state.

Since 1961, the total of state and District of Columbia electors has been 538; a simple majority of 270 is necessary for election. The presidential candidate who receives the most votes in a particular state wins all of that state's electoral votes (except for Maine and Nebraska, where electoral votes are awarded for winning a congressional district). The number of electors in each state is equal to the total number of senators and representatives it sends to the U.S. Congress.

Presidential electors are designated by each state legislature. Following a general election on the first Tuesday of November every four years, the electors meet to officially record the state's electoral votes. They meet simultaneously in all the states on the first Monday after the second Wednesday in December of presidential election years. On January 6, their votes are counted in the presence of both houses of Congress.

lected, or the chads were still attached to the perforations. Vote-counting machines could not tabulate them. Additionally, a candidate not expected to receive many votes in that county—Reform Party nominee Pat Buchanan (1938– )—was credited with 3,407 ballots in his favor. Voters (and Buchanan himself) acknowledged the count must have been a mistake. In nearby Broward County, another 6,686 ballots were disqualified. Similar problems were noted in adjacent Dade County. Gore requested manual (done by hand, rather than machine) recounts of the three counties as well as Volusia County, where some problems were also noted. All four counties had larger numbers of Democratic voters than Republicans.

Under Florida law, recounts must be conducted within seven days. Due to the problems with disqualified votes and the inability of machine counters to register them, however, legal proceedings began on whether to count voting cards manually, a more time-consuming process. Since recounts were due within seven days, large counties of Florida could not conduct manual recounts in time. Additionally, the legality of conducting manual recounts was challenged in court. On November 13, a federal judge in Miami, Florida, rejected a request by Bush's lawyers to end the hand recounts. Meanwhile, Florida's secretary of state, Katherine Harris (1957– ), called for an end to the manual recounts. She cited her legal authority to oversee election results, and her power was upheld in a Leon County court on November 14 (Leon County includes Florida's state capital, Tallahassee). Harris stated that the machine recount already conducted would be final, and that only overseas absentee ballots not yet counted would be added to the final total. (An absentee ballot is a vote cast by a citizen of a state who cannot be present at a polling place on election day.) Harris was scheduled to certify the results on Saturday, November 18.

Palm Beach County, Florida, election officials inspect a questionable ballot during a manual recount on November 11, 2000.
*Reproduced by permission of the Corbis Corporation.*

Machine recounts were completed on Wednesday, November 15. The recounts confirmed Bush as the winner of the state, but his margin had shrunk to 327 votes. Meanwhile, officials in Palm Beach, Broward, and Dade counties decided to conduct another recount, this time manually. Harris attempted to block them, but the ruling that had supported her power was appealed (challenged) by Gore's lawyers to the Florida Supreme Court.

Alleged partisan politics contributed to the controversy. Although Bush's brother, Jeb Bush (1953– ), the state's governor, chose to recuse (step aside from a situation to avoid a conflict of interest) himself from the entire recount process,

## The Electoral College Through the Years

**The Constitution (ratified in 1789):** Article II, Section 1, carefully defines the voting procedure to be followed by electors. Originally, the electors were to vote for the two most qualified persons without noting which of the persons was selected as president or vice president. The candidate receiving the greatest number of electoral votes, provided the votes of a majority of the electors were received, would be president, and the candidate winning the second largest number of votes would be vice president.

**1796:** The first flaw in the system occurred when John Adams and Thomas Jefferson were elected president and vice president, respectively. Political parties were not established back then, but the candidates had decidedly opposing viewpoints.

**1800:** A majority of electors voted for both Jefferson, head of the Democratic-Republican Party, and Aaron Burr (1756–1836; see box in **Thomas Jefferson** entry in volume 1), his running mate. They tied because electors voted for the two most qualified persons without noting which was selected as president or vice president. The election was referred to the House of Representatives, as mandated by the Constitu-

tion. Jefferson's opponents tried various ways to have Burr elected, but Jefferson was chosen president and Burr vice president after thirty-six rounds of voting.

**1804:** Congress enacted and the states ratified the Twelfth Amendment, providing for separate electoral votes for president and for vice president.

**1820: James Monroe** (1758–1831; see entry in volume 1) won the electoral votes from every state, but one elector voted differently than authorized. It was a symbolic gesture to ensure that **George Washington** (1732–1799; see entry in volume 1) remained the only president to have won all the electoral votes in an election.

**1824:** None of four candidates received the necessary number of electoral votes to become president. In such a case, the House of Representatives decides the outcome. A bitterly divided Congress selected John Quincy Adams over **Andrew Jackson** (1767–1845; see entry in volume 1), even though Jackson had won more electoral and popular votes.

**1836:** The Whig Party nominated three regional candidates for president, hoping to create a situation where neither candidate, including Democrat **Martin Van**

Harris, a Republican, had campaigned actively for Bush. The counties conducting the manual recount, on the other hand, were heavily Democratic. Republicans were accused of wanting to hurry the process, even if some voters were disenfran-

**Buren** (1782–1862; see entry in volume 1), received enough electoral votes to become president. In such a case, the election would be decided by the House of Representatives, where the Whigs were the dominant party. The strategy failed when Van Buren won the general election and accumulated enough electoral votes.

**1876:** A dispute over the voting results in four states left crucial electoral votes in doubt. Under existing law, it was the duty of Congress to resolve the dispute, but Congress was soon deadlocked. The Electoral Commission of 1877, authorized by Congress, resolved the issue in favor of Republican Rutherford B. Hayes.

**1887:** Congress enacted a law authorizing states to resolve all controversies regarding the selection of presidential electors. Congress may intervene to settle a dispute over the election of the presidential electors only when a state is unable to do so.

**1888:** Incumbent president **Grover Cleveland** (1837–1908; see entry in volume 3) outpolled **Benjamin Harrison** (1833–1901; see entry in volume 3), 5,540,309 to 5,444,337, in the popular vote but received only 168 electoral votes to Harrison's 233. Harrison won more of the larger states.

**1960: John F. Kennedy** (1917–1963; see entry in volume 5) defeated **Richard Nixon** (1913–1994; see entry in volume 5) in the popular vote by less than one percent. The scenario was repeated in 1968, when Nixon defeated Hubert Humphrey (1911–1978; see box in **Lyndon B. Johnson** entry in volume 5).

**1961:** The Twenty-third Amendment to the Constitution allowed the District of Columbia to vote for three electors.

**1969:** A challenge to the "winner-take-all" system of awarding electoral votes was rejected by the U.S. Supreme Court.

**2000:** Al Gore received more popular votes than George W. Bush, but was narrowly defeated in the Electoral College in one of the most hotly contested presidential elections in U.S. history. Bush did not become the clear winner until December 13—a little more than five weeks after election day—when Gore conceded the election following weeks of legal struggles and the involvement of Florida courts and the U.S. Supreme Court.

chised (stripped of their voting power) because of mistakes. Democrats were accused of trying to find more votes. Most Americans simply wanted to be assured of the integrity of the voting process.

On Friday, November 17, the Florida State Supreme Court ruled that it would hear arguments from lawyers representing the candidates, the secretary of state, and local officials about the certification and manual recount issues. The Supreme Court set Monday, November 20, as the court date and instructed Harris not to certify the results on Saturday. The counting of absentee ballots added another 603 votes to Bush's lead, giving him an official advantage of 930 votes. Some ballots cast by U.S. servicemen that were not properly postmarked were thrown out on Saturday, adding more fuel to the election controversy. Manual recounts of the original vote, that had started and stopped several times, continued in Palm Beach and Broward counties.

On Monday, November 20, lawyers for Bush and Gore presented arguments to the Florida Supreme Court in a nationally televised hearing. The justices interrupted speeches by the lawyers to focus on specific issues. The justices were concerned that vote counting could drag on toward the December 18, 2000, date when all state electors are supposed to convene in the respective states to officially record electoral votes. If recounts were not completed in time, Florida might not be able to certify electors, and all votes from the state would be lost. On the other hand, the justices were reluctant to discontinue manual recounts because that process might be the only way to count votes not tabulated by computers.

The Florida Supreme Court ruled unanimously (7-0) on Monday, November 21, that manual recounts could continue, and that the Florida secretary of state did not have the right to impose the November 18 date after local election officials had determined manual recounts were necessary. The court ruled that manual recounts had to be completed by Sunday, November 26, at 5:00 P.M., or 9:00 A.M. the next day if the secretary of state's office was not open on Sunday. Bush's lawyers appealed the ruling to the U.S. Supreme Court.

Meanwhile, officials in Dade County stopped their manual recount for lack of time. Controversies in Broward and Palm Beach counties erupted over whether or not to count "dimpled chads." A dimpled chad indicates that a stylus made an impression (a dent, or dimple) on a ballot, but the chad did not separate from the ballot, and, therefore, had not been counted. The question of whether a voter's intent had been compromised by the process of counting votes

# Closest Election Results in Presidential History

| Year | Presidential candidate | Popular votes | Electoral votes |
|------|------------------------|---------------|-----------------|
| 1824 | John Quincy Adams (Democratic-Republican) | 108,740 (29.5%) | 84 |
|  | Andrew Jackson (Democratic-Republican) | 153,544 (41.6%) | 99 |
|  | William H. Crawford (Democratic-Republican) | 47,136 (12.8%) | 41 |
|  | Henry Clay (Democratic-Republican) | 46,618 (12.6%) | 37 |
| 1844 | James K. Polk (Democratic) | 1,337,243 (49.5%) | 170 |
|  | Henry Clay (Whig) | 1,299,062 (48.1%) | 105 |
| 1848 | Zachary Taylor (Whig) | 1,360,099 (47.3%) | 163 |
|  | Lewis Cass (Democratic) | 1,220,544 (42.5%) | 127 |
|  | Martin Van Buren (Free Soil) | 291,263 (10.1%) | 0 |
| 1876 | Rutherford B. Hayes (Republican) | 4,036,298 (47.8%) | 185 |
|  | Samuel J. Tilden (Democratic) | 4,300,590 (51.0%) | 184 |
| 1880 | James A. Garfield (Republican) | 4,454,416 (48.3%) | 214 |
|  | Winfield Scott Hancock (Democratic) | 4,444,952 (48.2%) | 155 |
| 1888 | Benjamin Harrison (Republican) | 5,444,337 (47.8%) | 233 |
|  | Grover Cleveland (Democratic) | 5,540,309 (48.6%) | 168 |
| 1892 | Grover Cleveland (Democratic) | 5,556,918 (46.0%) | 277 |
|  | Benjamin Harrison (Republican) | 5,176,108 (42.9%) | 145 |
|  | James B. Weaver (Populist) | 1,041,028 (8.7%) | 22 |
| 1896 | William McKinley (Republican) | 7,104,779 (51.3%) | 271 |
|  | William Jennings Bryan (Democratic) | 6,509,052 (47.0%) | 176 |
| 1916 | Woodrow Wilson (Democratic) | 9,129,606 (49.3%) | 277 |
|  | Charles Evans Hughes (Republican) | 8,538,221 (46.1%) | 254 |
| 1948 | Harry S. Truman (Democratic) | 24,105,695 (49.5%) | 303 |
|  | Thomas E. Dewey (Republican) | 21,969,170 (45.1%) | 189 |
|  | J. Strom Thurmond (States' Rights Democratic) | 1,169,021 (2.4%) | 39 |
|  | Henry Wallace (Progressive) | 1,156,103 (2.4%) | 0 |
| 1960 | John F. Kennedy (Democratic) | 34,227,096 (49.7%) | 303 |
|  | Richard M. Nixon (Republican) | 34,107,647 (49.5%) | 219 |
| 1968 | Richard M. Nixon (Republican) | 31,710,470 (43.4%) | 301 |
|  | Hubert H. Humphrey (Democratic) | 31,209,677 (42.7%) | 191 |
|  | George C. Wallace (American Independent) | 9,893,952 (13.5%) | 46 |
| 1976 | Jimmy Carter (Democratic) | 40,977,147 (50.0%) | 297 |
|  | Gerald R. Ford (Republican) | 39,422,671 (48.1%) | 240 |
| 2000 | George W. Bush (Republican) | 50,456,167 (47.88%) | 271 |
|  | Al Gore (Democrat) | 50,996,064 (48.39%) | 266 |

Sources: James T. Havel. U.S. Presidential Candidates and the Elections. New York: Macmillan Library Reference USA, 1996; "Report: Gore Won Popular Vote by 539,897." Washington Post (December 21, 2000).

(dimpled chads are not recognized by a machine), or whether the legal standard for voting should prevail, was argued by lawyers representing the two candidates before the U.S. Supreme Court on Friday, December 1.

The results certified on Sunday, November 26, gave Bush 2,912,790 votes to Gore's 2,912,253—a margin of just 537 votes. Under that certification, Bush gained the state's 25 electoral votes for a total of 271—one more than needed to win the presidency. However, officials in Palm Beach County—who had missed the 5:00 P.M. deadline—continued counting until they finished just over two hours later. Because Harris would neither accept a partial manual recount nor extend the deadline, a previous machine recount served as the final tally for Palm Beach County.

On that Sunday evening, Bush made a brief speech announcing that his transition team was moving forward (a transition team prepares a president-elect to take power by working with a team representing the sitting president). However, more legal challenges were pending, and Gore addressed the nation briefly on Monday, asking for patience. On Tuesday, a Tallahassee circuit court judge rejected a Gore plea for a smaller recount, specifically of fourteen thousand ballots from Broward and Dade counties that clearly showed a vote but were not included in the machine counts.

On Friday, December 1, 2000, the U.S. Supreme Court heard arguments by lawyers representing Bush and Gore concerning the legality of the Florida manual recounts. The case had been initiated by Bush's lawyers following the ruling by the Florida Supreme Court for continuing manual recounts. On the following Monday (December 4), the Supreme Court returned the case to the Florida Supreme Court, ordering the court to clarify its earlier judgement. Meanwhile, on that same Monday, a Florida circuit court judge ruled that there was no basis for continuing manual recounts.

The topsy-turvy, dramatic events continued on Friday, December 8. Two judges ruled against Democrats in separate cases brought by private citizens of Florida concerning the applications of several thousand absentee ballots that had missing information and were corrected (and made legal) by Republican officials. Democrats wanted those ballots thrown out, which would have tipped the election to Gore. With courts ruling against Gore—by halting manual recounts and refusing to throw out the absentee ballots—the vice president's chances seemed dead. However, later that day, the Florida Supreme Court overturned the lower court's ruling against manual recounts and ordered the recounts to proceed again.

Recounts began again on Saturday, December 9, only to be halted by order of the U.S. Supreme Court later that day. The Court scheduled to hear an appeal by the Bush legal team against the Florida Supreme Court's ruling. In the hearing on Monday, December 11, U.S. Supreme Court justices expressed their concern about whether manual recounts were constitutional. Since state legislatures are authorized by the U.S. Constitution to make election laws, the Court feared that the Florida Supreme Court had overstepped its bounds by ordering the manual recounts. Lawyers for Gore argued that the state court had acted correctly, having served in its role of interpreting laws.

U.S. Supreme Court justices were also concerned about different standards used in different counties of Florida to judge whether previously untallied votes should be counted. Finally, the justices were concerned that time was running out. That concern was shared by the solidly Republican Florida state legislature, which moved to formally recognize electors for Bush based on the election results that had been certified by Florida's secretary of state.

On Tuesday, December 12, just before 10 P.M., the U.S. Supreme Court announced its official ruling: a bitterly divided court ruled 5-4 that the recounts were unconstitutional. It ordered a halt to all further recounts. The following evening, at 9:00 P.M., Vice President Gore conceded the election to Bush in a nationally televised address and called for the nation to unite behind the new president-elect. Bush followed with his own address at 10:00 P.M.

## "Work Together"

"After a difficult election, we must put politics behind us and work together to make the promise of America available for every one of our citizens," Bush stated in his first address to the nation as president-elect on December 13, 2000. Striking the right tone, according to most political observers, in an attempt to unite the nation and ease partisanship, he continued, "I am optimistic that we can change the tone in Washington, D.C." On that night, Bush said, "I believe things happen for a reason, and I hope the long wait of the last five weeks will heighten a desire to move beyond the bitterness and partisanship of the recent past."

In that speech, Bush made references to two other presidents who took office at a time of great national divisions. **Abraham Lincoln** (1809–1865; see entry in volume 2) had said, "a house divided cannot stand," in speaking of the dissolving Union near the outbreak of the Civil War (1861–65). Bush stated: "Our nation must rise above a house divided. Americans share hopes and goals and values far more important than any political disagreements." And **Thomas Jefferson** (1743–1826; see entry in volume 1), upon taking office in 1801 under the first transition of power from one party (the Federalists) to another (the Republicans, historically called the Democratic-Republicans), offered unity in saying, "We are all Federalists. We are all Republicans." Bush offered, "Republicans want the best for our nation," then paused, dramatically, before continuing, "and so do Democrats. Our votes may differ, but not our hopes."

But Bush took office under ominous conditions following the disputed election of 2000. History has shown that presidents who win controversial elections face formidable opposition. John Quincy Adams in 1824 and Rutherford B. Hayes in 1876 each became one-term presidents who could not govern effectively because of constant challenges by their opponents. Most politicians spoke of a spirit of cooperation once the presidential election of 2000 was finally over. Americans were watching to see whether or not those words became political action.

## Where to Learn More

Attlesey, Sam. "Governor Says Price Controls Sparked First Urge to Run." *Dallas Morning News,* November 21, 1999. [Online] http://www.dallasnews.com/specials/bush_campaign/career/1121bush1texpol.htm (accessed on November 20, 2000).

Bush, George W. *A Charge to Keep.* New York: Morrow, 1999.

"Bush Report." *Texas Monthly* (June 1999). Also [online] http://www.texasmonthly.com/mag/1999/jun/bush.html (accessed on November 30, 2000).

Ivins, Molly, and Lou Dubose. *Shrub: The Short but Happy Political Life of George W. Bush.* New York: Random House, 2000.

Minutaglio, Bill. *First Son: George W. Bush and the Bush Family Dynasty.* New York: Times Books, 1999.

Mitchell, Elizabeth. *W: Revenge of the Bush Dynasty.* New York: Hyperion, 2000.

Wade, Mary Dodson. *George W. Bush: Governor of Texas.* Austin, TX: W. S. Benson & Co., 1999.

Wukovits, John F. *George W. Bush.* San Diego: Lucent Books, 2000.

# Laura Bush

**Born November 4, 1946**
**Midland, Texas**

**Former teacher and librarian advocates
literacy and early childhood programs**

W hen Laura Bush came onstage to make the first major speech of the 2000 Republican National Convention, she was greeted with the wild cheering typical of such party gatherings. After pausing for a moment, she asked for quiet and said, "OK, that's enough." She probably felt like an elementary school teacher ready to begin class. In fact, she had been a public school teacher and a librarian for a decade.

She and her husband have complementary personalities; they are well-balanced opposites. **George W. Bush** (1946– ; see entry in volume 5) is more comfortable before large crowds, and is more talkative and energetic. Laura Bush is reserved and quietly persuasive. While he tackles big issues as a politician, she pursues programs related to education, libraries, and literacy. If she became first lady, she told the *New York Times,* she would focus on "areas I'm already interested in. Literacy, libraries and early childhood." In that respect, she is following in the footsteps of another first lady, her mother-in-law, **Barbara Bush** (1925– ; see entry in volume 5).

"[George and I] wanted to teach our children what our parents taught us—that reading is entertaining and important and fun."

*Laura Bush*

**Laura Bush.** *Reproduced by permission of the Corbis Corporation.*

## Influenced by a teacher

Born Laura Welch in Midland, Texas, on November 4, 1946, she was an only child. Her father owned a home-building business, and her mother worked as a bookkeeper for the business. Laura had a happy, quiet childhood. Her second-grade elementary teacher made such a great impression on her that Laura decided early on she wanted to be a teacher when she grew up.

When she was in the seventh grade, Laura Welch and George W. Bush attended the same junior high school in Midland, but they never met. She wore glasses and was studious; he was mostly sarcastic (according to his mother) and dreamed of being a baseball star.

Laura's happy youth was marred by a tragedy during her teen years. She was involved at age seventeen in an automobile accident in which a friend of hers was killed.

## Reading teacher

Laura attended Southern Methodist University, from which she earned her education degree in 1968. She taught reading in public schools in Dallas and then in Houston, where she had another near-miss in meeting George W. Bush. They lived in the same apartment complex. She resided in a quieter part of the complex, concentrated on her teaching position, and enjoyed her evenings by reading books. Bush preferred a more active lifestyle, what he has called his "young and irresponsible" era. He flew planes with the Texas Air National Guard, drove a sports car, and frequently attended parties.

Laura moved to Austin, Texas, where she studied and earned a master's degree in library science from the University of Texas. After her 1973 graduation, she became a librarian for the local public school system. On a visit back to Midland, during the summer of 1977, she attended an outdoor barbecue party where she was introduced by mutual friends to George W. Bush, who owned an oil business. A whirlwind romance began, including a first date in which they played miniature golf. The couple was married just three months later, in November 1977.

George Bush's father, **George Bush** (1924– ; see entry in volume 5), who had served as a U.S. representative from

Texas and in several positions in the administrations of presidents **Richard Nixon** (1913–1994; see entry in volume 5) and **Gerald R. Ford** (1913– ; see entry in volume 5), was already planning to run in the 1980 presidential election. At the time of their engagement, Laura agreed to marry George W. Bush after securing a promise that she would never have to make a political speech.

The following year, however, she did make a speech during her husband's unsuccessful bid for a seat in the U.S. Congress. After having spent their first year of marriage campaigning, the couple settled in Midland, where George W. Bush concentrated on his oil business. The couple's twin daughters were born in 1981 after illness complicated the pregnancy for Laura Bush. The twins were born five weeks premature and gradually grew healthy. They were named Jenna and Barbara after their grandmothers.

Laura lived quietly as a homemaker while Bush built his oil business in Midland. During that period in the mid-1980s, Laura convinced her husband that his occasional social drinking had become more regular, and he gave up alcohol.

## Promotes literacy and libraries

The Bush family moved to Washington, D.C., in 1987, as George W. Bush worked on his father's presidential bid. The elder Bush had served since 1981 as vice president to **Ronald Reagan** (1911– ; see entry in volume 5), who had defeated Bush, among others, for the Republican nomination for president in 1980. After her father-in-law was elected president in 1988, Laura Bush and her family returned to Texas. Her husband became the managing general partner of the Texas Rangers baseball team. His association with the Rangers, which ended in 1994, brought Bush to larger public attention in Texas. The team was beginning to enjoy success on the field, and an impressive new stadium, The Ballpark in Arlington, was built.

After the difficult and failed reelection bid of her father-in-law in 1992, Laura was not thrilled when her husband told her he wanted to run for governor of Texas against popular incumbent (an elected official currently in office) Ann Richards (1933– ). "I just wanted George to think about it, make sure it was really what he wanted," she later told the *New York Times*. Bush won the election and quickly gained national attention as a prominent governor. He was easily re-elected in 1998, which helped build a base for his successful run for the presidency in 2000.

Laura Bush was active as first lady of Texas. She hosted a luncheon at the University of Texas at which seven prominent Texas writers spoke. The success of that event encouraged her to establish the Texas Book Festival in 1996. The annual festival of books and authors raises funds for public libraries in the state. In 1998, she spearheaded the Early Childhood Development Initiative, a program that prepares children to learn to read before they enter school. She was involved with women's health issues through the National Governor's Association and pursued several programs to bring attention to the arts. Artworks by Texans were exhibited regularly at the state capitol.

Following the election of George W. Bush as president in 2000, literacy and education remained important pursuits for Laura Bush as she took on her role as the nation's first lady.

## Where to Learn More

Allen, Jodie T. "In Philadelphia, The Spouse that Soared." *U.S. News and World Report* (August 14, 2000). Also [online] http://www.usnews.com/usnews/issue/000814/laura.htm (accessed on November 30, 2000).

Anderson, Lisa. "Laura Bush: Stepping into the Spotlight." *Chicago Tribune* (August 1, 2000). Also [online] http://cnews.tribune.com/news/tribune/story/0,1235,tribune-elections2000-71468,00.html (accessed on November 30, 2000).

Bruni, Frank. "For Laura Bush, a Direction That She Never Dreamed Of." *New York Times* (July 31, 2000). Also [online] http://www.nytimes.com/library/politics/camp/073100wh-bush-laura.html (accessed on November 30, 2000).

Hollandsworth, Skip. "Reading Laura Bush." *Texas Monthly* (November 1996). Also [online] http://www.texasmonthly.com/archive/lbush/ (accessed on November 30, 2000).

"One Shall Be First: Laura Welch Bush." *People* (February 21, 2000). Also [online] http://people.aol.com/people/000221/features/firstlady3.html (accessed on November 30, 2000).

# Bush's Presidential Nomination Acceptance Speech

**Delivered on August 3, 2000; excerpted from *2000GOP.com* (Web site)**

*The Texas governor outlines his plans for a Bush presidency*

Texas governor **George W. Bush** (1946– ; see entry in volume 5) was well organized and financed early in his bid for the Republican nomination for president. He quickly emerged as the frontrunner among a large field of candidates and steadily gained strength while the other candidates gradually dropped from the race. He participated in some debates and gave many speeches, but he was still not widely known to the nation when delegates convened at the Republican National Convention in August 2000 to officially nominate Bush as the party's presidential candidate.

Bush's acceptance speech for the nomination, then, was considered extremely important. Before a national television audience, he had to impress voters that he had the ideas and personal qualities that would make them want to vote for him.

Bush succeeded. He was praised in the national press for his speech, and he received the kind of surge in support in polls of voters that usually follows a rousing acceptance speech at a national convention. The speech outlined the themes he planned to pursue if elected president.

"Prosperity can be a tool in our hands—used to build and better our country. Or it can be a drug in our system—dulling our sense of urgency, of empathy, of duty. Our opportunities are too great, our lives too short, to waste this moment."

*George W. Bush*

1625

## Things to remember while reading an excerpt from Texas governor Bush's presidential nomination acceptance speech:

- Bush began his speech by acknowledging his vice presidential running mate, Dick Cheney (1941– ; see box in **George W. Bush** entry in volume 5). He then expressed his gratefulness to his family: wife **Laura Bush** (1946– ; see entry in volume 5); daughters Jenna and Barbara; and parents, **George Bush** (1924– ; see entry in volume 5) and **Barbara Bush** (1925– ; see entry in volume 5). After claiming the administration of President **Bill Clinton** (1946– ; see entry in volume 5) and Bush's opponent, Vice President Al Gore (1948– ; see box in **Bill Clinton** entry in volume 5), had failed to realize the great potential of the times, Bush launched into a list of qualities he offered to voters in 2000.

- After praising the "greatest generation"—those who endured and triumphed through the Great Depression (1929–41) and World War II (1939–45)—Bush noted the promise of his own generation that began after World War II.

- Bush cited several specific areas he intended to concentrate on and improve as president: Medicare (government assistance to retired people to help cover medical costs); Social Security (the system where part of workers' tax dollars funds a program that provides retirement benefits); education; tax relief; and increased military spending. Those were the issues with which Bush felt he could impress voters. The speech, then, would serve to offer an interesting comparison between the pledges he made to voters and the results he would ultimately attain as president.

## *Excerpt from Texas governor Bush's presidential nomination acceptance speech*

*This is a remarkable moment in the life of our nation. Never has the promise of prosperity been so vivid. But times of plenty, like times of crisis, are tests of American character.*

*Prosperity can be a tool in our hands—used to build and better our country. Or it can be a drug in our system—dulling our sense of urgency, of empathy, of duty. Our opportunities are too great, our lives too short, to waste this moment.*

*So tonight we vow to our nation. . . . We will seize this moment of American promise. We will use these good times for great goals. We will confront the hard issues—threats to our national security, threats to our health and retirement security—before the challenges of our time become crises for our children. And we will extend the promise of prosperity to every forgotten corner of this country.*

*To every man and woman, a chance to succeed. To every child, a chance to learn. To every family, a chance to live with dignity and hope. . . .*

*[This] is a time for new beginnings. The rising generations of this country have our own appointment with greatness. It does not rise or fall with the stock market. It cannot be bought with our wealth. Greatness is found when American character and American courage overcome American challenges.*

*When Lewis Morris of New York was about to sign the Declaration of Independence, his brother advised against it, warning he would lose all his property. Morris, a plain-spoken Founder, responded . . . "Damn the consequences, give me the pen." That is the eloquence of American action.*

*We heard it during World War II, when General [Dwight D.] Eisenhower told paratroopers on D-Day morning not to worry—and one replied, "We're not worried, General. . . . It's Hitler's turn to worry now."*

*We heard it in the civil rights movement, when brave men and women did not say, "We shall cope," or "We shall see." They said, "We shall overcome."*

*An American president must call upon that character.*

*Tonight, in this hall, we resolve to be, not the party of **repose**, but the party of reform. We will write, not footnotes, but chapters in the American story. We will add the work of our hands to the inheritance of our fathers and mothers—and leave this nation greater than we found it. We know the tests of leadership. The issues are joined.*

*We will strengthen Social Security and Medicare for the greatest generation, and for generations to come. Medicare does more than meet the needs of our elderly, it reflects the values of our society. We*

**Repose:** Relaxation.

**George W. Bush: Presidential Nomination Acceptance Speech**     1627

*will set it on firm financial ground, and make prescription drugs available and affordable for every senior who needs them.*

*Social Security has been called the "third rail of American politics"—the one you're not supposed to touch because it shocks you. But, if you don't touch it, you can't fix it. And I intend to fix it. To seniors in this country . . . You earned your benefits, you made your plans, and President George W. Bush will keep the promise of Social Security . . . no changes, no reductions, no way.*

*Our opponents will say otherwise. This is their last, parting ploy, and don't believe a word of it. Now is the time for Republicans and Democrats to end the **politics of fear** and save Social Security, together.*

*For younger workers, we will give you the option—your choice—to put a part of your payroll taxes into sound, responsible investments. This will mean a higher return on your money, and, over 30 or 40 years, a **nest egg** to help your retirement, or pass along to your children. When this money is in your name, in your account, it's not just a program, it's your property.*

*Now is the time to give American workers security and independence that no politician can ever take away.*

*On education . . . too many American children are segregated into schools without standards, shuffled from grade to grade because of their age, regardless of their knowledge. This is discrimination, pure and simple—the soft bigotry of low expectations. And our nation should treat it like other forms of discrimination. . . . We should end it.*

*One size does not fit all when it comes to educating our children, so local people should control local schools. And those who spend your tax dollars must be held accountable. When a school district receives federal funds to teach poor children, we expect them to learn. And if they don't, parents should get the money to make a different choice.*

*Now is the time to make **Head Start** an early learning program, teach all our children to read, and renew the promise of America's public schools.*

*Another test of leadership is tax relief. The last time taxes were this high as a percentage of our economy, there was a good reason. . . . We were fighting World War II. Today, our high taxes fund a **surplus.** Some say that growing federal surplus means Washington has more*

**Politics of fear:** A term used to describe warnings by one party about the policies of another party.

**Nest egg:** Savings account.

**Head Start:** A program in which preschoolers are encouraged to learn to read and write.

**Surplus:** Remaining tax money after the country has paid its bills.

*money to spend. But they've got it backwards. The surplus is not the government's money. The surplus is the people's money.*

*I will use this moment of opportunity to bring common sense and fairness to the tax code. And I will act on principle. On principle . . . every family, every farmer and small businessperson, should be free to pass on their life's work to those they love. So we will abolish the* **death tax.**

*On principle . . . no one in America should have to pay more than a third of their income to the federal government. So we will reduce tax rates for everyone, in every bracket.*

*On principle . . . those in the greatest need should receive the greatest help. So we will lower the bottom rate from 15 percent to 10 percent and double the child tax credit.*

*Now is the time to reform the tax code and share some of the surplus with the people who pay the bills.*

*The world needs America's strength and leadership, and America's armed forces need better equipment, better training, and better pay. We will give our military the means to keep the peace, and we will give it one thing more . . . a commander-in-chief who respects our men and women in uniform, and a commander-in-chief who earns their respect.*

*A generation shaped by Vietnam must remember the lessons of Vietnam. When America uses force in the world, the cause must be just, the goal must be clear, and the victory must be overwhelming.*

*I will work to reduce nuclear weapons and nuclear tension in the world—to turn these years of* **affluence** *into decades of peace. And, at the earliest possible date, my administration will deploy missile defenses to guard against attack and blackmail. . . .*

*In Midland, Texas, where I grew up, the town motto was "the sky is the limit" . . . and we believed it. There was a restless energy, a basic conviction that, with hard work, anybody could succeed, and everybody deserved a chance. Our sense of community was just as strong as that sense of promise. Neighbors helped each other. There were dry wells and sandstorms to keep you humble, and lifelong friends to take your side, and churches to remind us that every soul is equal in value and equal in need. This background leaves more than an accent, it leaves an outlook.*

*Optimistic. Impatient with pretense. Confident that people can chart their own course. That background may lack the polish of*

**Death tax:** A tax on inherited wealth.

**Affluence:** Wealth.

*Washington. Then again, I don't have a lot of things that come with Washington.*

*I don't have enemies to fight. And I have no stake in the bitter arguments of the last few years. I want to change the tone of Washington to one of civility and respect.*

*The largest lesson I learned in Midland still guides me as governor. . . . Everyone, from immigrant to **entrepreneur,** has an equal claim on this country's promise.*

*So we improved our schools, dramatically, for children of every accent, of every background. We moved people from welfare to work. We strengthened our juvenile justice laws. Our budgets have been balanced, with surpluses, and we cut taxes not only once, but twice.*

*We accomplished a lot. I don't deserve all the credit, and don't attempt to take it. I worked with Republicans and Democrats to get things done. . . .*

*[When] problems aren't confronted, it builds a wall within our nation. On one side are wealth and technology, education and ambition. On the other side of the wall are poverty and prison, addiction and despair. And, my fellow Americans, we must tear down that wall.*

*Big government is not the answer. But the alternative to bureaucracy is not indifference. It is to put conservative values and conservative ideas into the thick of the fight for justice and opportunity.*

*This is what I mean by compassionate conservatism. And on this ground we will govern our nation. (2000GOP.com. [Web site])*

## What happened next . . .

Bush's speech was well received: he communicated his ideas forcefully, and his support in polls rose dramatically following the convention. His lead in the polls over challenger Al Gore was reduced following Gore's acceptance speech for the Democratic nomination for president three weeks later. The race remained close following three debates by the candidates and on to election day. The race was so close in fact, that the election was not over after the votes

**Entrepreneur:** Someone who invests money in people who have new ideas and helps finance their business venture.

were in. Bush lost the popular vote to Al Gore, but he won in the Electoral College, 271 to 266. The twenty-five electoral votes from the state of Florida proved decisive. After having won the original count as well as a recount, Bush had to endure several court challenges before he was finally awarded Florida's electoral votes and the presidency. He had been prematurely declared the victor at 2:45 A.M. on Wednesday, November 8, but it was not until December 13, following Vice President Gore's concession speech (and a decision in Bush's favor from the U.S. Supreme Court the previous day) that Bush could finally call himself president-elect.

## Did you know . . .

- In order to build support for his candidacy to become the Republican presidential nominee, George W. Bush invited many elected Republican officials to visit him before presidential primaries began. (Primaries are elections in individual states where voters express support for a particular presidential candidate. Delegates are awarded to candidates based on the number of votes they receive. A candidate must win a majority of a political party's delegates in order to be the party's presidential nominee.) Republican officials met with Bush at the governor's office in Austin, Texas, and at his ranch near Waco, Texas. The strategy worked, as Bush won early endorsements from many high-profile party members.

- Bush's tactic was similar to the "front porch" campaign of **William McKinley** (1843–1901; see entry in volume 3) in 1896. McKinley's campaign was run by a wealthy supporter, Mark Hanna (1837–1904). Hanna arranged to have trainloads of delegations visit the candidate at his home in Canton, Ohio. In that setting, McKinley could address them in a calm and dignified manner, appear presidential, and become familiar with people whose support he needed to become the nominee.

## Where to Learn More

"George W. Bush's Acceptance Speech." *2000GOP.com.* [Online] http://www.2000GOP.com/convention/speech/speechbush.html (accessed on November 20, 2000).

Minutaglio, Bill. *First Son: George W. Bush and the Bush Family Dynasty.* New York: Times Books, 1999.

Mitchell, Elizabeth. *W: Revenge of the Bush Dynasty.* New York: Hyperion, 2000.

# Where to Learn More

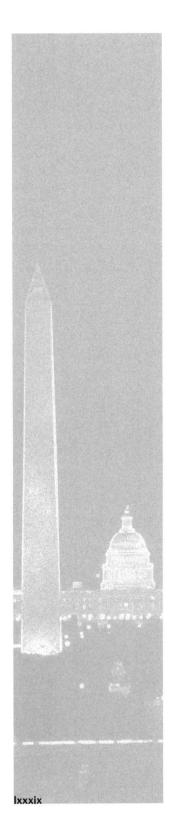

The following list of resources focuses on material appropriate for middle school or high school students. Please note that the web site addresses were verified prior to publication, but are subject to change.

## Books

Bailey, Thomas A. *The Pugnacious Presidents: White House Warriors on Parade.* New York: Free Press, 1980.

Barber, James David. *The Presidential Character: Predicting Performance in the White House.* 4th ed. Englewood Cliffs, NJ: Prentice-Hall, 1992.

Barzman, Sol. *Madmen and Geniuses: The Vice-Presidents of the United States.* Chicago: Follett, 1974.

Berube, Maurice. *American Presidents and Education.* Westport, CT: Greenwood Press, 1991.

Boller, Paul F., Jr. *Presidential Anecdotes.* Rev. ed. New York: Oxford, 1996.

Boller, Paul F., Jr. *Presidential Campaigns.* Rev. ed. New York: Oxford, 1996.

Boller, Paul F. Jr. *Presidential Wives: An Anecdotal History.* Rev. ed. New York: Oxford, 1998.

Brace, Paul, Christine B. Harrington, and Gary King, eds. *The Presidency in American Politics.* New York: New York University Press, 1989.

Brallier, Jess, and Sally Chabert. *Presidential Wit and Wisdom.* New York: Penguin, 1996.

Brinkley, Alan, and Davis Dyer, eds. *The Reader's Companion to the American Presidency*. New York: Houghton Mifflin, 2000.

Brogan, Hugh, and Charles Mosley. *American Presidential Families*. New York: Macmillan Publishing Co., 1993.

Bumann, Joan. *Our American Presidents: From Washington through Clinton*. St. Petersburg, FL: Willowisp Press, 1993.

Campbell, Colin. *The U.S. Presidency in Crisis: A Comparative Perspective*. New York: Oxford University Press, 1998.

Clotworthy, William G. *Presidential Sites*. Blacksburg, VA: McDonald & Woodward, 1998.

Cook, Carolyn. *Imagine You Are the . . . President*. Edina, MN: Imaginarium, 1999.

Cooke, Donald Ewin. *Atlas of the Presidents*. Maplewood, NJ: Hammond, 1985.

Cronin, Thomas, ed. *Inventing the American Presidency*. Lawrence: University of Kansas Press, 1989.

Cunliffe, Marcus. *American Presidents and the Presidency*. New York: Houghton Mifflin, 1986.

Dallek, Robert. *Hail to the Chief: The Making and Unmaking of American Presidents*. New York: Hyperion, 1996.

Davis, James W. *The American Presidency*. 2nd ed. Westport, CT: Praeger, 1995.

DeGregorio, William. *The Complete Book of U.S. Presidents*. 4th ed. New York: Barricade Books, 1993.

Fields, Wayne. *Union of Words: A History of Presidential Eloquence*. New York: The Free Press, 1996.

Fisher, Louis. *Presidential War Power*. Lawrence: University of Kansas Press, 1995.

Frank, Sid, and Arden Davis Melick. *Presidents: Tidbits and Trivia*. Maplewood, NJ: Hammond, 1986.

Frost, Elizabeth, ed. *The Bully Pulpit: Quotations from America's Presidents*. New York: Facts On File, 1988.

Genovese, Michael. *The Power of the American Presidency, 1789–2000*. New York: Oxford, 2001.

Gerhardt, Michael J. *The Federal Impeachment Process: A Constitutional and Historical Analysis*. 2nd ed. Chicago: University of Chicago Press, 2000.

Goehlert, Robert U., and Fenton S. Martin. *The Presidency: A Research Guide*. Santa Barbara, CA: ABC-Clio Information Services, 1985.

Havel, James T. *U.S. Presidential Candidates and the Elections: A Biographical and Historical Guide*. New York: Macmillan Library Reference USA, 1996.

Henry, Christopher E. *The Electoral College*. New York: Franklin Watts, 1996.

Henry, Christopher E. *Presidential Elections*. New York: Franklin Watts, 1996.

Hess, Stephen. *Presidents and the Presidency: Essays*. Washington, DC: The Brookings Institution, 1996.

Israel, Fred L., ed. *The Presidents*. Danbury, CT: Grolier Educational, 1996.

Jackson, John S. III, and William Crotty. *The Politics of Presidential Selection*. 2nd ed. New York: Longman, 2001.

Jamieson, Kathleen Hall. *Packaging the Presidency: A History and Criticism of Presidential Campaign Advertising*. 3rd ed. New York: Oxford, 1996.

Kessler, Paula N., and Justin Segal. *The Presidents Almanac*. Rev. ed. Los Angeles: Lowell House Juvenile, 1998.

Kruh, David, and Louis Kruh. *Presidential Landmarks*. New York: Hippocrene Books, 1992.

Kunhardt, Philip B. Jr., Philip B. Kunhardt III, and Peter W. Kunhardt. *The American President.* New York: Penguin, 1999.

Laird, Archibald. *The Near Great—Chronicle of the Vice Presidents.* North Quincy, MA: Christopher Publishing House, 1980.

Mayer, William G., ed. *In Pursuit of the White House: How We Choose Our Presidential Nominees.* Chatham, NJ: Chatham House, 1996.

Murray, Robert K., and Tim H. Blessing. *Greatness in the White House: Rating the Presidents.* 2nd ed. University Park: Pennsylvania State University Press, 1994.

Neustadt, Richard E. *Presidential Power and the Modern Presidents: The Politics of Leadership from Roosevelt to Reagan.* New York: The Free Press, 1990.

Patrick, Diane. *The Executive Branch.* New York: Franklin Watts, 1994.

*Presidents of the United States. A World Book Encyclopedia.* Chicago: Field Enterprises Educational Corp., 1973.

Riccards, Michael, and James MacGregor Burns. *The Ferocious Engine of Democracy: A History of the American Presidency. Vol I: From the Origins through William McKinley. Vol. II: Theodore Roosevelt through George Bush.* Lanham, MD: Madison Books, 1996.

Robb, Don. *Hail to the Chief: The American Presidency.* Watertown, MA: Charlesbridge, 2000.

Rose, Gary L. *The American Presidency Under Siege.* Albany: State University of New York Press, 1997.

Sanders, Mark C. *The Presidency.* Austin, TX: Steadwell Books, 2000.

Shenkman, Richard. *Presidential Ambition: How the Presidents Gained Power, Kept Power, and Got Things Done.* New York: HarperCollins, 1999.

Shogan, Robert. *The Double-Edged Sword: How Character Makes and Ruins Presidents, from Washington to Clinton.* Boulder, CO: Westview Press, 2000.

Sisung, Kelle S., ed. *Presidential Administration Profiles for Students.* Detroit: Gale Group, 2000.

Smith, Nancy Kegan, and Mary C. Ryan, eds. *Modern First Ladies: Their Documentary Legacy.* Washington, DC: National Archives and Records Administration, 1989.

Stier, Catherine. *If I Were President.* Morton Grove, IL: Albert Whitman, 1999.

Suid, Murray I. *How to Be President of the U.S.A.* Palo Alto, CA: Monday Morning Books, 1992.

Truman, Margaret. *First Ladies: An Intimate Group Portrait of White House Wives.* New York: Ballantine, 1995.

Vidal, Gore. *The American Presidency.* Monroe, ME: Odonian Press, 1998.

Wheeless, Carl. *Landmarks of American Presidents.* Detroit: Gale, 1995.

## Video

*The American President.* Written, produced, and directed by Philip B. Kunhardt Jr., Philip B. Kunhardt III, and Peter W. Kunhardt. Co-production of Kunhardt Productions and Thirteen/WNET in New York. 10 programs.

## Web Sites

*The American Presidency: Selected Resources, An Informal Reference Guide* (Web site). [Online] http://www.interlink-cafe.com/uspresidents/ (accessed on December 11, 2000).

C-Span. *American Presidents: Life Portraits.* [Online] http://www.american presidents.org/ (accessed on December 11, 2000).

Grolier, Inc. *Grolier Presents: The American Presidency.* [Online] http://gi.grolier. com/presidents/ea/prescont.html (accessed on December 11, 2000).

Internet Public Library. *POTUS: Presidents of the United States.* [Online] http:// www.ipl.org/ref/POTUS/index.html (accessed on December 11, 2000).

Public Broadcasting System. "The American President." *The American Experience.* [Online] http://www.pbs.org/wgbh/amex/presidents/nf/intro/intro. html (accessed on December 11, 2000).

University of Oklahoma Law Center. *A Chronology of US Historical Documents.* [Online] http://www.law.ou.edu/hist/ (accessed on December 11, 2000).

White House. *Welcome to the White House.* [Online] http://www.whitehouse. gov/ (accessed on December 11, 2000).

*The White House Historical Association.* [Online] http://www.whitehousehistory. org/whha/default.asp (accessed on December 11, 2000).

Yale Law School. *The Avalon at the Yale Law School: Documents in Law, History and Diplomacy.* [Online] http://www.yale.edu/lawweb/avalon/avalon. htm (accessed on December 11, 2000).

# Index

**Note:** *Italic* type indicates volume number; **boldface** indicates main entries and their page numbers; (ill.) indicates photos and illustrations.

Alien Enemies Act, *1:* 67, 68
  Naturalization Act, *1:* 67
  Sedition Act, *1:* 69
Alien Enemies Act, *1:* 67, 68
Alliance for Progress, *5:* 1284
Allied Powers (World War I), *4:*
    973–76, 1004, 1005, 1010,
    1046
Allied Powers (World War II), *4:*
    1147, 1150, 1181, 1221, 1235,
    1241, 1242
Alternative energy sources, *5:* 1448
Aluminum Company of America
    (Alcoa), *4:* 1022
Alzheimer's disease, *5:* 1489,
    1493–94, 1499
Amendment(s). *See* Bill of Rights;
    Constitution; specific amend-
    ment, e.g., Twelfth Amend-
    ment
"America First," *4:* 1025
American Ballet Theater, *5:* 1329–30
American Colonization Society, *1:*
    198
American Expeditionary Force (AEF)
    (World War I), *4:* 971, 1002–3
American imperialism. *See* Imperial-
    ism
American Indians. *See* Native Amer-
    icans
*American Individualism* (Hoover), *4:*
    1116
American (Know Nothing) Party, *2:*
    469, 484
*An American Life* (Reagan), *5:* 1489
American military, World War I, *4:*
    971, 976, 1002–3
"American Prince of Wales." *See*
    Adams, John Quincy
American Relief Administration
    (ARA), *4:* 1092, 1093 (ill.),
    1111
American Revolution, *1:* 10–16, 11
    (ill.), 82
  Adams, John and Abigail, *1:* 76
  Adams, John Quincy, *1:* 223
  Anti-British sentiment, *1:* 9
  Declaration of Independence, *1:*
    125–34
  Franklin, Benjamin, *1:* 17
  Jackson, Andrew, *1:* 260–61
  Jefferson, Thomas, *1:* 98–99,
    101–2
  Lafayette, Marquis de, *1:* 33 (ill.),
    186–87, 187 (ill.)
  Marshall, John, *1:* 64–65
  Monroe, James, *1:* 182–83, 205–6
  Paine, Thomas, *1:* 190
  privateers, *1:* 205
  Randolph, Edmund Jennings, *2:*
    362

Washington, George, *1:* 10–16,
    11 (ill.)
  Washington, Martha, *1:* 32–34
"American System" (Clay), *1:* 228,
    230–31
Americans, Reagan's view, *5:* 1502
Americans with Disabilities Act, *5:*
    1521
Americas, Monroe Doctrine, *1:* 200
Ames, Oakes, *3:* 657
*Amistad* case, *1:* 234, 245–46
  **closing argument** (John Quincy
    Adams), *1:* **245–53**
Anderson, John, election of 1980, *5:*
    1477, 1478
Anderson, Marian, *4:* 994 (ill.),
    1164
Andropov, Yuri, *5:* 1484
Angola, *5:* 1415
Annexation, Texas, *1:* 308
**Annual Address to Congress.** *See
    also* State of the Union Address
  Arthur, Chester A., *3:* **769–74**
  Buchanan, James, *2:* **539–48**
  Fillmore, Millard, *2:* **479–84**
  Grant, Ulysses S., *3:* 659
  Johnson, Andrew, *2:* **629–36**
  Roosevelt, Theodore, *3:* **909–16**
  Taft, William Howard, *3:* **949–56**
  Taylor, Zachary, *2:* **451–56**
*Antelope* case, *1:* 246
Anthony, Susan B., *3:* 785, 786–87,
    787 (ill.)
Anti-American sentiment, Iran, *5:*
    1450–51
Anti-Communism, *4:* 1143
Antidrug campaign, *5:* 1493
Antietam, Battle of, *2:* 568, 582
Anti-Federalist(s), *1:* 45, 60, 135–36,
    141, 153. *See also* Democratic-
    Republican Party; Federalist(s)
    vs. Anti-Federalist(s)
Anti-Imperialism League, *3:* 791
Anti-Jacksonians, *1:* 51; *2:* 364
Anti-Masonic Party, *1:* 300; *2:*
    461–62, 608
Antislavery. *See* Abolition
Antitrust laws, *3:* 915
Anti-union legislation, *4:* 1203
Antiwar (Vietnam War) protests, *5:*
    1334, 1335, 1337, 1366,
    1391–92, 1396–97
  Reagan, Ronald, *5:* 1475–76
  **"Silent Majority" Speech**
    (Nixon), *5:* **1391–97**
Apaches, *4:* 970
Apartheid, *5:* 1522
Appleton, Jane Means. *See* Pierce,
    Jane
Appleton, Jesse, *2:* 505

election of 1992, *5:* 1525, 1555
father of a president, *5:* 1528
foreign policy, *5:* 1512, 1522–23
Gulf War, *5:* 1512, 1523–25,
1537–38, 1543–44
Iran-Contra arms sales scandal, *5:*
1518–19
marriage and family, *5:* 1513,
1532
military service, *5:* 1513, 1532
Nixon, Richard, *5:* 1516
Operation Desert Storm, *5:*
1523–24
parachute jump, *5:* 1528
political career, *5:* 1515–19
presidency, *5:* 1520–28
retirement, *5:* 1528
**Bush, George W.,** *5:* **1595–1619,**
1597 (ill.), 1604 (ill.), 1608
(ill.)
campaign 2000, *5:* 1604–15
domestic policy, *5:* 1598–99,
1626
early years, *5:* 1599–1601
election of 2000, *5:* 1605–17,
1630–31
governor of Texas, *5:* 1602–5
marriage and family, *5:* 1601
political career, *5:* 1601–5
president-elect, *5:* 1617–18
**Presidential Nomination Accep-
tance Speech,** *5:* **1625–32**
Texas Air National Guard, *5:* 1600
Bush, Jeb, *5:* 1611–12
Bush, Jenna, *5:* 1601, 1623
**Bush, Laura,** *5:* 1604 (ill.),
**1621–24,** 1621 (ill.)
first lady of Texas, *5:* 1624
literacy and libraries, *5:* 1623–24
marriage and family, *5:* 1622–23
reading teacher, *5:* 1622–23
Bush, Prescott, *5:* 1512–13, 1599
Business and government
**Business and Government
speech** (Coolidge), *4:* **1077–83**
Coolidge, Calvin, *4:* 1057,
1077–78, 1081–82
Harding, Warren G., *4:* 1040,
1045
interstate, *3:* 911
Roosevelt, Theodore, *3:* 890, 895,
911, 928
**"Rugged Individualism" cam-
paign speech,** *4:* **1115–22**
Taft, William Howard, *3:* 933–35
Business monopolies. *See* Trusts
Butler, Pierce, *3:* 936 (ill.)
Butler, William O., election of 1848,
*2:* 439
Butterfield, Alexander, *5:* 1376

# C

Cabinet. *See also* administration of
each president
first, *1:* 20, 22 (ill.), 62
"Cabinet Government in the United States" (Wilson), *4:* 963
Cable News Network (CNN), Gulf
War coverage, *5:* 1544
Caledonia Furnace, *2:* 608
Calhoun, Floride, *2:* 417
Calhoun, John C., *1:* 156, 211 (ill.),
230, 270–71, 271 (ill.)
election of 1828, *1:* 267
nullification, *1:* 267–68
Van Buren, Martin, *1:* 299, 300
Whig Party, *2:* 370
California
acquisition from Mexico, *2:* 404,
405–6
counterculture youth and anti-
war protests, *5:* 1475
free state, *1:* 271; *2:* 371, 439–40,
452, 465, 466
Frémont, John C., *2:* 408–9
Nixon, Richard, *5:* 1360–61, 1365
Reagan, Ronald, *5:* 1474–76
*Call to Greatness* (Stevenson), *4:*
1247
Cambodia, *5:* 1287, 1331, 1370,
1371, 1373, 1375, 1396, 1415,
1417
"Camelot" (Kennedy White House),
*5:* 1287–90, 1299
*Camelot* (play), *5:* 1299
Camp David Accords, *5:* 1417,
1446–47, 1447 (ill.)
Carter, Jimmy, *5:* 1445
Campaign banners
Hayes and Wheeler, *3:* 688 (ill.)
Polk and Dallas, *2:* 402 (ill.)
Whig Party, *2:* 463 (ill.)
Campaign posters
Buchanan, James, *2:* 521 (ill.)
Frémont, John C., *2:* 524 (ill.)
Garfield and Arthur, *3:* 754 (ill.)
McKinley, William, *3:* 847 (ill.)
Whig candidate, *2:* 437 (ill.)
Campaign slogans
"54°40' or Fight!," *2:* 403, 405
"Give 'em hell, Harry!," *4:* 1190,
1205
"He kept us out of war," *4:* 973
(ill.), 974
"I Like Ike," *4:* 1236, 1245 (ill.),
1261 (ill.)
"It's the economy, stupid," *5:*
1558
"Keep cool with Coolidge," *4:*
1056

# J

# N

# O

Perkins, Frances, *4:* 1137, 1142–43, 1143 (ill.)
Perot, H. Ross, *5:* 1526–27, 1527 (ill.)
  election of 1992, *5:* 1525, 1527, 1555
  election of 1996, *5:* 1527, 1555, 1558, 1561
Perry, Matthew C., *2:* 468, 473, 498–99, 499 (ill.), 501
Perry, Oliver Hazard, *1:* 157
Pershing, John J. "Black Jack," *4:* 970–71, 971 (ill.), 972, 976, 1200
Persian Gulf crisis. *See* Gulf War
*The Personal Memoirs of U. S. Grant* (Grant), *3:* 661, 669, 672
Peru, *5:* 1467
"Pet banks," *1:* 289
Philadelphia, Pennsylvania, *1:* 78, 132, 164
Philippines, *3:* 851, 852, 858; *4:* 1100
  Eisenhower, Dwight D., *4:* 1240
  MacArthur, Douglas, *4:* 1208–9, 1240
  Pershing, John J. "Black Jack," *4:* 970–71
  Spanish American War, *3:* 887
  Taft, William Howard, *3:* 931, 944–45
Physical disability, New Deal legislation, *4:* 1141
Pierce, Barbara. *See* Bush, Barbara
Pierce, Benjamin (father of Franklin), *2:* 488, 489
Pierce, Benjamin (son of Franklin), *2:* 488, 494, 506
**Pierce, Franklin,** *2:* 468 (ill.), **485–503,** 487 (ill.), 492 (ill.), 494 (ill.), 496 (ill.), 500 (ill.)
  administration, *2:* 497
  Compromise of 1850, *2:* 495–97
  early years, *2:* 488
  election of 1852, *2:* 483, 493–94, 495, 521
  **Inaugural Address,** *2:* 494, **509–14**
  marriage and family, *2:* 489–90, 494, 505, 506
  military career, *2:* 490–93
  political career, *2:* 489, 493–94
  presidency, *2:* 495–501
  retirement, *2:* 501–2
**Pierce, Jane,** *2:* **505–7,** 505 (ill.)
  reclusive first lady, *2:* 507
  tragic loss of sons, *2:* 506
Pike, Zebulon, *1:* 114
*Pilgrim's Progress* (Bunyan), *3:* 918
Pinchot, Gifford, *3:* 896–97, 899 (ill.)

Pinckney, Charles C., *1:* 66, 115
  election of 1800, *1:* 109
  election of 1804, *1:* 109
  election of 1808, *1:* 155, 165
Pinckney, Thomas, election of 1796, *1:* 61
Pittsburgh, Pennsylvania, *4:* 1022
Plains Indian Wars, *3:* 769, 770
Platform, political. *See* Political platform
Platt, Thomas Collier, *3:* 758, 888
Plymouth Notch, Vermont, *4:* 1054, 1055–56, 1074, 1075
Pocahontas, *4:* 991
Podgorny, Nikolai, *5:* 1369 (ill.)
Poland
  Communist era, *4:* 1252
  democratization, *5:* 1482, 1522
  war relief, *4:* 1092
  World War II, *4:* 1147
Polio (Roosevelt, Franklin D.), *4:* 1162
Polish Relief Commission, *4:* 1105
Political appointees, *3:* 721. *See also* Patronage system
Political cartoons
  1856 presidential campaign, *2:* 469 (ill.)
  Polk and Webster, *2:* 407 (ill.)
Political machine, *3:* 751–53
Political parties, Washington's view, *1:* 46–47
Political patronage. *See* Patronage system
Political platform, lacking in Harrison/Tyler campaign, *2:* 364–65
Politics, international. *See* International politics
**Polk, James K.,** *2:* 354, **393–413,** 395 (ill.), 400 (ill.), 402 (ill.), 407 (ill.)
  annexation of Texas, *2:* 372, 386, 419, 420
  Calhoun, John C., *1:* 271
  early years, *2:* 395–97
  election of 1844, *2:* 372, 401, 403–4
  gallstone surgery, *2:* 396
  **Inaugural Address,** *2:* 404, **419–25**
  Jackson, Andrew, *2:* 397
  marriage, *2:* 397, 416, 417
  political career, *2:* 397–404, 416
  presidency, *2:* 404–11, 417
  retirement, *2:* 411
  slavery issue, *2:* 410–11
  Taylor, Zachary, *2:* 436
Polk Place, *2:* 411, 415, 417–18
**Polk, Sarah,** *1:* 167; *2:* 381, 411, **415–18,** 415 (ill.)
  marriage, *2:* 416

popular first lady, *2:* 417

private political involvement, *2:* 415, 416–17

*Poor Richard's Almanack, 1:* 17

Pope, John, *3:* 649

Popular vote, *1:* 19, 61, 109, 155, 193, 227. *See also* election results under specific president

Populism, *3:* 821, 823, 886

Populist Party (People's Party), *3:* 824, 848

Postmaster General. *See also* administration of specific president

first, *1:* 20

Postwar South. *See* Reconstruction

Potawatomi, *2:* 435

Potsdam conference, *4:* 1196, 1198 (ill.), 1221, 1222

Potsdam Declaration, *4:* 1197

Pottawatomie Creek, *2:* 528

Poverty

King, Martin Luther, Jr., *5:* 1293

"War on Poverty," *5:* 1326, 1343

Powell, Colin, *5:* 1544

Powers, Abigail. *See* Fillmore, Abigail

Powers, Francis Gary, *4:* 1251

Prendergast, Tom, political machine, *4:* 1191, 1193

Presbyterians, *2:* 396

President(s)

dark horse, *2:* 403, 493; *3:* 688, 721–22

father-son, *1:* 71, 219; *5:* 1528, 1597

first press conference, *4:* 959

lame duck, *2:* 635; *4:* 1145

married in office, *2:* 380

physically challenged, *4:* 1132–33

served nonconsecutive terms, *3:* 777

Supreme Court chief justice, *3:* 940

youngest, *3:* 889

Presidential candidates, military leaders as, *2:* 468 (ill.)

Presidential election(s). *See* election by year under each president

closest results in presidential history, *5:* 1615

federal supervision, *3:* 697

first, *1:* 18–19

Presidential elector(s), selection, *5:* 1613

**Presidential Nomination Acceptance Speech** (George W. Bush), *5:* **1625–32**

"Presidential Polonaise" (Sousa), *2:* 381

Presidential powers

commander in chief, *4:* 997

limitations, *2:* 347–49

Lincoln, Abraham, *2:* 551, 566

McKinley, William, *3:* 860

Roosevelt, Franklin D., *4:* 1154, 1173

Presidential primaries, *5:* 1631

Presidential succession, *2:* 357–58, 366–67

Presidential veto

Hayes, Rutherford B., *3:* 695, 696

Jackson, Andrew, *1:* 276

Johnson, Andrew, *2:* 619

President's Commission on Mental Health, *5:* 1457

President's Commission on the Status of Women, *4:* 1165

President's Committee on Equality of Treatment and Opportunity in the Armed Services, *4:* 1229, 1230

*The President's Daughter* (Britton), *4:* 1015

President's (Presidential) Palace, *1:* 70, 79, 121. *See also* White House

President's Science Advisory Committee, *4:* 1250

President/vice president

born in same county, *2:* 339

different parties, *2:* 607

youngest-ever combined ticket, *5:* 1555

Press

Clinton, Hillary Rodham, *5:* 1583–85

Ford, Gerald R., *5:* 1414, 1415

news agencies call election 2000, *5:* 1608, 1609

Press conference(s)

with first lady, *4:* 1035

first presidential, *4:* 959

Preston, Thomas J., Jr., *3:* 801

*The Princeton, 2:* 380

Princeton University, *3:* 794, 800; *4:* 963, 964–65, 995

Privateers, *1:* 205

"Proclamation 4311, Granting a Pardon to Richard Nixon" (Ford), *5:* 1408–9, 1427

*Profiles in Courage* (John F. Kennedy), *2:* 617; *5:* 1279, 1302

Progressive "Bull Moose" Party, *3:* 900, 937

Progressive Party, *4:* 1204

Progressivism, *3:* 886, 927; *4:* 968

Prohibition, *4:* 1058–60, 1115

Harding, Florence, *4:* 1036

Harding, Warren G., *4:* 1020

repeal, *4:* 1102

# X

# Y

# Z